THE CULTURE OF LANGUAGE IN MING CHINA

The Culture of Language in Ming China

SOUND, SCRIPT, AND THE REDEFINITION
OF BOUNDARIES OF KNOWLEDGE

Nathan Vedal

Columbia University Press
New York

This publication was made possible in part by an award from the James P. Geiss and Margaret Y. Hsu Foundation

Columbia University Press
Publishers Since 1893
New York   Chichester, West Sussex
cup.columbia.edu
Copyright © 2022 Columbia University Press
All rights reserved

Library of Congress Cataloging-in-Publication Data
Names: Vedal, Nathan, author.
Title: The culture of language in Ming China : sound, script, and the redefinition of boundaries of knowledge / Nathan Vedal.
Description: New York : Columbia University Press, [2021] | Includes bibliographical references and index.
Identifiers: LCCN 2021023360 (print) | LCCN 2021023361 (ebook) | ISBN 9780231200752 (trade paperback) | ISBN 9780231200745 (hardback) | ISBN 9780231553766 (ebook)
Subjects: LCSH: Chinese philology—History. | China—Intellectual life—1368-1644. | China—Intellectual life—1644-1912.
Classification: LCC PL1051 .V43 2021 (print) | LCC PL1051 (ebook) | DDC 407.2/051—dc23
LC record available at https://lccn.loc.gov/2021023360
LC ebook record available at https://lccn.loc.gov/2021023361

Cover image: Diagram connecting linguistic, musical, and calendric categories from Qiao Zhonghe 喬中和 (1573–1652), *Yuanyun pu* 元韻譜, *juanshou*, 44a. Image courtesy of the National Library of China.
Cover design: Chang Jae Lee

In memory of my mother, Cherie Louise Manning

Contents

Note on Language   ix

Introduction   1

PART I   Sound and Script

1   The Number of Everything: Music, Cosmology, and the Origins of Language   17

2   Letters from the West: Sanskrit, Latin, and Phonetic Legibility in Ming China   46

3   Script, Antiquity, and Mental Training: Metaphysical Inquiry Into the Nondiscursive Potential of Writing   73

PART II   Singing and Speaking, Reading and Writing

4   Opera and the Search for a Universal Language   105

5 Reading the Classics for Pleasure:
Prose as Verse, Verse as Music   136

PART III   Philology: The Making and Remaking of a Discipline

6   Afterlives: Ming Methods and Their Competition in the
Eighteenth and Nineteenth Centuries   167

7   The Reinvention of Philology: Specialization,
Disciplinarity, and Intellectual Lineage   199

Epilogue   224

Acknowledgments   231
Notes   235
Selected Bibliography   285
Index   305

Note on Language

I employ a modified version of Yuen Ren Chao's "General Chinese" (*tongzi* 通字) throughout this book to transcribe Ming dynasty Chinese. Originally designed to be pronounceable in any modern topolect, it reflects distinctions in Ming dynasty phonology fairly well for the purpose of understanding the phonological categories being discussed by Ming scholars. In employing these transcriptions I make no claims about actual Ming-era pronunciation. The purpose is rather to abstract key phonological characteristics, many of which no longer exist in modern Mandarin. I use Mandarin *pinyin* for graphs where the term itself, rather than the pronunciation, is important. I have modified Chao's system, which alters the spelling of each syllable to indicate tonal change, by using the standard pinyin tonal diacritics; that is, ¯ for level tone (*ping* 平), ˇ for rising tone (*shang* 上), and ` for falling tone (*qu* 去). This Ming transcription is further distinguished from pinyin in the text by being nonitalicized and contained within angle brackets < >.[1]

Names of historical figures are accompanied by Chinese characters (and dates when determinable) on their first occurrence.

THE CULTURE OF LANGUAGE IN MING CHINA

Introduction

What is the nature of language? Are there general principles that unify all languages in the world? What is the most effective system to notate speech? Writing in the early seventeenth century, Wu Jishi 吳繼仕 (fl. 1579–1611) proposed a program for the student interested in such questions. According to Wu, one should first master the principles of cosmology, calendrics, and musical pitches. Only then could one proceed to the methods of linguistic study.[1] This program of learning has little clear relation to the study of language as we understand it today, although the questions it addressed belong to the present-day field of linguistics. Wu was no outlier, however.[2] The study of language, or philology, which captivated scholars throughout the sixteenth and seventeenth centuries, was bound up with subjects beyond the strictly linguistic. My purpose in this book is to unravel the logic underlying this interconnectedness of knowledge and its implications for our understanding of late imperial Chinese scholarly practices. The sixteenth through nineteenth centuries witnessed profound transitions in notions of intellectual validity, rigor, and method. As one of the most prestigious fields of learning in late imperial China, philology was at the heart of these transformations.

As early as the eighteenth century, Chinese critics characterized the fusion of disparate branches of learning as misguided and representative of a benighted age when literati valued abstract philosophical musing over concrete textual study. This image of Ming intellectual culture has largely remained to the present day. Intellectual change in China has often been delineated according to which disciplines (based on our modern definitions) attracted the greatest attention at a given time. By instead tracing shifts in the very notion of disciplinary learning, I offer an alternative perspective on intellectual change in China reflecting historical rather than present-day categories. As the assumptions underlying knowledge production changed, so too did the connections between and boundaries surrounding disciplines.

Philology is upheld in the current literature as the defining feature of the eighteenth-century intellectual landscape. During this period, scholars intent on shedding their predecessors' preoccupation with metaphysical philosophy turned their attention toward the study of texts and language. The problem with this narrative is that philology had become a central locus of scholarly inquiry already in the Ming. This book examines shifts in philological practice, and modes of knowledge production more broadly, from the sixteenth through eighteenth centuries. It explores the emergence of new methods of notating linguistic sounds, analyzing Chinese graphs, and establishing pronunciation norms across a broad range of Ming thinkers, from Buddhist monks and Confucian classicists to opera librettists and poets. Ultimately, however, this book is not primarily about the history of language study in China, but how language study reflects major intellectual transitions in a pivotal age. By documenting shifts in the study of language over the course of three centuries, it reveals a profound change in the methodology of learning from an assumption of interconnectedness among various branches of knowledge to their separation.

Why Did Philology Matter in Late Imperial China?

Philology was a venerated subject in many regions of the early modern world.[3] It was the key to interpreting ancient texts and therefore served as a point of access to the moral, political, and cultural underpinnings of various civilizations. Its methods of textual research were also fundamentally transferable and came to find application in many other disciplines.[4] The central question this book seeks to answer is how late imperial scholars studied language and in what ways their practices reflect broader intellectual and literary trends. Fascination with language has deep resonances in the Chinese tradition.⁵ Nevertheless the study of language reached new heights during the sixteenth century, evidenced by the explosion of treatises, dictionaries, and other philological texts recorded from the period. In late imperial China a substantial body of creative and innovative thinkers devoted themselves to philological endeavors. What use did they see in this seemingly innocuous discipline?

I employ "philology" as a translation of the Chinese term *xiaoxue* (小學), or "the lesser learning."⁶ Although such a label might imply the inferior status of philology in comparison to more lofty philosophical pursuits, late imperial scholars were quick to point out that there was nothing "lesser" about the study of language. As one seventeenth-century thinker observed, "The lesser can be a part of the greater, but the greater cannot encompass the lesser."⁷ In his view, only through philology could the "noble truths" of the ancient Classics be conveyed in the present. Another scholar wrote that although philology was termed "the lesser learning," he would never dare call it a "lesser Way" (小道).⁸ By the mid-eighteenth century, book catalogs typically outlined *xiaoxue* as comprising three branches of study: *yunxue* (韻學 "the study of rhymes"), *xunguxue* (訓詁學 "the study of glosses"), and *zixue* (字學 "the study of graphs"). *Yunxue*, or phonology, referred to the study of the sounds of language. *Xunguxue* was primarily aimed at glossing the meaning of terms. *Zixue*, usually translated as paleography or grammatology, involved the study of historical character forms. Ming book catalogs, although less standardized, roughly hewed to these categories as well.⁹ Given the breadth of content falling under the purview of philology, some scholars specialized in one area, rather than philology as a whole. As the sixteenth-century bibliographer Hu Yinglin 胡應麟 (1551–1602) commented, "Among those broadly learned from past to present, none have been able to master all [elements of philology]."¹⁰ Nevertheless, Hu categorized it as one branch of learning (*yi duan* 一端) with multiple subfields (*menjing* 門徑).¹¹

Philology mattered in late imperial China. By establishing an order for words and their pronunciation, scholars contended that they were solidifying the bedrock of their civilization. Today the term *philology* has a pedantic connotation, but the philologist in late imperial China played a central role in the period's intellectual life. Some of the implications of linguistic study become clear in the following dictionary preface by the mid-seventeenth-century scholar Sima Yan 司馬衍:

> Alas, ever since there have been errors in writing, the meanings of words have been corrupted; since the meanings of words have been corrupted, the minds of people have become confused; since the minds of people have become confused, the affairs of the world have been ruined; since the affairs of the world have been ruined, heresies have arisen; and since heresies have arisen, the Way of the sages has perished![12]

Sima Yan traced what he perceived as the corrupt morals of his age to errors in the contemporary form of written script, which had damaged people's ability to fully comprehend the foundational classical texts. As vessels of moral knowledge, the Classics were considered essential sources for personal cultivation. Philology was an indispensable part of reading and interpreting the textual tradition. Without it, one could not effectively grasp the teachings of the ancient sages or appreciate the poetry of great literary figures. It was the philologist, therefore, who was responsible for providing readers with uncorrupted access to the core texts of a cultured civilization.

Sima Yan observed the potential negative effects of improper script forms on societal mores. Some of his contemporaries extended this argument, contending that the study of language was not only important for making sense of ancient texts; it could also reflect something profoundly human, the inner workings of our mind. As another seventeenth-century scholar detailed:

> The dots and strokes [of script] are the form of the mind, the rhymes and tones are the sounds of the mind, and the glossing of meaning is the coherent principle of the mind. . . . If one were to claim that [philology] is merely about recognizing difficult graphs to conceal ignorance and distinguishing errors to correct pronunciation, with no effort to relate it to the human mind and body, and ultimately no relation to our moral nature, this would truly be superficial.[13]

Language was fundamentally a product of the mind. Correcting pronunciation or written graphs was therefore not just about reading and writing but could also alter our behavior. Effectively correcting our ability to read, write, and utter language would require a broader rectification of the mind at work. Ming thinkers claimed that the language of antiquity was reflective of the way ancient sages thought and saw their attempts to recover this language as bearing great implications for our potential to become moral actors.

While some Ming scholars sought to transcend the distance between past and present, others pioneered methods to clearly differentiate ancient and contemporary language. Most famously, Chen Di 陳第 (1541–1617) proposed that the phonology of Chinese in antiquity differed systematically from that of his current language.[14] Others marveled at the changes in terminology and word usage that had occurred over time. Zhao Yiguang 趙宧光 (1559–1625), for instance, levied "the distinctions between ancient and present terms" as justification for the necessity of etymological research—without it, he opined, future readers would not even be able to tell what language old texts were written in.[15] The emergence of a notion of historical change, a basic assumption in linguistics today, spurred on new avenues of philological research and validated its relevance to some contemporary literati.

The importance of philology in late imperial China went beyond textual knowledge and morality; it extended to the political arena as well. The courts of both Ming and Qing China devoted energy to defining linguistic standards, although their power to enforce these standards may have been limited. Alluding to a passage in a classical ritual text, scholars in late imperial China frequently referred to a key role of the ruler as ensuring that his people "write in a shared script" (*shu tongwen* 書同文). The first Ming emperor, Zhu Yuanzhang 朱元璋 (1328–1398), commissioned a dictionary to further this goal by providing a model for character forms and pronunciation. He also prescribed linguistic registers for writing and speaking at court.[16] While the Ming court quickly lost linguistic authority in practice, the political and societal implications of language were widely acknowledged. Court involvement in linguistic matters can be traced back at least as early as the Qin dynasty (221–206 BCE) when the first emperor of Qin commissioned a sweeping unification of the Chinese script. Compared to earlier and later periods, the Ming court was relatively unconcerned with language standardization. The lack of a widely accepted court standard served as a call-to-arms for literati who believed such standards to be an essential part of a functioning society. Philological scholars claimed to inherit the mantle of establishing a "shared script," thereby assuming the governmental responsibilities of "scholarship, governance, ritual, music, and education."[17] Just as local governance took on new forms in the hands of gentry during this period in the absence of state oversight, so too did scholarly practices that capitalized on the lack of court involvement.[18]

Debates surrounding standards for a unified Chinese language were perhaps most visible in literary circles. New varieties of regional opera called into question earlier assumptions about the proper form of literary language. Within these sung genres, pronunciation was especially important, both for performers in making themselves intelligible to audiences and for librettists in selecting rhymes. Opera theorists and pedagogues went to great effort to defend particular linguistic standards, while innovating new systems for notating them. Poetry, as well, was a central arena of philological research. Although anyone in the sixteenth century would agree that poetry should rhyme, there was considerable debate concerning what words rhymed together, particularly when imitating ancient poetic styles. One's application of rhyming and the knowledge of phonology that this displayed was another layer of connoisseurship one could deploy within the social composition of poetry.[19]

Concern with literacy and proper pronunciation, especially in the context of classical recitation, was pervasive in late imperial China, when the ability to cite freely from the Classics was de rigueur among elites. A joke from the late Ming relates the story of a village schoolteacher, who after death is given the option of choosing his form in the next life. Curiously, he decides to be reincarnated as a dog. When asked why, he misquotes a line from a classical ritual text: "When confronted with wealth, do not *cur*-lessly obtain it; when confronted with calamity, do not *cur*-lessly avoid it." The teacher's misreading of "careless" for "cur-less" is based on his confusion of visually similar graphs.[20] Ming collections of humorous stories abound with such parody of the inability to recognize graphs, lack of phonological knowledge, and nonstandard accent.[21] Underlying these jokes was a clear message regarding the relationship between linguistic proficiency and status in late imperial Chinese society.

Philological ability allowed one to participate in this culture, to compose poetry in dialogue with one's peers, to make arguments about the Classics, and to recite these texts aloud in the presence of others. An understanding of the essential terminology and methods of philology was also expected of any member of the educated elite. Civil service examination questions routinely tested such learning, which was also presented in encyclopedic surveys of knowledge for literati.[22] These same examinations were responsible for the enforcement of language standards, particularly in terms of the written form of graphs. Not every scholar in late imperial China specialized in philology, but the texts discussed in this book would have been generally intelligible to a contemporary elite audience.

Resituating the Ming in China's Intellectual History

As early as the late seventeenth century, Gu Yanwu 顧炎武 (1613–1682) evaluated the scholarship of the preceding two centuries in harsh terms as misguided and imprecise. This picture of Ming scholarship was solidified in the late eighteenth century when the Qianlong emperor commissioned court scholars to compile the *Siku quanshu* (四庫全書 Complete library of the Four Treasuries), an enormous project that involved collecting, evaluating, and in some cases censoring the Chinese literary and intellectual tradition from past to present. Editors charged with composition of the annotated bibliography accompanying the *Siku quanshu* provided brief evaluations of each text. Much of their severest criticism was directed toward texts from the Ming, which they routinely described as "mishmash learning" (*douding zhi xue* 餖飣之學), "baseless" (*fei you genju* 非有根據), and "preposterous" (*duzhuan* 杜撰).[23] Modern attempts to characterize intellectual change in late imperial China have tended to accept this eighteenth-century presentation of the Ming intellectual landscape.[24] According to conventional representations of late imperial intellectual history, scholars from the fourteenth through seventeenth centuries largely neglected technical and textual learning in favor of metaphysical speculation. Beginning in the late seventeenth century and increasingly through the eighteenth, scholars came to reject abstract philosophy in favor of concrete learning, especially philology, as part of a new turn in intellectual culture. Numerous proposals have been advanced to explain the causes of intellectual transition in this period, but most take for granted the eighteenth-century narrative of what had changed.[25]

The flourishing world of textual study in the Ming has generally been neglected by historians, in large part as a result of the negative depiction generated by eighteenth-century scholars intent on demonstrating their departure from the past. The purpose of this book is not to place China's "philological turn," as the eighteenth century has recently been fruitfully conceptualized, two centuries earlier than previously thought.[26] Instead, by sidestepping the biased appraisals of later Qing scholars and removing the teleological endpoint of Qing philology, I pursue an inquiry into the nature of learning in this period based on historical actors' categories. Rather than evaluating Ming philological thinkers according to present-day standards, I aim to describe the logic and motivations underlying their methods of learning. Many Ming scholars were aware of approaches that would eventually gain sway in the eighteenth century, and which may seem more rational according to today's standards. They consciously rejected these methods based on their belief in the necessity of validating knowledge within a greater integrative system of learning.

Recent studies of select "great minds" of Ming scholarship have remedied received narratives by demonstrating areas of innovation, particularly in realms of technical scholarship.[27] Related work has sought the roots of Qing textual study in a set of exceptional Ming thinkers, showing that eighteenth-century philology did not develop ex nihilo.[28] Following recent research on the history of scholarship in early modern Europe, however, I posit that an intellectual context is not best measured by its few most outstanding minds.[29] I survey a substantial body of material, little-studied in the historical literature, in order to provide a broad picture of sixteenth- and seventeenth-century humanistic thought. Instead of identifying the few individual thinkers whose methods might be interpreted as foreshadowing the dominant modes of linguistic study in the Qing, I seek to contextualize Ming philology on its own terms. Some of the figures and works presented in this book were highly influential, both for contemporaries and for future generations, often in surprising ways. Others were ephemeral. On its own, each individual text of the latter category may provide little insight into contemporary intellectual culture. In the aggregate, important trends in late Ming thought that have been invisible become apparent. This approach also provides the necessary context with which to evaluate subsequent centuries. Did the eighteenth and nineteenth centuries represent a drastic reversal of previous trends or a natural evolution out of past scholarly methods? As will become clear from the present study, there is some truth to both perspectives. For instance, much-heralded advances of late nineteenth-century philology, such as a push toward phonographic writing systems, have roots in sixteenth-century discourse. On the other hand, the period between the sixteenth and nineteenth centuries witnessed a significant transition in notions of valid learning and knowledge production.

Research on history of the humanities has increasingly turned to the working methods of scholars according to the premise that the world of ideas is not separate from the broader social and material conditions under which they arise.[30] The collaborations delineated in this book across disparate Ming communities of learning reflect this concern with the nature of scholarly interaction and communication. They also provide insight into reading and composition practices, such as the use of reference books, that molded how these ideas were circulated, interpreted, and put to use. Previous research has documented the role of institutions, such as academies and the civil service examinations, in creating scholarly allegiances, especially in the Qing period.[31] The present study, by focusing on the role of communities of knowledge in constructing disciplinary affiliation, highlights the way in which a shared disciplinary interest (in this case language) could overcome institutional barriers, such as the lack of court support. The study of language in the Ming brought together communities of learning, which overlapped in unexpected ways, ranging from classicists (*ru* 儒) to Buddhist clergy (*seng* 僧) to practitioners of the literary arts (*wenren* 文人). This ecumenical approach to knowledge was reflective of a search for comprehensiveness, which promoted a notion of validity based on communal expertise. Ming scholars valued specialization in language, but the locus of authority was not exclusively *ru*, as it would increasingly grow to be in the Qing. Philologists saw themselves as part of a shared intellectual project composed of a past scholarly tradition and a contemporary community of likeminded scholars. Only by drawing on the linguistic expertise of scholars in disparate domains of learning did Ming philologists believe they could derive a comprehensive description of the nature of language.

This book provides an alternative understanding of late imperial Chinese intellectual culture; it also addresses issues of broad concern in the study of knowledge production. The nature of scholarly disciplines in history has received significant attention, particularly in the context of debates over the historical existence of a division between the "Two Cultures" of scientific and humanistic study.[32] It is well-established that boundaries of knowledge in the past differ from the present, but by what mechanisms were these boundaries established, and how did they shift over time? How were disciplines conceived in the past? Beyond simply observing that disciplinary boundaries were flexible in the early modern world, this book reconstructs the rationales underlying the negotiation of categories of knowledge. Although the interconnections among certain branches of learning in late imperial China may seem arbitrary to the modern eye, they operated according to rules that were widely accepted among contemporaries. An accurate understanding of the categories of scholarly pursuit in the early modern world can provide the basis for assessing the presence of historical divisions between and within scientific and humanistic learning, as well as tracing shifts in these divisions across time. The purpose of this book is to analyze the formation of a specific, and centrally important, discipline in late Ming China. By situating this study within the scope of contemporaneous—rather than anachronistic present-day—disciplinary boundaries, it offers an alternative method of contextualizing the history of knowledge.

Conceptualizing this shift in terms of the formation and transformation of "disciplinary" learning in China offers two benefits: it highlights how the scholarly environment of the sixteenth century differed significantly from previous periods, and it sheds new light on what changed over the course of the eighteenth century. Hence this book traces two significant shifts in conceptions of knowledge in China in the late imperial period. The first is the rise of a contemporary community of study defined by a shared interest in philology in the sixteenth century. Scholars over the course of the sixteenth and seventeenth centuries formed disciplinary communities, which valued the specialized knowledge of their contemporaries. This disciplinary configuration of knowledge tended to highlight the significance of ongoing collaborative study in the production of new knowledge. What we might refer to by contrast as the various "traditions" of learning in earlier periods, while similarly marked by a generic difference in the content of knowledge, primarily emphasized a communion with authorities of the past. The contested nature of disciplinary boundaries throughout the late imperial period reflects a second transition, evident in the narrowing of philology as a discipline in the eighteenth century. In the sixteenth century the boundaries surrounding these new disciplinary communities of knowledge were broad; philology (*xiaoxue*) bridged linguistic, musical, cosmological, and literary fields of learning. Over the course of the eighteenth century these boundaries narrowed considerably, and the category of *xiaoxue* came to focus predominantly on matters clearly related to the language of classical texts. The methods of philology remained influential beyond the study of language, and expert philologists of the Qing such as Dai Zhen 戴震 (1724–1777) and Qian Daxin 錢大昕 (1728–1804) were highly proficient in a wide variety of scholarly subjects, from mathematics to astronomy. But the study of language itself no longer required forging connections between them.

Structure of the Book

Philology in the Ming served as a nexus of scholarly and literary endeavors across multiple subjects. Part 1 of this book examines the role of cosmological, religious, and philosophical communities of learning in the generation of new linguistic knowledge in the Ming. Chapter 1 explores the cosmological and musical underpinnings of Ming philology, which were rallied as tools for uncovering *self-so* features of language that could not be documented solely on the basis of human observation. Ming scholars aimed to surpass regional bias by calculating the precise number of existing sounds in the universe, regardless of their presence in Chinese. The linkage of linguistic sound to the perceived natural processes of the universe also generated new attention toward phonographic scripts, which were capable of transcribing sounds posited by cosmological theory that did not exist in Chinese.

Although Ming scholars paid considerable attention to phonographic writing, they did not unequivocally accept such scripts as useful. Chapters 2 and 3 consider these discussions of writing within Buddhist and Confucian Learning of the Mind communities of learning. Chapter 2 focuses on the phonographic scripts most accessible to Ming scholars, namely those associated with the Sanskrit language. Debates concerning Sanskrit among Buddhist scholars and lay literati fueled an extensive discussion of the nature of writing systems. This chapter questions teleological assumptions of progress in the study of writing systems by presenting the reasons underlying the rejection of phonographic scripts in China. It also proposes the concept of phonetic legibility through which alphabetic writing conveyed phonetic information, but not semantic or grammatical content, to Ming readers. Chapter 3 places the discussion of phonographic writing within the broader discourse on Chinese script, which Learning of the Mind thinkers conceptualized in terms of the nondiscursive potential of Chinese graphs. Analyses of ancient graph forms yielded new theories of script as a mirror of the structure of the mind, laying the foundation for philology as a moral pursuit. These theories also provided the basis for new proposals on the most effective methods for indexing and retrieving information in lexicographic and encyclopedic texts.

While theoretical discussions of the nature of language occupied considerable scholarly attention, translating theory into practice was essential for the literary activities that preoccupied the elite in late imperial China. Part 2 turns to the engagement between literature and textual philology, highlighting the deep interconnections between classical and literary scholarship in this period. Chapter 4 delves into the world of literary practice, as classical philologists and literary figures collaborated on defining the standards and methods of linguistic description. Opera librettists, confronted with the challenges of intelligibility in new regional sung genres, invested great effort in describing a universal singing pronunciation. In so doing, they attracted the attention of contemporary classicists who imagined broader applications for these operatic methods. Chapter 5 explores how Ming scholars applied literary philology to the appreciation of the Classics of antiquity. Classicists envisioned new reading strategies that uncovered the literary and musical qualities of ancient texts. By focusing on the linguistic features of classical texts, scholars read prose as verse and verse as music.

The texts considered in parts 1 and 2 were primarily composed during the Ming dynasty but also include several works produced in the immediate decades following the Ming fall. Scholarly trends do not cleave precisely to dynastic dates, but by the early eighteenth century, a new epistemological stance toward the generation of philological knowledge was beginning to take form. Part 3 traces the afterlives of Ming texts and methodologies within this context and extending through the nineteenth century in order to illustrate how incorporating this largely forgotten history of Ming philology has significant implications for our understanding of late imperial intellectual change. By examining a set of Ming texts as they were cited and printed in new formats over the course of the Qing dynasty, chapter 6 reveals the impact of Ming scholarship that the anti-Ming discourse of the era obscures. Chapter 7 traces the formation of disciplinary communities in the late Ming and suggests reasons for why the notion of discipline narrowed in the eighteenth century. Federico Marcon has documented a similar process of disciplinary narrowing in early modern Japanese natural history (*honzōgaku* 本草学).[33] To a great extent, this transition occurred as a result of interaction with Western disciplinary conceptions of natural history. Such is not the case with philology in China, for which there was relatively little engagement with European methods. In this final chapter, an investigation of the construction of intellectual genealogies of philology in the eighteenth century indicates that the formation of a pantheon of largely Qing philological thinkers and the relegation of Ming scholars from the history of the field occurred over several generations, involving a shift toward new sources of authority and a redefinition of proper disciplinary methods.

The epilogue considers how a study of Ming philology historically situates the even more distant and seemingly unrelated language reform projects of the first half of the twentieth century, which ultimately produced the pinyin Romanization system and simplified graphs in current use in mainland China. In some cases, twentieth-century reformers pulled directly on Ming linguistic discourse; in others, superficial resemblances belie fundamental differences in aim. My purpose in highlighting these antecedents is not to argue that Ming innovation anticipated modern language reform, but rather to provide the context for a more nuanced explanation of what shifted in China's language politics over the course of the late imperial and modern period.

This book offers an unfamiliar picture of the Ming scholarly landscape. In so doing, it aims not only to restore what has been obscured, but also to reflect on how this changes our understanding of subsequent periods. That the intellectual culture of this period was much richer than the commonplace depiction of Ming philosophical iconoclasm and literary excess should not be surprising.[34] What is more unexpected is the centrality of philology in particular to Ming thinkers. Scholars, literary figures, and officials collaborated across fields in pursuit of linguistic systems that could facilitate reading of the Classics and composition of poetry and opera. Individualism and iconoclasm were balanced by a new priority on communal knowledge and the value of expertise. The communities of linguistic knowledge that formed during the Ming differ profoundly from those of later periods. Yet they initiated a discourse on language and produced new forms of scholarly interaction with concrete ramifications through the nineteenth century and into the present.

PART I

Sound and Script

CHAPTER 1

The Number of Everything

Music, Cosmology, and the Origins of Language

The Ming was a period of great literary and scholarly efflorescence. By the early sixteenth century the economic stagnation of the previous century had begun to change course.¹ Commercial publishing had revived alongside the growth of literary audiences.² Manuscript and limited-circulation private printing also took on new dimensions as literati sought to establish their authority within this diverse book market.³ Participation in the civil service examination system ensured the social and (to the successful few) political value of education. Particularly in the second half of the sixteenth century and into the seventeenth, the retreat of the court from scholarly patronage resulted in the formation of independent communities of learning devoted to technical, metaphysical, and political thought.

The explosion of scholarly and literary production in the period was also accompanied by a set of epistemological concerns: Where was the locus of authority? How could authenticity be evaluated? Should information be accessible to all or limited to a select audience of elite viewers? Assessing validity was of critical importance to late Ming literati, particularly in an environment of commercial and intellectual competition. Conceptions of valid knowledge shared among Ming literati had earlier origins, most notably in the discourse of Song dynasty Learning of the Way (*daoxue* 道學) thinkers. Prominent Song thinkers argued that there existed two kinds of knowledge: "knowledge [acquired] through hearing and seeing" (*wenjian* zhi 聞見之知) and "knowledge [acquired] through virtuous nature" (*dexing zhi zhi* 德性之知). As Ya Zuo has persuasively shown, "knowledge through virtuous nature" reflected a process of "modeling," which places a given "thing" in relation to a greater system.[4] For Learning of the Way thinkers, this system was bound together by the Coherence (*li* 理) possessed by every thing and affair in itself, as well as all things taken together. Through a process of learning, one would progressively understand the Coherence of particular things with the ultimate goal of becoming aware that this Coherence was inherent in one's mind as well. "Knowledge [acquired] through hearing and seeing," on the other hand, was based primarily on secondary knowledge, derived from sensory observation or learned from others and texts. For Learning of the Way thinkers, it was useful only to the degree it enabled one to become aware of Coherence.

The tension between these sensory and system-building methods of learning comes into sharp focus within the field of phonology, or the study of linguistic sound. Some Ming scholars were skeptical of the potential of human perception to accurately describe language, as well as the role of the philologist in defining standards. They did not employ terms that correspond precisely to present-day notions of "prescriptivism" and "descriptivism." Awareness of regional variation, however, as well as linguistic change across time, gave rise to a similar discourse of "correct" (*zheng* 正) and "originary" (*yuan* 元) forms of language. The two need not be oppositional; some claimed that recovering an "originary" pronunciation was necessary for "correcting" later linguistic corruptions. Often, however, one of these two notions served as the primary motivation behind the composition of a given philological text. Was the role of the scholar to establish a standard for others to employ in poetic composition or speech, correcting past errors? Or was it to devise an impartial system capable of encompassing all variations, one that was concerned primarily with the fundamental nature of sound? A clear example of this distinction is visible in how thinkers treated the issue of regional speech variation. Some philologists aimed to "correct" errors in pronunciation, which had crept into the poetic tradition as a result of the regional biases of dictionary compilers. Others conversely claimed that there was no "greater or lesser" among various forms of spoken Chinese; instead the task of the philologist was to devise a system that could take into account all varieties.[5] The Ming dynastic dictionary, *Hongwu zhengyun* (洪武正韻 Correct rhymes of the Hongwu reign), clearly adopted the former model. Its preface emphasized the pernicious influence of southeastern speech on earlier rhyme systems and sought to eliminate the vestiges of regional pronunciation.[6] A wealth of commercial rhyme books and dictionaries similarly offered standard pronunciations for literary usage. But the dominant mode of philological study among late Ming literati involved investigation into the origins of sound, capable of encompassing variation across time and place.

The epistemological victory of this approach lay in an increasingly prevalent discourse surrounding the value of *self-so* (*ziran* 自然) knowledge, which informed representations of "originary" phonology. Ming scholars configured *self-so* knowledge as impartial, not constructed by cultural or social norms, in opposition to "partial" (*si* 私) and "man-made" (*renwei* 人為) knowledge that reflected the learning or perception of an individual observer. A common refrain of praise in Ming scholarly texts went: "How could it be the product of man?" (*qi renwei* 豈人為).[7] This discourse was especially prevalent in discussions of the fountainhead of cosmological thought in China, the *Classic of Changes* (*Yijing* 易經). One routinely sees, for instance, claims that the sixty-four hexagrams of the *Changes* "emerge from the *self-so* quality of heavenly Coherence (*tianli* 天理), and must be different from the artificial labor of man-made [products]," or that they were evidence of "the *self-so* marvel of Coherence and Number, and not man-made."[8] As Dagmar Schäfer has shown, the two concepts did not have to be in opposition.[9] Some thinkers saw humans as capable of channeling what is *self-so*. The representative philological texts considered in this chapter, however, generally framed the two as opposing categories.

The notion of a dichotomy between nature and artifice has deep roots in the Chinese tradition and is evident already in texts from the Warring States period.[10] During the Ming, this dichotomy came to be focused on the relationship between *self-so* and "man-made" knowledge. The best evidence of something being *self-so* in the eyes of Ming scholars was its universality. What was so-of-itself originated in the "heavenly Dao" (*tiandao* 天道) accessible to all, whereas the "man-made" was a product of "personal opinion" (*sijian* 私見) belonging to one individual.[11]

Self-so knowledge was rooted in the notion of *li* (理).[12] Originally a generic term for "pattern," *li* gained new metaphysical significance as it was developed by the foundational Learning of the Way thinkers in the eleventh and twelfth centuries. For these thinkers, *li*, conventionally translated as "Coherence," provided a model for understanding individual things, as well as the interconnection between all things in the universe and the shared underlying morality of the human mind. The power of this concept, especially for Ming thinkers, was its ability to incorporate diversity within a framework of unity. In the famed words of one of the early Learning of the Way thinkers, "Coherence is one, but its manifestations are differentiated" (理一分疏). Each individual thing, be it a physical object like a tree or a relationship like that between parent and child, had a Coherence that governed its structure, development, and function. This Coherence could be articulated in ways that were specific to that particular object or situation. But ultimately each particular instance of Coherence was held to reflect the shared unitary Coherence present in all things.[13] Coherence therefore could explain how a specific thing worked, but also how all things fit together with one another. Ming thinkers self-consciously affirmed that anything that was *self-so* (in contrast to the "man-made") had to be coherent and representative of the *self-so* world as a unitary integrated system.

The notion of a unitary Coherence was essential to the late Ming pursuit of *self-so* knowledge. While most contemporaries would agree that *self-so* knowledge was superior to "partial" or "man-made" knowledge, the question remained as to how to prove that one's work represented what was *self-so*. The shared discursive appeal to *self-so* knowledge belied differing notions of what actually constituted the *self-so*, but one of most widespread Ming solutions to this problem within the study of language is highlighted in the use of correlations across various fields of learning. Following the logic of a unitary Coherence, these correlations were taken to reflect the underlying interrelationship of differing branches of knowledge. In practice, this effort did not result in the condensing of all knowledge into one framework. Rather, subjects with certain shared concerns, such as language and music, which both involved the study of sound, came to be grouped together. By extrapolating the demonstrable truths of one subject and correlating them with phenomena in other, related subjects, Ming scholars claimed to have discovered the key to *self-so* learning. The concept of Number (*shu* 數) also came to assume a newly elevated position in discussions of valid knowledge, based on the perception that arithmetical calculations reflected objective truths and were "commensurate" (*xiangtong* 相通) with, rather than secondary to, Coherence.[14]

Ming thinkers' adoption of the Learning of the Way discourse was often used toward profoundly different ends from those envisioned by their predecessors. In the Song, "knowledge through virtuous nature" and the investigation of Coherence could be used as a methodology to study specific things. But the ultimate point of such an exercise as promoted by Learning of the Way thinkers was to reveal the underlying unified Coherence in all things. This concern was fundamentally a moral issue because the point of understanding Coherence in particular things lay in deriving a universal basis for ethical decision making. In the Ming, the invocation of Coherence within fields of technical scholarship was not necessarily directed at questions of morality but could instead serve as the basis for a methodology aimed at surpassing the limits of human perception in generating knowledge.

As Thomas Gieryn has described, producers of knowledge demarcate boundaries to assert legitimacy.[15] In their pursuit of scholarly validity, Ming scholars drew boundaries around fields of knowledge that differed from earlier periods. The establishing of correlations between language and other subjects was typically framed as an improvement on previous linguistic methods by virtue of the *self-so* qualities of these interconnections. If something could hold true in multiple subjects, it could not be the product of an individual biased observer's creation. While from today's perspective Ming systems of knowledge appear highly contrived, contemporary justifications were rooted in the sense that they bypassed the artificiality of human construction. This justification fueled cosmology-based systems for modeling the sounds of language. It also served as a central point of defense for the Chinese script, which was heralded for its nondiscursive *self-so* potential, comparing favorably against what were perceived as arbitrary phonographic writing systems (see chapters 2 and 3).

The cosmological correlations Ming thinkers drew across different branches of knowledge interacted with other methods of knowledge production, including those that today would be considered empirical. Fang Yizhi 方以智 (1611–1671), for instance, incorporated discussions of physical sound production alongside his cosmological systematization of phonology. Jiao Hong 焦竑 (1540–1620), often heralded today for his interest in reconstructing ancient pronunciations on the basis of textual evidence, was deeply invested in the cosmological studies of contemporary philologists.[16] A growing body of literature on early modern Europe has examined the central role of esoteric modes of humanistic and philological practices in the period's intellectual life.[17] While clearly nonempirical from today's perspective, these practices coexisted in their time with empirical approaches and also lent methods critical to the development of natural science in Europe.[18] Coming to terms with the cosmological thinking of late imperial Chinese scholars is essential to understanding the intellectual culture of the period beyond those select few thinkers whose priorities align with those of present-day readers and similarly reveals surprising connections to later innovations.

Cosmology and Phonology

In his magnum opus on principles of linguistic sound, Chen Jinmo 陳藎謨 (c. 1600–1692), one of the great seventeenth-century scholars of language, observed:

> The world refers to [the study of] sounds and graphs as the "lesser learning" (*xiaoxue* 小學). Those who write in flourishing styles loathe it and put it aside, while the textual scholars are narrow-minded and do not understand it. Thus for thousands of years there has been no one to reveal its origins. Granted it is only one branch of the Six Arts, but if one does not study broadly and investigate texts for years, it cannot be verified. Yet it is not something textual scholars (*kaojiu ren* 考究人) can comprehend. If one does not over the course of several years deeply seek enlightenment, it cannot be understood. Yet it is not something those who seek enlightenment (*canwu ren* 參悟人) can explain. I therefore consider it the closest thing to cosmology (*xiangshu* 象數).[19]

This striking passage, which depicts the study of language as a mystical enterprise combining practices of textual study and religion, is as incomprehensible to the modern reader as it appears misguided. Making sense of such theories is the task facing a reconstruction of philology in sixteenth- and seventeenth-century China before the rise of Evidential Learning approaches to the study of language in the eighteenth century. Cosmology strongly informed the study of language in Ming China and continued to influence linguistic thought through the nineteenth century. If we wish to understand how late imperial Chinese scholars thought about language, we need to understand this relationship.

Evidential Learning (*kaozhengxue* 考證學), which emerged as a scholarly trend in the late eighteenth century, typically involved the comparison of linguistic usage in ancient texts. It continues to inform the field of

Chinese historical linguistics today, and its methods remain intelligible to the present. Chen Jinmo, using a related term for evidential research (*kaojiu*), claimed that the analysis of texts should not be the sole focus of linguistic study. Ming scholars were aware of concrete evidential methods but consciously rejected them. They instead proposed an alternative, which sought to embed language within a sphere of related fields. This system of knowledge, they argued, was superior to the limited scope of any individual field.

Chen Jinmo specifically related philology to the study of *xiangshu* (象數, lit. "Image and Number"), which I translate as cosmology. The term *xiangshu* originally referred to a school of *Classic of Changes* interpretation, which focused on the symbolic representations of cosmic processes within the text. By late imperial times the term referred not only to specialized *Changes* studies, but more broadly to analyses of universal processes based in numerology. By drawing a connection between philology and cosmology, Chen argued not simply that they were equally abstruse, but that there existed concrete links between the two. Chen's viewpoint would have been widely accepted by his contemporaries. During the mid-sixteenth through the seventeenth centuries, phonological scholars redefined the boundaries of their study to incorporate cosmological methods, which established correlations between the cosmos and the sounds of language.

In the early twentieth century, Chinese political thinkers such as Liang Qichao 梁啟超(1873–1929) and Chen Duxiu 陳獨秀 (1879–1942) came to see the cosmological and numerological thought of the sixteenth century as the "premodern cast of Chinese traditional society": irrational and unscientific.[20] Such negative appraisals tended to be based on a positivist notion of scientific progress, framed in comparison with the West. Contrary to most accounts, Ming scholars cared a great deal about philology and more specifically phonology.[21] Moreover, innovation in the field of phonology came about largely through the efforts of the cosmological scholars who would later be deplored for their inhibiting influence on Chinese modernity. As a result of their cosmologically motivated desire to notate all possible sounds in the universe, late Ming scholars separated linguistic sound from written script, advancing innovative ways for notating language without Chinese graphs.

The debate for many Ming phonological thinkers was not whether cosmological properties could be used to characterize linguistic sound but over the best way to understand these properties. Most thinkers predicated their methods on the cosmological premise that music and language were fundamentally related by virtue of their shared properties of "sound-based *qi* (vital force)" (*shengqi* 聲氣).[22] A common refrain in late imperial acoustic scholarship referred to the fact that "rhyme and music reflect each other inside and out."[23] Music had borne an extensive set of cosmological associations ever since its genesis as a field of study in antiquity.[24] In particular, the study of music in early texts was frequently combined with calendrics, both of which had a considerable basis in arithmetical calculations and were believed capable of making patterns of the cosmos knowable to humans. Language, on the other hand, was not heavily associated with the study of cosmology in early China. To be sure, the written script and linguistic utterances were characterized as reflections of nature, but their study was not seen as important to revealing universal processes.[25]

In the medieval period, literary figures began to develop associations between music and language, arguing that certain aspects of the Chinese syllable reflected pitches of the musical scale.[26] Shao Yong 邵雍 (1011–1077) in the Song dynasty was perhaps the first to merge all three scholarly traditions (music, cosmology, and language) by applying certain cosmological associations long assumed to inhere in musical pitch to linguistic categories. During the early and mid-Ming, phonological scholars increasingly solidified this conception of the shared cosmological basis for all varieties of sound.[27] By the late Ming this fusion of cosmology, music, and language came to be reflected in the titles of many contemporaneous works of acoustic scholarship. Cheng Yuanchu 程元初 (fl. 1609–1614), for instance, wrote a pair of works entitled *Lülü yinyun guashu tong* (律呂音韻卦數通 Comprehending the twelve musical pitches, syllable initials and rhymes, and the numbers of the *Yijing* trigrams) and *Huangzhong yinyun tongkuo* (黃鍾音韻通括 A comprehensive examination of the initials and rhymes based on the pitch C). Other acoustic studies combining music and language indicated their concern with all forms of "sound-based *qi*" by referring more broadly to "sound" (*sheng*), "tone" (*yin*), or "pitch" (*lü*), such as *Yinsheng jiyuan* (音聲紀元 Recording the origins of sound), *Tailü* (泰律 Grand pitches), and *Taigu yuanyin* (太古元音 Primordial tones of distant antiquity). Such categorical overlap is evident in a seventeenth-century bibliographical catalog, which even listed a study of musical pitches with no explicit discussion of language under its phonology section (*yunxue*).[28]

Totalizing thinkers of the late Ming inherited the Learning of the Way claim that the universe constituted a coherent system. In an approach occasionally characterized in the sources as "integrative" (*cuozong* 錯綜), scholars would address problems that could not be easily solved within the confines of a single field by drawing correlations from others. The term *cuozong* possessed a technical meaning within *Changes* scholarship and later in mathematical treatises for a particular combinatorial method. It also came to be applied to the combination of various branches of learning, alongside related terms for "synthesizing," such as *zong* 綜, *guantong* 貫通, *jian* 兼, and *he* 合, as well as references to the "mutually complementary" (*xiang wei biaoli* 相為表裏) nature of various fields, such as music, cosmology, and language.[29]

It was this notion of mutual complementarity that justified Chen Jinmo's linkage of cosmology with philology. As Chen's older contemporary, the prolific lexicographer Lü Weiqi 呂維祺 (1587–1641), put it: "The Way of the six principles of graph formation [derived from *Shuowen jiezi*] is indeed mutually complementary with the diagrams and eight trigrams [of the *Classic of Changes*]" (六書之道，實與圖書八卦相表裏).[30] Lü elaborated that this relationship not only invoked the supposed origins of Chinese graphs in the written forms of the trigrams but also reflected the cosmological significance of analyzing graphs. Similar statements throughout the period's philological literature, offering, for instance, that "the applications [of written graphs] are mutually complementary with music" (用與樂相表裏) or that "[linguistic] sound and cosmology are mutually complementary" (聲音與象數相表), indicate a widespread contemporary approach to linguistic scholarship that prioritized establishing how things fit together within a grander system of *self-so* knowledge.[31] This methodology was also framed negatively by its critics as "forging artificial connections" (*qianhe* 牽合 or *fuhui* 附會).[32] For its proponents, so long as a theoretical linkage could be established between two fields, thus validating their mutual complementarity, then the known facts of one could be used to solve for unknowns of the other. Hence the putative shared originary sound linking music and language allowed late Ming scholars to apply musical knowledge, such as the arithmetically derived number of pitches in the musical scale, to linguistic problems like the number of rhyme groups in Chinese. Earlier theories of cosmic resonance (*ganying* 感應) that argued that things of a similar category respond to one another underlay these correlations, as well as the more recent Learning of the Way proposal that a unitary Coherence (*li* 理) manifests itself in different forms to link all things in the material world.[33] For Learning of the Way thinkers, investigating

Coherence in external things would ultimately enable one to realize the Coherence within the human mind, allowing one to become a moral actor. But Ming scholars did not uniformly see philology as a moral enterprise.[34] As opposed to earlier cosmologists, they were also generally less interested in speculating on how the universe as a whole functions than on how universal principles could be applied to answer particular linguistic questions. As a result, Ming scholars invoked Coherence and correlation in service of philological research, rather than employing linguistic facts as proof of generalizable universal phenomena, as past thinkers had.

The Ming witnessed the emergence of a widespread community of language specialists, but the content of this specialization involved a broadening of the valence of subjects associated with language. In search of a new *self-so* basis for discussing language, scholars drew on analogies across many fields. Music and cosmology were particularly appealing to contemporary thinkers, given the widespread belief in the *self-so* quality of their foundation in arithmetical calculations. This widespread trend based on the cosmological premise that all sound was fundamentally related instigated striking innovations in the study of language, from the creation of new phonographic writing systems to numeric codes that long predate similar innovations in the twentieth century.

Why Cosmology? On the Limits of Human Perception

What was the appeal of applying abstract cosmological properties to the study of language? A recurring theme among Ming scholars was the need to surpass the limits of human perception and bias. The issue of bias was particularly relevant within a linguistic context due to the existence of numerous, mutually unintelligible regional varieties of spoken Chinese, or topolects.[35] Some advocated for a unified standard, particularly within the context of literary composition and operatic performance (see chapter 4). In contrast to this desire to establish unity, cosmological thinkers tended to embrace the diversity of Chinese languages. Ge Zhongxuan 葛中選 (1577–1636) referred to this diversity, including even non-Chinese languages, as "all the royal sounds of heaven and earth."[36] Wu Jishi similarly argued that, "as to the differentiation among sounds southern, northern, eastern, and western, this is all simply a matter of humans and is not the natural disposition of heaven."[37] Scholars such as Ge and Wu argued that a cosmological approach allowed for the study of sound in a more general way than focus on a particular regional variety of Chinese would permit.

Wu Jishi and Ge Zhongxuan went to great lengths to expound the correlations between universal processes and sound, which they believed could surpass the artificiality of a system created by humans. Wu, for instance, correlated each of his rhyme groups with elements significant in geomancy and cosmology, such as solar periods, winds, and *Yijing* trigrams. Wu's contemporaries developed similar systems under the premise that they reflected "self-so sounds" (*ziran zhi yin* 自然之音), which "could not have emerged from human creation."[38] These geomantic and cosmological properties were also believed to explain the diversity of Chinese topolects. Fang Yizhi, among others, described "regional speech" (*fangyan* 方言) as the product of "*self-so qi*"; pronunciation variation was a result of the differing *qi* properties of particular regions.[39]

In the view of these thinkers, most prior phonological scholarship was too subjective, asserting one particular topolect over another as more correct, or relying on fragmentary textual evidence from antiquity to assert claims about ancient pronunciations. The perceived cosmological processes underlying the natural world provided these scholars with a way of abstractly discussing sound without reference to time, place, or texts. This approach is particularly striking when juxtaposed against the single most famous statement regarding phonology to emerge from the Ming dynasty: "That time divides into past and present, that space divides into north and south, that graphs undergo transformations, and sounds undergo shifts must all be the necessary result of changing circumstances."[40] This novel argument for the nature of linguistic change over time was proposed by Chen Di in the preface to his seminal *Mao Shi guyin kao* (毛詩古音考 An investigation of ancient pronunciations in the *Classic of Poems*), first printed in 1606, and it is widely acclaimed today for its influence on the study of historical phonology in China. Many of Chen's contemporaries read his study, although its premises were evidently not so widely accepted. Cosmological scholars saw Chen's work as misguided in its focus on a rupture with antiquity, which did not recognize the universal cosmological basis of sound. Wu Jishi, for instance, opined that "although past and present differ, sounds have not changed."[41] Wu further argued that cosmology afforded a way to escape adhering to the sounds of a particular time or region: "I have followed the *self-so* sounds of heaven and earth, notating them one by one, without regard for north and south or their peoples."[42] Concretely, Wu, as well as many of his contemporaries, proposed a combination of rhyme table methods and the use of phonographic scripts in order to comprehensively document linguistic sounds, including regional and putative ancient pronunciations.

Cosmological and musical correlations addressed not only the concern of human bias, most notably regional preferences, but also limitations of the human body itself. As Wu Jishi argued, a cosmological approach could allow scholars to surpass the constraints of human aural perception: "There are limitless sounds in the universe, and all of them enter [us] through our ears (皆從耳入). Thus the sages' hearing was attuned, their conceptualization was conforming, and their mind was comprehending. The Way of sound is great. . . . [My] method in *Yinsheng jiyuan* follows the ear but is comprehended through the mind and does not solely rely on the ears (非徒任耳)."[43] Wu Jishi claimed that even if one tried to be impartial in recording sounds, it would ultimately be futile because our perception of sound is limited by what we as individuals are capable of hearing. Wu extensively recorded differences in regional pronunciation as proof of the futility of relying on the biased human ear. Contemporary phonologists largely agreed that an overreliance on oral and aural evidence resulted in the parochial avoidance of linguistic sounds that "the Chinese could not pronounce" (華人所不能道) or could not differentiate by ear.[44] To go beyond the constraints of human perception, there would have to be another way to comprehensively describe sound, and cosmology was seen as providing the methodology.

The Beauty of Number

To understand more completely the appeal of a cosmological approach to knowledge, it is necessary to examine a critical term within its discourse: Number (*shu* 數, capitalized to differentiate it from its basic sense). In the context of late imperial Chinese cosmology, Number is best understood not in the basic sense of a unit of counting, but instead as the numerical relationships underlying the functioning of the universe.[45] Perhaps the most exemplary usages of Number in the Chinese intellectual tradition are the binary of *yin* and *yang*, as well as the Five Phases. The numerical basis of these concepts was fundamentally relational and did not represent fixed quantities. The phases, for instance, were used to indicate change over time as one phase progresses to the next (in the order wood, fire, earth, metal, and water). The time period could vary, from the progression of seasons over the course of a single year to a much grander scale, such as the succession of dynasties over hundreds of years. The five-part sequence therefore indicated a relationship between time points, rather than a specific unit of time.

Ming scholars understood Number to be a fundamental property of sound. Fang Yizhi, for instance, promoted the concept that "sound and Number share the same origin" (*sheng shu tong yuan* 聲數同原). By acknowledging that the universe is constituted of the "intermingling of *self-so* Coherence and Number," Fang argued that one could observe the universal and originally unitary origins of sound. He claimed that the evidence for this lay in the fact that although "the languages of the five directions differ, their cries and gurgles are naturally the same."[46] He observed that differentiations among language were not evident in infants, who all make the same utterance of "*wa wa*" (哇哇) at birth. The notion that the language of infants was regionally undifferentiated hearkens back to the classical claim that "the children of various tribal peoples all produce the same sound at birth, and only differ in their customs (*su* 俗) as they age," or as one Ming scholar paraphrased it: "all produce the same sound at birth, and only differ in their language (*yu* 語) as they age."[47] Seventeenth-century philologists frequently invoked the language of infants as representing an originary form of language.[48] Fang Yizhi's contemporary Chen Jinmo, for instance, claimed in similar terms that "at birth all sounds are alike" (墮地時聲盡相同), with regional differences emerging only later in a child's youth.[49] Yet another referred to the utterances of a newborn baby as "purely of heaven and uncontaminated by humans" (純乎天而不雜以人), a state of affairs that would change as the child was exposed to the speech of its parents.[50] The opera theorist Li Yu 李漁 (1610–1680) even advocated taking advantage of the unfixed nature of infant and young adult speech by training singers in pronunciation at a young age before their accent was corrupted by regional influence.[51]

This phenomenon raised a set of questions as significant for Ming thinkers as for modern-day neuroscientists and linguists: Why are all humans born with an innate ability for language? And how is it that this ability decreases with age? In an observation largely confirmed by present-day understandings, Fang Yizhi noted that only as infants developed (*zhang* 長) did the physiological constraints of regional languages become settled. However, Fang Yizhi and his contemporaries were primarily concerned with the first question concerning the universal nature of early-stage language.

Fang Yizhi's explanation for the universality of language hinged on the basis of language in the universal categories of Number. As a result, he proposed an elaborate phonological classification system, involving numerological correspondences between the seasons of the year, cardinal directions, and speech sounds. The prevalence of such methods requires us to ask why such scholars were persuaded by the utility of Number, and how they demonstrated its relationship to language.

Music, Arithmetic, and the Objectivity of Number

Ming thinkers generally considered Number to be essential in cementing the connection between the two fundamental instantiations of sound: music and language. In their view, all sound was the product of some kind of movement of *qi*, which existed prior to its categorization as tone, either musical or linguistic. Both music and language were therefore simply differing manifestations of sound-based *qi*.

Ming scholars frequently referred to this originary form of sound as "primordial sound" (*yuansheng* 元聲 or *yuanyin* 元音). Although the term existed in earlier periods, "primordial sound" became a topic of widespread acoustic study only in the Ming.[52] Primordial sound was neither fundamentally linguistic nor musical. Some scholars believed it to be manifested in the sounds of nature, especially wind and thunder.[53] One thinker opined that it was the sound created at the beginning of the universe "when heaven and earth first split apart."[54] Only later was the primordial sound channeled into musical and linguistic contexts, through either the human voice or musical instruments.

Ming thinkers would generally agree that the reason musical harmony was pleasing to the ear was its *self-so* properties. This perceived natural quality of music was evident to Ming scholars in the arithmetical derivation of pitches, which were calculated based on the length of the pitch-pipe for the pitch C (*huangzhong* 黃鐘).[55] Frequent court debates from as early as the third century concerned the methods of ascertaining the correct length of the C pitch-pipe.[56] Once this length was established, however, the method of calculating the subsequent pitches most often followed the practice known as "adding and subtracting one third" (*sanfen sunyi* 三分損益).

In this method, the length of the pitch-pipe would alternatingly have one-third of its length subtracted and added to produce the rest of the scale. For instance, if the length of the C pitch-pipe was set at nine "inches" (*cun* 寸), then the subsequent pitch-pipe would have one-third of its length subtracted, yielding a length of six "inches." This length produces a pitch a fifth higher than the original pipe (in this case G). The product would then have one-third of its length added, yielding a pitch-pipe length of eight "inches," producing the pitch a fourth lower than the preceding pipe (in this case D). This alternating operation could be performed twelve times before (almost) returning to the original C pitch an octave higher.[57]

The perceived efficacy of an arithmetical calculation to determine pitch was bolstered by a belief in the *self-so* nature of Number itself. The renowned music theorist Han Bangqi 韓邦奇 (1479–1556), for instance, insisted that the arithmetically based model of pitch derivation reflected "the *self-so* qualities of Number (數之自然), and is not the product of the manipulations of private opinion or human effort."[58] Another seventeenth-century scholar, Ying Huiqian 應撝謙 (1615–1683), opined that "the arithmetical calculations of musical pitches, although complicated, presumably have profound meaning, given that they reflect the *self-so* qualities of Number and are neither possible through the efforts of humans nor merely one school of thought."[59] Even Zhu Zaiyu 朱載堉 (1536–1611), the greatest musical thinker of the Ming, often upheld as a pioneer of empiricism in China, wrote that the "miracle of arithmetic calculation . . . emerges from the true principle of heaven and earth's *self-so* quality . . . it is not created through the machinations of human effort."[60] These numerical and therefore *self-so* calculations were believed to surpass musical taste, which various late imperial musical treatises held to be subject to the corrupting influence of "vulgar music" aimed solely at "pleasing the ear."[61]

Underlying these appeals to the *self-so* nature of arithmetically derived musical pitches was a desire to establish a set of communal scholarly norms. The concern with "human effort" voiced by so many scholars of this period was that it was not universal; any individual's effort could yield different results. Ying Huiqian's invocation of "one school of thought" (*yi jia zhi xue* 一家之學) reflects a broader seventeenth-century discourse regarding the significance of communal standards in validating scholarship. While the phrase "one school of thought" appears in medieval texts as praise for creative scholarship, it began to acquire a negative connotation as early as the eleventh century. By the late imperial period, scholars levied the phrase as a common criticism against those who did not meet contemporary disciplinary norms.[62] Arithmetical calculations were perceived as something impartial that would obtain the same result under any circumstance and were not subject to interpretation.[63]

As another manifestation of "primordial sound," Ming scholars claimed that language was also subject to the same *self-so* numerical properties as music. Rhyme tables came to be permeated with musical terminology on the basis of its perceived natural characteristics. Such tables, which may have originated as early as the tenth century, had historically aimed to comprehensively describe the sound system of Chinese by creating abstract categories for each aspect of the Chinese syllable (such as initial, final, and tone; see the text box). Seminal rhyme tables from the twelfth century claimed that there existed sixteen distinct finals in the Chinese language. Perhaps the clearest expression of the newfound nexus of music and language in the Ming is the replacement of these categories with a variety of twelve-part categorizations in imitation of the twelve musical pitches, as well as five- and seven-part systems intended to reflect the pentatonic and heptatonic scales employed in Chinese music. Scholars argued that this method of categorizing linguistic sound, in addition to more accurately accounting for the shared basis of linguistic and musical sound, would improve the aesthetic quality of vocal music by ensuring the proper correspondence between pronunciation and sung pitch.[64] The generation of twelve pitches through a process of arithmetical calculation lent the number twelve epistemological authority as a *self-so* quantity for sonic categories. Although Ming philologists produced many competing twelve-part linguistic categorization systems, they nevertheless all shared the conviction that musical constants should govern our understanding of language.

CHINESE PHONEMES, TONES, AND THE REPRESENTATION OF PHONETIC INFORMATION

The phonological structure of the Chinese syllable is an (optional) initial phoneme (the most basic linguistic unit of sound) combined with a final. The initial is composed of a consonant, and the final is composed of a vowel, occasionally followed by a consonant. The final may also contain a medial vowel, which is a short vowel sound, located between the initial and the main vowel. For example, the Mandarin syllable *jiang* comprises the initial [*j*-] combined with the final [-*iang*]. The final is itself made up of the medial vowel [-*i*], the main vowel [-*a*], and the consonant [-*ng*]. Initial phonemes are also distinguished by voicing, which refers to the presence or absence of vocal cord vibration (familiar in English from the contrast between phonemes such as /s/ and /z/). In Chinese historical phonology, the term *rhyme* is often used interchangeably with *final*, although some scholars omit the medial vowel in discussing rhymes. The term *articulation* refers to the physical place (palatal, dental, and the like) and manner (nasal, stop, and so on) of the production of a particular linguistic sound.

Traditional analyses of Chinese phonology, dating back to the fifth century, identify four tonal categories: level (*ping* 平), rising (*shang* 上), falling (*qu* 去), and entering (*ru* 入). The first three tones were characterized by a tonal contour; the final or "entering" tone was characterized by its ending in a stop consonant (<-p>, <-t>, or <-c>). The entering tone, still present in many topolects such as Cantonese, no longer exists in Modern Mandarin.

There existed several methods of indicating pronunciation with Chinese graphs. The most prevalent in the late imperial period was the *fanqie* (反切, occasionally 翻切) method by which the pronunciation of a single Chinese graph, representing one syllable, is "spelled" by means of two graphs. The first *fanqie* graph represents the initial of the glossed graph, while the second graph represents the final. For example, <dhūng> 同 can be glossed in *fanqie* as <dhū> 徒 + <hūng> 紅 (in other words, the initial <dh-> + the final <-ūng>).

Rhyme tables provided even more detailed phonological information. In such tables, the head of each column was typically an initial, while rows were organized according to elements of the final (including rhyme, medial vowel, and tone). Similarly to *fanqie*, syllables glossed in the body of a rhyme table represented the combination of an initial (at the head of its column) and a final (at the head of its row). For an example of the standard matrix format of a rhyme table, see figure 2.2.

Music served not only as a direct source for mapping the Chinese sound system, but also as a methodological analogy for understanding acoustic principles in language. Zhao Yiguang, for instance, argued that the principles of phonology "resemble" (*sihu* 似乎) those of music. Because the C pitch-pipe was the basis from which the other eleven pitches were calculated, Zhao termed it "the origin of myriad sounds." Linguistic sound, too, had an origin: the phoneme *a* (阿). In his view, when combined with other linguistic sounds it could generate all possible syllables. Zhao argued that there were concrete differences between music and language, such as how many musical pitches exist compared to how many syllables do. From a methodological perspective, however, they could be held to have "no discord in principle."[65] Such analogies between language and musical-arithmetic derivations would come to be employed as a justification for the study of non-Chinese phonographic scripts, such as Sanskrit, which represent sound through the combination of letters with no inherent meaning of their own (see chapter 2).[66]

Number as a Finite Constraint on Language

Number was perceived as a fundamentally *self-so* property of sound. Arithmetical calculations also allowed scholars to determine a fixed number, which could represent all possible sounds in the universe. The fascination with identifying the precise number of possible sounds traces back to the eleventh-century thinker Shao Yong. His writings, which emerged from a long tradition of correlative thinking, emphasized a mechanistic system in which numerical cycles based on the number four (among other numbers) explained and constrained the functioning of the universe and the progression of history. For Shao Yong, theory overrode observation and the rules of Number and category could explain all phenomena. Shao's work was based on the premise that the universe operates according to knowable principles that change according to a numerical process. By demonstrating that these numerical processes apply to language as well, Shao provided another example of his theory in action. Shao Yong did not see himself as a phonologist, nor did he intend his work to contribute to the field of phonological scholarship. Rather he framed his rhyme tables as another demonstration of how the cosmological system underlying all phenomena was consistent. Shao Yong's analysis of the cosmological underpinnings of language, which had little influence during his lifetime, came to be adopted again in the late Ming dynasty. In contrast to their original purpose as a reflection of greater cosmological processes, Ming scholars saw these methods as directly relevant for the purposes of phonological description.

Shao's magnum opus, the *Huangji jingshi shu* 皇極經世書 (Book of the august ultimate traversing the ages), is our main source for understanding his thought. This text contains a set of rhyme tables, where Shao applied to spoken sounds the combinatory schemes found in the rest of the work. Later Chinese rhyme tables frequently included blank spaces where the author could not find a Chinese graph that matched the phonological description for a particular position in the table. Shao was remarkably different: he prescribed a precise number for how many phonological positions in his tables should contain no graph based on cosmological principles. According to Shao's calculations, there should be exactly 48 (out of 160) finals with no corresponding graph, and 40 (out of 192) initials with no corresponding graph. By multiplying the total number of initials (192) and finals (160), which were themselves derived from a set of cosmological calculations, Shao proposed the existence of 30,720 possible sounds. These calculations were based not on a sense of linguistic reality, but instead on his conception of the cosmological processes underlying all things in the universe.

Shao Yong had devised a solution for how many syllables could possibly exist. This question of precisely how many syllables, or linguistic units, exist did not concern many thinkers after Shao Yong until the late Ming when cosmological approaches to phonology reemerged in response to new phonological debates. Some Ming scholars, such as Yuan Zirang 袁子讓 (*jinshi* 1601) and Lü Weiqi, simply cited Shao Yong's numbers. Others, such as Ge Zhongxuan, Wu Jishi, Chen Jinmo, and Fang Yizhi, came up with entirely new proposals for determining the precise number of existing syllables on the basis of calculations that aligned parts of the syllable with cosmologically significant elements, such as musical pitches, generating numbers ranging from roughly six thousand to ten thousand possible syllables.[67] They seem to have been aware of each other's work, and their creation of separate systems implies disagreement.[68] However, they shared the belief that the universe comprises a coherent and knowable system; their divergences were primarily related to differing conceptions of how universal processes affect sound.

Ming cosmologists claimed that there existed a finite (*ding* 定) number of sounds in the universe, resulting from their generation by the "*self-so* origins of heaven and earth." Written language, on the other hand, contained infinite possibilities because it was an artificial creation.[69] Defining the number of sounds as a finite quantity had several implications. Fang Yizhi, for instance, claimed that it could reveal the underlying link between all spoken languages. What appeared to be differences in pronunciation from various regions of the world were the result of differences in articulation, in Fang's view—a physiological issue, rather than a question of the fundamental sound.

Ge Zhongxuan offered another possibility for the importance of documenting the numerical properties of sound. Ge criticized Chen Di, who has been frequently upheld as the originator of critical historical phonology in China for his study of rhyming in the *Classic of Poems* (*Shijing* 詩經). Chen Di attempted to uncover ancient pronunciations and gloss them with a graph approximating that pronunciation in modern spoken language, Most modern scholars of the history of Chinese phonology consider Chen's work a major step forward from the earlier "forced" or "harmonized" rhyming method (*xieyun* 叶韻), in which readers adjusted the pronunciation of graphs on an ad hoc basis to fit the rhyme scheme in an individual poem. Chen's argument that the ancients did not change pronunciations at will and that each graph typically had only one fixed pronunciation in antiquity was deeply influential for later seventeenth- and eighteenth-century phonologists. For Ge Zhongxuan, however, Chen's approach was too subjective (*ziwo zuo* 自我作).[70] Ge argued that Chen's method, which ultimately glossed graphs with a modern pronunciation, was simply masquerading as a representation of antiquity. Ge claimed to have derived the number of possible sounds in the universe, including those of antiquity, and that he was able to document all these possibilities in his rhyme tables. Ge differentiated his way of cataloging ancient pronunciations from Chen Di's by characterizing his own approach as one that recognized that "sounds also contain Number" (聲亦有數).[71] An abstract system based on Number and cosmology appeared to Ge to be a more reliable method of discussing linguistic change over time than studying the sparse remaining textual record. In particular Ge believed that the superiority of his own method lay in its ability to theorize linguistic sounds without relying exclusively on existing graphs or sounds of the modern spoken language. He further developed a system of phonographic writing, which allowed him to notate the great number of sounds he had derived in his rhyme tables.[72]

Ge's argument had considerable implications for practices of classical recitation. In an education system in which literacy was acquired primarily through recitation, and a culture in which the ability to cite the texts of antiquity was highly valued, how one chose to pronounce these texts mattered.[73] Ge may not have fully grasped Chen's concept of linguistic change over time—he even embraced the *xieyun* method as "at least a convenient method for reciting the *Classic of Poems*."[74] However, the basis of his repudiation of Chen Di was not complacent adherence to tradition, a criticism often leveled at supporters of the *xieyun* method. Instead, Ge believed that his newly developed abstract system of phonological representation based on cosmology was ultimately a more valid way of conceptualizing the differences in rhyming between antiquity and the present.

Ming scholars, despite their widespread incorporation of Shao Yong's cosmological methods, tended to be skeptical of his claim that the principles of phonology could be extrapolated to describe the functions of the universe more broadly. In their adaptation of Shao Yong's methods, Ming scholars criticized Shao for his evident lack of concern for the implications of his work for the study of phonology. Qiao Zhonghe 喬中和 (1573–1652) described Shao Yong's contribution as "assiduous yet too forced" in its desire to fit everything into an immovable universal system.[75] Although Qiao's own phonological study was highly abstract and rooted in cosmological theory, he would occasionally make exceptions in order to account for the discrepancy between his system and a sense of linguistic reality. Yuan Zirang similarly referenced "questionable" aspects of Shao's tables, which Yuan altered to bring them in line with other phonological texts.[76]

Ming proposals for the number of sounds in the universe derived from Shao Yong's contention that cosmological categories, such as natural elements or musical harmonics, were relevant to phonology. As opposed to Shao Yong, however, they interpreted these numbers as directly relevant to the study of language, rather than merely a reflection of broader cosmological phenomena. On the basis of these numbers, Ming scholars even called for new methods of phonetic notation capable of transcribing all possible sounds.

The Ease of Examining Numbers: Chen Jinmo and the Perfection of Shao Yong's Method

In addition to promoting the *self-so* nature and finite constraint of Number, proponents of cosmological phonology also claimed to be capable of generating simpler explanations of linguistic principles than had previously existed. One of the major targets of Ming philological criticism was a genre known as "methods of study" (*menfa* 門法), which attempted to explain the intricacies of Chinese phonology contained in rhyme tables with highly esoteric language. Ming scholars routinely criticized these texts for obscuring more than they clarified.[77] Number, and its associated arithmetical practices, came to be upheld as a means to explain basic phonological principles in a way that avoided complex theoretical explanation or even the use of Chinese graphs.

The late Ming saw the innovation of several systems for representing sounds outside of Chinese graphs. All these systems were premised on the concept of Number, as a reflection of the relationship between language, music, and cosmology, and as a limiting factor on the quantity of existing sounds. One phonological system from the period even sought to substitute Chinese graphs with numbers. The creator of this system, Chen Jinmo, was a disciple of the cosmologist Huang Daozhou 黃道周 (1585–1646).[78] Chen was from Zuili 檇李 (present-day Jiaxing 嘉興) in Zhejiang province; he studied as a government student (*zhusheng* 諸生) until the end of the Ming, when he abandoned his formal studies. In addition to his expertise in phonology, Chen was highly proficient in mathematics and compared Western and Chinese mathematical practices.[79] Chen justified his combination of these two fields and the creation of a numeric method of phonetic representation by asserting "the ease of examining numbers" (數之易稽), which would obviate the challenges present in other modes of phonetic transcription.[80]

In his *Huangji tuyun* (皇極圖韻 Supreme principles for diagramming rhymes), printed in 1634, Chen Jinmo presented a system of numerical phonetic notation that abstracted linguistic sound from the Chinese script. Chen's study, as a reflection of broader contemporary concerns with phonetic notation, represents a significant turning point in Chinese linguistic thought. Unlike some contemporary cosmologists, however, Chen did not see phonographic scripts as the key to comprehensive phonological description. Instead, he presented an alternative, and even more radical, way of thinking about the sounds of language: although it did not abandon Chinese graphs entirely as a reference, it offered a conception of sound removed from any existing script.

In *Huangji tuyun*, Chen constructed a set of nine rhyme tables modeled after one of the most influential diagrams of the Chinese cosmological tradition: the *Luoshu* 洛書 (Luo [River] writing) diagram (figure 1.1). The *Luoshu* diagram was, according to legend, first observed by the Great Yu (Da Yu 大禹), the mythical first emperor of the Xia dynasty, on the back of a turtle emerging from the Luo River. There are, however, no extant versions of the diagram prior to the Song dynasty. The diagram is a magic square, comprising a 3 x 3 matrix, in which any three numbers (represented by circles) added vertically, horizontally, or diagonally equal fifteen.[81]

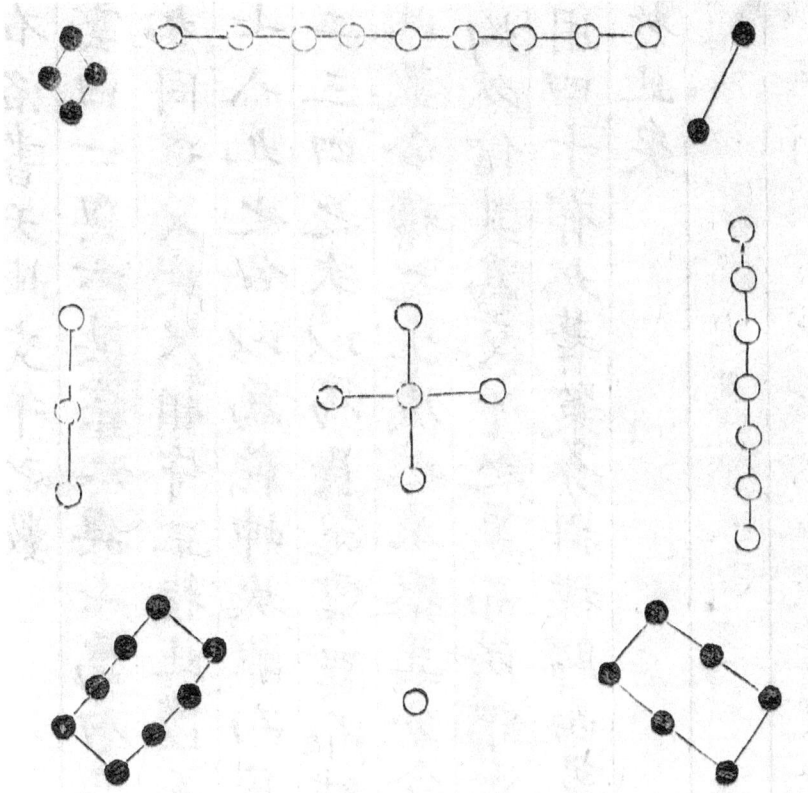

Figure 1.1 The *Luoshu* diagram. Zhang Li, *Yixiang tushuo neipian* (1673 edition at Harvard-Yenching Library), j. 1, 8b. (Image courtesy of Harvard-Yenching Library.)

Learning of the Way thinkers infused this diagram with great cosmological significance. Seventeenth-century scholars would frequently make use of such cosmological diagrams to establish correlations between various subjects.[82] Philological texts, in particular, came to regularly adopt cosmological diagrams to illustrate the relationship between language, music, calendrics, and other branches of learning (for example, figure 1.2).[83]

Each of Chen Jinmo's nine tables comprises nine squares that mimic the 3 x 3 matrix of the *Luoshu* diagram.[84] Each square contains four distinct syllables (figure 1.3A). In an effort to signal that his discussion of sound was not tied to the sounds of the Chinese language, Chen replaced all graphs in his tables with numbers (figure 1.3B). For instance, Chen assigned the number 1 to <cūng> 公, 2 to <ciōng> 弯, 3 to <gī> 奇, and

THE NUMBER OF EVERYTHING [39]

Figure 1.2 Cosmological diagram linking tonal categories, musical, numerological, and calendrical concepts. Ma Ziyuan, *Chongding Ma shi dengyin* (1708 edition at Harvard-Yenching Library), *zimu tushuo*, 19b. (Image courtesy of Harvard-Yenching Library.)

4 to <nī> 倪. Chen's tables were constructed according to a complicated fusion of numerological and phonological principles. They were ultimately intended, however, to simplify phonetic description by virtue of the absence of graphs. Chen proposed that the units in his tables could be combined to form syllables according to the *fanqie* method of using one graph to represent the initial and a second graph to represent the final. For instance the first calculation he illustrated would see the combination of the initials of graphs 1, 2, 3, and 4 with the finals of graphs 33

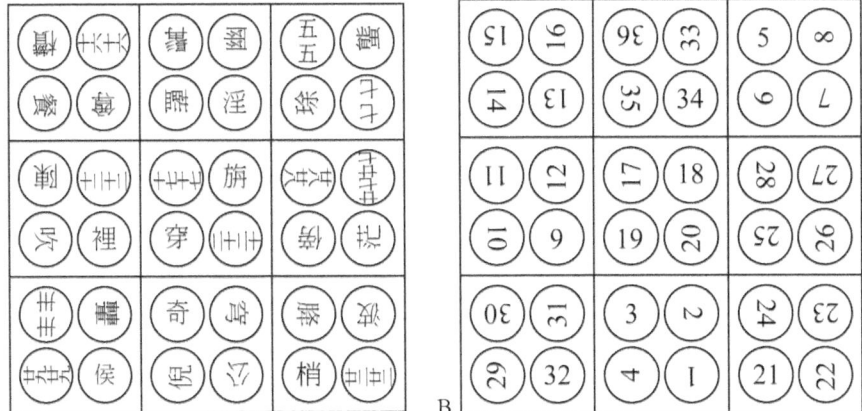

Figure 1.3 Chen Jinmo's numerical phonetic notation tables. To further abstract the linguistic sounds represented in the reference table (A) from specific Chinese graphs, Chen replaced the graphs in the table with numbers, which I translate here into Arabic numerals (B). Chen Jinmo, *Huangji tuyun*, 47b–48a.

(<iēu> 幽), 34 (<yīm> 淫), 35 (<lām> 藍), and 36 (<rōm> 髶). One set of combinations and their resultant syllables is:

$$1 + 33 = 公 <c-> + 幽 <-iēu> = <ciēu>,$$
$$1 + 34 = 公 <c-> + 淫 <-īm> = <cīm>,$$
$$1 + 35 = 公 <c-> + 藍 <-ām> = <cām>, \text{ and}$$
$$1 + 36 = 公 <c-> + 髶 <-ōm> = <cōm>.$$

The other possible combinations of this set of graphs (35 + 1, 35 + 2, and so on) yield a total of sixteen combinations. When completed across all nine tables, the combination process yields 1,296 total syllables in the level tone (144 syllables per table x 9 tables). By interpolating the remaining three tones, it yields 5,184 syllables (1,296 syllables x 4 tones).

Chen occasionally doubled this number to 10,368 to represent heaven calling to earth (all finals combining with all initials) and the duplicate syllables of earth responding to heaven (all initials combining with all finals).[85] By replacing all the graphs with numbers, except for those in the original reference table, Chen went beyond his contemporaries in terms of abstraction. In the context of a phonological tradition that up until this

THE NUMBER OF EVERYTHING

period had primarily associated pronunciations directly with the Chinese script, this numeric approach is a striking development. To a greater degree than any previous system, Chen seems to have isolated the study of sound from Chinese or other phonographic scripts. Many of his contemporaries, as well as later scholars such as Pan Lei 潘耒 (1646–1708), bemoaned the overreliance on script in discussing Chinese phonology.[86] Chen's approach spoke to these concerns by creating a system of phonetic notation that partially abstracted sound from Chinese graphs.

Chen Jinmo believed that Shao's findings were incomplete, as a result of his perceived reliance on the phonological information present in the Tang-dynasty rhyme book *Tangyun* 唐韻.[87] By implying that Shao was copying an older work from the standard tradition, Chen, like many of his contemporaries, defined Shao as a phonologist in some sense. For some of Chen's Ming contemporaries, this attributed identity was a positive way to reinforce Shao's scholarly credentials, but Chen's motivation was to assert that he could accomplish what Shao had been unable to do: create a truly comprehensive description of sounds that went beyond the limitations of the previous phonological tradition.

Some of the most striking innovations in the history of Chinese linguistics occurred at the hands of Ming cosmologists. Ge Zhongxuan, for instance, similarly sought to go beyond the potential of either Chinese graphs or existing phonographic scripts by constructing a new phonetic notation system that indexed the initial, medial vowel, voicing, and tone of a syllable in a single compound graph.[88] Wu Jishi, among others, experimented with integrating existing phonographic scripts into Chinese writing (see chapter 2). Their conviction that Number, music, and language constituted an interconnected system underlying the production of sound led to the pursuit of new methods of phonetic notation. Not content to simply delimit the number of possible sounds through cosmological calculations, many cosmologists also attempted to create systems capable of notating every sound. That they conceived of this effort as including sound more generally, and not just human speech, is evident in the refrain, variously worded, that their systems could be applied not only to human language but "even [to the sounds of] insects, birds, and beasts."[89] Some Ming scholars saw the role of the phonologist as restoring orthodoxy or correctness (*zheng* 正) to the corrupted contemporaneous language and thus sought a universal standard for recitation of the Classics and spoken koiné. The new attention to cosmology within linguistic study during this period, on the other hand, represented a desire to be comprehensive and impartial rather than prescriptive. By removing their systems from subjective description based on a specific topolect or a standard koiné, cosmologists claimed to create a comprehensive index of sounds. Cosmological speculations on sound produced various innovative systems, which were among the first to isolate phonetic sounds from the Chinese script. These notation systems would initiate a search for transcribing Chinese in phonographic scripts that would continue well into the twentieth century.

Conclusion: Objective or *Self-So*?

Cosmology studies had steady adherents beginning from the Han dynasty, experiencing an intensification in the Song dynasty as a result of Shao Yong's scholarship. During the Ming an interest in the cosmological applications of Number came to be applied more widely, including within areas that were not the traditional purview of cosmology. The interaction between cosmological and empirical approaches in this period was complicated, neither approach completely subjugated to the other. This widespread revival of cosmology within a new scholarly context has parallels in contemporaneous seventeenth-century Europe, which Daniel Stolzenberg has described as a "complex moment when empiricism and esotericism coexisted."[90] Sixteenth- and seventeenth-century Chinese phonologists employed seemingly esoteric methods alongside observation and textually based forms of linguistic study, viewing cosmology as a necessary supplement to convey the impartiality of their linguistic systems.

The opposition of *self-so* and "man-made" was a powerful argument in linguistic contexts, reaching back at least to the Song dynasty.[91] The idea that written language emerged from "nature" can be traced to some of the earliest writings on language in China, which claim that the Chinese script was modeled after the tracks of birds.[92] This discourse of a *self-so* basis for language took on a new intensity within the context of Ming integrative learning. Analogies and correlations drawn across fields of learning served as the ultimate proof of something being *self-so*, according to the logic that this unitary Coherence reflected a natural order. The "evidence" (*zheng* 證 or *ju* 據) presented in eighteenth-century works of Evidential Learning was primarily textual. Ming thinkers also believed their study to be based in a kind of evidence. As Chen Jinmo explained when asked by a fictional interlocutor about the basis (*ju*) of his cosmological approach to the study of language: "The Coherence is simply in accordance with what is *self-so*" (理因乎自然而已).[93] Qu Jiusi 瞿九思 (1546–1617) similarly described the process of designing a universal acoustic theory that could "obtain the correct sounds of heaven and earth": the first step, in his view, was to understand the Coherence (*li* 理) underlying these correlations between language and music. So long as the system was correct, then all of the specific components (such as pronunciation) would fall into place "on their own."[94] Sixteenth- and seventeenth-century thinkers sought such systems in response to an anxiety about the limits of the textual legacy of antiquity and human perception. Ming scholars believed the same *self-so* numerical properties that governed musical pitches should have precise equivalents in speech, based on their shared origin as "primordial sound." On this assumption scholars created numerous categorizations of linguistic sound according to what they perceived as musical constants.

The Ming concern with *self-so* knowledge merits comparison with the epistemic value in modern science of "objectivity." "To be objective," as Lorraine Daston and Peter Galison argue, "is to aspire to knowledge that bears no trace of the knower—knowledge unmarked by prejudice or skill, fantasy or judgment, wishing or striving."[95] Ming thinkers described *self-so* knowledge in strikingly similar terms as overcoming the biases of personal judgment. Ming criticisms of "man-made" (*renwei*) knowledge framed bias as an unavoidable aspect of observation, resulting from the limitations of human perception. Calls for "objectivity" in the nineteenth-century West similarly arose from a critical view of observation-based systems of knowledge collection. Earlier proponents of observation, such as Bacon and Linnaeus, premised their findings on experience and witnessing but also incorporated an explicit element of interpretation to curate what they had observed.[96] The discourse surrounding objectivity sought ways, mechanical or otherwise, to limit the role of interpretation in the generation of information.

There are clear differences between the notion of "objectivity," developed in the mid-nineteenth-century West, and Ming *self-so* knowledge. *Self-so* knowledge frequently involved a process of "modeling," in which an abstract system is devised on the basis of first principles.[97] "Objective" knowledge, in the nineteenth-century Western sense, did not fully abandon the potential of human observation and sought through other means to limit the influence of personal bias in the recording of observation.

Self-so knowledge attempted to bypass bias through the creation of universal categories, which were not necessarily observable. In this sense, Ming thinkers pursued a mode of validating new knowledge that is counterintuitive to our notion of objectivity. It is also quite removed from what have often been identified as precursors to scientific objectivity in the West: the Baconian desire for impartiality by limiting the reliance of "facts" on a unifying theory or system, and Robert Hooke's solution to the limits of human perception through the incorporation of "artificial" instruments into the process of knowledge-making.[98] By juxtaposing these two epistemologies I do not mean to suggest that Ming scholars were attempting to achieve "objectivity" in the Western sense, which stemmed from a fundamentally different ontological relationship between the self and objects.[99] Nor do I intend to obscure the efforts of late imperial empiricists who shared a great deal with thinkers like Bacon, or to diminish possible parallels between Qing Evidential Learning and the Western notion of objectivity. Instead, by noting this discursive similarity between models of unbiased knowledge, I would like to illustrate an alternative trajectory of knowledge production in China, which goes beyond the teleological model of a shift from benighted Ming philosopher to enlightened Qing evidential scholar. Framed from this perspective, one sees over the course of the late imperial period the development of opposing epistemological values, directed at a set of shared questions, such as the most effective way to understand ancient pronunciations. An unlikely source of linguistic innovation, cosmology also highlighted certain constraints of the Chinese writing system, spurring on China's first widespread engagement with alternative phonographic scripts. It is to this new concern with phonographic writing that we will shift our gaze in the following chapter.

CHAPTER 2

Letters from the West

Sanskrit, Latin, and Phonetic Legibility in Ming China

Ming thinkers, when confronted with the limitations of the textual record of antiquity, human perception, and the Chinese script, turned to music and cosmology to bolster their arguments about language. The recognition that there existed more linguistic sounds than the Chinese script was capable of notating prompted cosmology-inspired thinkers to devise new phonetic notation systems. Such scholars were also aware of existing phonographic scripts, employed by other contemporary cultures. Sixteenth- and seventeenth-century literati were exposed to the Latin alphabet, primarily through Jesuit missionaries. Clerks at the Translators Institute trained in the phonographic writing systems of neighboring states, such as Korea, Mongolia, and Tibet. However, within the realm of philological discussion, one writing system received far and away the greatest attention: Sanskrit. As a language with deep and conflicted religious roots in China, Sanskrit served as the focal point for debate about the merits of different writing systems.

This engagement with Sanskrit reflects critical aspects of scholarly identity in Ming China. Philology, as a field of knowledge, was generally subsumed under the "Classics" (*jing* 經) bibliographical category. Its primary purpose was to provide the tools necessary to accurately interpret the language of classical texts. As a result, most scholars affirmed the fundamentally *ru* (儒) nature of language study. Interpretations of the term *ru* vary: common English translations include "Confucian," "scholar," and "classicist."¹ Any translation is complicated by the fact that the term had different meanings in different periods and contexts. It was typically used in contrast to what were thought of as nonclassical and nonnative traditions of learning. *Ru* was therefore frequently paired in opposition to *fo* (佛), or Buddhism, as a belief system introduced from outside of China.² Consultation with Buddhist experts in Sanskrit, however, was widely accepted as a way to supplement existing methods of phonological description within the classical study of philology during the Ming. Such an ecumenical approach to the study of language came under attack in some quarters during the eighteenth century, with Ming scholarship coming to be characterized as "neither *fo* nor *ru*" (不佛不儒).³ While the lack of a categorical distinction increasingly grew to be a point of issue over the course of the eighteenth century, Ming scholars did not see the two as at odds in practice, even within as "classical" a field as philology. Like their better-known eighteenth-century successors, Ming classicists saw philology as central to the definition of *ru* identity. But in contrast to eighteenth-century scholars, they did not view antiquity as providing the core basis for this linguistic study. Many scholars instead favored Buddhist linguistic techniques and theories, which they considered useful tools in their quest for comprehensive linguistic description.

Sanskrit study in the Ming highlights the unexpected collaboration of literati scholars and Buddhist monks. It also provides access to late imperial Chinese perceptions of phonographic writing, largely undocumented in the current literature. The assumption among historians of writing that phonographic scripts represent the most rational and efficient writing systems has come under increasing scrutiny. David Lurie, for instance, has shown how early Japanese methods of reading Chinese script were more dependent on the capacity of those graphs to convey meaning than sound, despite their ability to do the latter.⁴ In other words, Japanese readers benefited substantially from the logographic capability of Chinese graphs to represent words rather than solely their phonographic potential to represent sound.⁵ Thomas Mullaney has argued that Chinese inputting methods in the twentieth and twenty-first centuries have proven graph-based writing to be as efficient as phonographic writing in the digital age, if not more so.⁶ The arguments that Ming scholars rallied in support of Chinese graphs vis-à-vis Sanskrit illustrate the depth of interaction among late imperial thinkers with phonographic writing and reveal some of the reasons they chose not to adopt it.

The Chinese script is the subject of countless studies.[7] As a unique example of logographic script among the writing systems of the world today, it has been invoked as a source of both national pride and shame beginning from the late nineteenth century.[8] Chinese graphs have piqued Western interest since as early as the seventeenth century. Originally viewed as a possible key to universal writing in this period, later Western observers came to criticize the inefficiency of nonphonographic writing. Twentieth-century Chinese reformers and Western observers alike have posed the question: Why did China not adopt phonographic writing? The teleological assumptions about the evolution of writing inherent in such a question have been elaborated elsewhere.[9] The Ming case provides further evidence for the culturally and historically contingent nature of notions of efficiency in writing. Researchers of writing have typically claimed that the lack of script reform in China before the twentieth century was the result of a lack of exposure to or consideration of phonographic scripts.[10] In the sixteenth century, however, we can observe an important moment of interaction with phonographic scripts in China. Chinese scholars were not unaware of the capabilities of phonographic writing, in which graphs represent sound alone. Instead, it was precisely this exposure to phonographic writing that confirmed their views about the superior potential of the Chinese script. Late Ming thinkers did not view phonographic scripts as inherently more intuitive than the logographic Chinese script. The value of phonographic writing, as some scholars saw it, was its ability to document more sounds than was possible with Chinese graphs alone. They therefore argued for the utility of Sanskrit as a tool for corroborating or complementing traditional phonological methods. Even among those who advocated for the theoretical study of Sanskrit and Latin scripts, few saw advantages in phonographic writing for daily use.

The maintenance of China's relationship with its neighbors has always involved interaction with non-Chinese languages and relied on interpreters to some extent.[11] Over the course of the seventh through fifteenth centuries, many of these neighboring regions developed phonographic writing systems, which captured the attention of Chinese officials and scholars. In the Yuan dynasty, Mongol rule prompted greater administrative concern with phonographic and non-Chinese writing in general. The Mongols themselves employed a phonographic writing system adapted from the Old Uyghur script in the thirteenth century. Integral to the Yuan emperor Qubilai Khan's (r. 1260–1294) vision of multilingual rule was the commission of the 'Phags-pa script, intended both to represent the Mongolian language of the ruling house and to "transcribe" (*yixie* 譯寫) other languages, including Chinese. Schools were established to promulgate this script, which appears to have gained considerable currency during the Yuan.[12] Widespread knowledge of 'Phags-pa script quickly disappeared following the Ming conquest, but the establishment of new institutions of foreign relations in the fifteenth century involved an even more concerted effort among Chinese officials to examine non-Chinese languages.[13] In particular, the Translators Institute (Siyi guan 四夷館) instructed translators in various writing systems of the Chinese periphery, while the Interpreters Institute (Huitong guan 會同館) trained oral interpreters.[14] Despite the increased study of the phonographic scripts of neighboring empires in the Ming, there is little reference to such writing systems in late Ming philological texts. For the most part, translation was considered a technical skill, rather than a focus of literati scholarship.

The presence of Jesuits in late sixteenth-century Ming China may have played a role in the heightened interaction with phonographic writing among literati. Prominent missionary-scholars, like Matteo Ricci (1552–1610) and Nicolas Trigault (1577–1628), collaborated with literati to promote the Latin alphabet. Some contemporary Chinese philologists incorporated this alphabet into their linguistic studies. The most influential phonographic scripts in Ming China, however, were those associated with Sanskrit, the original language of many of the Buddhist texts widely circulated in China. Since the medieval period, members of the Buddhist clergy had maintained the importance of referring to the Sanskrit version of Buddhist texts, not to be closer to the semantic meaning of the original texts, but in order to recite chants with more accurate (and therefore more efficacious) pronunciation. Efforts to establish the philosophical compatibility of Buddhist and Confucian thought during the Ming also facilitated new avenues of research through collaborations between classicists and Buddhist monks, whose knowledge of phonographic Sanskrit writing was a focal point of Ming philology. In contrast to the bulk of earlier Sanskrit study in China, Ming scholars not only focused on the religious implications of Sanskrit script but also attempted to integrate the script into secular philological texts.

Increased attention to the nature of writing systems during this period was linked to broader intellectual trends. Chapter 1 highlighted a central concern among Ming thinkers with generating *self-so* knowledge, which was not limited by human perception. Hence there emerged numerous propositions for the total number of linguistic sounds that could theoretically exist, regardless of their presence in Chinese or the ability of humans to produce them. Phonographic writing assumed new significance in this context as a result of its presumed utility for notating these sounds. Discussions of the merit of various writing systems also hinged on an evaluation of their *self-so* qualities. Sixteenth- and seventeenth-century philologists would come to argue that phonographic writing was ultimately less *self-so* than Chinese. Alphabets were seen as arbitrary inventions with no fundamental connection to language. The Chinese script, many argued, was based in nature and relayed meaning through its very form. Their reasoning reflected concerns not only with the theoretical basis of writing but also with efficiency. Despite the tendency of modern critics to herald the inherent efficiency of phonographic writing, the Ming case reveals the contingent nature of such assumptions. Presented with the alternative, Ming scholars largely defended the use of Chinese script on the basis of both its theoretical and its functional superiority.

Rhyme Masters and Religious Sanskrit Study in Ming China

Sanskrit study in China between the third and twelfth centuries was largely related to the explication and recitation of Buddhist texts. Medieval scholars emphasized the significance of learning Sanskrit because the efficacy of chants and spells was considered to be linked to the chanter's ability to utter them with accurate pronunciation.[15] The first clear mentions of Sanskrit as a language in China occur in texts from the third and fourth centuries. During this period Chinese monks, like Faxian 法顯 (337–422), traveled to India and mastered Sanskrit for the purpose of scriptural translation. Concurrently, Indian and Central Asian scholars in China, including most famously Kumārajīva (344–413), produced influential translations of Buddhist sūtras and composed studies of Sanskrit phonology. Knowledge of Sanskrit among the Chinese elite was initially limited to a small group of monks who made pilgrimages to India. There is evidence that by the late fourth century, however, this knowledge was already spreading to scholars outside this circle.[16] Sanskrit was historically notated with a number of phonographic scripts, which shared a set of generic features characteristic of an *abugida* (otherwise termed alphasyllabary, pseudoalphabet, or semisyllabary).[17] In such scripts a single graph represents a consonant-vowel combination, the assumed vowel being *a* unless altered by a diacritic. For example, the graph for *k* (क in Devanāgarī, for instance) would be read *ka*, unless modified by a series of diacritics indicating a different vowel (for example, *kā* का or *ku* कु).

The inaccurate notion that Sanskrit studies in China had effectively ended by the twelfth century is a commonplace in studies of the history of Sanskrit in China.[18] This assumption neglects the renaissance of Sanskrit studies that occurred in the sixteenth and seventeenth centuries. Scholars in this period turned to Sanskrit, and phonographic scripts more generally, in order to supplement Chinese logograph-based approaches to phonology. Major lexicographical works were produced by monks in the mid-Ming.[19] These in turn came to be cited in the non-Buddhist philological literature. During this period the philological role of Buddhist monks increased—or perhaps their scholarly activities were better recorded by secular scholars. In particular, a new specialty in phonology seems to have emerged among certain monks, who came to be known as "rhyme masters" *yunzhu* 韻主, "rhyme master monks" *yunzhu heshang* 韻主和尚, or "rhyme teachers" *yunshi* 韻師. As the seventeenth-century scholar Liu Xianting 劉獻廷 (1648–1695) recounted: "During the mid-Ming, the study of graded rhymes (*dengyun* 等韻) flourished in the world. . . . [Rhyme master monks] purely enlightened students by reciting rhymes. Scholars looked at Chan meditation as the greater gate to enlightenment and graded rhymes as the lesser gate to enlightenment (*xiao wumen* 小悟門)."[20] The graded rhymes Liu refers to are the phonological classification schemes that emerged in the production of rhyme tables within late Tang Buddhist communities and would come to play a large role in later classical studies of Chinese phonology.

Within Buddhist circles, the practice of rhyme recitation and phonological expertise had long been linked with efficacious Sanskrit chanting. As Liu Xianting's comment on the "lesser gate to enlightenment" suggests, Buddhist monks in the Ming still considered phonology a worthwhile task for the purposes of achieving an understanding of Buddhist truths. One such figure, Renchao 仁潮 (fl. 1584–1607), a northern monk who traveled extensively to temples in southeastern China,[21] carefully documented the importance of Sanskrit study:

> Only the Huayan letters (華嚴字母) [that is, Sanskrit in Chinese transcription] have been transmitted today. But without knowing their

origins, even though those who recite them are a multitude, they do not know why they are letters (*zimu* 字母), how they establish names, how they are applied, or how they can be used to grasp the dharma. Because the ancients transcribed them into Chinese, they thereupon lost their transmission. I once inquired among Western monks, and only then understood the method of generation of letters.[22]

Beginning in the sixth century, an increasing number of medieval Buddhist exegetical works came to discuss Indic scripts, going beyond an earlier focus primarily on pronunciation.[23] Despite the presence of this medieval tradition of script analysis, later monks still relied primarily on transcriptions of Sanskrit syllables into Chinese graphs, which would have obscured the differences between a phonographic script and Chinese. Renchao believed that it was not sufficient to imitate the sounds of Sanskrit with reference to Chinese transcription.

For Renchao, efficacious pronunciation of Sanskrit syllables could be achieved only with a thorough understanding of the script and its potential to represent sounds that Chinese graphs could not. As he elaborated in another text, both the sounds and script of Sanskrit were intrinsically numinous:

> Sanskrit graphs (*fanzi* 梵字) are like the ancient [Chinese] "seal" script (*guzhuan* 古篆).[24] At the beginning of the universe there was already this writing, and over the course of tens of thousands of years, there has been no change from past to present. This is different from the writing here where "seal" and "clerical" scripts have changed and been corrupted [into the contemporary standardized graphs]. It originally came from brahma heaven (*fantian* 梵天), and is thus called Brāhmī writing (*fanshu* 梵書). . . . Thus where one writes Sanskrit graphs, demons keep their distance; when one chants Sanskrit sounds, ghosts and spirits pay their respects in awe. It must be that it is the jade tone of the heavenly emperor (Indra)—who would dare not submit? For this reason, when the Buddhas explain the dharma, they all use Sanskrit sounds. The eight groups of spiritual beings obey and transmit them. As a result, one may call to heaven and heaven will respond; one may summon insects and the insects will obey. Only the sounds of Sanskrit are the most numinous and spirit-like for comprehending the hidden and the apparent. . . . Only the use of

Sanskrit writing can make the dirty clean, the ignorant wise, the prematurely dead long-lived, the sick healthy, destroy evil and assist the correct, and bring benefit to all beings. There are sixty-four kinds of writing in the world . . . among the sixty-four scripts, Sanskrit is the first. Thus one may know that Sanskrit is the king of scripts.[25]

Renchao's argument was built on a faulty description of the history of Sanskrit scripts. In reality, the Sanskrit language could be represented in numerous scripts developed in different historical periods. In fact, one of the most widespread scripts for rendering Sanskrit in Renchao's own time was quite different from the Siddham script that had initially captured scholars' attention in medieval China.[26] Renchao's misrepresentation, whether willful or not, of Sanskrit script as unchanged since antiquity allowed him to claim that the script itself acted as a direct and uncorrupted line to the origins of the universe.

Already in the early ninth century, Kūkai 空海 (774–835), the great Japanese Buddhist scholar of Esoteric Buddhism who studied Chinese and Sanskrit in China, asserted that the act of reading and writing Sanskrit graphs was itself an important part of Buddhist practice. Ryuichi Abe has argued that Kūkai understood the value of the phonographic Sanskrit script, the individual letters of which signified nothing, to be its ability to represent the underlying unreality of all things.[27] Renchao instead ascribed the same magical potential long understood to inhere in Sanskrit chanting to the script itself. Hence, in his view, the script could drive off demons and prolong life. In addition to the uncorrupted antiquity he saw in the script, Renchao justified his exaltation of the script in an allusion to the *Lalitavistara sūtra*, in which the Buddha claims that sixty-four scripts exist in the world. He interpreted the fact that the Buddha lists Sanskrit first as indicating that it is the most important script.

Zhao Yiguang and Secular Sanskrit Study in Ming China

Scholars outside the Buddhist clergy routinely consulted with Renchao and other Buddhist monks who specialized in phonology. This central feature of Ming Sanskrit study differentiates it from earlier periods when Sanskrit rarely attracted the interest of classicists.[28] Some, like Tan Zhenmo 譚貞默 (1590–1665), a high official and classical scholar, engaged in this study with the goal of learning to efficaciously practice Sanskrit writing and chanting for ritual purposes.[29] Most classicists, however, primarily indicated a concern with the applications of their Sanskrit study to the field of Chinese philology.

Accounts of travel to Buddhist temples across northern and southeastern China are recorded in secular philological texts of the mid- and late Ming.[30] Certain temples in particular appear to have established a tradition of rhyme study. An influx of Tibetan monks in the Ming, heralded for their superior knowledge of Sanskrit, may have spurred this specialization.[31] An account of the process of working with such monks is contained in Zhao Yiguang's *Xitan jingzhuan* (悉曇經傳 Authoritative study of Sanskrit script), printed in 1611.[32] According to Zhao, if one encountered trouble in understanding the phonology of traditional rhyme tables, one could consult a "rhyme teacher" monk who would elucidate the pronunciation of each syllable and demonstrate the shape of the lips and mouth with his hands. Zhao also went into considerable depth on the chanting of rhyme tables as a method for understanding phonology, based on the practice of rhyme teachers.[33] The process evidently involved slow, rhythmical chanting of syllables accompanied by rhythmic beating.[34] The reciter would begin by clarifying the pronunciation of syllable initials before systematically chanting the contents of the rhyme table, combining the initials and rhymes into a single syllable. Liu Xianting also considered this practice of "chanting rhymes" (*chang yun* 唱韻) to be the primary method of Buddhist phonological instruction, describing the "Sanskrit intonation" (梵音) of a rhyme chart as "elegant and pleasing to the ear."[35] The precise connection between Sanskrit pronunciation and the recitation of a Chinese rhyme chart is not made clear in these texts. Presumably the appeal of Sanskrit-proficient monks was their ability to pronounce syllables that did not exist in Chinese but were recorded in Chinese rhyme charts as theoretically possible. Scholars outside of the clergy came to adopt the practice of rhyme chanting and by the mid-seventeenth century may have been its primary practitioners. Liu Xianting, writing in the late seventeenth century, recounted how Chen Jinmo, a major secular philologist, "specialized in chanting rhymes." By contrast, Liu's attempt to study the practice with Buddhist monks was hindered by his inability to find one proficient in phonology.[36]

During the Ming dynasty, philologists came to believe that Sanskrit was relevant to a complete understanding of phonology. The case of Zhao Yiguang (1559–1625) neatly illustrates this phenomenon and its implications for new possibilities in scholarship that arose in the late Ming. Zhao was a member of the literary elite of Suzhou prefecture. Although he was a distant descendant of the Song dynasty royal house, official service was not a major factor in his recent family history. His father had failed the examinations and pursued a life of scholarship and writing, a path that Zhao Yiguang would repeat. In addition to authoring many scholarly works, Zhao was also one of Suzhou's best-known book collectors and publishers.[37] His contemporaries widely recognized him as being among the foremost philological scholars of his age, and his authority in this domain is demonstrated by frequent references to his work in seventeenth-century scholarship.

Zhao Yiguang's *Xitan jingzhuan* is only partially preserved and leaves many questions unanswered. Nevertheless, the remaining portions of the text provide valuable insight into how classical study in the late Ming could interact with scholarship generated in a Buddhist context. The ability of the gentry to assemble at and fund the construction of Buddhist temples has been attributed, in part, to ecumenical attitudes during this period toward the synthesis of Buddhist and Confucian teachings.[38] This attitude is visible even within classical scholarship in a discipline such as philology, which was formally considered a branch of Confucian classical learning. As Zhao wrote in the preface to *Xitan jingzhuan*: "Gautama (Qutan 瞿曇, i.e., the Buddha) and Confucius (Xuanni 宣尼) were both able to preach. Buddhism (*fo* 佛) achieves breadth, while Confucianism (*ru* 儒) achieves the generalities. Buddhism achieves what is close, while Confucianism achieves what is far away. . . . There is no greater or lesser among them, and they alternately serve as lord and minister."[39] Zhao signed this preface as "a disciple of Confucius" (孔氏之徒) and referred to his approach throughout the text as that of "us *ru*" (吾儒). He also framed the neglect of phonology among his fellow classical scholars as "the shame of us *ru*" (吾儒家之恥).[40] Confucians, in his view, had relinquished the authority to speak on linguistic matters. To rectify this shortcoming among contemporary classicists, Zhao considered it necessary to draw from the Buddhist tradition of phonological scholarship.

Zhao Yiguang's presentation of the complementary potential of Buddhist and classical philology is paralleled by the philosophical compatibility between Buddhism and Confucianism among contemporary thinkers.[41]

Zhao and his contemporaries were likely receptive to Buddhist scholarship as a result of the current intellectual and religious climate. Chen Jinmo similarly promoted Buddhist spelling methods in the phonological analysis of Chinese, while continuing to align himself with "us Confucians/*ru*" (吾儒).[42] Other seventeenth-century philologists invoked Confucius's famed dictum to search for the rites in the wild if they cannot be found among the civilized as justification for consulting Buddhist experts in phonology.[43] Zhao Yiguang's example highlights this ambivalence. His pointed self-identification as "a disciple of Confucius" suggests that he understood the term *ru* to refer to Confucians (rather than as a generic term for scholars) and the field of philology to belong to the Confucian tradition. At the same time, his proclamations of the equivalent validity of the two traditions, alongside his consultation with monks indicate his belief in their complementarity.

The well-documented crisis facing *ru* identity later in the eighteenth century led to a search to recover the fundamental *ru* Way embodied by the "former *ru*" (*xianru* 先儒) of antiquity.[44] Zhao Yiguang faced a similar crisis. Like eighteenth-century thinkers, he criticized the "vulgar *ru*" (*suru* 俗儒) and "dogmatic *ru*" (*furu* 腐儒) among his contemporaries and referred to the "shame" of *ru* learning for abandoning philology.[45] He too desired to restore something that had formerly belonged to *ru* learning that was no longer transmitted.[46] He likewise saw philology as central to this renewed *ru* identity. But in contrast to the dominant representation of *ru* identity in the eighteenth century, recovering this Way did not require reaching back to the putative practices of antiquity. Instead he believed that philology, a core field within *ru* learning, had continued to flourish within Buddhist practice. And while the methods of antiquity were necessarily confined to discussions of Chinese script and ancient pronunciation, the expertise of contemporary Buddhist thinkers, which involved comprehensive documentation of linguistic sounds, better suited the philological questions of the day.

Zhao Yiguang wrote one of the most extended studies of Indic scripts and phonology to be produced in premodern China. He was not alone, however, in his belief that Sanskrit phonology and its relation to Chinese were significant, and many encyclopedic surveys of phonological methods included a discussion of Sanskrit.[47] A perennial issue for late imperial philologists was the degree to which the seminal medieval methods of phonological analysis were of native or Indic origin. Major scholars of the eighteenth century rejected the premise that Buddhists could have introduced these methods and attempted to reveal their indigenous origins.[48] In the Ming, however, there was a trend toward acceptance of this foreign influence. Zhao Yiguang and his contemporaries argued strongly in favor of recognizing the Sanskrit origins of Chinese linguistic methods. Present-day researchers have gone to great lengths to demonstrate that Sanskrit models informed the Tang rhyme table tradition, but their conclusions must be inferred from circumstantial evidence.[49] In the late Ming, philologists explicitly invoked Sanskrit writing, directly incorporating examples of the script within their studies.

Zhao Yiguang was convinced that important Chinese phonological methods had Indic origins, and he framed his study as an extension of this long tradition.[50] In addition, like his consultant Renchao, he believed that Sanskrit sounds were best represented with a Sanskrit script, as opposed to the Chinese transcriptions used in most Buddhist writings of his time.[51] Inspired by the possibilities for phonological description offered by a phonographic script, Zhao advocated for the incorporation of Sanskrit script into Chinese phonological methods as well. While he did not see the phonetic system of Sanskrit script as infallible or entirely able to represent the sounds of Chinese, he felt it could be used to approximate sounds more accurately than could a notation that relied solely on the logographic Chinese script. Accordingly, he created a rhyme table in which he supplied Sanskrit graphs for theoretical sounds with no corresponding Chinese graphs.[52] Such rhyme tables were typically riddled with blank spaces, indicating a theoretical sound that did not exist in Chinese. Zhao claimed to have been able to fill in the gaps by phonetically spelling such sounds in Sanskrit writing. He also employed the traditional rhyme table format to explain the spelling system of the Sanskrit alphasyllabary in a way that would be accessible to a contemporary audience (see figure 2.1).

Zhao argued that phonographic scripts were simpler to learn than Chinese: "Although the transformations [of the Sanskrit script] are limitless, it is very simple to grasp the method. It is not like Chinese writing in which recognizing one [graph] is only one and recognizing ten [graphs] is only ten. Even if one comprehensively acquires tens of thousands, it is difficult to go farther than a step."[53] Zhao had a more sophisticated understanding of the nature of Sanskrit scripts than did some of his contemporaries. By interacting directly with the script, rather than Chinese transcriptions of Sanskrit, he recognized that a prescribed number of graphs could be used

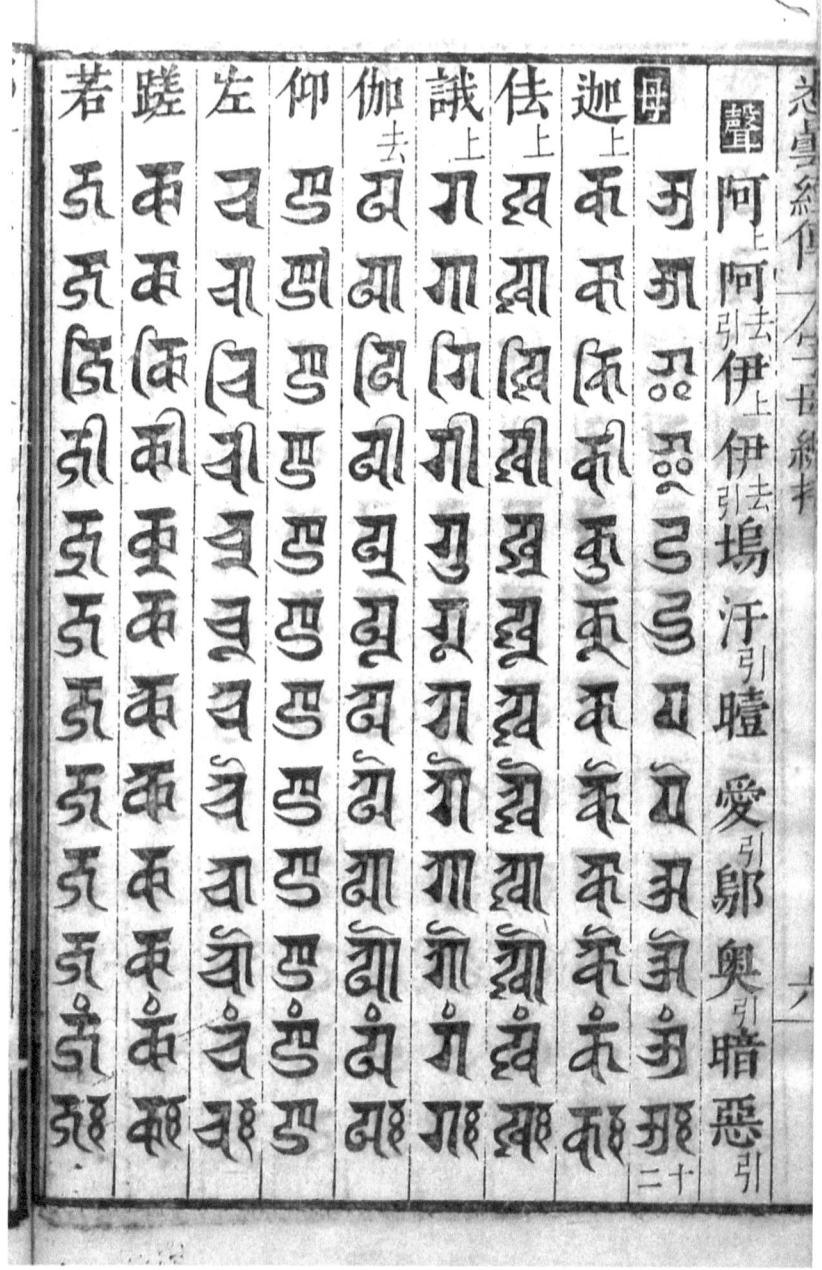

Figure 2.1 A Sanskrit rhyme table. This description of how Sanskrit consonants are modified to combine with vowels, which mirrors the standard Chinese rhyme table, comes from an extant portion of Zhao Yiguang's *Xitan jingzhuan* (*zimu zongchi*, 6b). The top row (labeled "initials" 母) represents consonants, while the first column (labeled "finals" 聲) represents vowels. The first column would be read, in Sanskrit, as *ka*, *kā*, *ki*, *kī*, and so on, while the second column would do the same with the initial *kh*-. (Image courtesy of the Nanjing Library.)

to generate many sounds. Zhao Yiguang was not a script reformer in the sense of wanting to replace or systematically modify the Chinese script. He could, however, acknowledge the limitations of Chinese graphs, and he saw phonographic writing as having supplementary value for the purposes of rhyme table phonology.

Even more strikingly, Zhao argued in a dictionary of ancient graph forms that the Chinese script in its modern form had in part derived from phonographic Sanskrit writing. In his view, "when the Sanskrit language came east, it changed our Chinese graphs" (梵語東來，易我華字).[54] According to his analysis, certain Chinese graphs were made up of two elements, both unusually bearing phonetic significance. For example, he identified the graph <shěn> 矧 (a particle meaning "besides") as composed of two graphs, <shǐ> 矢 and <yěn> 引, the former representing the syllable initial (<sh->) and the latter representing the syllable final (<-ěn>). Zhao argued that this combination of initial and final mirrored the method of phonetic spelling, which he believed was introduced to China with Sanskrit. The canonical interpretation of <shěn> 矧, on the other hand, would see <shǐ> 矢 ("arrow") as containing semantic significance, and only <yěn> 引 as bearing phonetic information. What is most innovative about Zhao Yiguang's interpretation is that it breaks free from the six principles of graph formation (*liushu* 六書) prescribed in the Han dynasty *Shuowen jiezi* (說文解字 Explanation of simple and compound graphs). There is no such principle in this foundational text characterized by multiple phonetic elements. Few other contemporary scholars would venture outside of these canonical principles, although linguists today largely reject the framework of *Shuowen jiezi* as an entirely accurate way of understanding the Chinese script. Zhao envisioned Sanskrit not only as allowing for more comprehensive phonetic representation of linguistic sounds than the Chinese script, but also as a model for reinterpreting the very nature of the Chinese writing system.

Zhao Yiguang is an example of one possible Ming *ru* identity. It is one that resonates with broader Ming concerns that are useful to contrast with those of the eighteenth century. Zhao's rejection of the ancient canon of philological texts, and the principles outlined in *Shuowen jiezi* in particular, is striking in light of the work's status as the central object of philological attention in the eighteenth century.[55] Zhao Yiguang conceived of language as ever-evolving, particularly as a result of the introduction of Buddhism to China, which was something a text from antiquity could not capture. Hence, in a dictionary entry on the word "pagoda" (*ta* 塔), he wrote: "Because there was no such thing [as a pagoda, in China] before the Han dynasty, there is therefore no such graph in *Shuowen jiezi*."[56] Zhao was a devoted scholar of *Shuowen jiezi*, producing a massive study of the text. However, he freely discarded core principles from the work and considered it insufficient on its own. Previous scholars had failed in their attempts to comprehensively document Chinese graphs within their lexicons, he believed, by not taking into account the extent of Sanskrit-influenced Buddhist vocabulary in China. Although Zhao did not criticize antiquity to the degree some of his contemporaries would, he made clear that its recovery was not the primary goal of the *ru* classicist.

The motivation underlying Zhao Yiguang's approach aligned with that of other contemporary scholars who attempted to devise comprehensive systems for documenting linguistic sounds. Zhao similarly claimed that the purpose of his Sanskrit study lay in providing a comprehensive basis for understanding ancient rhyme usage as well as contemporary regional pronunciations.[57] Cosmologists, who shared this aim, attempted to bridge the gap between differences in historical and regional pronunciation by generating systems that could catalog all possible sounds. Zhao Yiguang, among other contemporary scholars, focused on the concrete methods of notating such sounds by adopting and adapting phonographic writing systems.

The Phonetic Legibility of Phonographic Writing in the Ming

Despite the presence of Sanskrit inscriptions in Buddhist temples, as well as the attention to Sanskrit writing in the work of scholars such as Zhao Yiguang, I have found little evidence to suggest a widespread ability among Ming Buddhist monks or classicists to actually read a text written in Sanskrit for semantic content and translate it into Chinese. The early tradition of Sanskrit grammatical analysis aimed at translation did not continue in a sustained fashion past the Tang dynasty. David Lurie has posited a continuum of "alegibility" to "legibility" in the uses of writing in Japan. Alegibility involves writing for symbolic purposes, such as inscriptions or tattoos, where the reader derives meaning not from linguistic knowledge of the semantic or phonetic information contained within the graph, but instead from the symbolic associations conveyed by a particular writing system or graph. Legibility represents a mode of reading in which semantic interpretation is directly related to the inscribed text.[58] Sanskrit in Ming China falls somewhere between these two categories. A Sanskrit inscription or chant may not have been "legible" to a Ming reader, who would be unable to access semantic and grammatical information from such a text. On the other hand, the script served more than a symbolic function, given that it conveyed precise phonetic information to those who had mastered the alphasyllabary. Ming scholars of phonographic writing obtained a kind of alphabetic literacy, which rendered syllabic and alphabetic scripts phonetically, if not semantically, legible.

This usage of Sanskrit to represent sound was similar to the phonographic usages of the Chinese script itself. Dhāraṇī chants could be transcribed from Sanskrit with Chinese graphs to facilitate recitation. Similarly, non-Sinitic names and terms were routinely transcribed in Chinese by means of graphs employed solely for the purpose of notating their pronunciation.[59] In rhyme tables and rhyme dictionaries, as well, Chinese graphs could be systematically employed as phonographs. Was there any difference in substance, then, between existing phonographic usages of the Chinese script and new conceptions of Sanskrit as a tool for phonetic representation? There is perhaps no single answer to this question. Some Ming thinkers argued that there was no distinction between the two, making the usage of Sanskrit unnecessary.[60] Others maintained that there was something unique about phonetic graphs, which separated them even from phonographic usages of Chinese. As we saw in the case of the early Esoteric Buddhist tradition, phonographic writing could be upheld for its abstraction of reality from form. For Ming philologists, it was the abstraction of sound from meaning that made a phonographic script an invaluable tool.

Ming scholars embraced phonographic scripts, not as a wholesale replacement of Chinese graphs, but as a useful supplement. The great encyclopedist and philological thinker Fang Yizhi (1611–1671), for instance, employed phonographic scripts as a comparative phonological tool. Fang believed that similar principles could be derived from both Chinese and non-Chinese spelling methods. These similarities suggested the existence of fundamental phonological properties of human speech, which went beyond any written representation of language. This proposition of the universality of linguistic sound further resonated with the broad Ming concern regarding artificial or "man-made" knowledge. Fang claimed that his study of Latin, Sanskrit, and Chinese scripts had revealed to him that the phonological principles of rhyming shared among these languages were "natural" (*tianran* 天然, lit. "heavenly-so") and not an "artificial creation" (*zaozuo* 造作).⁶¹ The use of phonological scripts in the context of Chinese language study served a similar purpose to the efforts of cosmologists to separate linguistic sound from any particular writing system. Linguistic sound was "natural," with the various writing systems merely representing different artificial approaches to representing these sounds.

This interest in fusing phonographic and Chinese writing for phonological study, suggested in both Zhao Yiguang's and Fang Yizhi's studies, is visible in the work of Zhao's contemporary, Wu Jishi. A cosmologist with great interest in Chinese phonology, Wu Jishi integrated letters from the Latin alphabet into his rhyme tables under Zhao Yiguang's influence. Similarly to both Chen Jinmo and Fang Yizhi, Wu Jishi was committed to cosmological methods of language study, suggesting further the linkage between cosmology and phonological innovation revealed in the previous chapter. Wu's acoustic study *Yinsheng jiyuan* (音聲紀元 Recording the origins of sound) was based in the numerology of the twelfth-century scholar Shao Yong and attempted to correlate sound with universal processes by aligning phonological features with cosmologically significant things, such as musical pitches, solar terms, and geomantic winds. Importantly, this approach allowed him, along with like-minded contemporaries, to assert that Chinese script was not the key to understanding phonology. Wu created rhyme charts that recorded many possible syllables for which no Chinese graph existed, and he cited Zhao Yiguang's claim that "the marvelous functions of sound are not contained in graphs" (音聲妙用不在文字) and that the reader should even "pay extra attention to those [sounds] without a [corresponding] graph."⁶²

In an attempt to link the cosmological origins of sounds with precise phonological categories, Wu created twenty-four rhyme groups to match the twenty-four solar terms of the lunar calendar, creating further categorizations according to musical pitch. Within each rhyme table, he listed a set of sixty-six initials (*yin* 音), arranged by place of articulation. Under each initial, Wu listed four graphs in the order of the four Chinese tones. The pronunciation of each graph thus combines the initial; the given rhyme, or final (*sheng* 聲); and the tone. For instance, in his fourteenth rhyme group, <-ie>, Wu listed four graphs under the initial <z-> 精 (see figure 2.2). The combination of the initial <z-> plus the final <-ie> across the four tones yields the following readings: <ziē> 嗟, <ziě> 姐, <ziè> 借, and <ziet>

節. Empty circles represented syllables that Wu believed exist but for which there was no matching Chinese graph.[63]

In the hope of filling in as much of the tables as possible, Wu occasionally inserted letters from the Latin alphabet as a way to represent sounds that did not exist in Chinese (see figure 2.3).[64] Wu placed most Latin letters in the row of the level tone. For example, the letter *H* appears in the level-tone row for the combination of the initial <x-> with the final <-ia> (thus pronounced <xiā>) (figure 2.3A). The letter *Z*, however, appears in the rising-tone row for the combination of the initial <sz-> and the final <-ie> (thus pronounced <sziě>) (figure 2.3B). There is insufficient evidence to determine how Wu came into contact with Western languages, but it seems possible that if he was exposed to a spoken Western language (perhaps Portuguese), he may have believed it to be tonal. One must surmise

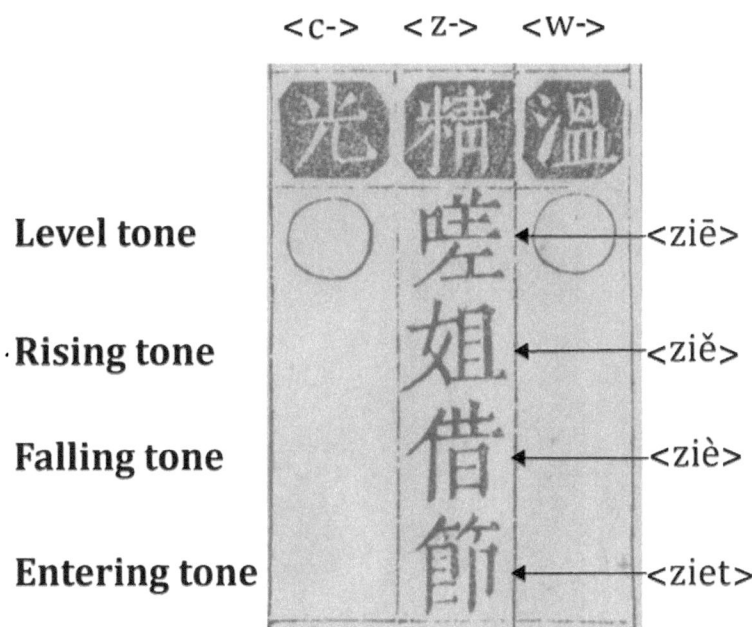

Figure 2.2 Wu Jishi's <-ie> Rhyme Group. Wu's *Yinsheng jiyuan* organizes syllables in a given rhyme group according to the initial and arrays them in the standard sequence of the four tones. (Image courtesy of the National Library of China.)

that Wu, or others involved in the printing process, were not terribly familiar with the Latin alphabet, given that letters were occasionally written backward (figures 2.3C and 2.3D).

Wu Jishi would likely have been unable to read Western-language texts, and his proficiency in the Latin alphabet was limited. Still, his use of the alphabet was more than decorative. Similarly to the use of Sanskrit by Zhao Yiguang and other late Ming scholars, alphabetic writing conveyed phonetic legibility for Wu Jishi, who employed it to represent phonological information. Such alphabetic literacy would have required training, and given the paucity of instructional materials for phonographic scripts in the

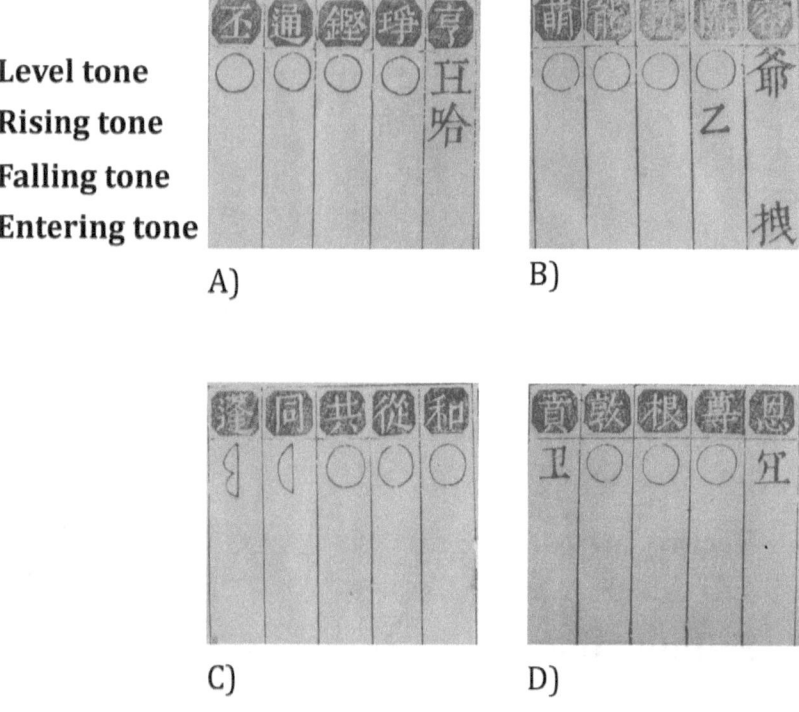

Figure 2.3 Wu Jishi's use of the Latin alphabet. Most Latin letters appear in the level-tone rows (in A, C, D), although Z appears in the rising-tone row (B). Sometimes Latin letters appear backward (in C and D). Wu Jishi, *Yinsheng jiyuan*, j. 2, 10b, 16a. (Images courtesy of the National Library of China.)

early seventeenth century, interaction with a tutor was the most likely point of access for these scholars. We know that Zhao Yiguang studied with Buddhist monks, and we can surmise that Wu Jishi likely had contact with Jesuit missionaries (or Chinese converts). Philologists did not typically express an interest in reading documents, such as Buddhist sūtras or the Bible, in their original languages. Nor did they invest considerable effort in using phonographic writing as a transcription tool, a role it would come to serve in the Manchu Qing dynasty and more prominently with pinyin annotation in China today. They were attracted, however, by the potential of foreign scripts for phonetic notation of individual phonemes or syllables for the purposes of theoretical linguistic study. This study was focused on sound in the abstract, divorced from specific semantic contexts.

As scholars in the late Ming increasingly sought to devise comprehensive systems for describing linguistic sounds, some turned to phonographic scripts for supplement or corroboration. In certain cases, as the examples of Zhao Yiguang and Wu Jishi illustrate, phonographic scripts were used to supply sounds that would be difficult to represent with Chinese graphs. In other cases, such as that of Fang Yizhi, these writing systems were seen as more clearly illustrating the universal principles underlying indigenous methods of spelling through the combination of graphs. Perhaps the great difference between Sanskrit and Chinese also led scholars to believe that accounting for the sounds of both languages would effectively encompass all possible sounds. Wen Deyi 文德翼 (fl. 1630s), for instance, in prefacing a work that claimed to describe all linguistic sounds in the universe, wrote that the author had "exhausted the sounds of Chinese and Sanskrit."[65]

In addition to the benefits of phonographic scripts for phonological analysis, some found the organization of sounds in the Sanskrit alphasyllabary especially compelling. In particular, several scholars reported that the fact that the alphasyllabary begins with the phoneme *a* indicated that it followed a natural *self-so* pattern because this is the first sound a child makes.[66] We can infer possible influences of Sanskrit phonological analysis on earlier periods of Chinese phonology. In the late Ming, however, the discussion of Sanskrit was explicit and made possible by both an increasingly relaxed attitude among literati toward Buddhism and a scholarly world in which disciplinary boundaries of classical learning were more fluid than they would become in later centuries. Finally, a desire for comprehensiveness and impartiality drove scholars to incorporate non-Chinese scripts to aid in developing more complete forms of phonological representation.

Disadvantages of Phonographic Writing in a Culture of Logography

Ming literati enjoyed considerable exposure to phonographic scripts and were attracted to their potential utility in systems of theoretical linguistic description. There are few clear instances, however, suggesting a sense that such scripts were superior to the Chinese writing system. In one rare case, Wang Kentang 王肯堂 (d. 1638), a classical scholar with deep interests in Buddhism, claimed that in Tibet the use of phonographic writing had created an entirely literate society.[67] Scholars like Zhao Yiguang and Fang Yizhi would acknowledge certain advantages in phonographic writing. Nevertheless, the consultation of phonographic scripts did not necessarily equate to a view of Chinese graphs as fundamentally inadequate. The use of phonographic scripts as phonological tools in the late Ming did force contemporary Chinese scholars to acknowledge the clear differences between these writing systems and their native script. The majority of contemporary scholars, however, saw the utility of phonographic scripts as, at best, corroborative. At the same time, the increasing presence of these scripts in philological discourse gave rise to concerted efforts to assert the superiority of Chinese writing.

Script reform, as it existed during the Ming, involved attempts to assign specific meanings to particular forms of graphs, which had previously been considered interchangeable. Zhao Yiguang, for instance, believed that the recovery of ancient script forms would overcome the confusion caused by interchangeable graphs, approximating the kind of differentiation of words possible with a phonographic script (see chapter 3).[68] In some cases, it is possible that the desire for reform was linked to an awareness of Sanskrit. However, such reform was primarily directed toward a rectification of Chinese graph forms, rather than the adoption of an entirely new writing system. Research on the history of the Chinese script and script reform has tended to characterize the majority of premodern Chinese scholars as possessing a stagnant view of script, which explains their failure to adopt phonographic scripts.[69] But Ming scholars' responses to the increased use of such scripts reveal that their ideas about the nature of writing were hardly ossified. Ming thinkers felt the need to address alternative writing systems. Their reactions, even in defense of the Chinese script, are evidence of the broad influence such scripts had on conceptions of writing and language in this period.

The late Ming case highlights the culturally and historically contingent nature of perceptions of script efficiency. Despite their attention to phonographic scripts for theoretical linguistic study, late Ming scholars did not perceive them wholly favorably for the purposes of written communication. Hao Jing 郝敬 (1558–1639), for instance, wrote:

> Chinese is refined; each graph constitutes one meaning. Sanskrit is disorderly; several graphs constitute one sound, and several sounds constitute one meaning. For example, Chinese Nengren (Ch. 能仁, He who is able to care for others) is Sanskrit *Shijiamouni* [Ch. 釋伽牟尼, Sk. Śākyamuni]. Chinese Shizun [Ch. 世尊, World-honored one] is Sanskrit *Lujianata* [Ch. 路迦那他, Sk. Lokanātha]. . . . There are many [examples] of this nature. Reading them in Sanskrit, one must bind together the excessive sounds (約其繁響). But with Chinese writing, one graph clearly has one sound.[70]

Zhao Yiguang had contended that Chinese graphs posed challenges for readers because each graph "muddles together both sound and meaning" (*yinyi xianghun* 音義相溷).[71] Hao Jing, by contrast, considered this aspect of the Chinese script to be precisely its virtue. Chinese, in his view, was more straightforward because meaning was embedded in each individual graph, and each graph represented an entire syllable. Hence in Chinese he saw a direct correspondence between "meaning" (*yi* 義), "sound" (*yin* 音), and "graphs" (*zi* 字). In Sanskrit, phonographic "graphs" were only equivalent to "sound" with no intrinsic meaning of their own. While earlier Buddhist theorists such as Kūkai had upheld the metaphysical significance of the absence of meaning in phonographs, philologists were concerned with issues of perceived efficiency.[72] Some scholars questioned even the potential of phonographic writing to clearly convey pronunciation, given the use of multiple letters within a single syllable.[73] Hao Jing lamented the fact that in order to obtain meaning from a Sanskrit text, one must go through the burdensome phonological operation of putting multiple sounds together. Only after correctly combining sounds and associating the resulting syllables with a word could one then reach the semantic content. The association of phonographic spelling with theoretical phonology may have made the prospect of reading a script that operated on this phonetic principle appear taxing and unapproachable. For an audience accustomed to the correspondence of an entire syllable with a single graph (in most cases representing a semantic unit), phonographic writing conveyed neither sound nor meaning as directly as the Chinese graph.

Some scholars also saw existing phonographic scripts as imprecise. Liu Xianting, for example, criticized the phonographic systems of Manchu (*nüzhi guoshu* 女直國書), Latin (*ladeng hua* 蠟等話), and Sanskrit (*fanyin* 梵音) and proposed a rhyme table method with Chinese graphs that he believed could better describe sounds.[74] While Liu drew inspiration from phonographic writing, he ultimately saw existing scripts as flawed.[75] In particular he believed that contemporary phonographic scripts contained superfluous vowels, which in his view simply comprised redundant tonal variations of the same vowel. A rhyme table, in his view, conveyed more precise phonological information than these scripts. Liu, like many of his contemporaries, seems to have based his understanding of phonographic scripts largely on Chinese transcriptions and did not see them as providing a superior system for notating all possible sounds. Using solely Chinese graphs, Liu proposed that with his rhyme table system "all [sounds] could be recorded." He even envisioned creating an anthology of rhyme tables to encapsulate all the varieties of speech in China, with a separate volume for each region, the thought of which made him "deliriously happy."[76]

Gu Yingxiang 顧應祥 (1483–1565), a prominent classicist, believed that the contemporary appeal of Sanskrit writing remained linked to perceptions of its magical potential when properly chanted. Gu attempted to debunk this notion as part of a larger argument regarding the superior qualities of the Chinese script:

> [It is] further claimed, "The Chinese are not skilled with sound. When Indian monks chant for rain then rain responds, when they chant for a dragon then a dragon appears. Within the blink of an eye, changes occur in accord with the sounds. Even though Chinese monks may imitate their sounds, they have no experience, and have not perfected the Way of sound."[77] I consider this to be the techniques of illusion. The people of China also have those who can

summon thunder and rain through incantation. But illusions among the Chinese are few, while among the Western monks they are many. China is a bright, sunny place; thus illusions are few. Foreign lands are dark, hidden places; thus illusions are many.[78]

In Gu's view, the geomantic properties of the region determined the effects attributed to the power of accurately pronounced Sanskrit letters. In other words, the language itself did not inherently possess magical properties.

Gu further characterized the letters of phonographic writing systems in unflattering terms as "coiling worms," invoking a criticism typically reserved for illegible calligraphy.[79] By contrast, Chinese graphs operated according to constant principles that governed their form. Even more important, he argued, Chinese graphs were necessary for China on the basis of its more highly developed culture:

> For what purpose are graphs created? They are created to order all under heaven (*zhi tianxia* 治天下). The people of China have the mutual relations of lord and minister, superior and inferior, as well as the mutual bonds of rites, music, punishment, and governance. Their graphs must be many. Although the sparse records of those foreign peoples each have their foreign graphs, they are not many. It is not only Indians; the graphs of the Hui Muslims and foreigners outside the southwestern reach of our transformative civilization (*huawai* 化外) are all this way. It is because they lack an influential cultural heritage.[80]

For Gu, the multitude of Chinese graphs was necessary to encompass the extent of China's civilization. Some of Gu's contemporaries opposed the use of Sanskrit by rejecting the notion that Sanskrit letters were in fact simpler than Chinese. Gu, by contrast, effectively acknowledged the simplicity of Indic writing but claimed that for just this reason it was unsuitable for China, which possessed a civilization that could only be communicated with a vast number of graphs. This argument was based on the assumption that graphs are equivalent to ideas. Gu was perturbed by his contemporaries' arguments that Indic scripts and the Chinese script could in some sense be commensurate, or at least supplement each other. Gu conceived of the script itself as a record of culture; foreign phonographic scripts were separate from the Chinese script, therefore, not just in how they functioned, but also in their ability to communicate ideas. By defining the purpose of writing as giving order to the world, rather than simply notating speech, he reframed the complexity of Chinese writing as a reflection of its sophisticated civilization.

One of the enduring virtues of the Chinese script to some Ming thinkers was its basis in nature, be it the patterns of bird tracks or a reflection of the workings of a sagely mind. Despite the attempts of Buddhist theorists, such as Renchao, to establish a similarly numinous origin for Sanskrit writing, philologists largely viewed Sanskrit and other phonographic scripts as lacking this natural basis. Yuan Changzuo 袁昌祚 (1538–1616), for instance, derided Sanskrit for "forging" (*duan* 鍛) graphs (*zi* 字) together out of multiple sounds (*yin* 音).[81] The use of a metallurgic term to describe a script was damning. Phonographic writing was artificial, something that possessed no intrinsic meaning until it was hammered into the form of a recognizable word. Chen Shiyuan argued that phonographic scripts "were only passed on orally and understood aurally" (惟以口傳而耳聽).[82] In other words, there was no added value in the script itself. One of the few scholars to claim the superiority of phonographic scripts argued that the sole purpose of writing was "to notate sound" (*jisheng* 記聲).[83] His contemporaries would largely disagree with this assessment. Gu Yingxiang would claim, for instance, that writing was invented "to order all under heaven." Such scholars could embrace phonographic writing as a tool for linguistic analysis. They did not, however, see the potential of such scripts to replace what they saw as the more efficient, meaning-laden, and cosmologically sound Chinese writing system.

The notion that the Chinese script communicates "ideas" is almost universally refuted in the study of writing systems today. This belief is typically traced to early modern Western thinkers, such as Leibniz and Kircher, who, rather than denigrating a lack of phonological efficiency, sought the potential of universal language in Chinese graphs. Their perception of the unique attributes of the script was not entirely different from conceptions of writing in China in the same period.[84] Ming scholars such as Gu Yingxiang presented a vision of script that conveyed not only meaning and sound but also thought process and civilization. However, as opposed to the universalist assumptions of European thinkers, this understanding of the power of logographic writing did not necessarily suggest the potential of universal communication to a Chinese audience. Gu Yingxiang seems to have doubted that Chinese graphs could serve a society outside China's "transformative civilization." Despite the practical uses of Chinese graphs for communication across East Asia in the early modern period, scholars expressed uncertainty about the capacity for even their immediate non-Chinese neighbors to fully grasp the nature of the Chinese script. Liu Xianting, for instance, commented on the numerous errors in Korean usage of the Chinese script, decrying their "inability to understand the intricacies of the principles underlying graphs (*liushu* 六書)." In his view, the lack of civilization reflected in Korean attempts to employ Chinese writing made them "assuredly barbarians" (固夷狄也).[85] Some Chinese scholars may have lacked faith in the potential of a writing system so deeply tied to a civilization to be effective beyond China. As we shall see in chapter 3, Ming thinkers developed new propositions for the underlying metaphysical significance of Chinese graphs that would further reinforce notions of their unique capacity to convey more than just language.

The use of phonographic scripts, which emerged in the Ming dynasty as a way of supplementing traditional methods of phonological description, continued well into the Qing. The establishment of the Manchu language as a new "state language" (*guoyu* 國語), itself written in a phonographic script, ushered in a heightened sense of the utility of phonographic writing.[86] Although perhaps overshadowed by the Manchu script, specialized studies of Sanskrit writing continued to be published (see chapter 6). The idea that phonographic scripts are inherently superior to logographic writing, a viewpoint assumed by much Western scholarship, was not evident to Ming and later scholars. As late as the turn of the twentieth century, the great scholar and revolutionary thinker Zhang Taiyan 章太炎 (1869–1936) observed the prevalence of phonographic scripts in neighboring regions, caustically inquiring, "Could it be that their cultures are superior to that of China?" According to Zhang, in reading a phonographic script, one could "only recognize the sound (音) but would certainly be unable to know the meaning (義)," in contrast to the Chinese script, where, for instance, Japanese readers who could not speak Chinese would still understand the semantic content of Chinese graphs.[87] Nevertheless, Sanskrit and other phonographic scripts had an enduring influence on phonologists who saw their potential to create a comprehensive phonetic notation system. These techniques were developed by a community of late Ming scholars who consulted with monks specializing in the scripts and phonology of Sanskrit and Tibetan, and to a lesser degree Jesuits with knowledge of the Latin script. While monks continued to emphasize the practice of phonology for the purposes of self-realization, secular scholars applied their methods in the pursuit of a comprehensive and inartificial system of linguistic description.

CHAPTER 3

Script, Antiquity, and Mental Training

Metaphysical Inquiry Into the Nondiscursive Potential of Writing

Sanskrit scripts featured in many Ming discussions of writing, suggesting a more widespread interaction with phonographic writing in late imperial China than generally recognized. At the same time, there were few proposals to adopt such scripts for use outside of philological research. In contrast to the early twentieth century, when reformers attempted to implement various forms of phoneticization in the service of mass literacy, there was no consensus during the Ming that phonographic scripts were easier to use. Apprehension about the efficiency of phonographic writing abounds in Ming texts. A sense of the uniqueness of the Chinese script as the most *self-so* writing system was bolstered by arguments from practitioners of a particular brand of Confucian thought that emerged in the mid-Ming. Often considered to have played a large role in China's supposed turn from textual and scientific pursuits, these thinkers produced influential new theories concerning the nature of writing and methods of knowledge organization. In particular they claimed that Chinese graphs conveyed not only semantic meaning and sound, but also an additional nondiscursive sense reflecting the cognitive processes of the ancient sages.

Ever since the eighteenth century, discussions of the mid-to-late Ming have traced a lack of intellectual innovation and the rejection of reading and scholarly inquiry to Wang Yangming 王陽明 (1472–1529) and his promotion of a new trend in Confucian thought known as the Learning of the Mind (*xinxue* 心學).[1] The Learning of the Mind is typically characterized as a turn toward internality, which eschewed reading texts in favor of self-reflection. It arose in part as a response to the Song dynasty Learning of the Way thinker Zhu Xi's 朱熹 (1130–1200) proposal that the way to understand the Coherence (*li* 理) pervading all things was to observe it in the external world, as well as in the texts of the classical tradition. Through a cumulative process of observing and learning, one would ultimately apprehend the Coherence within one's own mind. With this knowledge, one would then be able to act as a moral person, whose behavior was in accordance with the Coherence of the situation. Wang Yangming, whose teachings espoused the new Learning of the Mind approach to moral self-realization, argued that the mind was equivalent to Coherence. In Wang's view, by eliminating selfish desire and recognizing one's unity with all things, one could uncover the innate goodness (*liangzhi* 良知) present in the mind. In this way, he believed that the intellectual work of apprehending Coherence could be effectively replaced by activating the mind's innate ability to know the good.

A tendency in studies of the period to focus on Wang Yangming's influence on sixteenth- and seventeenth-century intellectual culture has obscured the fact that a broad set of Ming Learning of the Mind scholars saw philological study as a valid method for realizing moral values. These thinkers viewed written language not solely as a medium of communication, but more significantly as the framework of perception. By identifying how the sages constructed graphs, they claimed one could understand precisely how the sages' minds operated. To aid in both the study of ancient writing and moral cultivation, new genres of philosophical dictionaries emerged, designed to be read from beginning to end. Such dictionaries attempted to reveal a consistent logic underlying the formation of Chinese graphs, which could influence how people acted in the world. In pursuing philological endeavors, Learning of the Mind scholars instigated a sweeping debate about the nature of writing, the history of language, and the commensurability of ideas across languages.

The Learning of the Mind exploration of writing resonated with broader contemporary discussions and criticisms of phonographic scripts. Ming scholars routinely criticized phonographic writing as less efficient at conveying information than the logographic Chinese script. The level of meaning imputed to individual graphs by Learning of the Mind thinkers was one reason for this assessment of the power of Chinese writing. In contrast to semantically rich Chinese graphs, phonographic letters were generally considered meaningless on their own. This focus on how writing conveys meaning had implications for broader issues in the organization of knowledge in ways that parallel contemporary debates in early modern Europe. The emergence of alphabetic order in Europe as an organizational framework in dictionaries and encyclopedias aroused skepticism among those who considered it arbitrary for placing unrelated items next to each other.[2] In China, this concern manifested itself in the question of whether it was more efficient to index material on the basis of the form and sound of graphs, which would similarly align semantically unrelated items, or according to thematic linkages. Learning of the Mind thinkers saw the form of graphs on the individual level as a window into the minds of the ancient sages but considered thematic organization more logical when dealing with graphs in the aggregate.

The venues of discussions of script in the Ming are particularly significant in light of the Qing dynasty assessments that largely inform our current understanding of Ming intellectual culture. For eighteenth-century Qing court scholars, the perceived lack of "concrete learning" in the Ming was a result of the perversion of Confucian thought, embodied most clearly in the Learning of the Mind teachings of Wang Yangming and attempts to establish unity between Buddhist and Confucian thought.[3] According to this narrative, philology, as the pinnacle of concrete learning, emerged as a way of reclaiming the correct teachings of Confucius. This representative field of "concrete learning," however, was not only widely practiced in the Ming; some of its most ardent proponents lay among Learning of the Mind thinkers, as well as literati seeking to link Buddhist and Confucian learning. These communities of philological learning fueled interregional scholarly connections from the resource- and education-rich lower Yangzi delta region to the mountain temples dotting northeastern and southeastern China (see chapter 2).

Wei Jiao and Philology in the Learning of the Mind

Wang Yangming was one the most influential thinkers in the Confucian tradition since Zhu Xi. His Learning of the Mind teachings served as the basis for significant developments in Confucian thought into the eighteenth century. During the sixteenth and seventeenth centuries, however, there was no consensus on what exactly constituted the Learning of the Mind.

Generally Learning of the Mind thinkers were in agreement that Coherence was not external to the mind. Most also felt that literary culture (*cizhang* 詞章) was not the key to understanding the workings of the mind. Some also saw philological analysis of the Classics as antithetical to true learning.[4] However, Wei Jiao 魏校 (1483–1543), an influential contemporary of Wang Yangming, devised an alternative Learning of the Mind in which the minds of the sages were accessible only through the script they employed.

Wei Jiao enjoyed a distinguished official career. He was born in Kunshan 崑山 county in Suzhou prefecture, and after obtaining his *jinshi* degree in 1505 he began his career as department director at the Nanjing Ministry of Justice. He later assumed the position of vice intendant of education in Guangdong, where he earned a reputation for his strongly anti-Buddhist policies, including orders for the destruction of Buddhist relics and confiscation of temple estates. An innovative educator, he established a community school plan that came to be emulated by later intendants. Dismayed by the educational advantages of students in urban centers, Wei created a rotation system in which students from the countryside would travel to more established urban schools for a period of study.[5] His final years in office were spent in the capital as chief minister of the Court of Imperial Sacrifices and head of the Directorate of Education. In 1530 he retired and returned to Suzhou, where he shifted his priority to scholarship and teaching, counting among his students many luminaries of Suzhou literary and intellectual life.[6]

Wei Jiao's name is paired with Wang Yangming's in Ming texts as representative of a polarity in the Learning of the Mind.[7] As one contemporary averred, "Those who think Wang Yangming is right consider Wei Jiao to be in error, while those who think Wei Jiao is right consider Wang Yangming to be wrong."[8] Wei Jiao and Wang Yangming disagreed with each other on philosophical grounds; they also belonged to opposing political factions.[9] Wang Yangming's teachings suggested that reading and textual study were inconsequential in the grander task of moral self-cultivation. Wei Jiao, on the other hand, saw philological scholarship and morality as intertwined.

Wei Jiao's most influential work is a dictionary, entitled *Liushu jingyun* (六書精蘊 Essential meanings of the six principles of graph formation). Printed in 1540 by his nephew Wei Ximing 魏希明 (1502–1540), *Liushu jingyun* is focused primarily on ancient script forms and is organized thematically (rather than according to the shape or sound of graphs).[10] The "six principles of graph formation" in the work's title refers to the framework of graph analysis defined in the seminal first-century dictionary *Shuowen jiezi*.[11] This allusion to *Shuowen jiezi* belies the significant departure *Liushu jingyun* represented from the previous etymological tradition. While he acknowledged the existence of all six "principles," Wei Jiao focused his attention primarily on the single principle of "combined-meaning" graphs (*huiyi* 會意). Combined-meaning graphs, which are today understood to account for only a small number of existing graphs, are typified by each component of the graph containing semantic significance. The graph therefore tells a story in some sense, as the overall meaning is conveyed by the relationship between the constituent parts. For instance, the graph "to look" (*kan* 看) was traditionally interpreted as a combined-meaning graph, composed of a hand (*shou* 手) and eye (*mu* 目), suggesting the act of shielding the eyes as one looks into the distance. Wei Jiao employed the reasoning of combined-meaning graphs to characterize the bulk of Chinese writing in order to reveal the messages the sages intended to convey in each graph.

Wei Jiao believed that uncovering the meaning behind the construction of ancient graphs could reveal the mind (*xin* 心) of the sages. As he stated in the preface to his dictionary, "Writing is nothing other than a painting of the mind (心之畫), that which embodies the principles of everything in heaven and earth. The ancient script 'apprehended before me that which is common in my mind with everyone else's.'"[12] The generic description of Chinese graphs as a "painting of the mind" originated with Yang Xiong 揚雄 (53 BCE–18 CE), a foundational Han dynasty classicist and scholar of language. Ming dynasty Learning of the Mind scholars routinely appropriated this language as a justification for philology. According to Wei Jiao, written language was a representation of the shared unity of the human mind. As with other Learning of the Mind thinkers, he believed that all humans possessed the same, fundamentally good mind, which became corrupted only through the influence of selfish desire. By "observing the painting of the mind of the ancients," as Wei claimed in an entry in his dictionary, "one can understand their Learning of the Mind" (知其心學).[13] Explaining the purpose of his work in a letter to another scholar, Wei claimed that he was revealing the "methods of the minds of the ancients"

(古人之心法).¹⁴ The notion of "methods of the mind" (*xinfa*) had a long history in Learning of the Way thought, relating to the mental training required in the process of moral self-cultivation, and achieved even greater prominence within Learning of the Mind discourse.¹⁵ Throughout the entries in his dictionary, Wei Jiao referred to these "methods of the mind" as well as the ancient "creators of graphs" (制字者), whose intent was mirrored in the script they designed.¹⁶ Wei's focus on intent and the artificial creation of graphs at the hands of humans is somewhat at odds with the conventional representation of writing as stemming from observation of the natural world. However, he posited that the commonalities of the uncorrupted mind observable in ancient graphic forms represented not artifice, but rather the product of "what is naturally so" (天然而然).¹⁷ By understanding the process by which the sages created writing, Wei believed that we could comprehend the way the minds of the sages worked and emulate their moral behavior.

Wei Jiao was not the first to attempt to unlock aspects of antiquity through an analysis of the construction of graphs. In the eleventh century the leading statesman Wang Anshi 王安石 (1021–1086) proposed a new way of understanding Chinese graphs in a dictionary titled *Zishuo* (字說 Explanations of graphs), which he submitted to the emperor and ultimately promulgated throughout the school system. Wang similarly believed every component of a given graph to have semantic importance for the graph's overall meaning. He argued that understanding the way the sages had constructed graphs would provide insight into the coherent system that underlay society and government in antiquity. For example, he claimed a genetic relationship between the graphs for "heaven" (*tian* 天) and "husband" (*fu* 夫), which in his analysis were both constructed from the same two components, "great" (*da* 大) and "one" (*yi* 一). Wang explained the relationship between the two graphs as denoting that "the husband is heaven to his wife" (夫者妻之天故也). According to Wang, that a husband is still not as great as heaven could be inferred from the fact that the graph "one" 一 occurred at the top of "great" 大 in the graph for "heaven" (天), symbolizing the fact that nothing surpasses heaven.¹⁸ By systematically analyzing these relationships, Wang claimed we could reconstruct the sociopolitical system of antiquity in the present day.

Wang Anshi believed ancient graphs reflected the coherence of the natural world, something only the ancient sages had been able to perceive. In his view, the fact that they were created by humans (雖人之所制) was secondary to their basis in the natural order of "what is so-of-itself" (出於 自然).[19] Wei Jiao, on the other hand, was more interested in the mental processes underlying the sages' construction of graphs. Wei would agree that graphs ultimately revealed "what is naturally so," but his concern was primarily with the human aspect of their derivation.

Wei Jiao's dictionary focused on Zhou dynasty seal script (*zhuan* 篆) forms of graphs, which had been standardized in the third century BCE. Today we have access to considerably older forms of the Chinese script, including most famously the oracle bone writing of around 1000 BCE, which came to light as a result of archaeological excavations at the turn of the twentieth century. In the Ming dynasty, seal script was the best understood writing system of antiquity, although there did exist a tradition of scholarship on other early scripts. Wei Jiao's commitment to seal script is evident from the fact that the entire text of Wei's dictionary, including definitions and the preface, is written in a modified seal script.

For Wei Jiao, alongside other Learning of the Mind thinkers, understanding antiquity and ancient values meant experiencing and living them. His contemporary Wang Gen 王艮 (1483–1541), for instance, famously insisted on wearing what he considered to be ancient garments.[20] Wei channeled antiquity through his use of ancient scripts both in the context of his dictionary entries and in other texts. By practicing the composition of ancient graph forms, Wei Jiao believed we could inhabit the minds of the sages of antiquity. His commentary to the seminal classical text of the court-sponsored Confucian curriculum, the *Great Learning* (*Daxue* 大學), begins with a transcription of the text in an ancient script.[21] Even brief notices Wei wrote to his students would sometimes employ archaic variant graphs.[22] The contemporary popularity in Suzhou of ancient graph forms in calligraphy and seal carving may have rendered this script familiar to his contemporaries, but Wei Jiao's primary justification was not aesthetic.[23] An earlier calligraphic discourse held that the regular script (*kaishu* 楷書), developed in the third century CE and codified by the Tang court in the seventh, reflected moral rectitude.[24] For scholars of the ancient script like Wei Jiao, it was precisely the opposite, with regular script representing a departure from ancient morals. Instead, Wei believed that the earliest forms of written graphs that he was aware of demonstrated the intentions of the ancient sages in ways that the later simplification of graphs glossed over.

Wei Jiao's concerns were not primarily philological, but rather with shedding insight on contemporary issues and debates in the Learning of the Mind. For example, in an explanation of the graph "to obtain" *de* 得 (the ancient form that Wei employed is shown in figure 3.1), he wrote: "得 <dec>, pronounced with the initial of <dō> and the final of <zec> (多則切), is composed of the graphs for 'to see' (見) and 'hand' (手). Why is that? What our vision can reach is empty and not necessarily real. But if we hold something in our hands, then it is something we possess ourselves. This should persuade people that knowledge and action are united (*zhixing heyi* 知行合一)."[25]

The unity of knowledge and action (*zhixing heyi*) was a central tenet of the Learning of the Mind. Orthodox Learning of the Way doctrine, based on the codifications of Zhu Xi, claimed that one must first observe things and acquire knowledge before putting it into action. In other words, one must first learn what is morally correct, or else one's actions may immoral. According to Learning of the Mind thinkers, knowledge and action could not be separated. Just as one could know the flavor of something only by actually tasting it, knowledge, and particularly moral knowledge, could be realized only in the course of performing an action. Wei Jiao felt he had achieved a concrete way of demonstrating that this had been the view of ancient sages through his philological exegesis of graphs. Most previous analyses of the graph *de* 得 had interpreted the upper component of the graph to be a "shell" (*bei* 貝), which served as a form of money in antiquity.[26] Having a shell or money in one's hands was thus representative of obtaining something. Wei Jiao interpreted the upper component instead as the similar-looking graph "to see" (*jian* 見), which he understood to represent knowledge. By combining this symbol of knowledge with one of

Figure 3.1 Seal script form of "to obtain" (*de* 得). This alternative form is likely derived from one of the major thirteenth- to fourteenth-century paleographic dictionaries, such as *Liushu tong* (六書統). (Image courtesy of Staatsbibliothek zu Berlin—PK, Libri sin. N.S. 637. http://resolver.staatsbibliothek-berlin.de/SBB0002352700000000. Present location: Biblioteka Jagiellońska, Kraków.)

action (a hand, *shou* 手), Wei could claim that the original form of the graph, as a reflection of the sages' minds, proved the validity of this doctrine.

Wei Jiao repudiated traditional graphical analyses, corralling them uniformly into combined-meanings interpretations that supported his philosophical platform. The graph "to obtain" had long been understood to be a combined-meanings graph, and Wei Jiao's reinterpretation simply constituted a reevaluation of the graph's constituent parts. Wei, however, even more radically rejected the conventional phonetic-semantic interpretations by which most graphs had been traditionally analyzed. The reduction of a component part of the graph to a phonetic element was often, in Wei's view, a result of the "Learning of the Mind of the sages not being transmitted."[27] To rectify this shortcoming, Wei devoted the majority of the entries in his dictionary to providing explanations of ancient graph forms, which emphasized the semantic importance of all components of the graph, dismissing the fundamental significance of phonetic information.

As in the case of "to obtain" *de*, Wei Jiao's extended definitions tied the component parts of the graph to a larger Learning of the Mind message. In "knowledge" (*zhi* 知), for instance, Wei discoursed specifically on *liangzhi*, the innate understanding of goodness that Learning of the Mind thinkers advocated recovering.[28] In other examples, he sought to demonstrate that certain graphs implied the fundamental unity of all things in the world.[29] Recognition of this unity was a central tenet of Learning of the Mind as the basis of all morally informed decisions. Wang Yangming argued that the removal of selfish desire could lead to the recognition of unity with all things and cautioned against seeking this knowledge outside of the mind.[30] Wei Jiao proposed the alternative that this unity could fruitfully be explored in the written texts of antiquity, through insight the writing system provided into the "methods of the minds" of the sages.

Wei Jiao's concern with the minds of the sages is exemplified in his attention to documenting their intentions in the creation of graphs. For instance, in his interpretation of the graph "to experience" *li* 歷 (see figure 3.2), Wei highlighted the component *yan* 厂, which originally referred to a house built precariously on a cliff, or more generally as Wei Jiao glossed it here, "a perilous place." Wei claimed that this component is present because "the creators of graphs desired that humans experience all manner of perils (制字者欲人備嘗險阻), in order to 'stimulate their minds and make

Figure 3.2 Seal script form of "to obtain" (*li*) 歷. (Image courtesy of Staatsbibliothek zu Berlin—PK, Libri sin. N.S. 637. http://resolver.staatsbibliothek-berlin.de/SBB0002352 700000000. Present location: Biblioteka Jagiellońska, Kraków.)

their spirit endure, improving that which they are incapable of.'"[31] According to Wei Jiao, the original form of graphs served not only as the inscribed representation of a word or idea, but also as a tool constructed with the intention of altering behavior. Hence on a surface level the graph *li* 歷 meant "to experience," but on a symbolic level it conveyed the worldview of the ancients. Properly interpreting this graph would teach the reader to embody this worldview and, in this case, to accept difficult circumstances as a necessary part of self-cultivation.

Liushu jingyun defined a total of 1,468 graphs. This number of entries is a far cry from even early dictionaries, such as *Shuowen jiezi*, which contained 9,353 graphs, not to mention major seventeenth-century dictionaries, such as *Zihui*, which contained over 33,000.[32] However, previous philosophical lexicons geared toward introducing the reader to critical terms within a particular school of thought typically contained only a handful of graphs, with the most famous such text, *Beixi ziyi* (北溪字義 [Chen] Beixi's interpretation of graphs), including fewer than thirty entries. Wei Jiao clearly did not aim to provide a comprehensive gloss of all graphs for the purposes of reading or composition. Nevertheless the considerable breadth of his text compared to narrower philosophical lexicons indicates the significance of his appropriating the format of a dictionary. The ideas of the sages were evidently not imparted only in conceptually significant terms like the "Way" or "Coherence." Even more mundane terms, such as "to obtain" and "to experience," as well as terms for body parts and plants, for instance, could convey profound philosophical messages by virtue of the script's reflection of sagely intent. Wei Jiao's dictionary outlined a coherent philosophical platform, but it was also relevant to practices of reading. The inclusion of roughly 1,500 graphs, although relatively few by the standards of Chinese lexicography, suggested that Chinese writing was intended to systematically convey meaning at multiple levels, from the semantic to the symbolic.

Wei Jiao's Students, Spinoffs, and the Contemporary Appeal of Nondiscursive Readings

Wei Jiao's dictionary achieved a good deal of fame during his lifetime. Prior to printing, Wei circulated the manuscript among a coterie of scholars, requesting assistance in writing the definitions. In a revealing letter to Zou Shouyi 鄒守益 (1491–1562), a student of Wang Yangming's, Wei wrote: "The graph 'knowledge' (*zhi* 知) in the third *juan* of *Liushu jingyun*, the graph 'centrality' (*zhong* 中) in the fourth *juan*, the graph 'sort' (*ge* 格) from the sixth *juan*, and the graph 'numinous' (*ling* 靈) from the second *juan* have some relation with the contents of your previous letter. I wish that you might read through them and amend any mistakes."[33] This epistolary solicitation of advice is not an isolated case. Wei requested revisions from a host of prominent officials and thinkers.[34] Recounting the publication process in his colophon, the printer Wei Ximing noted Wei Jiao's reluctance to publish the work so long as he could continue to improve it.[35] The improvements Wei sought were evidently developed out of collaborative discussion of Learning of the Mind and philological values with leading contemporary scholars.

In addition to widely distributing manuscripts of his work, Wei transmitted his approach to philology through his students, who in turn produced dictionaries reflecting Learning of the Mind values. These works cited and paraphrased entries from *Liushu jingyun*, and also presented themselves as the product of discussion with Wei Jiao. The most influential of these texts was another thematically organized dictionary of ancient script forms entitled *Tongwen beikao* (同文備考 A complete study of the unified script) by Wei Jiao's student Wang Yingdian 王應電. *Tongwen beikao* was printed by Wang Zongmu 王宗沐 (1524–1592), himself a noted Learning of the Mind scholar. Wang Yingdian's dictionary contained considerably more graphs than Wei Jiao's and made a more concerted effort to engage with other contemporary philological trends.[36] Nevertheless, it maintained a highly ethical dimension.

Wang Yingdian urged readers not to be misled by the seemingly insignificant moral implications of a dictionary. Some he imagined might see his dictionary as a contribution only to "art" (*yi* 藝) and the techniques of properly composing graphs in calligraphic styles. But the implications of this "art" were much broader in his view: "It is not acceptable to refer to this [art] as something apart from the Way (*dao* 道). By observing their [i.e., the sages'] writing, we can see the Way. When we illuminate their Way, then moral education is established. Is it really merely art?"[37] This representative contemporary viewpoint envisioned morality as intertwined with the technical study of language. In a basic sense this was true because one needed to be able to read in order to access the moral and textual legacy of the Classics. Similar arguments in favor of philology as a necessary skill for reading the Classics had existed since the medieval period.[38] In the Ming this argument was extended to include the study of the construction of individual graphs as a moral exercise.

The content of *Tongwen beikao* was heavily imbued with Learning of the Mind values. As with Wei Jiao, Wang Yingdian chose the ancient graph forms he believed best conformed with the intent (rather than sound) of the graph. Hence, for "virtue" (*de* 德), he followed Wei Jiao in choosing an obscure form 悳, composed of the graphs "upright" (*zhi* 直) and "mind" (*xin* 心), claiming that "when humans are first born, they are upright. This is the heavenly nature of their original mind."[39] This differs from an earlier, and in fact still accepted, exegesis of the graph as composed of a semantic and phonetic element. Citing Wei Jiao, Wang also disputed the common form of the graph "to believe" (*xin* 信), composed of the graphs "person" (*ren* 人) and "speech" (*yan* 言), as he denied that the speech of a person in and of itself can be believed.[40] Both chose instead an alternative graph composed of "speech" (*yan*) and "mind" (*xin*). This graph, they argued, better reflected the intent of the sages by indicating that truth emerged from a correspondence between one's speech and one's mind.

The persistence of Wei Jiao's methods went beyond his students and lasted past his lifetime. For example, one seventeenth-century scholar, Wu Shilin 吳士琳, composed a dictionary of ancient graph forms entitled *Zhengyun yi* (正韻翼 An aid to correct rhymes [of the Hongwu reign]). Despite the work's title, which might suggest its status as a commentary on the early Ming dynastic rhyme book *Hongwu zhengyun*, *Zhengyun yi* focused on graph analyses largely based on Wei Jiao's model. Little is known about Wu Shilin, except that he was active in the late seventeenth century in Xin'an 新安, Anhui province. Wang Deyuan 汪德元, a lecturer at the renowned center of classicism in Xin'an, the Ziyang Academy 紫陽書院,

helped Wu in editing his dictionary, perhaps for use in instruction at the academy.[41]

Invoking Wei Jiao, Wu Shilin claimed that "the Learning of the Mind of the ancients was deep and subtle, yet it remains everywhere in the form of the 'paintings of their mind' [i.e., written graphs]."[42] Like Wei Jiao, Wu believed that ancient writing contained moral messages, which reflected the teachings of the Learning of the Mind. For example, he tied the ancient form of the graph for "to learn" (*xue* 學) to the recovery of "innate goodness" (*liangzhi*), which Wang Yangming had urged people to restore.[43] The work itself is clearly modeled after Wei Jiao's, and in some cases his definitions are taken almost word-for-word from *Liushu jingyun*, as well as from *Tongwen beikao*.[44] Although Wu Shilin had no direct connection to Wei Jiao, his dictionary clearly inherited its methods and accepted the premise that script could provide access to the moral thinking and behavior of the sages.

By the seventeenth century, Wei Jiao's method of parsing the underlying moral message of graphs had achieved a significant place within the period's philological discourse.[45] While superficially similar folk etymologies have a considerable history in China, such discussion in elite circles as something philosophically and philologically significant was new.[46] Wang Anshi's attempt to reveal the meaning behind the construction of graphs fell out of favor in the eleventh century, in part due to his contentious political influence within the Song court. In the late Ming, such interpretations were increasingly persuasive, reflecting the widespread acceptance of Learning of the Mind thought, as well as skepticism toward the validity of classical methods of philology that had dominated much earlier linguistic discussion. Sixteenth- and seventeenth-century scholars questioned the authority of *Shuowen jiezi* and sought a new basis for analyzing the written Chinese script. *Shuowen jiezi* would enjoy a resurgence of interest in the eighteenth century, but some late Ming scholars took issue with its methods as based in faulty assumptions about the nature of Chinese graphs.[47] Others claimed that in fact morality-based graph exegeses were not fundamentally different from those of *Shuowen jiezi*—both shared the premise that graphs were produced by sages and not "constructed randomly" (苟然而成者).[48] Hence the discrepancies between the *Shuowen* tradition and Learning of the Mind approaches could in some cases be reconciled as an interpretive debate, rather than a fundamental methodological difference.

This fusion of *Shuowen* and Learning of the Mind approaches is evident in the writings of one of the most audacious seventeenth-century philologists, Liu Ning 劉凝 (1620–1715). Recent research has documented how Liu, a Christian convert, parsed Chinese graphs to elucidate Christian theology and history.[49] His attention to the analysis of graphs, as cited in a dictionary by the scholar-missionary Joseph Henri Marie de Prémare (1666–1736), has been identified as foreshadowing the philological inclination of later Evidential Learning methods. However, Liu's handwritten marginalia on a copy of Zhao Yiguang's massive commentary on *Shuowen jiezi* indicates that his philological thought was developed through a reading of this central piece of Ming philology. Within the marginalia Liu further revealed his indebtedness to Wei Jiao's students, whom he cited throughout, as well as Wang Anshi's similar method of graph parsing.[50] Liu, who was relatively critical of Zhao Yiguang, maintained that the metaphysical reading of graphs for understanding antiquity, which began with Wang Anshi and continued through the Ming, was in fact useful in corroborating graph forms in *Shuowen jiezi*. It also evidently provided a method he could apply in his Christianized readings of graph forms.

The appeal of Wei Jiao's methods to a contemporary audience was rooted in a widespread belief in the nondiscursive, symbolic capability of Chinese graphs to communicate meaning outside of their use within a sentence. Early discussions of writing in China had linked the script with the trigrams of the *Changes*, which were referred to as "images" or "symbols" (*xiang* 象). These symbols were, as Mark Edward Lewis has observed, "not translatable into ordinary language."[51] Late Ming scholars of the *Changes* devoted special attention to the relationship between ancient graph forms and the images they represented.[52] Wei Jiao embraced the nondiscursive capacity of graphs to convey a second layer of information beyond their direct semantic definition. For Wei Jiao, however, the symbolic capacity of the graph did not displace its ability to function as a unit of ordinary writing. Instead he envisioned multiple capabilities of the Chinese graph: he cited pronunciation glosses from the Ming dynastic dictionary acknowledging their capacity to convey phonetic information and also provided brief synonymic glosses defining their basic semantic content. This information reflected the discursive utility of graphs, while his extended philosophical discussions of their construction spoke to additional nondiscursive implications of graphs to communicate beyond the level of the word and sentence. Just as nearly contemporaneous attempts in early modern Europe would "translate" a single purportedly nondiscursive Egyptian glyph into an essay, Wei Jiao also believed that the nondiscursive sense of the graph could be conveyed with lengthy verbal explanation.[53]

David Lurie has observed that writing is "often associated with pictorial or symbolic visual designs with conventional meanings that overlap with or complement the meaning of the graphs themselves."[54] For Lurie, the distinction between the true "meaning" and the "symbolic" sense can be characterized as the difference between "alegible" and "legible" uses of writing, the ubiquitous Chinese graph tattoo in Western culture being a readily accessible example of the former. Wei Jiao's articulation of the symbolic meaning inherent in the Chinese graph relied instead on multiple forms of legibility. For Wei the surface legibility of the graph incorporated its basic semantic and phonological properties, an understanding of which would facilitate one's understanding of the graph within the context of a sentence. The symbolic power of Chinese graphs as Wei Jiao understood it relied not on the magical properties of the script or generic associations between specific graphs and conventional meanings, but rather on the interaction of the component parts particular to each graph. Wei Jiao proposed that a precise understanding of these component parts generated a layer of meaning that complemented the basic semantic definition of the graph. This practice involved a mode of reading that transformed the most elemental aspects of each graph into a meaningful unit for apprehending the teachings of the sages.

Wei Jiao's analysis of graphs differed in aim from the contemporaneous European fascination with the perceived "ideographic" quality of Chinese graphs to convey ideas directly, independent of language. Some European scholars did cite Wei Jiao's work, and Figurists employed similar methods of parsing the component parts of graphs to reveal a deeper meaning.[55] For European thinkers, the Chinese script had the potential to serve as a universal written language that communicated solely in ideas. Their concerns with universality were not shared by Ming thinkers, who tended to uphold the specificity of their writing system to Chinese civilization (see chapter 2). Moreover, while early modern European discourse adopted and amplified the prevalent Chinese view of the writing system as based in nature, Wei Jiao proposed the significance of the production of graphs at the hands of sages.[56] He pursued not a recovery of natural principles, but instead sagely intent.

Philological Trends within the Learning of the Mind

The implications of Wei Jiao's scholarship resonated deeply within the community of thinkers engaged in the Learning of the Mind. His dictionary was seen as making a powerful case for written texts as a concrete window into the minds of the sages. In a postface to Wei's dictionary, Lu Ao 陸鰲 (*jinshi* 1502) defended the work against the potential criticism that Wei neglected the fundamental task of "restoring the Way of antiquity," which was "to rectify the minds of people." Lu countered that this rectification could not "come out of nothingness." By focusing his attention on philology, Lu argued that Wei had placed "explicating the Learning of the Mind" on solid ground, as well as provided the necessary tools for students to understand the Classics.[57] Wei's nephew, Ximing, who was ultimately responsible for printing the work, similarly claimed in a colophon that this text was not to be misinterpreted as primarily a philological work: "My uncle's work does not lie in the six principles of graph formation. It lies in the explication of the Learning of the Mind."[58] Lu Ao and Wei Ximing averred that philological and metaphysical endeavors need not be opposed. Likely echoing Wei Jiao's own intentions, however, they argued that the primary intent of the work lay in its philosophical message, rather than as a philological reference work on the Chinese script.

This notion that philology was a useful tool for moral exploration was echoed among prominent contemporary Learning of the Mind thinkers. For instance, Luo Hongxian 羅洪先 (1504–1564), one of the most influential proponents of Wang Yangming's teachings, associated closely with both Wei Jiao and Wang Yingdian. Luo Hongxian wrote a colophon for Wang Yingdian's *Tongwen beikao*, connecting Wang's etymological scholarship to the "teachings of the sages." Luo indicated that despite certain reservations about aspects of Wang Yingdian's work, he was in agreement that the learning of the ancient sages had been obscured by the transformation of the Chinese script over time. Paraphrasing the "Appended Phrases to the *Classic of Changes*" (*Xici* 繫辭), Luo acknowledged that "writing cannot fully express speech," and texts alone cannot convey the teachings of the sages fully.[59] However, by way of justifying Wang Yingdian's dictionary, Luo observed that without texts one would be even more lost. Luo's discussion calls to mind the immediately following passage within the "Appended Phrases," which represents the seminal claim to the nondiscursive capacity of images: "Speech cannot fully express ideas. But could it be that the ideas of the sages cannot be seen? The Master said: 'The sages created images to fully express ideas (聖人立象以盡意).'"[60] Luo Hongxian maintained that "ancient script" (*guwen* 古文) was the sole relic of the "ideas" (*yi* 意) of the sages and considered the ancient form of graphs to be closely modeled on the original trigram "images." When the later evolution of the script had departed from its basis in the images of the *Changes*, it had obscured "the subtle essence of the sages." To Luo Hongxian, the study of ancient Chinese script provided an essential window into the minds of the sages. Along with other contemporaries active in the Learning of the Mind center of Jiangxi, Luo Hongxian, who is also known for his influential cartographic scholarship, endorsed reading and the accumulation of knowledge as valid pursuits. Wei Jiao's brand of scholarship provided such scholars with a concrete example of how close textual study could benefit moral learning.

Gu Yingxiang 顧應祥 (1483–1565), an idiosyncratic sixteenth-century thinker, went further in attempting to justify Wei Jiao's philology by arguing that the study of graphs had always been a part of the Learning of the Mind tradition. To make this claim, Gu cited a passage from the collected sayings of Lu Xiangshan 陸象山 (1139–1193), a famed Song dynasty philosopher whose early emphasis on the mind as Coherence was influential for Ming developments in Learning of the Mind thought. In the quoted passage, Lu Xiangshan intimated that ancient graph forms were preferable to modern in some contexts. Gu Yingxiang elaborated on this premise by claiming that the study of ancient graphs could lead to the recovery of one's original, fundamentally good mind: "If today's scholar can restore his lost mind (收其放心) while writing graphs, causing each dot and stroke to have a precedent and not violate the ancient, then he will be very near the Way."[61] Gu Yingxiang tied the study of graphs to the origins of the Learning of the Mind. He further believed that practicing the composition of ancient graph forms could help one become a moral person. By ensuring that one's writing was based on ancient "precedent," one could inhabit the minds of the sages.

Like Luo Hongxian, Gu Yingxiang had reservations about Wei Jiao's methods. In another text, Gu praised Wei Jiao's scholarship on ancient graph forms but questioned the logic of a wholesale return to writing in the ancient script. Gu saw the transformation of script over time as a natural condition of historical change (*shishi shiran* 時勢使然).[62] Moreover, it would be difficult to replace a standard script that had already been established for so long. As Gu pointed out, even Confucius was willing to bend to popular custom over antiquity if there were reasonable justification.[63] Gu proposed a compromise: When the occasion called for writing in ancient script styles one should attempt to faithfully emulate the ancient, presumably according to Wei Jiao's analyses. In other cases, regular script, as prescribed in the dynastic standard *Hongwu zhengyun*, would be acceptable.[64]

Leading Learning of the Mind scholars were reading the philological works of Wei Jiao and his school. On the one hand, they seemed to share a sense that Wei was somewhat eccentric in the degree to which he advocated studying and practicing the ancient script. They agreed with the basic premise, however, that the ancient script contained important traces of the minds of the sages. Wei Jiao himself did not argue that philology was the sole component of moral study. As he wrote in a letter to the prominent Learning of the Way scholar Zhang Bangqi 張邦奇 (1484–1544), "Reading the works of the sages now, one should aim to experientially understand them oneself. If you get mired in the language and graphs (滯於言語文字間), then you will chase the branch and forget the root."[65] He similarly criticized Han dynasty commentators for looking at the Classics solely from a philological perspective.[66] The distinction seems to be that Wei did not see philology as an end in itself. However, he believed its methods provided crucial insight into the minds of the sages and should therefore not be neglected. Although he borrowed graph forms and phonetic glosses from earlier philological texts, Wei Jiao primarily consulted with contemporary Learning of the Mind thinkers in his composition of the dictionary and framed the text as a contribution to the practice of moral cultivation.

The Learning of the Mind was divided in the Ming dynasty. Wang Yangming, the formative figure in codifying this school, opposed Wei Jiao's teachings. Others doubted that the ancient script was morally enlightening. As one contemporary of Wei's scathingly opined, "If explanations of graphs were sufficient to illuminate the Way, then Confucius's disciples should have written *Shuowen jiezi*!"[67] However, Wei Jiao's claim for philology in service of the Learning of the Mind may have been persuasive for some contemporary thinkers, who were averse to Wang Yangming's discrediting of reading as a path to moral knowledge. In the mid-to-late Ming, philology was not seen as necessarily separate from metaphysical moral learning.

It could instead be a tool for revealing sagely truths, and even providing concrete evidence in support of Learning of the Mind teachings.

Learning of the Mind in the World of Philology: Thematic Ordering

Wei Jiao's dictionary was primarily intended to convey teachings of the Learning of the Mind. It was nevertheless highly influential in the world of philological scholarship. Learning of the Mind teachings resonated with the broader concerns of producing valid knowledge among contemporary philologists. In the preface to a text that would retrospectively be reinterpreted in the eighteenth century as a progenitor of Evidential Learning, Gu Yingxiang claimed that the basis of the Learning of the Mind in the ultimately infallible workings of the human mind provided a valuable standard for linguistic research. He further explained: "In general, any learning of the ancients that has been passed down to later generations is only its remnants (*ji* 跡). But if one examines *self-so* sounds (*ziran zhi yin* 自然之音), seeking accord with one's own mind, then one will be near the Way."[68] This approach to scholarship, which emphasized the *self-so* qualities of the human mind above textual evidence, stands in sharp contrast to the better-understood philological activities of the eighteenth century. Late Ming scholars recognized that they had only limited access to the range of texts that would have been available in antiquity. In the view of some thinkers, the innate knowledge present in the mind provided a standard for scholarly judgment that surpassed the textual record of "remnants."

Over the course of the sixteenth and seventeenth centuries, numerous dictionaries in the style of Wei Jiao's *Liushu jingyun* were produced, and Wei's text came to assume a place as one of the standard reference works on the etymology of graphs. Whether or not Wei Jiao intended it to be employed as a lexicon, its widespread use as a philological text is evident from many contemporary bibliographical catalogs where it is included under sections related to philology.[69] By the end of the dynasty, Wei Jiao was consistently mentioned alongside other prolific lexicographers, such as Yang Shen and Zhao Yiguang, as one of the dynasty's most significant etymological thinkers.[70]

Wei Jiao's method of parsing graphs to unveil their moral message remained contentious in some circles. However, another aspect of his dictionary gained even broader traction: namely, the thematic organization of entries. In premodern China there existed three primary methods of dictionary entry lookup: (1) those based on sound (usually arranged according to rhyme), (2) those based on script (involving features such as the number of strokes in and shared components among graphs), and (3) thematic or semantic arrangements. The famous seventh-century rhyme dictionary *Qieyun* (切韻 Divided rhymes), and in particular its eleventh-century successor *Guangyun* (廣韻 Expanded rhymes), set the model for sound-based systems, while the second-century CE *Shuowen jiezi* was the progenitor of script-based approaches. These first two methods were commonly employed in lexicographical works. The thematic approach, represented in the early lexicon *Erya* (爾雅 Approaching elegance), was employed primarily in encyclopedias until lexicographic texts in the Song, Yuan, and Ming reclaimed it as an organizational principle (see table 3.1). Wei Jiao and his students inherited and further modified this form of thematic categorization. In so doing, they instigated a broader discussion among their contemporaries concerning how to classify and categorize information.

Despite earlier precedents for thematic ordering in the thirteenth and fourteenth centuries, late Ming philologists tended to invoke Wei Jiao's categories. Wei Jiao had implemented a thematic organizational system on the basis of his Learning of the Mind convictions, but other philological scholars adopted it because they viewed it as a more effective method of indexing lexical information. The seventeenth-century scholar Han Qia 韓洽 criticized the philosophical bent (以義理為先) of Wei Jiao's definitions as "hackneyed" and "superficial" but nevertheless saw Wei's work as containing some philological value.[71] In particular, Han upheld the organizational system of Wei Jiao's over the stroke-based systems of other contemporary works: "At present I broadly adhere to [Wei Jiao's] *Liushu jingyun* and [Wang Yingdian's] *Tongwen beikao*, dividing sections according to heaven, earth, humans, and things."[72] Criticizing other organizational systems as "merely explanations for illiterates, having nothing to do with the study of graphs," Han Qia saw thematic arrangements as more philologically convincing.

Han Qia specifically targeted the lookup system developed in the early seventeenth-century *Zihui*, in which a reader could consult a graph by identifying one component as the "classifier" (*bushou* 部首) and counting the remaining strokes in the graph. The graph in question would be located in a section dedicated to that classifier, further indexed according to number of strokes. This method of organization is commonly identified today as

TABLE 3.1
Thematic Categories Compared in Song Through Ming Dictionaries

Liushu gu 六書故 (13th century)	Liushu tong 六書統 (xiangxing category)* (14th century)	Liushu benyi 六書本義 (14th century)	Liushu jingyun 六書精蘊 (16th century)	Liushu zongyao 六書總要 (16th century)
Origins of the six principles of graph creation	System of the six principles of graph creation	Original meaning of the six principles of graph formation	Mysterious essence of the six principles of graph formation	Comprehensive summary of the six principles of graph formation
數 (Numbers)	天文 (Heavens)	數位 (Numerical positions)	象數 (Images and numbers)	數位 (Numerical positions)
天 (Heaven)	地理 (Earth)	天文 (Heavens)	天文 (Heavens)	天文 (Heavens)
地 (Earth)	人品 (People)	地理 (Earth)	地理 (Earth)	地理 (Earth)
人 (Man)	宮室 (Dwellings)	人物 (Humans)	人倫 (Human relations)	人倫 (Human relations)
動物 (Animals)	衣服 (Clothes)	草木 (Plants and trees)	人體 (Human form)	身體 (Human form)
植物 (Plants)	器用 (Implements)	蟲獸 (Insects and beasts)	宮室 (Dwellings)	飲食 (Food)
工事 (Crafts)	鳥獸 (Birds and beasts)	飲食 (Food)	飲食 (Food)	衣服 (Clothes)
雜 (Miscellaneous)	蟲魚 (Insects and fish)	服飾 (Attire)	衣服 (Clothes)	宮室 (Dwellings)
疑 (Indeterminate)	草木 (Plants and trees)	宮室 (Dwellings)	器用 (Implements)	器用 (Implements)
	怪異 (Anomalies)	器用 (Implements)	草木 (Plants and trees)	鳥獸 (Birds and beasts)
			鳥獸 (Birds and beasts)	蟲魚 (Insects and fish)
			蟲魚 (Insects and fish)	草木 (Plants and trees)

Note: This table is adapted from Nathan Vedal, "Later Imperial Lexicons," in *Literary Information in China: A History*, ed. Jack Chen et al. (New York: Columbia University Press, 2021), 85.

* *Liushu tong* is organized according to the "six principles of graph formation," and the section for each principle contains a unique, albeit related, subset of thematic categories. Included here are the thematic categories for the first principle (*xiangxing* "image and form" graphs).

one of the major philological breakthroughs in Chinese history, and contemporary accounts indicate that *Zihui* was a popular reference work in its time.[73] Its successors *Zhengzi tong* (正字通 Comprehensive correction of graphs) and the renowned Qing court dictionary *Kangxi zidian* 康熙字典 embraced this model of graph lookup. Han Qia's complaint that such a method had "nothing to do with the study of graphs" was echoed by other scholars, however, who routinely claimed that it "misunderstood the meaning of graphs" (不知字意).[74] The long-lasting contribution of *Zihui* in terms of practicality has obscured the fact that its acceptance was not immediate in all circles. Some contemporaneous scholars believed that categorizing graphs according to isolated components and stroke counts was arbitrary and ignored a crucial layer of meaning, often moral, conveyed in the written form of the graph itself. A proper dictionary, in the view of such scholars, should reflect the thematic linkages inherent in the script.

Wu Yuanman 吳元滿 (fl. 1584–1605), a prolific lexicographer of the late Ming, criticized earlier attempts at thematic categorization for interspersing human-related categories with animal and plant-related ones. For instance, Dai Tong's 戴侗 (*jinshi* 1241) *Liushu gu* placed the categories for "animals" 動物 and "plants" 植物 between those for "humans" 人 and "works and affairs" 工事. Wu Yuanman praised Wei Jiao for being the first philological scholar to recognize that all things related to human activity should be placed before those of plants and animals.[75] For such scholars, the organizational system of a dictionary was reflective of broader universal and natural principles. Wu Yuanman provided even more elaborate justifications for the hierarchy embedded in such categorizations, ranging from moral attributes to distinguishing animals based on their method of producing offspring.[76] In Wu Yuanman's eyes, Wei Jiao had established the precedent for a more logical organization of graphs in a dictionary.

Morally based thematic categorizations were developed in depth by Learning of the Mind thinkers, such as Wei Jiao. One need not adhere to the Learning of the Mind, however, to accept the underlying premises of these categorizations and their application to philology. Han Qia and Wu Yuanman both criticized the influence of metaphysical philosophy on philological study.[77] But they also saw Wei Jiao's organizational theories as innovative and useful, despite the metaphysical thrust of Wei Jiao's original text.

The contemporary obsession with the order of categories in dictionaries carried over into discussions of the sequence of the entries themselves. A twelfth-century Learning of the Way glossary of philosophically significant terms, *Beixi ziyi*, appears to have assumed sequential reading and provided one model for sequential ordering.[78] But it did not explicitly address the logic of its arrangement. In one exemplary sixteenth-century work, *Renzi ce* (認字測 Conjectures on the recognition of graphs), the compiler Zhou Yu 周宇 (fl. 1580s), actually offered an explanation for his specific ordering of graphs. For example, Zhou explicated the sequence of the graphs "heaven" (*tian* 天), "great" (*da* 大), "correct" (*zheng* 正), and "center" (*zhong* 中) in his lexicon as follows: "Only heaven is great, therefore [the graph] 'great' comes after [the graph] 'heaven.' When there is something great it must be correct, and therefore [the graph] 'correct' comes after [the graph] 'great.' When something is correct its way is centered, and therefore [the graph] 'center' comes after [the graph] 'correct.'"[79] And so Zhou proceeded to outline the ordering of each and every dictionary entry, placing emphasis on the sequence of each individual graph. This attention to the sequence of entries implies that his dictionary was in some sense meant to be read from beginning to end in order to capture the significance behind the progression from one entry to the next.[80] In his view the dictionary was intended to contain two levels of meaning: that of the individual entry, and that of the relationship of entries to one another, as conveyed by their ordering.

Previous thematic dictionaries typically incorporated a classifier-based lookup system within their overarching categories.[81] Wei Jiao's *Liushu jingyun*, by contrast, ordered graphs within a category by semantic linkages, similarly indicating the potential for a sequential reading of the text. Wei commissioned a student of his to provide glosses of obscure seal forms in the upper margins of the text (figure 3.3). Most glosses appear only at the first appearance of a graph, suggesting that readers were intended to consume the text sequentially, familiarizing themselves with the glosses as they proceeded.[82] Graphs within a given thematic category were also organized according to semantic relationships rather than shared classifier, and the definitions in many instances were dependent on one another. For instance, within the category "Images and Numbers" (*xiangshu* 象數), the term "circle" (*yuan* 圓), which Wei glossed as "the substance of heaven," precedes "square" (*fang* 方), which he defined as "the substance of earth."[83] The two graphs do not share a classifier but are instead a conceptual pair representing a complementary bipolarity within Wei Jiao's cosmology.[84] A more complex example of these principles of ordering is evident in the following sequence of graphs within the category "Patterns of Heaven" (*tianwen* 天

文): "to divine" (*bu* 卜), "omen" (*zhao* 兆), "to divine" (*bu* 卟), "to divine" (*zhan* 占), "divination" (*shi* 筮), "auspicious" (*ji* 吉), "inauspicious" (*xiong* 凶). The last two graphs, "auspicious" and "inauspicious," form a complementary bipolarity, similar to that of "circle" and "square." Wei reflected this complementarity in his definitions, respectively, "reaping good fortune by following the Way" and "reaping calamity by going counter to the Way."[85] The progression of the graphically related *bu* 卜 and *bu* 卟 is interrupted by the unrelated graph "omen" (*zhao* 兆). The purpose of this

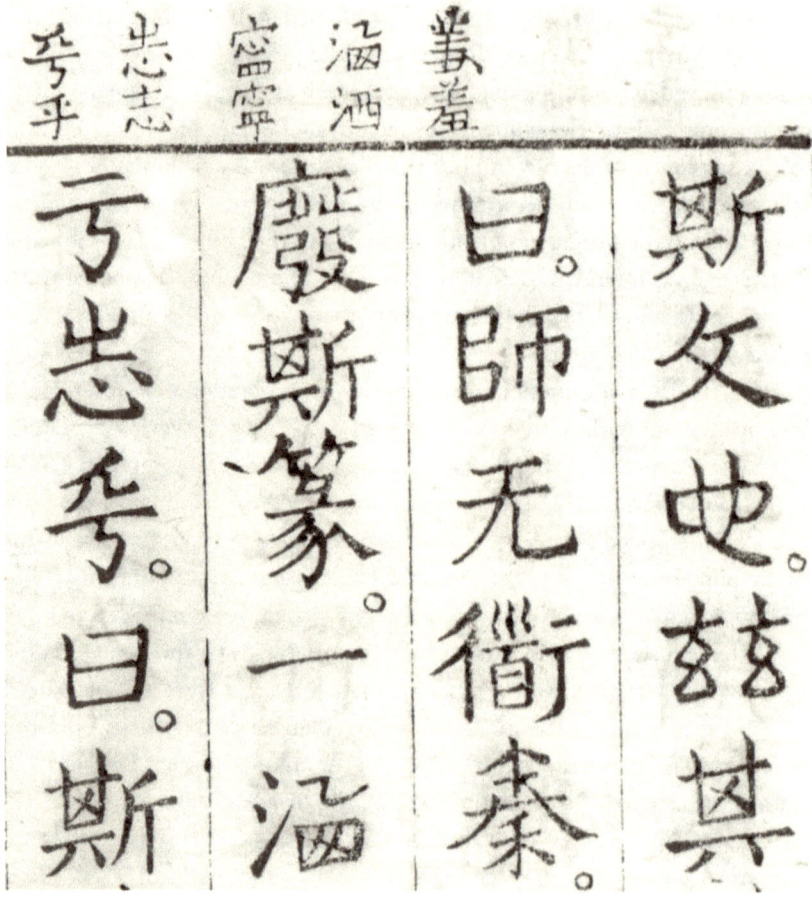

Figure 3.3 Upper margin glosses of seal form graphs in Wei Jiao's dictionary. Wei Jiao, *Liushu jingyun*, *xu*, 6a. (Image courtesy of Staatsbibliothek zu Berlin—PK, Libri sin. N.S. 637. http://resolver.staatsbibliothek-berlin.de/SBB0002352700000000. Present location: Biblioteka Jagiellońska, Kraków.)

ordering was presumably to explain the term "omen," contained within the definition of *bu* 卜. The graphs "omen" (*zhao* 兆), "divination" (*shi* 筮), "auspicious" (*ji* 吉), and "inauspicious" (*xiong* 凶) have no graphical relationship to one another but are nevertheless included in this section because of their relevance to the topic of prognostication.

Ultimately Wei Jiao's organizational strategy frequently resulted in graphs with the same classifier being grouped together, given that his interpretations of component parts of the graph, including the classifier, were often shared across entries. However, the reasoning underlying this organization was not graphic or phonetic, but rather semantic. Wei Jiao's work, and the texts it inspired, viewed a purely classifier or sound-based organization as fundamentally arbitrary. By virtue of its relational ordering of graphs within overarching thematic categories, Wei's dictionary was a tool for mental training, to be read from beginning to end (or at least in sections, rather than focusing on individual graphs) and taken as seriously as any moral tract.

Learning of the Mind in the World of Philology: Opposition to Overanalysis of Graph Forms

Wei Jiao's methods of graph analysis not only influenced contemporary practices of lexical organization but also served as a catalyst for discussion of the nature of writing. Wei's argument that the writing of antiquity reflected sagely values rather than scribal happenstance fell within a much broader debate about the history of writing in Ming linguistic thought. Some sided with Wei and the notion that individual graphs had precise and unchanging meanings. For example, Zhao Yiguang similarly saw an understanding of the construction of graphs as integral to comprehending antiquity, as well as writing in the present day. As with Wei Jiao, this translated into practice. Zhao Yiguang typically printed his works in the contemporary regular script, as opposed to the deliberately archaic script of Wei Jiao's work. However, he employed many uncommon variant graphs derived from ancient forms, occasionally providing glosses for less recognizable graphs (figure 3.4). For example, he used two different graphs to represent the varied senses of the graph <xao> 好. In a grammatical distinction that premodern philologists characterized as "active" (*dong* 動) versus "inactive" (*jing* 靜), <xao> 好 when pronounced in the falling tone

(<xào>) is a transitive verb meaning "to like," while in the rising tone (<xǎo>) it is a stative verb meaning "to be good." For most scholars, this distinction simply affected reading pronunciations of a single graph (好). Zhao Yiguang, on the other hand, shared Wei Jiao's conviction that the ancients would have necessarily created a different graph for each possible meaning. He therefore adopted an alternative archaic form, 㛿, for the transitive usage of the graph.[86] Zhao also adapted contemporary practices of cursive calligraphy for application to ancient script forms, creating a unique hybrid form of calligraphic script.[87]

Despite the considerable influence of Wei Jiao's methods in the late Ming, some contemporaries took issue with his approach to graph analysis. Wei Jiao may have never intended his work to be consulted by philologists, or at least understood as a contribution to linguistic, rather than moral, learning. Philological scholars nonetheless did read it. Their responses indicate how Wei's Learning of the Mind provoked heated debated about the purpose of writing.

Figure 3.4 Zhao Yiguang's archaic regular script and annotations. Zhao Yiguang, *Shuowen changjian, zixu*, 3a. (Image courtesy of Harvard-Yenching Library.)

Implicit in Wei Jiao's graph analyses was the sense that there was sagely intent behind the exact form of a particular graph. Variant forms either were unorthodox or were intended to express a specific shade of meaning. This stood in contrast to the notion that many graphs in antiquity were interchangeable (*tongyong* 通用), an argument that had considerable persuasive power for premodern scholars and informs the study of ancient texts to this day. Perhaps the most famous example of its use in practice is Zhu Xi's emendation of the first line of the *Great Learning*, a foundational classical text, to read "the Way of great learning lies in renewing the people (*xinmin* 新民)" over the received text "the Way of great learning lies in loving the people (*qinmin* 親民)." This seemingly minor change had considerable implications and became a major source of debate as Wang Yangming came to assert the latter reading in support of his valuation of internal over external cultivation.[88] The increasingly pressing question for philological and moral thinkers was whether or not to view the texts of antiquity as historical products. Could it be that the development and use of writing in antiquity was at a different stage from the present (i.e., were graph forms and usage in flux in antiquity)? Or were the sages faultless, and our inability to maintain ancient usage a result of contemporary moral and scholarly decay?

Critical responses to Wei Jiao's approach to etymology developed elaborate propositions for how to understand written language. The issue at stake was whether the form of written script represented ideas or whether graphs were, as one scholar put it, merely "vessels" (*qi* 器) for conveying words.[89] The classical commentator Hao Jing 郝敬 (1568–1639) opposed Wei Jiao's methods in a dictionary of his own. After achieving his *jinshi* degree, Hao Jing held a number of official positions from the county to capital level. His ability to offend, however, resulted in his demotion to the lowest rank following his capital appointments. As a result, he retired from officialdom and devoted himself to classical scholarship. Hao Jing wrote a dictionary, entitled *Dushu tong* (讀書通 Comprehensive analysis of reading), that like Wei Jiao's work, had grander aims than simply glossing graphs. As the title of the work suggests, it also comprised a theory of reading and approaching the Classics. Although Hao did not explicitly mention Wei Jiao, his criticisms of contemporary scholarship were clearly a response to etymological methods like those of Wei Jiao, which put emphasis on deciphering the underlying meaning of words based on the form of their graphs. As Hao explained, "the ancients used graphs like they used money. Money cannot be used as clothing and food; clothing and food are simply bought with it. Graphs cannot serve as moral principles (文字不可當義理); moral principles are simply borrowed from them."[90] He further averred that "the ancients valued meaning (*yi* 義) in their use of graphs and did not emphasize the strokes or forms of the graphs."[91] In Hao's view, the many variations in graphs "were all manmade (*you ren zuo* 由人作).[92] Invoking the widespread Ming concern with human artifice, Hao Jing highlighted the imperfection of human effort, rather than the sagely intent Wei Jiao had emphasized. Wei Jiao and Zhao Yiguang insisted on a strict distinction of graph forms, discarding those they felt were unorthodox and assigning specific meanings to the remaining variants. Hao Jing, however, argued that learning to properly read the Classics was a matter of mastering the inherent flexibility of the Chinese script. A single graph might bear multiple possible structural variations, but a reader's focus should be on the meanings of the terms themselves, rather than their written representations.

Jiao Hong, one of the great thinkers of the late Ming, similarly believed that graphs refer to things but are not intrinsically meaningful. Hence he praised one contemporary's observation that Chinese *tian* 天 and Xiongnu *tängri* (*chengli* 撐犁) both refer to the same "heaven."[93] Jiao argued that excessive attention to "moral principles" (*yili* 義理) contained in graphs was misguided. To support this claim, he cited a passage from a twelfth-century encyclopedia that listed numerous examples of graph variants from antiquity, described as "all products of the sages' hands."[94] Wei Jiao and his followers believed so strongly in the intentionality behind the sages' writing that variants could be embraced as meaningful for capturing different senses of a term. Jiao Hong pointed out that the vastness of variation precluded the possibility of such an interpretation. A small number of advocates for phonographic script in the Ming had proposed the primary significance of writing as "recording sound" (*jisheng* 記聲), making an alphabet the most effective conveyor of linguistic information.[95] The majority of Ming thinkers did not agree with this conception of writing and affirmed the superiority of the logographic Chinese script. Even among those who upheld Chinese graphs, however, there was debate over what the source of their superiority was. Hao Jing and Jiao Hong posited that writing was concerned with notating words and concepts, which existed universally. Hao Jing argued for the superiority of the Chinese script in terms of its efficiency in conveying information (see chapter 2), but he did not perceive the additional layer of meaning Wei Jiao claimed to exist within the graphs themselves.

The efforts of both Learning of the Mind advocates and their opponents in the sixteenth and seventeenth centuries fueled a robust discourse on the nature of written language. In Wei Jiao's view, there existed a level of nondiscursive meaning contained in the individual graph, beyond the immediate semantic information it conveyed within a sentence. Wei Jiao's approach to graph exegesis emphasized intentionality and the existence of a single correct version of each graph (for a given meaning). Its popularity also generated rebuttals from prominent scholars, who saw writing as a functional tool for the communication of meaning. In their opinion, words and concepts were universal and could be related in any language, even if the Chinese script may relay these meanings more efficiently. One opponent even felt the need to respond on Wei Jiao's own terms to demonstrate his superiority as a scholar. At the conclusion of his lengthy and metaphysically dense definition of the graph "centrality" (*zhong* 中), he wrote: "I needn't have gone into such philosophical depth here. But because my predecessor [Wei Jiao] did so, if I did not do the same, I fear those who are fond of philosophy (好講道理者) would still think his explanation [of the graph] superior."[96] This comment, tongue-in-cheek as it may have been, reflects the considerable influence of Wei Jiao's definitions and the increasingly expected ability to acknowledge the potential moral implications of written script.

During the sixteenth century moral thinkers were deeply involved in philological projects, and textual study came to be seen as a method to transcend history and access the enduring principles of antiquity. Wei Jiao and his followers analyzed writing based on the notion that each graph was developed to convey a precise moral message. Wei's development of a thematic organizational system of information retrieval was influential even for contemporary and later scholars who did not accept his metaphysical interpretation of graphs.

The relationship of cognition and language remains an issue of linguistic, neurobiological, and philosophical concern in the present day. Although today much-disputed, the Sapir-Whorf hypothesis, which in its strongest interpretation has been understood to suggest that one's native spoken language directly affects one's perception of the world, continues to inspire neurolinguistic research.[97] Ming thinkers saw the potential of written language to alter the operation of the mind. By adopting the script forms used in antiquity, they argued, one could train one's mind to think like a sage. A vague link between calligraphic forms and morality had existed for centuries, but late sixteenth-century thinkers explained concretely why script and mind were connected. In their view, ancient graphs were constructed in a purposeful manner, containing a level of meaning that reflected the thought patterns of the sagely mind.

The philological efforts of Learning of the Mind thinkers also had bearing on notions of efficiency in information retrieval. The late Ming is typically recognized for a critical advance in indexing methods, resulting from the perfection of the classifier-stroke count method in *Zihui*. A closer look at debates surrounding the development of this method indicates that it was far from immediately welcomed. As in many premodern cultures, thematic ordering was claimed to reflect better the workings of the mind and therefore to provide a more efficient indexing system.[98] In contrast to the arbitrary logic of alphabetical indexing, thematic arrangements also conveyed additional layers of information, ranging from hierarchies within human society to biological relationships. Phonetic and form-based indexing would eventually dominate lexical and encyclopedic organization in the twentieth century, by virtue of their perceived efficiency and objectivity. More recently digitization has made alphabetic and form-based lookup systems increasingly irrelevant, and the hyperlink has emerged as a new kind of thematic relational indexing system. For mid-to-late Ming Learning of the Mind thinkers, the graph itself was an index, containing an embedded layer of information central to reconstructing meaning and reforming the mind.

PART II

Singing and Speaking, Reading and Writing

CHAPTER 4

Opera and the Search for a Universal Language

What makes opera pleasing to the ear? Is it the quality of the singing voice, the lyrics, the music, or some combination of these elements? For late Ming audiences, these three aspects of performance were intimately connected. The choice of words within an aria was regulated by musical and prosodic requirements, which could be fulfilled only if sung with the correct pronunciation. The formal stipulations of the musical accompaniment and prosody were also well established. But who determined the correct pronunciation? With the rise of regional operatic forms over the course of the Ming dynasty, pronunciation debates brought together the seemingly unrelated communities of classicists and opera librettists, who sought to settle this question. Philology was formally classified within the bibliographic tradition as a branch of classical studies and therefore concerned primarily with exegesis of the Classics, a more or less stable set of ancient texts associated with Confucian thought. Texts of the operatic tradition, on the other hand, were recent in origin, for the most part coming from no earlier than the thirteenth century. In addition, operatic language was decidedly unclassical, often embracing vernacular modes of expression. Yet in the Ming dynasty, the linguistic analysis of opera was seen to be an essential tool for answering broad questions into the nature of language, and as such an integral part of the classical philologist's enterprise. In creating methods to train singers and writers in operatic genres, opera theorists developed new ways of discussing linguistic sound, which in turn attracted the attention of classicists.

Language study went hand in hand with literary production in imperial China. The discipline of Chinese phonology itself formed largely within a literary context in the fifth century. To be sure, earlier philological texts employed various forms of phonetic description. The second-century *Shuowen jiezi*, for instance, employed the "read as" (*duruo* 讀若) method, which glossed graphs with a common homophone. The early commentarial tradition on the Classics also incorporated new phonetic methods, including most notably the *fanqie* method of glossing a single graph with two common graphs (one to represent the initial, the other the final). The codification of tones, however, central to all later phonological discussions, emerged from a context of standardizing literary norms within the poetic circle of Shen Yue 沈約 (441–513).[1] Although their designation of four tonal categories, level (*ping* 平), rising (*shang* 上), falling (*qu* 去), and entering (*ru* 入), was established for the sake of producing aesthetically pleasing poetry, it has remained in use among linguists up to the present.

The establishment of literary linguistic norms reflected a long-standing concern with linguistic standardization in China. Awareness of regional differences in relation to a putative standard in spoken Chinese traces back to references in the Classics themselves, as well as the work of Han classicists, such as Yang Xiong (53 BCE–18 CE). Concern with regional varieties of Chinese took on new significance in the medieval era when pronunciation came to be discussed as a reflection of one's aristocratic upbringing. This awareness of linguistic diversity in China led to some of the first attempts to characterize the nature of speech in different regions. In a statement often cited by later Ming scholars, Lu Fayan 陸法言 (fl. 601), the primary compiler of the seminal phonological lexicon *Qieyun*, observed: "As for the Wu and Chu regions [of southern China], [the pronunciation] occasionally suffers from being too light and shallow (*qingqian* 輕淺); in the Yan and Zhao regions [of northeastern China], [the pronunciation] often infringes on being too heavy and turbid (*zhongzhuo* 重濁); in the Qin and Long regions [of northwestern China], the falling tone sounds like the entering tone; as for the Liang and Yi regions [of southwestern China], the level tone sounds like the falling tone."[2] Lu Fayan's contemporary Yan Zhitui 顏之推 (531–591) similarly observed pronunciation variation in speakers from different regions and made the case that there should exist a single correct standard.[3]

The linguistic ideals of these early medieval scholars were formalized in the Tang dynasty bureaucracy where pronunciation was one of the categories evaluated as evidence of proper cultivation in the official appointment process.[4] As Meow Hui Goh has observed, despite the co-option of the phonology codified in Lu Fayan's *Qieyun* by the Tang and later states, the original context of Lu Fayan's composition was "private" and perhaps to some extent exclusive. Lu Fayan drew a distinction between "desiring to expand the literary path" (欲廣文路), for which serious phonological study was unnecessary, and "showing appreciation for true connoisseurship of sound" (賞知音), for which it was required. The precise meaning of this polarity is still debated, but the locution clearly denotes an opposition between an expansive view of literary practices that does not demand excessive attention to phonological detail and a narrow audience of those who appreciate refined literature.[5] In its original context, *Qieyun* was geared toward the establishment of poetic standards among a circle of cultivated connoisseurs, who set themselves apart from others by virtue of their pronunciation. The concern of its compilers, as far as we can tell, was not to achieve widespread currency or to aid in communication, but rather to codify acceptable literary usage in elite settings.

The compilers of *Qieyun*, by laying out the features of proper literary readings, perhaps unintentionally demonstrated that pronunciation was not solely a matter of pedigree but could be learned. Despite the origins of this phonological discourse outside of officialdom, the state had good reason to take *Qieyun* and the issue of language standards seriously. Beginning from some point in the seventh century, the Tang state began to institute poetry on the *jinshi* exam as a means for recruiting officials into the bureaucracy. Although the *jinshi* exam added a nonpoetry track in the eleventh century, the poetry track remained popular until its discontinuation in the Yuan dynasty. Candidates and examiners needed a standard to apply in writing and grading poems submitted on the exams, and *Qieyun* provided a model for the state to adopt.[6] The Tang and Northern Song imperial courts produced several other influential rhymebooks, inspired by the *Qieyun* model, as a standard for poetic composition in an examination setting.

In addition to the necessity of standards on the examination, the nature of the imperial bureaucracy required a spoken standard to facilitate the communication of officials, who from the Tang onward could not serve in their home region and were frequently shifted to new positions throughout the empire. This common official language (*guanhua* 官話 or *guanyin* 官音)

appears to have existed in some form for much of Chinese history. Explicit references to such a language become much more common in the Ming, suggesting the increasingly standardized nature of the official language.[7] It is only beginning in the eighteenth century, however, that there is clear evidence of state investment in codifying the official spoken language and providing opportunities for training in its proper pronunciation.

Discussions of regional difference and standardization assumed a new form in the Ming. The expansion of literary audiences in the sixteenth century contrasts with the concerns of medieval aristocratic connoisseurs, while the lack of a poetry track on the examinations made such literary standards less pressing to the state. The responsibility for creating a standard that could be appreciated by increasingly broad audiences thus fell on the shoulders of literary figures and scholars outside of the court. The Ming witnessed many proposals for literary and spoken language standards, based on both northern and southern varieties of Chinese. In the absence of a widely accepted official standard, privately compiled poetic rhyme books flourished. New operatic genres in particular became a venue to consider issues of intelligibility, history, and aesthetics in the establishment of linguistic norms. Even more significant was a new sense that literary philology was relevant not only for the functional purpose of literary composition but also provided essential insights into the nature of language that could be generalized and applied more broadly to the study of both ancient Chinese and the establishment of contemporary spoken standards. Texts originally written for the purposes of operatic composition were reinterpreted as systematic treatises on the Chinese language. Literary figures and classical scholars collaborated during this period on the basis of their shared goal to uncover fundamental principles of language. These collaborations fueled a reconceptualization of the component parts of the syllable and how best to phonetically represent them.

Opera and Linguistic Standardization in the Ming

Librettists tended to be concerned with establishing a fundamental unified pronunciation, which could serve as a standard for recitation and singing. The standardized form of language employed in literary texts, and occasionally by extension speech, was referred to by a variety of terms, including not only "official pronunciation" (*guanhua* 官話 or *guanyin* 官音), but also "elegant pronunciation" (*yayan* 雅言 or *yayin* 雅音), "common pronunciation" (*tongyu* 通語 or *tongyin* 通音), and "correct pronunciation" (*zhengyin* 正音).⁸ Similarly to Renaissance Italy, where editors such as Pietro Bembo (1470–1547) played a decisive role in the establishment of vernacular linguistic standards, Ming opera editors and connoisseurs saw language standardization as an essential part of their occupation.⁹ Zang Maoxun 臧懋循 (1550–1620), for instance, editor of the famed Ming compilation of Yuan dynasty northern-style opera *Yuanqu xuan* (元曲選 Selection of Yuan plays), wrote of the necessity of conscientiously attending to "the voicing of syllable initials and tones of final rhymes."¹⁰ Zang's editorial contributions include a revision of perhaps the most famous operatic work in the Chinese tradition, Tang Xianzu's 湯顯祖 (1550–1616) *Peony Pavilion* (*Mudan ting* 牡丹亭). His motivation in editing this renowned work was Tang Xianzu's lack of attention to phonological and prosodic details.¹¹ Zang Maoxun was by no means alone in his criticism. *Peony Pavilion* was revised at least six times by various editors in the late Ming. Judging from extant copies of these revisions, prosodic issues were at the top of the list for correction. Tang Xianzu himself responded to revisions of his work, claiming: "In the past there were those who disdained Wang Wei's 王維 (701–761) painting of a banana palm in a winter scene and cut out the palm to replace it with a plum tree. Well, it remained winter, but it was not Wang Wei's winter scene."¹² For Tang Xianzu, an overemphasis on technical details would interfere with artistic expression. His contemporaries largely did not agree with this premise, and opera critics overwhelmingly expressed a concern with the phonological and prosodic details of arias and recitatives. A common trope among critics was that Tang Xianzu had great talent, but his ignorance (willful or otherwise) of the technical aspects of composition affected the performability, as well as the aesthetic value, of his operas.¹³ There nonetheless existed no universally accepted standard with which to correct the mistakes of earlier and contemporary dramatists.

Debates about the standards for assessing correct pronunciation abound in works of late Ming operatic scholarship. This interest could lead to meticulous philological analysis as a method for justifying one's pronunciation claims. He Liangjun 何良俊 (1506–1573), for example, recounted his discussion with fellow theorist Dun Ren 頓仁 as follows:

> Master Dun never set aside the rhymebooks *Zhongyuan yinyun* (中原音韻 Tones and rhymes of the central plains) and *Qionglin*

yayun (瓊林雅韻 Elegant rhymes of celestial forest). Hence he was right 80 or 90 percent of the time about closed and opened mouth sounds [syllables ending in <-m> and <-n>, respectively], the four tones, and voicing distinctions. But when the text was not clear, there would occasionally be errors. For example, Ma Zhiyuan's 馬致遠 (1250–1321) *A Lone Goose in Autumn over the Palaces of Han* contains the lyric: "Felt-covered cart loaded with parting's grief, rattling halfway down the hill" (載離恨的氈車半坡裏響). He said the graph "felt-covered" 氈 [commonly written as 毡] should be closed-mouthed [pronounced <dyām>]. I replied, "氈 should be open-mouthed [pronounced <dyān>]." He said, "My research into rhymes is quite extensive. This graph is based on the written element <dyām> 占 and should be closed-mouthed." I replied, "If it were based on <dyām> 占, then it should indeed be closed-mouthed. But this is nothing more than an abbreviated form created by scribes. This graph was originally based on <dǎn> 亶. <dǎn> 亶 is open-mouthed, and if you look into the correct form of the graph <dyān> 氈, it is not based on <dyām> 占." He only then believed me that it should be open-mouthed.[14]

The crux of this debate hinged not on contemporary pronunciation of 氈 "felt-covered," but rather the history of the written form of the graph. The majority of Chinese graphs contain a phonetic element in addition to a semantic component. These phonetic elements have long served as evidence for adducing historical pronunciations of graphs. In the example given, Dun Ren based his pronunciation <dyām> on a version of the graph for "felt-covered" written 毡, which contains the phonetic element 占 (ending in the phoneme <-m>). He Liangjun, most likely having consulted *Shuowen jiezi* or a comparable dictionary of ancient graph forms, asserted that an older version of the graph was written 氈, which contains a different phonetic element, 亶 (ending in the phoneme <-n>). For He Liangjun, this indicated that the graph 氈 should instead be pronounced <dyān>. This passage suggests the high degree to which historical philological investigation could inform the prescription of contemporary singing pronunciations.[15] In this case philology, or what Dun Ren referred to as "research into rhymes" (*yunshang kaosuo* 韻上考索), involved tracing ancient pronunciations according to the methods in common use among contemporary classicists. Opera editors attempted to design an idealized form of Chinese, not necessarily based on a specific dialect or contemporary norm, but instead on historical linguistic principles. This anecdote also provides insight into the process of composition and reading, which clearly relied heavily on the use of reference books. Dun Ren annotated the pronunciation of operas primarily on the basis of a set of opera dictionaries from the fourteenth and fifteenth centuries, while He Liangjun's disputation almost certainly relied on a paleographical dictionary.

Research on late Ming literary culture tends to associate those who have come down to us as the greater literary figures with freedom and creativity as opposed to stodgy adherence to the rules.[16] With the exception of a handful of figures like Tang Xianzu, however, Ming librettists and editors generally tended to emphasize the necessity of studying and understanding phonology. The fascination with minutiae of pronunciation and singing has sometimes been characterized as part of an elite strategy to form a boundary for ascension into true circles of connoisseurship.[17] Recent research has also illuminated the aesthetic ramifications of prosodic and musical rules in Ming opera.[18] I would like to suggest that operatic language debates were not solely intended for the eyes of fellow librettists. Literary figures both pulled on a contemporary tradition of philological scholarship and directed their message to an audience of classicists. Opera theorists incorporated abstract cosmological discussions of sound into instructional materials for singers, adopting materials and methodologies from the cosmologists we encountered in chapter 1. Building on these methods of phonological categorization, they innovated new ways of describing linguistic sound that influenced broader philological debates among classicists. While these fields would increasingly grow apart over the course of the Qing dynasty, literary and classical modes of scholarship cross-fertilized each other in the sixteenth and seventeenth centuries.

The Ming concern with linguistic standardization occurred in a relative vacuum of official attention to linguistic matters. There is little evidence from Ming China of court influence in the creation of language standards, and in particular vernacular standards, as would be the case in early modern Europe and later in the Qing dynasty.[19] To be sure, the Hongwu emperor's commissioned dictionary, *Hongwu zhengyun*, was intended to supply the dynastic standard for script and rhymed composition. The courts of previous dynasties had similarly commissioned lexicographic works. In earlier periods, however, the requirement of poetic genres on the civil service examination obliged literati to pay attention to these rhymebooks, as deviations from the official rhymes could lead to disqualification for candidates and punishment for examiners who were unable to identify such mistakes.[20] The lack of poetic genres on the Ming exams perhaps made it so that elites did not feel compelled to pay attention to the official standard, and numerous scholars commented on the neglect of this text in contemporary usage. In addition, literary figures lambasted the text's basis in southern regional standards, which were inapplicable to northern literary genres.[21]

Aside from this early attempt to establish a standard, there were few later Ming official language policies. The Hongzhi emperor (1470–1505) did approve a memorial requesting to make the use of a Mongolian-influenced dialect in the capital a punishable offense, on account of its perceived deleterious effect on morals.[22] Neither the emperor nor his officials proposed a concrete alternative to this dialect, other than what they referred to vaguely as "the correct pronunciations of China" (*zhonghua zhengyin* 中華正音). There is evidence of one or more de facto koines in the Ming, but how information about this language was circulated or regulated remains unclear.[23] The next significant and concrete imperial directive regarding a common language would have to wait until a 1728 decree from the Yongzheng emperor of the Qing.[24] The idea of an "official speech" (*guanhua* 官話) was routinely invoked but only loosely conceptualized in the Ming. It was not until the eighteenth century that the imperial government, along with various philological scholars, made clear attempts to codify the "official speech."[25]

One scholar, perhaps with the goal of exculpating the Ming court's inability to promote a standard, observed that "a sage in the position of emperor can cause his empire to write in the same script, but not to speak with the same pronunciation."[26] To substantiate this claim, he pointed to examples of notoriously unsagely rulers, such as Empress Wu Zetian (624–705), who had invented a special set of graphs for officials to adopt, suggesting that authority alone was sufficient to effect a change in writing. Despite the perceived difficulty of standardizing speech, late Ming opera theorists took up the mantle of creating a standard pronunciation in the face of imperial neglect. Debates about linguistic correctness in Ming opera resonate even in the modern and contemporary eras, where speakers of non-Mandarin topolects have continued to assert their inheritance of an "authentic" uncontaminated version of Chinese.[27] Ming linguistic discussions reveal similar concerns with the history of language and description of dialects for the purpose of establishing an empire-wide linguistic standard. This discourse emerged not out of a directive from the central court, but from within the discussions of opera theorists. Their interest in standardization was primarily related to aesthetic concerns and the desire to increase intelligibility of performed works but also extended to the consideration of ancient phonology and a common spoken pronunciation.

Aria Dictionaries as Classical Lexicons and Sources for a Standard Chinese Language

A focal point of Ming opera debates was the Yuan dynasty rhymebook *Zhongyuan yinyun* (中原音韻 Tones and rhymes of the central plains). Compiled by Zhou Deqing 周德清 (1277–1365) in 1324, *Zhongyuan yinyun* quickly became an authoritative reference work for opera composition, a status it retained throughout the late imperial period. In a striking departure from the earlier tradition, Zhou Deqing attempted to codify the contemporary pronunciation of the "Central Plains" of North China, rather than adhere to medieval standards of linguistic description. Most contentiously from the perspective of some language theorists, this text eliminated the entering tone (characterized by a stop final, <-p>, <-t>, or <-c>), which had existed as one of the four tonal categories of Chinese phonological analysis since the fifth century. Because this tone was no longer present in most northern varieties of Chinese, Zhou Deqing considered it unnecessary to artificially preserve in sung genres, despite its persistence in poetry composition.[28] In the Ming there were competing interpretations of the validity of the phonological system outlined in *Zhongyuan yinyun*. Some saw it as preserving essential distinctions of an older idealized form of Chinese that had disappeared from many contemporary languages, both northern and southern. Others saw it as representing only a single topolect, and inferior as a universal standard. In this way, a text originally intended as a reference for librettists came to be cited in theoretical discussions of how to define general characteristics of Chinese phonology as well as the possibility of a shared common language.

In the original context of its composition in the early fourteenth century, *Zhongyuan yinyun* invoked a standard of empire-wide linguistic unity but was created explicitly for the purpose of aria composition and the challenges of singing (*ge* 歌). Despite its origins as a guide for the librettist,

Zhongyuan yinyun came to be understood as a treatise on the nature of the Chinese language more broadly during the Ming. Xiao Yuncong 蕭雲從 (c. 1596–1673), for instance, claimed that *Zhongyuan yinyun* could substantiate the theoretical phonological system of the Song cosmologist Shao Yong.[29] Wang Jide 王驥德 (d. 1623), a major Ming opera theorist and librettist, even compiled a no longer extant dictionary that purportedly corroborated the rhymes of the ancient *Classic of Poems* with those of *Zhongyuan yinyun*.[30] The use of *Zhongyuan yinyun* as a text to theoretically discuss the Chinese language of antiquity raises a number of questions. How could a thirteenth-century dictionary of aria rhymes corroborate fifth-century BCE poetry? Who would the intended audience of such a dictionary be?

The answer to these questions is provided most explicitly by Zhao Yiguang, a leading Ming philologist, who made the case for the utility of *Zhongyuan yinyun* as a classical dictionary:

> Although *Zhongyuan yinyun* may seem too small and disorderly, this work is nevertheless of great benefit to the Classics (*jingzhuan* 經傳). People today only take it as a tool for application in aria composition—what a pity! In antiquity there was no literary elite in the South. Thus the Classics all used northern pronunciations. Northern pronunciations lack the entering tone. Although this may seem incomplete, if you try to harmonize the entering tone in a musical tune, it will be too rough and will not match the music. Further, wherever their customs have spread, the three tones rule. If this book did not exist, when southerners read the Classics, they would mostly be shrike-tongued (*jueshe* 鴂舌). Ever since this book appeared, ancient pronunciations have been comprehensible, and when the ancient pronunciations are comprehensible, the ancient tunes are as clear as though in the palm of your hand.[31]

Zhao Yiguang was from Suzhou in southeastern China, and his native language would have preserved the entering tone. He was therefore sympathetic to the criticism of Zhou Deqing's system as "incomplete" (*weiquan* 未全). His conception of classical history, however, overrode pride in his native language. If indeed the ancient sages had originated in the North China Plain, then Zhou Deqing's dictionary could be considered a record of their speech. Zhao Yiguang adduced further evidence to this effect by citing a passage from the *Mencius* characterizing the speech of southerners as "shrike-tongued."[32] The referent in Mencius's discussion is unclear and could be describing non-Chinese southern languages, but Zhao Yiguang, among other Ming scholars, invoked this case to illustrate that southern Chinese topolects were considered less pure in classical antiquity.[33] Zhao argued that the northern pronunciations documented in *Zhongyuan yinyun* could therefore be applied to the recitation of the Classics and even corroborate ancient melodies accompanying sung genres.

It is often averred that southerners disparaged the lack of linguistic conservatism in northern topolects, hindering the spread of the northern standard as a Mandarin during the Ming.[34] Contemporary accounts, however, document many southern scholars who looked to the North for a linguistic standard. Southern philological scholars could embrace northern standards for historical, aesthetic, and metaphysical reasons. For instance, the opera critic Xu Fuzuo 徐復祚 (b. 1560), a native of Changzhou in Suzhou prefecture, argued against the use of southern standards in literary composition on aesthetic grounds. In Xu's view, there should be a single standard, which followed distinctions present in the northern language and therefore eliminated the entering tone.[35] This standard was both the most singable and pleasant to the ears.[36] At issue for Xu Fuzuo was the nature of the stop consonant (<-p>, <-t>, <-c>) in the entering tone. Like Zhao Yiguang, he considered this tone "too rough" for refined singing.

An influential Learning of the Way thinker, Cai Qing 蔡清 (1453–1508), argued instead on the basis of cosmological principles that the northern language should be adopted as the standard. Cai claimed that although *Zhongyuan yinyun* was on the surface concerned with the language of humans, as a study of sound it was in fact primarily about "the spontaneous movements of the dynamic processes of the universe (氣機之自動) and the spontaneous calls of the heavenly pipes (天籟之自鳴)." Viewing *Zhongyuan yinyun* as a treatise on sound and its cosmological basis in *qi*, Cai argued that Zhou Deqing had carefully selected its northern basis: "It must be that the central *qi* of heaven and earth is in China, and the central *qi* of China is in the Central Plains. When *qi* achieves its centrality, then sounds achieve their proper nature."[37] "Centrality" or "equilibrium" (*zhong* 中) was an essential Learning of the Way concept representing the ideal balance of *qi* in human nature. The term "Central Plains" invoked in Zhou Deqing's *Zhongyuan yinyun* refers to the North China Plain, which had long been associated with the core of Chinese civilization. Cai Qing aligned the cultural and metaphysical "centrality" of the "Central Plains" as justification for adopting a northern linguistic standard. Zhao Yiguang and Xu Fuzuo were both from the Suzhou region, while Cai Qing was from Fujian. None saw their native southern topolects as suitable for a literary standard, and instead they rallied diverse historical, aesthetic, and metaphysical reasons for preferring the North.

A concern with standardization and awareness of regional differences led to early attempts to document differentiation within Chinese topolects. Ling Mengchu 凌濛初 (1580–1644), a renowned author of vernacular fiction and opera critic from Kuaiji, Zhejiang, analyzed several dialects within the Wu topolect group, comparing them to Zhou Deqing's northern standard. He found that two dialects (those of Kuaiji and Piling prefectures) were "stricter" (猶嚴) by virtue of their maintaining distinctions present in the northern language but lost in many southern languages.[38] Despite his attention to southern topolects, Ling saw the northern standard outlined in *Zhongyuan yinyun* as representing the purest form of Chinese. The characterization of certain dialects as "stricter" implies that they had not deviated from an imagined standard. Other less conservative dialects simply did not hold to this standard as strongly. It would be a stretch to consider Ling Mengchu's documentation of regional speech as a precursor to the modern science of historical Chinese linguistics, which seeks different historical layers of the language in various modern dialects. However, the Ming concern over which topolects best reflected archaic Chinese fueled new attention toward the history of spoken Chinese languages and set the stage for broader discussions of which language would best serve as a common standard for the Chinese state.

Xu Fuzuo understood the very existence of topolects in China as a result of people's deficient understanding of phonology. According to Xu, if phonology (*yunxue* 韻學) and its methods (such as *fanqie*) were standardized and widely studied, perhaps there would not exist topolects and variant pronunciations. Just as Ling Mengchu heralded the "strictness" of certain dialects according to a particular standard, Xu Fuzuo characterized departures from this standard as "errors" (*miuzhe* 謬者). In Xu Fuzuo's eyes, Zhou Deqing was the consummate philologist, who had "consulted regional and vulgar variants and corroborated them against past and present standards . . . generating a relative balance."[39] The bolstering of Zhou Deqing's philological credentials still served a purpose in the context of opera composition. For Xu Fuzuo, it explained why Zhou Deqing's northern standard would be the most widely intelligible form of Chinese to a broad audience. But by repositioning Zhou as a philologist, rather than exclusively an opera librettist, Xu and others initiated what would become an increasingly close connection between opera and classicism in the discussion of language.

While many southerners defended northern speech standards, Wang Shizhen 王世貞 (1526–1590), one of the most influential literary men of his age and also from Suzhou prefecture, disputed the authority of the North, claiming: "North of the Yangzi river, [the language] was gradually contaminated by northern tribal tongues (*huyu* 胡語)."[40] The South, by contrast, was far removed from the historical military conquests by tribal peoples on China's northern borders and therefore persevered an unadulterated form of Chinese.[41] Fang Yizhi defended the northern language against Wang Shizhen's claim, which he found historically and linguistically dubious.[42] Others flipped this criticism the other way, claiming that southern languages represented the harmful influence of non-Chinese southern barbarian tongues (*man* 蠻, *yiyu* 彝語) and were "incomprehensible without translation."[43] Still others attempted to reconcile these competing notions of authenticity by claiming that Zhou Deqing had incorrectly employed the term "Central Plains," implying the origins of Chinese civilization. While the true language of the Central Plains would indeed be the purest form of Chinese, Zhou Deqing had merely documented the later accretions of "northern barbarians" (*beidi* 北狄).[44]

Gu Yanwu famously derided the premise of taking any existing form of regional speech as a unified standard.[45] In its place he advocated for a wholesale adoption of ancient pronunciation.[46] Nevertheless, Li Guangdi, a major court scholar and native of the southeastern province Fujian, attested that Gu had declared the speech of Fujian to be the true "ancient pronunciation" (*guyin* 古音).[47] This suspicious claim says more about Li Guangdi's priorities, as a defender of Fujian's cultural position, than it does about Gu Yanwu.[48] At the heart of pronunciation debates were questions of historical and often regional identity, which served for the basis of asserting a particular version of Chinese as "correct." The proposed correct speech, however, was rarely simple advocacy of a particular regional standard. Instead it involved a consideration of the historical evolution of the Chinese language and relied on arguments about the causes and nature of historical linguistic change, in pursuit of an original uncorrupted speech form.

Zhongyuan yinyun functioned as a crucial text for envisioning what a shared pronunciation could look like, but its focus on a particular variety of northern pronunciation caused issue for some. One mid-Ming scholar tellingly criticized *Zhongyuan yinyun* for what he perceived as its overreliance on spoken dialect (*fangyu shiyan* 方語市言). In his view, "if one only uses one's eyes and ears to find differences and similarities, how will one achieve the proper nature of all regions?"⁴⁹ This statement reflects the concern with the personal bias of an individual's "eyes and ears," which permeates Ming linguistic thinking, and the pervasive skepticism among Ming literati toward to the validity of "knowledge [acquired] through hearing and seeing" (*wenjian zhi zhi* 聞見之知) (see chapter 1). In a world of pervasive forgery and increasingly broad circulation of information, the veracity of which was often dubious, Ming intellectuals sought reliable standards of validating knowledge.⁵⁰ These standards often rhetorically advertised their potential to circumvent the individual's fallible faculties of perception.

Late Ming promoters of a correct universal pronunciation tended to highlight what they saw as the correct features present in various topolects, rather than asserting the validity of a single topolect over all others. Later seventeenth- and eighteenth-century classicists largely inherited this stance. The phonologist Pan Lei, a Jiangnan scholar who had read widely in opera phonetics, described the ideal pronunciation as "neither the southern pronunciation nor the northern pronunciation, but rather the innate pronunciation within everyone (*renren benyou zhi yin* 人人本有之音)."⁵¹ Jiang Yong 江永 (1681–1762) similarly argued that the spoken language of any specific region is "regional pronunciation" (*fangyin* 方音). The "correct pronunciation" (*zhengyin* 正音) would necessarily cull the most suitable elements from each region to form an appropriate standard.⁵² By asserting that these pronunciations were "innate," scholars fended off the potential criticism that such a standard would be artificial. The selection of elements from various topolects was thus framed as a project of reconstruction rather than invention.

While some Ming opera theorists promoted *Zhongyuan yinyun* or a particular regional standard, many others proposed an authoritative pronunciation based on a combination of elements culled from various regional speeches. In this regard their proposals resembled both much earlier attempts at standardization, such as those of Lu Fayan in the early eighth century, and later cases, such as Chao Yuen-Ren's "national language" of the 1920s, as an amalgam of languages native to no one.⁵³ Lu Fayan's standards were intended for use by a limited audience of elite literary figures; Chao

Yuen-Ren's "national language" was aimed at an entire nation. The Ming discussion of language standards stood somewhere in between. It emerged within a literary context with the immediate purpose of facilitating composition in an elite genre, but certain scholars extended these discussions to the consideration of classical reading pronunciations, as well as a shared spoken language.

Shen Chongsui and the Late Ming Theorization of Pronunciation

The most prominent figure at the intersection of operatic and classical philology was the opera theorist Shen Chongsui 沈寵綏 (d. 1645), who played a formative role in the codification of the new operatic form of Kunqu (Kun opera 崑曲, typically referred to in contemporary sources as "Kun melodies" *kunqiang* 崑腔 or *kunshanqiang* 崑山腔). Kunqu takes its name from its birthplace, Kunshan, located in Jiangnan province within the Ming intellectual and cultural center of Suzhou prefecture. The origins of Kunqu trace back to the fourteenth century, but the genre was formally codified over the course of the sixteenth and seventeenth centuries. One of the primary goals of this codification process was the establishment of a standard pronunciation for singing in the Kunqu style. Typified by its erudite language and slow, melodious singing style, Kunqu presented unique challenges of intelligibility, which necessitated particularly close attention to phonetic precision. Given its southern origins, the rise of Kunqu opera also occasioned further debate over the relative merits of northern and southern varieties of Chinese.

Despite Shen Chongsui's seminal influence on Kunqu, little is known about his life. As a native of Suzhou prefecture, where the genre had emerged, Shen saw himself as an inheritor of the tradition of Kunqu studies. First printed in 1639 (and again shortly thereafter in 1649), Shen Chongsui's *Duqu xuzhi* (度曲須知 Prerequisites for aria composition/singing) is a foundational text of opera theory and pedagogy. It is best known for its precise descriptions of pronunciation for librettists and singers. Although the text clearly filled the functional needs of opera performance, it also incorporated highly theoretical discussions of language. Most notably, Shen Chongsui included a set of rhyme tables from Chen Jinmo's *Huangji tuyun* (Supremely august principles of diagrammed rhymes). As discussed in chapter 1, Chen Jinmo's text represented a bold reinvention of the phonological tradition, experimenting with the replacement of Chinese graphs with numerals. The inclusion of material from Chen Jinmo's work raises a question critical to understanding late Ming literary and intellectual practices: Why and in what context would Shen Chongsui, an opera pedagogue, read a book by Chen Jinmo, a classical philologist and mathematician?

Throughout *Duqu xuzhi*, Shen Chongsui suggests that earlier opera librettists had only a superficial understanding of phonology and did not grasp the underlying nature of Chinese phonology. He claimed that the foundational codifier of Kunqu opera, Wei Liangfu 魏良輔 (1480–1566), had discussed phonology in only a general sense, causing later readers to merely "see that it was so, and not understand why it was so."[54] He further averred that many contemporary literary figures only understood how to match rhymes and avoid basic errors in prosody but were not trained in the "principles of sound" (*yinli* 音理).[55]

Shen Chongsui believed that these deeper principles were reflected in the cosmological basis of sound. The prefatory material to *Duqu xuzhi* is replete with cosmological description of the origins of sound, suggesting the value of *self-so* knowledge in a literary context. Shen's own preface claimed that linguistic sounds "originated in the *self-so* qualities of heaven and earth," while another preface asserted that "those who thoroughly comprehend tones and pitches necessarily have always expertly understood *yin-yang* and comprehended the patterns of the stars."[56] Shen's son Biao 沈標, in the preface to a later edition of *Duqu xuzhi*, highlighted the influence of Shao Yong's cosmological explanations of the nature of sound, which he claimed had prompted his father to seek out the work of Chen Jinmo. It was upon reading Chen's *Huangji tuyun* that his father "realized the marvel of heavenly *self-so* harmony in *fanqie* [i.e., the combination of two graphs to illustrate the pronunciation of a single syllable]." Echoing other Ming critiques of textual and observation-based knowledge, Shen Biao noted that many *ru* scholars had wasted considerable effort trying to reconstruct ancient music and pronunciation on the basis of "incomplete writings and relics."[57] In contrast to the damaged textual and material legacy of antiquity, Shen Biao contended that a *self-so* phonological system based on cosmological correlations would generate pronunciations that were more appealing to the ear and better ensure the proper correspondence between melody and words.

The relevance of cosmology, essential to the philological renaissance of the Ming, can be found throughout Ming opera discussions. For example, *Xiaoyu pu* (嘯餘譜 Formularies for the remnants of howling [i.e., singing]), an influential assemblage of texts for the composition of lyrics and arias first printed in 1619, includes, as one might expect, *Zhongyuan yinyun* and its Ming successor *Zhongzhou quanyun* (中州全韻 Complete rhymes of the central states). The compilation begins, however, with a set of Shao Yong's cosmological tables correlating rhymes and musical pitches (figure 4.1). A preface to the first edition suggests the reason for this inclusion, claiming that "the vital force of heaven and earth assembles in the hearts of humans and is expressed in song. Thus those who investigate sound explicate the solar periods and seasons according to a description of the sounds of the mind. But this linkage is subtle and elusive—if one does not explore the origins of the universe (*tiandi zhi yuan* 天地之元), how could one easily distinguish these?"[58] The compiler, Cheng Mingshan 程明善 (fl. 1619), also edited a contemporary theoretical treatise on the nature of linguistic sound and its relation to Number and music.[59] Despite its apparent intent as a compilation of opera handbooks, *Xiaoyu pu* appears to have circulated widely among phonologists. The turn-of-the-eighteenth-century scholar Xiong Shibo 熊士伯 (fl. 1642–1719), for instance, documented his consultation of *Xiaoyu pu* throughout his dense theoretical treatise on phonology, *Dengqie yuansheng* (等切元聲 The primordial sound of graded rhymes and divided syllables).[60]

Shen Chongsui's interaction with the work of cosmological scholars was not mere lip service. Throughout the text, Shen carried out a dialogue with Chen Jinmo's earlier study. Shen Chongsui did not agree with all of Chen's conclusions, particularly on the correct pronunciation of certain syllables. From a theoretical standpoint, however, he asserted the validity of Chen's framework as "heavenly *self-so* and infallible," adding that "there exist no other sounds from different regions or times past."[61] In Shen's eyes, Chen may have misidentified the pronunciation of specific graphs, but that did not affect the validity of his tables as an encapsulation of all possible sounds in the universe.

Shen Chongsui's most distinctive contribution to the study of Chinese phonology was his division of the Chinese syllable into three parts, rather than two as was the case in the earlier *fanqie* method.[62] He referred to these three parts as the head (*tou* 頭), belly (*fu* 腹), and tail (*wei* 尾) of the

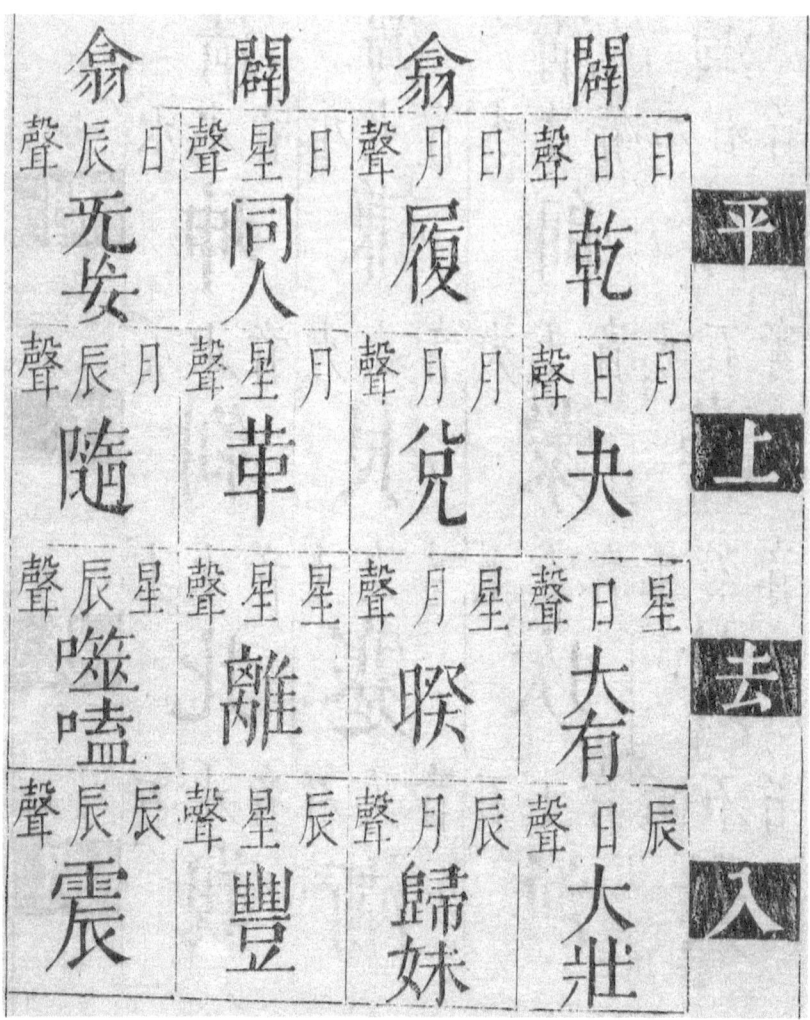

Figure 4.1 Cheng Mingshan's compilation of materials for aria composition features diagrams correlating various linguistic attributes and numerological categories. Cheng Mingshan, *Xiaoyu pu*, j. 1, 16a. (Image courtesy of Harvard-Yenching Library.)

syllable. The head represents the initial consonant and sometimes a medial vowel. The belly contains the main vowel, as well as the final, while the tail represents the final alone. For example, he detailed the graph <iēu> 憂 as composed of the head <ī> 依, belly <ēu> 歐, and tail <ū> 鳴. Segmentation of the syllable into three parts would potentially allow for greater specificity in phonological description, especially when the final contained a diphthong (which is not always clear from two graph spellings). Particularly within the context of Kunqu opera singing, which featured the prolonged intonation of each syllable, Shen had provided a standardized way for singers to conclude the pronunciation of each graph. Shen also argued that this method could clarify distinctions in his normative version of Chinese that a southerner might overlook.

In devising this new method, Shen claimed to have established a superior approach for training singers and standardizing sung pronunciation. He placed particular emphasis on the "tail" of the syllable and created new terminology to distinguish the endings of syllables. With practice, he argued, all singers, regardless of their birthplace, could train themselves to accurately recognize and articulate these distinctions. To aid with this practice, Shen provided heavily annotated arias from famous operas, designed for "slow rehearsal" (figure 4.2).[63] A reader could practice, for instance, the challenging opening to an aria from *Story of the Western Chamber* (西廂記 *Xixiang ji*): "Clouds gather away in the clearing void, the icy wheel suddenly swells up (雲斂晴空，冰輪乍湧)."[64] The first four graphs of this phrase (<yūn liēm dziēng kūng> 雲斂晴空) contain three similar final phonemes Shen claimed were frequently confused by singers: <-n>, <-m>, and <-ng>. Shen's annotations directed the reader to these differences while highlighting other essential attributes of their pronunciation.

Shen's methodological innovations are typically attributed to his concern with opera aesthetics, but it is worth considering why he felt it necessary to devise a new system in the first place, given the existence of other methods for describing pronunciation. Shen acknowledged that his three-part division largely replicated information already present in the two-part *fanqie* division, but he maintained that his method would benefit those less familiar with the intricacies of phonology. Shen presented his own method as simpler than earlier approaches, rendering pronunciations that could be "understood on sight," rather than requiring in-depth phonological knowledge.[65] At the root of the problem of phonological representation for Shen was the nature of Chinese graphs. In a striking passage, he decried the fact that there exist linguistic sounds that could not be notated by existing graphs as "an obstruction to composition." The culprit, in Shen's eyes, was none other than Cang Jie himself, the legendary creator of the Chinese script, whose "incompleteness" he could only "retrospectively resent."[66] This surprising criticism of a foundational figure in Chinese civilization appears in the work of other contemporaries, who likewise derided Cang

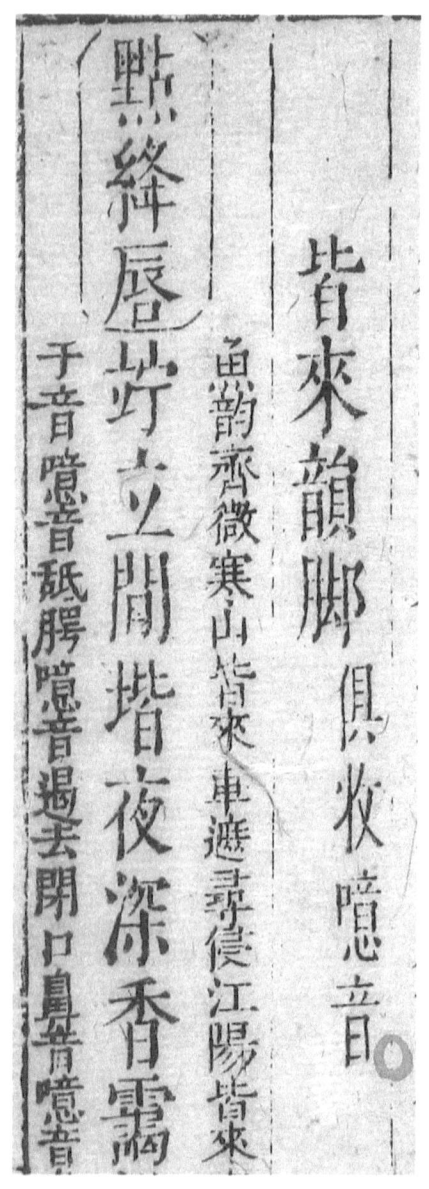

Figure 4.2 Shen Chongsui's annotations of opera arias provided detailed phonological information for each graph. Shen Chongsui, *Duqu xuzhi* (1639 edition at Harvard-Yenching Library), *shang juan*, 21a. (Image courtesy of Harvard-Yenching Library.)

Jie's efforts, and parallels a broader skepticism toward the authority of antiquity among Ming thinkers.[67] On the one hand, we have seen how scholars such as Wei Jiao could claim that ancient graph forms provided access to the minds of the sages (see chapter 3), and various opera theorists believed that ancient pronunciations predated later phonological corruptions. At the same time, critiques of antiquity, as well as skepticism toward our ability to truly access the ancient on the basis of limited remaining sources, grew increasingly pervasive over the sixteenth and seventeenth centuries. This relegation of antiquity from a position of inherent authority to a fallible historical period would ultimately provoke considerable pushback from eighteenth-century literati, who restored a vision of antiquity as the fundamental source of ethical and scholarly practice (see chapter 7).

For scholars like Shen Chongsui, there should ideally exist a graph for every conceivable sound in the rhyme table. That not being the case, he would have to devise a clearer way to detail the pronunciation of any given syllable accurately. Shen admitted his inability to adequately describe all possible linguistic sounds using Chinese graphs alone.[68] He nevertheless believed he had created a system that captured the intricacies of Chinese phonology, which had to some degree been obfuscated by the nature of the writing system. Shen's substantial interaction with the tradition of classical philology, from which he drew methodological inspiration, may have underlain his conviction that his methods could be applied beyond simply aria composition. For instance, he claimed that his principles of phonological glossing were useful "even for examination candidates," who could overcome recitation issues or thorny philological problems in classical texts as a result of his emphasis on pronunciation in place of inherently unstable written graphs.[69] Shen aimed his work primarily at singers and librettists but framed his method as having important implications for the classical study of phonology.

Ultimately Shen Chongsui argued that the opera theorist was uniquely positioned to practice philology and could even surpass the classicist:

> Today people focus exclusively on competing in the civil service examinations, and the field of philology (*zixue yi mai* 字學一脈, lit. the study of graphs, but including phonology here) has virtually extinguished.... The *ru* classicists and literati view it as trivial and do not discuss it. We can only rely on librettists/singers (*duquzhe* 度曲者) who

still maintain a trace (of this field) within their sung lyrics. It is because the classicists focus on phrase and line (*zhangju* 章句), while singers investigate pitches (*yinsheng* 音聲); those who mindlessly recite texts (*chanbi* 呫嗶) are too hurried to discuss such issues in depth, while those who sing know that sounds ought to be slowly measured.⁷⁰

From Shen's perspective, the examination system had corrupted the classical enterprise by encouraging scholars to focus their attention exclusively on the massive feats of memorization necessary for exam success. The power of Shen Chongsui's claim lay in its repositioning of philological authority. As in the case of Zhao Yiguang, who justified the incorporation of Buddhist methods by noting the lack of concern with phonology among contemporary classicists (see chapter 2), Shen framed his work as responding to absence. With contemporary *ru* scholars not giving philology its due attention, Shen could downplay their role in the production of new philological knowledge. He instead asserted the authority of those involved in the composition and singing of opera, for whom attention to phonological detail remained essential. Examination preparation among classicists necessitated being "hurried" (*mang* 忙) in pursuit of vast reading requirements, while singing in the Kunqu style invited the prolonged intonation of single graphs. The term Shen employed to characterize philology as a "field," *mai* 脈 (lit. vein), implies the transfer of teachings through a master-disciple relationship. It was the breakdown of this transfer, one that Shen would acknowledge had originally belonged to classicists, that justified the authority of the opera theorist who maintained a sincere interest in a field of former classical attention.

Li Yu and Opera as a Universal Standard

Discussions of phonology within the operatic and literary sphere remained one of the major arenas for philological research well into the 1680s. The importance of philological research in opera composition in the late seventeenth century is exemplified by one of the age's most renowned literary figures, Li Yu 李漁 (1610–1680), whose creative genius is reflected in short stories, operas, essays, and literary criticism.⁷¹ Li's network of literary and scholarly friends was considerable, and he consciously positioned himself among them to secure his own social position and reputation.

Technical matters such as prosody, music, and rhyming are generally considered to be the one arena in which he lacked originality.[72] Li Yu was not one of the great phonological scholars of the early Qing, but his compilation of three lexicons concerned with rhyming, and sponsorship of other lexicographical texts, reflects his considerable interest in the subject. A closer reading of these texts reveals that Li Yu was not merely recycling material from the older phonological tradition but was paying attention to current debates in the field. He was also a member of a much broader scholarly network that dominated the philological scene in the late seventeenth century. Recent studies on the substantial impact of publishers and editors in producing and shaping literary taste have enriched our understanding of the role of collaboration in seventeenth-century literary production.[73] This collaboration extended into intellectual exchange with classical scholars, who shared opera theorists' concern with understanding the nature of language and sound production.

Li Yu's interest in phonology was linked to the demands of precision in writing opera lyrics. In his view, out of the many regulated literary forms, from eight-legged essays and parallel prose to regulated verse, filling in the lyrics to a given tune was the strictest and most difficult linguistically: "The length of phrases, the number of graphs, the tone (level, rising, falling, or entering) of a sound, the voiced or unvoiced, *yin* or *yang* nature of the rhyme all have a set, immovable form."[74] A librettist would therefore need to be highly qualified in identifying these phonological features in order to pen a lyric. Attention to phonology was also essential for an aesthetically pleasing performance. He therefore claimed that the study of pronunciation was a singer's "top priority" (首務).[75] Li Yu inserted himself into contemporary discussions of how to characterize Chinese rhymes and displayed considerable familiarity with current research on phonology.[76] Most notably, Li was paying attention to the latest developments in methods of "spelling" Chinese sounds. He observed that recent lexicons maintained the traditional *fanqie* method of using only two graphs to gloss pronunciation, which he considered insufficiently detailed, particularly in the context of singing "slow arias" (*manqu* 慢曲). In its place he embraced Shen Chongsui's method of dividing the syllable into three segments (which Li referred to as "head," "tail," and "remaining sound" *yuyin* 餘音, as opposed to Shen's "head," "belly," and "tail"). Li described these three phonetic components of the graph as a "natural creation" (天造地設) rather than an artificial abstraction, and essential for intelligible and pleasing singing.[77]

Li Yu was also motivated by issues he identified in contemporary lexicographical practice. Li disparaged lexicographers of his day who competed for inclusion of the most graphs in their dictionaries. This tendency had, in his view, created a situation in which poets "spent little time crafting lines and a great deal of time looking up rhymes" (覓句時少，選韻時多).[78] This comment reinforces the importance of reference works for the composition of poetry and arias in late imperial times. It also indicates a mismatch between the goal of lexicographers to comprehensively document the written language and users who might benefit from a curated lexicon. As Li Yu observed, many graphs were inappropriate for poetic composition as rhyme words, because of either their vulgar nature or purely lexical impossibility, as in the case of the first graph of two-graph compounds (such as the <hu> of <hu dhiep> 蝴蝶 "butterfly"), which typically could not appear in isolation.[79] To include such graphs in a rhyme dictionary provided users with unnecessary information, which he believed could slow the process of composition.

Li Yu's interest in Shen Chongsui's tripartite division of the syllable was due to its utility for training singers, while his lexicographic compilations were motivated by a desire to increase efficiency for librettists and poets. However, he saw careful attention to operatic philology as having applications beyond the literary. Although not typically considered to be at the forefront of phonological research, opera scholars joined pathbreaking classicists, such as Chen Di, in promoting a notion of historical change in the Chinese language, which would later capture the attention of eighteenth-century Evidential Learning scholars.[80] As early as the fourteenth century, Zhou Deqing had observed that "it is a multitude today who are mired in antiquity and dispute the present, and who do not recognize the principle of historical change (*shibian* 時變). . . . They will actively cite [the medieval standards of] *Guangyun* as evidence, and endure the criticism of being 'shrike-tongued' without regret."[81] Evidential Learning scholars tended to embrace the notion of historical change in order to better understand the language of the past. Zhou Deqing and Li Yu, on the other hand, expressed their recognition of historical change in order to justify their focus on contemporary spoken norms. At the core of Li Yu's philological practice was a belief that the phonology of sung texts ought to reflect actual spoken practice, in contrast to those who argued for an artificial standard based on ancient texts. As he wrote in the preface to his dictionary of poetic rhymes, "If the people of antiquity were present today, then the sounds they produced would necessarily be the same as people today."[82] In this charge against intentional archaism, Li held that linguistic sound should not be understood as an unchanging constant, but instead as continually evolving. In his opinion, if one were to imitate the ancient rhymes that no longer worked in the Chinese of his time, one would only succeed in "grating against everyone's teeth and offending their ears."[83] Li further averred that the Classics themselves were rife with dialectal usage, reflective of the origin of the sages in the Northwest. For the sages, these regionalisms "emerged from their mouths spontaneously" (*sui kou er chu* 隨口而出) and exemplified the nature of the Classics as a record of their natural speech. It also meant, however, that even the Classics "could not entirely serve as a model" for a common language, given the contemporary understanding of dialect as a deviation from "correct pronunciation."[84] For Li Yu, irreconcilable differences between ancient and modern pronunciations, as well as the perceived usage of dialect, made the Classics of limited utility as language standards.

In contrast to the Classics, Li Yu viewed opera (*chuanqi* 傳奇) as the true "universal writing" (*tianxia zhi shu* 天下之書).[85] It was therefore inappropriate to include colloquialisms and regional speech, which would not be intelligible throughout the empire. Because opera embodied most perfectly the principles of universal language, Li argued that pronunciation training in the manner of singers was "not merely designed for the study of singing" (不止為學歌而設) and was as much the responsibility of traveling officials as it was of performers. Recognizing the challenges of a bureaucratic system in which officials were repeatedly transferred to locations outside of their native linguistic region, Li observed: "It is often the case that an official speaks and his clerk does not understand, or that a commoner comes to dispute an injustice and the official does not comprehend, bringing about mistaken floggings and the reversal of rewards and punishments. How could one say that the injury sound (*shengyin*) can cause people is trivial?"[86] He argued that officials as well could therefore benefit from the linguistic training that singers receive, in order to "purge their regional pronunciations" (洗滌方音) and govern more effectively. Li's vision of linguistic unity contrasted a putative "correct pronunciation" (*zhengyin*) against "regional pronunciation" (*fangyin*). "Correct pronunciation" was the standard of sung pronunciation for opera, but Li also envisioned it as a speech standard. He did not provide a concrete description of what this lingua franca would look like. Within the context of opera training, Li Yu saw the northern dictionary *Zhongyuan yinyun* as the authoritative standard but believed that certain regions in Suzhou prefecture adhered most closely to the distinctions outlined in that text.[87] Despite his praise of conservative features of Wu topolects, such as Suzhou dialect, he did not advocate for their usage as a universal sung or spoken language.[88] Instead, Li appears to have proposed adapting it according to what he termed an "official pronunciation" (*guanyin* 官音), given that an emphasis on any local speech, even that of the Wu region, would not be universally intelligible. Depending on the location of the performance, he suggested that actors may insert the local dialect in specific places for comedic effect. But here too his emphasis remained on intelligibility and the training of singers, who would need to accurately imitate the local language. In his words, "The more people who understand [the words], the more people are laughing."[89]

Li Yu may have been a unique literary genius, but he was also a man of his times. As with other figures of opera composition and theory beginning from several generations prior, Li Yu published dictionaries and proposed methods for analyzing Chinese phonology. He also maintained correspondence with leading contemporary phonologists, establishing himself as a member of the broader phonological community, in both his citation of and communication with other scholars. Li's influence as a lexicographer persisted well into the eighteenth century, when his dictionaries were alternately praised or criticized as sources for the discussion of theoretical phonology.[90]

The Classical Assimilation of Opera Theory

Shen Chongsui and Li Yu contextualized their discussions of opera pronunciation within the broader classical tradition of linguistic analysis. The emphasis on classical philology within the work of opera theorists suggests their desire to speak to a broader audience of readers. This implication is all the more compelling considering the fact that classicists did indeed read and comment on their work, emphasizing its utility for classical philology.

Li Yu, who lived in Hangzhou for around ten years, belonged to a network of prominent phonologists in the Hangzhou region, including most notably Mao Xianshu 毛先舒 (1620–1688), Mao Qiling 毛奇齡 (1623–1716), and Chai Shaobing 柴紹炳 (1616–1670).[91] The leading members of this network constituted a poetry society, which centered on the self-proclaimed

"Ten Masters of Xiling" (西泠十子), of whom Mao Xianshu was the leader.[92] Such poetry societies (*shishe* 詩社) in the early years of the Qing dynasty served as gathering places of intellectual and political discussion and were often associated with loyalty to the fallen Ming.[93] Some of the Hangzhou scholars pointedly refused serving the Qing government, with Chai Shaobing even reportedly rejecting the Zhejiang provincial governor's recommendation during the Kangxi emperor's search for promising "recluse scholars" (山林隱逸之士) in 1669.[94] Others, such as Mao Qiling, responded to such calls, shifting from an initial position of resistance to achieve notable positions in the Hanlin Academy and central government agencies. Despite active court efforts to bring the highest level of scholarship to the capital, the most prolific of these philological thinkers remained in Hangzhou, acting as local teachers and scholars. Largely adherents of the Learning of the Mind rather than the orthodox Learning of the Way values promoted by the early Qing court, scholars such as Mao Xianshu saw themselves as inheriting the tradition of late Ming Learning of the Mind thinkers, such as Liu Zongzhou 劉宗周 (1578–1645). Chai Shaobing and Mao Xianshu positioned themselves as the leaders of this extensive circle of likeminded phonological scholars based in Hangzhou, the members of which included Wu Baipeng 吳百朋 (1614–1670), Sun Zhi 孫治 (1619–1683), Shen Qian 沈謙 (1620–1670), Shi Guizhang 施閏章 (d. 1683), Huang Yanbo 黃彥博 (*jinshi* 1664), Wu Renchen 吳任臣 (d. 1689), Lu Fanchao 陸繁弨 (d. 1700), Zhong Heng 仲恆, Xu Fen 徐汾, and Zhang Jingguang 張兢光, among others.[95] Members of the group prefaced one another's works and referenced one another's scholarship, promoting a sense of intellectual and literary community.

Some members of this network produced lexicographical works aimed specifically at composition within a particular genre. Zhong Heng, for instance, published a *Ciyun* (詞韻 *Ci* rhymes), which cited the discussions of local poets with regard to phonology, and also appended a short text by Chai Shaobing, edited by Mao Xianshu.[96] Others, like Wu Renchen, published general lexicographical studies, such as the *Zihui bu* (字彙補 A supplement to the *Assemblage of Graphs*), which made additions to *Zihui*, the crowning achievement of Ming lexicography. The centrality of philology among the Hangzhou elite attracted some of the region's most famous luminaries. Hong Sheng 洪昇 (1645–1704), for instance, a native of Hangzhou and librettist of the renowned opera *Palace of Eternal Life* (*Changsheng dian* 長生殿), authored a dictionary titled *Shi Sao yunzhu* (詩騷韻注

Commentary on the rhymes of the *Shijing* and *Lisao*). It too was prefaced by Mao Xianshu.[97]

Mao Xianshu and Chai Shaobing did not write opera, as Li Yu and Hong Sheng did, but they were well-regarded composers of poetry and *ci* lyrics. Their scholarship alternated between theoretical discussions of ancient Chinese phonology and practical application in contemporary literary forms. The nature of this late seventeenth-century philological network suggests crucial aspects of late Ming–early Qing scholarship obscured by eighteenth-century evaluations of the period. The late eighteenth-century court narrative of philology identified a single thinker, Gu Yanwu, as the originator of Evidential Learning and the dominant practitioner of philology during the period. The Hangzhou philologists, who are largely excluded from this narrative, in fact influenced Gu Yanwu's scholarship.[98] For the most part, however, the Hangzhou network did not endorse his methods, and its members were equally at home discussing phonology with opera theorists, such as Li Yu.[99] Although Gu Yanwu's name would eventually gain prominence in the mid-eighteenth century, it was the Hangzhou scholars whose work was most closely identified with linguistic innovation well past the turn of the eighteenth century (see chapter 7).

Li Yu engaged in correspondence with Mao Xianshu on various topics, including phonology. In one telling letter (for which only Mao's half of the correspondence is preserved), Mao commented on the lack of attention to proper linguistic tones in contemporary operatic composition. Pointing to Tang Xianzu and his *Peony Pavilion* as the originator of this trend, Mao implored Li to consider phonology as a central task of the "creator" (*zuozhe* 作者) of literary works.[100] Although Mao Xianshu did not write opera, he nevertheless found opera to be a useful arena for discussing Chinese phonology, writing a dictionary designed for this particular literary context, titled *Nanqu zhengyun* (南曲正韻 Correct rhymes for southern arias). He also composed a treatise entitled "A Dialogue on the Entering Tone in Southern Arias" ("Nanqu rusheng ke wen" 南曲入聲客問), in which he discussed both the nature of the entering tone in a theoretical sense and practical issues of composing arias with an entering tone rhyme.[101]

Mao's scholarship was deeply steeped in that of the late Ming and was influenced strongly by Shen Chongsui, the late Ming theorist of opera pronunciation. As Mao wrote in a general treatise on the study of linguistic sound, "If one wishes to be clear on the principles of rhyme, one must first understand the tripartite explanation of the initial (*sheng*), tone (*yin*), and final (*yun*). It must be that the completeness of one graph necessarily has a head, belly, and tail."[102] Shen's tripartite division of the Chinese graph is commonly acknowledged to have had a lasting influence on discussions of pronunciation within operatic circles. As Mao Xianshu's example shows, it also shaped conceptions of phonology outside of the strictly operatic. Mao explicitly addressed the original context of Shen's work commenting, "[Shen's *Duqu xuzhi*] clearly distinguished the subtleties of the principles of sound (*shengyin zhi li* 聲音之理). It is not only something one should study in composing arias but is also a meritorious servant of phonology (*yunxue* 韻學)."[103] While he recognized the primary aim of Shen's work as a guide for singers and librettists, Mao claimed that its system of phonological categorization illustrated something fundamental about the "principles of sound."

Mao Xianshu applied the practice of slow chanting, advocated in Shen Chongsui's recommendations for opera students, within his broader philological study. In an epistolary debate on phonology with Chai Shaobing, Mao defended his pronunciation prescriptions on the basis of "slowly intoning a graph" (慢聲讀之). Chai replied that this approach was merely aping Shen Chongsui's method of "head, belly, and tail," which was applicable only to singing. Mao responded that the combination of multiple phonemes to create a single syllable was "an axiomatic principle of phonology (韻學定理)." He further noted that when a child is born, it immediately cries out with a wail that contains multiple phonetic values. "How would it know about the so-called head, belly, and tail? Thus we know that this matter did not originate in singing, nor did it begin with Mr. Shen."[104] For Mao Xianshu, Shen's method was describing a general linguistic phenomenon, evident even in the speech of an infant. Shen Chongsui had recognized the utility of documenting this phonetic principle in the context of opera composition, but that did not diminish its validity as a method of general linguistic analysis.

Shen Chongsui's method was influential beyond Mao Xianshu and his circle. Other contemporary classicists, such as Pan Lei, Zhao Shaoji 趙紹箕 (fl. 1674), Han Qia, and Shen Jiao 沈鼒 (fl. 1657), employed the notion of the head, belly, and tail of a graph in their analyses of Chinese phonology.[105] The great early Qing court scholar and phonologist Li Guangdi praised Shen Chongsui's work as having captured more perfectly the cosmological principles of language than the foundational work of Shao Yong. He even criticized Gu Yanwu, who would later be upheld as the originator of Evidential Learning, for being seemingly unaware of the work of Shen Chongsui and other opera phonologists.[106]

Chen Jinmo himself, whose tables had featured in Shen Chongsui's work, adopted Shen's tripartite spelling method in phonological studies he wrote later in life.[107] In his words: "If scholars realize that there are a head, belly, and tail [within each graph], and when these three items are completely furnished, then the many distinctions present in sound (聲音繁碎) will not be confused."[108] Chen also copied verbatim Shen Chongsui's extended explanation of his own earlier work (including the sections that proclaimed Chen's own genius), claiming: "I created it, but Shen detailed its methods."[109] He further addressed what he saw as instances of misinterpretation in Shen's characterization of his original work.[110] Chen Jinmo's interaction with Shen Chongsui's adaptation of his own text indicates several key features of seventeenth-century scholarly culture. Most important, it highlights the fluidity of philological learning in the seventeenth century as contemporary communities of scholars applied a range of methodological and functional priorities toward a shared goal of linguistic description. Beginning in the late Ming, scholars increasingly framed their work in dialogue with the ongoing research of fellow specialists (see chapter 7). Chen's self-quotation of his own earlier writing, embedded within Shen Chongsui's citations, highlights the degree to which this collaborative ideal involved textual conversation with current scholars. The markedly different venues of this research, one a theoretical treatise on sound, the other a handbook for singers and librettists, illustrate the pull of a shared disciplinary interest in language, which transcended the boundaries of literature and classicism that would solidify in the eighteenth century.

Texts on operatic singing pronunciation, such as *Zhongyuan yinyun* and *Duqu xuzhi*, were decidedly in the Collections (*ji* 集) category of literary texts in the *Siku quanshu* and later Qing bibliographies.[111] Seventeenth-century bibliographies, on the other hand, tended to place *Zhongyuan yinyun* in the philology subsection of the Classics (*jing* 經) category.[112] Such categorizations acknowledged the potential of opera texts to address the concerns of a classicist audience. This recognition is strongly evident within the world of seventeenth-century classical philology. Scholars of language regularly consulted, cited, and adapted theories developed within a context of sung drama. Claims that such theories were not intended solely for singing suggest that a certain degree of justification was required to make use of these materials. Nevertheless, a number of the most influential and prolific philologists of the period explicitly shared their indebtedness to the operatic community.

The late Ming witnessed an explosion of literary and philological activity. The popularity of opera as an elite art gave rise to fundamental questions about the Chinese language and the potential for a unified standard. The practical challenges of intelligibility in singing instigated particularly fine-tuned attention to pronunciation, while the desire for broadening audiences made the call for universality all the more pressing. The contours of this standardization debate were significantly different from those of the twentieth and twenty-first centuries, but the engagement with history and notions of linguistic authenticity bear remarkable similarities. The literary origins of these discussions may suggest the need to rethink assumptions about the discourse of Chinese language reform and its relationship with the unique political circumstances of modern China. Nationalism and foreign interactions underlay modern language reform movements, but notions of a common language in China have a considerably more complicated history. Opera is only one part of this story, a more complete picture of which awaits future study. In the following chapter I turn to another aspect of Ming literary philology that sought not standardization for the present, but rather plurality in the reading of classical texts.

CHAPTER 5

Reading the Classics for Pleasure

Prose as Verse, Verse as Music

The intersection of classical and literary learning in the Ming manifested in multiple areas. As shown in the previous chapter, it could involve the inclusion of texts and methods from new sung genres into the canon of classical studies. Recent research has similarly demonstrated how thinkers such as Li Mengyang 李夢陽 (1472–1529) envisioned the composition of poetry as an aspect of Confucian learning.[1] Erudite scholars, such as Yang Shen 楊慎 (1488–1559), linked the philological study of graph forms and phonology in ancient texts with textual connoisseurship and literary composition practices in the present.[2] Vernacular lexicographers in the seventeenth century, although primarily focused on perceived colloquialisms in the Classics, even began to apply philological techniques of etymological analysis to the forms of spoken language represented in vernacular literature but absent from the classical literary tradition.[3] This chapter focuses on another critical facet of literary-classical practice: the application of new methods of poetic and even musical reading to the foundational texts of antiquity. These methods sought to restore the fundamentally poetic qualities of writing in antiquity, which some Ming scholars believed were obscured by moralistic approaches to the Classics. These scholars further distinguished poetry in antiquity from this generically poetic mode of all ancient writing by investigating the perceived musical basis of the *Classic of Poems* (*Shijing* 詩經).

The incorporation of literary issues into the classical discipline of philology forces us to consider the relationship of the broad categories of the literary (*wen* 文) and classical (*jing* 經) in Ming China. Recent studies have demonstrated that considerable interplay existed between these seemingly unrelated fields throughout Chinese history. As Bruce Rusk has shown, literary and classical discourses complemented each other and played a significant role in defining the other.[4] Although long separated as bibliographic categories, overlap between literary and classical endeavors traces back to at least the medieval period, when Confucian learning was commonly referred to as *wenjiao* (文教, "literary" or "cultured" teachings). Composition in this context served as a form of moral cultivation. Literary forms represented normative patterns, and engaging with these patterns was akin to practicing rituals, which trained the individual how to respond to the world.[5] A significant shift occurred in the late Tang dynasty when classicists proposed that normative literary models were in fact constraining and prevented the writer from making a sincere argument. What followed was a sweeping reconceptualization of writing as an exercise in the expression of ideas and an embodiment of the morality of the ancient sages.

This notion that literary composition could embody moral values proved extremely influential for eleventh-century thinkers. However, foundational Learning of the Way thinkers beginning with the brothers Cheng Yi 程頤 (1033–1107) and Cheng Hao 程顥 (1032–1085) developed a new vision of morality that framed literary composition as secondary to true moral learning. According to these thinkers, the pursuit of morality was based on mental cultivation. Literary values were portrayed as a distraction from the investigation of Coherence that trained the mind to understand the basis of morality (see chapter 1).[6] Given the influence of these ideas, particularly following their institutionalization in the civil service examination curriculum, the tension between literature and morality became a point of concern for much of the late imperial period. Early Ming court scholars, such as Song Lian 宋濂 (1310–1381) and Wang Wei 王禕 (1322–1374), attempted a reconciliation of the two, pursuing what Peter Bol has termed a "revalidation of the literary enterprise."[7] By arguing that literature was also a path toward uncovering Learning of the Way morality, such thinkers reasserted *wen* as an aspect of classical practice. By the late Ming, views on literature and morality had diverged into multiple competing discourses, ranging from Learning of the Mind proposals for the abandonment of literary practice to new archaist movements that resonated with those of the late Tang.

Literary philology in the Ming asserted a new kind of relationship between *wen* and *jing*. The question for much of the period leading up to the late Ming was whether literature constituted a valid path toward moral cultivation. Even among those who believed that it did, the kinds of *wen* that provided access to moral values were primarily highly formal genres, such as ancient-style prose and regulated verse poetry. The seventeenth century witnessed the emergence of new reading practices that transformed vernacular novels with substantial violent and sexual content, for instance, into morality textbooks.[8] Operatic texts occupied a particularly uneasy place in Chinese conceptions of *wen*, as the "licentious tunes" of opera were open to criticism as a morally corrupting influence.[9] For literary philologists, however, it was precisely opera's position at the intersection of music and language that made it appealing. Given the widespread belief that music and language represented variations of the same fundamental sound, some felt that opera was the ideal venue to investigate the precise nature of the relationship between the two fields. Enthusiasm for applying literary techniques to the study of the Classics was also premised on a new appreciation of the perceived literary quality of classical texts. To fully appreciate these texts meant recovering their underlying poetic and musical aspects, an endeavor for which philology was well suited.

Literary figures had long proclaimed their indebtedness to the Classics, but the Ming moment represents something more unusual, as textual scholars openly claimed inspiration from literary theorists and saw their work as sharing a mutual goal. The notion that the Classics could serve as stylistic exemplars for literary production was not new. Liu Xie's 劉勰 monumental fifth-century treatise on literary theory *Wenxin diaolong* (文心雕龍 The literary mind and the carving of dragons) declared the Classics to be "the ancestors of all words" (群言之祖) and the model for all literary composition.[10] This understanding of the Classics as repositories of not only the wisdom of antiquity but also compositional style remained at the heart of prose composition education in imperial China. In particular, Tang and Song dynasty thinkers, whose prose would serve as models for Ming writers, famously advocated for a return to "ancient-style prose" (*guwen* 古文), which they believed was the only faithful way to communicate ideas. These earlier trends were primarily concerned with how to use the past as a model for composition in the present. As Bruce Rusk has observed, in imperial China this "lending out from classical studies to other fields was acknowledged," but the opposite influence from other fields on classical studies was much less readily granted.[11] This general tendency to obscure the literary influences on classical interpretation makes the late Ming moment particularly notable. Ming philologists explicitly theorized the poetic and musical elements of the Classics, not only for the purposes of composition, but also for a fuller appreciation of the Classics themselves.

Zhang Xianyi and the Versification of a Classic

The use of commentary in the seventeenth century as a means to bolster the status of literary, and in particular vernacular, texts by according to them similar modes of close reading as those applied to classical works is well-documented.[12] Less understood are the reasons underlying the reverse phenomenon, wherein literary modes of reading were applied to the Classics. The literary analysis of classical texts, which commented on stylistic and aesthetic features of ancient writing, appeared in numerous venues in Ming China. Prose anthologies geared toward the study of composition frequently analyzed such seemingly dry texts as the *Tangong* (檀弓), a chapter on mortuary practices in an early Confucian ritual text, for their perceived literary brilliance.[13] Interlinear commentaries on literary and classical texts shared generic features, reflected most clearly in the highly marketable anthologies of examination essays on the Classics.[14] While such compilations were still explicitly geared toward the use of classical texts as models for composition, they may well have functioned as guides to the appreciation of classical texts in their own right.[15] Reading the literary elements of the Classics served as an interpretive framework for appreciating ancient texts within the context of late Ming literary culture. By highlighting the literary function of the Classics, Ming commentators asserted the relevance of reading the Classics as materials that could be valued for their aesthetic qualities.

The ability of Ming readers to view the Classics as works designed for literary appreciation is reflected in the late sixteenth-century *Du Yi yunkao* (讀易韻考 A study of the rhymes in reading the *Changes*). This text sought to transform the *Classic of Changes* (*Yijing* 易經), an ancient divinatory text and oftentimes prosaic commentary on cosmology, into a lyrical work of verse.[16] Its author, Zhang Xianyi 張獻翼 (1534–1601), little known today, was an influential member of the Suzhou literary elite. Zhang was famed for his extravagance later in life, which ended, according to the rumors, when he was murdered by the enraged husband of a woman with whom he had had an affair, or, according to another story, upon his encounter with a bandit who intruded on his soirée with a courtesan in an abandoned garden. Despite his considerable reputation during his lifetime, it is due to this ignominious end, according to one account, that much of Zhang's literary output was not preserved.[17] In Suzhou, Ming China's cultural capital, Zhang kept close company with the region's most famous literary and visual artists, including Wang Shizhen, Wen Zhengming 文徵明 (1470–1559), and the Huangfu 皇甫 brothers—Chong 冲 (1490–1558), Xiao 涍 (1497–1556), Pang 汸 (1505–1584), and Lian 濂 (1508–1564).

The contemporary appeal of Zhang Xianyi's lyrical approach to the *Changes* is reflected in the work's prefaces. Wang Shizhen claimed in his 1579 preface that "ever since Cheng Yi transmitted its Coherence and Zhu Xi transmitted its Numbers, those who study the *Changes* have entirely abandoned other commentaries."[18] Wang here invoked what from the Song dynasty forward had been the two primary modes of analyzing the *Changes*: Studies focusing on the Coherence of the *Changes* sought moral messages in the abstruse cosmological statements of the text; Zhu Xi's numerological approach viewed the text as primarily of significance in prognostication.[19] From Wang Shizhen's perspective, Zhang Xianyi's study offered an important alternative—namely, a discussion of the *Changes* that treated it as a work to be incanted or sung aloud in the manner of verse. For Wang Shizhen, if anything, Zhang had not gone far enough in discussing the rhymes of texts in antiquity. By his account, when Zhang approached him with his study, Wang exclaimed, "Among [texts] of antiquity that communicated in poetry, how could there only be the *Changes*?"[20] For instance, Wang noted that the speeches of legendary rulers in the *Shangshu* also rhymed and could be interpreted as verse. In addition, he averred: "The application of *yin* and *yang* is communicated through the five tones and twelve pitches. Could the words the sages appended [to the *Changes*] include those that cannot be intoned or sung?"[21] As the foundational cosmological text in the Chinese the tradition, the *Changes* was widely regarded as a reflection of the processes of *yin* and *yang*. Wang Shizhen noted that these same processes governed musical pitch, and a complete understanding of the text would therefore take into account its fundamental musicality and be communicated in verse. Evidently Wang envisioned the *Changes* as a text to be read out loud, chanted, and perhaps even sung, by virtue of its rhyming qualities. Wang Shizhen also observed the attention to chanting in Buddhist circles as an educational tool, noting that the sages would have certainly recognized the superior ability of rhymed and sung text to communicate a message.

Zhang Xianyi's brother, Zhang Jin 張津, in a colophon to *Du Yi yunkao*, similarly promoted the notion that the sages produced rhyming texts for ease of learning and as a textual representation of cosmological principles. Zhang Jin described the existence of rhyming in the *Changes* as "a *self-so* principle" (自然之理) and "inevitable circumstance" (必然之勢), the primary purpose of which was to "numinously transform things and cause the common people to adapt to them so that they should be heartened and unwearied."[22] He also justified the importance of literary phonology by invoking the Song cosmologist Shao Yong's phonological efforts to describe universal processes "exhausting the changes of sounds, and thereupon expounding the subtleties of written script, connecting with musical pitches, and corresponding with the myriad things in heaven and earth." Zhang Xianyi and his peers could envision the *Changes* as a literary text for several reasons. One is an assumption that all texts in antiquity, be they explicitly literary or not, rhymed and were intended for reading and singing out loud. Equally significant was the notion that these texts were originally written to be accessible to the common people, which necessitated a singable, rhyming format. Finally, as a reflection of greater cosmic processes, rhymed writing better mirrored natural correspondences.

Zhang Xianyi's effort was neither the first nor the last to focus on the phonological features of the *Changes*. As early as the sixth century Lu Deming 陸德明 (c. 550–630) compiled the *Zhouyi yinyi* (周易音義 Phonological explanations of the *Changes*), which built on an earlier tradition of no longer extant *Changes* glossing and formed the basis for several later studies.[23] Such texts were focused primarily on recitation, a fundamental aspect of classical education in medieval and late imperial times, detailing the pronunciation of every graph in the text. They were not concerned with rhyming or the literary aspects of the writing. As Bruce Rusk has noted, later texts related to the *Changes*, such as *Jiao shi Yilin* (焦氏易林 Master Jiao's forest of *Changes* interpretation) and *Cantong qi* (參同契 Token of the three's unity), were also heralded as model works of verse in the Ming.[24] As unlikely candidates as these later divinatory texts would seem to be for inclusion in poetry collections, Ming readers could anthologize them as verse alongside material from the *Classic of Poems*. However, these later texts were written in consistently rhyming lines, typically constituted of four syllables, making the connection to the four-syllable line poetry of the *Poems* relatively understandable.[25]

Zhang Xianyi attempted to transform the entire *Changes*, including even its most prosaic sections, into an extended verse text. The commentaries of the Cheng brothers and Zhu Xi, mentioned in Wang Shizhen's preface, provided one method for understanding the coherence of the text. Zhang Xianyi had found another that lay within the style. To validate this versified reading of the *Changes*, Zhang highlighted the rhyming nature of each line. We can take one line from the opening chapter of the *Changes* as an example: "a flying dragon is in the sky, it is advantageous to see the great man" (<fuī līong dzàe tiēn, lì cièn dhà rēn> 飛龍在天, 利見大人).[26] Zhang Xianyi claimed that the first phrase rhymes with the second, which requires "sky" (<tiēn> 天) and "man" (<rēn> 人) to rhyme.[27] These two syllables rhymed in the contemporary Mandarin, making his case intuitively reasonable. To solidify his claim, Zhang cited the use of the graph "sky" <tiēn> rhyming with "man" <rēn> in texts from throughout the poetic tradition, ranging from as early as the *Poems*, which would have been roughly contemporaneous with the *Changes*, all the way to the fourteenth century. By highlighting the way in which the great masters of the poetic tradition used this rhyme pattern of <tiēn> and <rēn>, Zhang Xianyi attempted to demonstrate that the *Changes* aligned with all manner of works that were commonly accepted as verse and should belong to this same tradition.

The example of <tiēn> and <rēn> as rhyming words seems plausible, and the two graphs are today still considered to have rhymed in Old Chinese. In addition, as in the case of later divinatory texts such as *Jiao shi Yilin* and *Cantong qi*, the phrase is made up of two four-syllable lines, mirroring the meter of the *Poems*. However, Zhang Xianyi applied this same method of reading throughout the entire text in an effort to transform the *Changes* into verse, forcing extremely unpoetic lines to rhyme in what would from today's perspective seem to be a very implausible manner. Take, for instance, the following line: "The action of heaven is strong. The noble man, in the same manner, never ceases to strengthen himself" (<tiēn hāeng gièn> 天行健, <cīun zǐ yǐ dzì giāng but sic> 君子以自強不息).[28] Zhang Xianyi bizarrely argued that these phrases form a rhyming line, observing a rhyme neither at the natural break nor within an internally consistent pattern, but between the second graph "motions" (<hāeng> 行) and the final graph "cease" (<sic> 息).²⁹ To rhyme these two graphs, Zhang claimed that <sic> should be pronounced <siāng> (襄),³⁰ while <hāeng> should be pronounced <hāng> (杭), yielding a line (with rhymes in bold) that could be read <tiēn **hāng** gièn>, 天行健, <cīun zǐ yǐ dzì giāng but **siāng**> 君子以自強不息. The only evidence Zhang offered for this wildly altered pronunciation of <sic> is a chant recorded in a seventh-century Buddhist encyclopedia. Beyond the anachronism of using a seventh-century CE text to corroborate one from the fifth century BCE, Zhang in fact resorted to changing the pronunciation of surrounding graphs in the seventh-century chant as well, to prove that <sic> would have necessarily been pronounced <siāng> in the later context.

Zhang Xianyi would also apply such reading strategies to lines in the "Appended Phrases" (繫辭 Xici) and "Providing the Sequence of Hexagrams" (序卦 Xugua), later additions to the text of the *Changes* traditionally ascribed to Confucius, which provided a metaphysical interpretation for the content of the main text. Although Qing dynasty and present-day studies have largely dismissed these prosaic commentarial sections as sources for ancient rhymes, Zhang Xianyi attended to these extended prose discussions as closely as he did the rest of the text. In the following example, Zhang highlighted the perceived rhymes underlying an elaborate, and rather prosaic, passage:

> The *Changes* make evident both that which has already happened and scrutinizes what is yet to come, thus subtlety comes to light, revealing what is hidden; [the hexagrams] are elucidated in such a way that they suit their names, differentiating things and rectifying language, to form decisive phrases that are complete.³¹
>
> <fū yec> 夫易, <jāng wāng ēr trat lāi> 彰往而察來, <ēr vuī xiěn chǎn iēu> 而微顯闡幽, <kāi ēr dāng miēng> 開而當名, <bhièn vut jàeng iēn> 辨物正言, <dhòn szī zec bhùy yǐ> 斷辭則備矣.

Zhang transformed this passage into the following "rhymed" reading (with rhymes in bold):

<fū **yec**> 夫易,
<jāng wāng ēr trat **ic**> 彰往而察來[億],

<ēr vuī xiĕn chăn iēu> 而微顯闡幽,
<kāi ēr dāng miēng> 開而當名,
<bhièn **vut** jàeng iēn> 辨物正言,
<dhòn szī zec **bhet** yĭ> 斷辭則備[勃]矣.³²

For certain graphs, Zhang's altered pronunciations may have some historical grounding. It is also probable that, as in the present-day Suzhou dialect where the various stop endings of the entering tone (<-p>, <-t>, <-c>) have merged into one, <yec>, <ic>, <vut>, and <bhet> (all four of which he claimed to rhyme with each other) would have roughly rhymed in Zhang Xianyi's local dialect.³³ As in the previous example, however, the inconsistent placement of these "rhyme words" defies any conventional contemporary notion of the role of rhyme in verse. Zhang assumed the entirety of the received *Changes* text to constitute a coherent whole. The basis of this coherence was its stylistic structure, which in his view relied primarily on rhyme. These rhymes could appear at the end of a line, or internally, or both, as Zhang sought any form of phonic symmetry to connect its phrases.

Zhang Xianyi further offered multiple possible readings for many phrases in the *Changes*. For instance, he provided the following alternative reading of the previous passage, tracing the beginning of the rhyme pattern to the preceding line:

<gī sruāi shèy jī **yī** yē> 其衰世之意[噫]邪,
<fū yec> 夫易,
<jāng wāng ēr trat **yī**> 彰往而察來[怡],
<ēr vuī xiĕn chăn iēu> 而微顯闡幽,
<kāi ēr dāng miēng> 開而當名,
<bhièn vut jàeng iēn> 辨物正言,
<dhòn **szī** zec **bhuēi** yĭ> 斷辭則備[陪]矣.³⁴

Zhang employed the adverb "also" (*you* 又) before his alternative readings, suggesting that they were equally plausible pronunciations. In another passage he proposed that a single graph, "virtue" (德 <dec>), could be pronounced with four alternate readings: 荅 <dap>, 丟 <diēu>, 篤 <douc>, or 得上聲 <dĕ>. Without specifying a preferred reading, Zhang outlined how the choice of each pronunciation would alter the readings of other graphs in the passage.³⁵ Zhang's goal therefore does not seem to have been to uncover the systematic differences of language in antiquity. Instead he routinely provided differing readings of the same line, illustrating a multiplicity of ways to versify the text.

This notion of a plurality of plausible readings contrasts with the dominant reading approach to the Classics, bolstered by its institution in the required commentaries for the civil service examination, which asserted orthodoxy through singularity. It is paralleled, however, by the contemporary emergence of a trend in literary commentary that allowed for the possibility of multiple valid interpretations.[36] It also reflects new propositions for the philosophical compatibility of Confucianism and Buddhism, as well as the applicability of Buddhist scholarly methods to classical fields of learning. As we saw in chapter 2, late Ming scholars incorporated Buddhist methods of Sanskrit study into Chinese philology. A similar attention to Buddhist scholarship is evident in Zhang Xianyi's preface to *Du Yi yunkao*, which begins with the citation of a passage from a Buddhist sutra regarding the significance of phonology: "There has never been [a graph] that could be explained without obtaining its pronunciation."[37] Wang Shizhen's preface similarly related Sanskrit chanting to *Changes* recitation.[38] Within the text itself, Zhang regularly cited Buddhist texts and lexicons as relevant sources for corroborating pronunciations in the *Changes*, a work that Zhang characterized as the pinnacle of *ru* learning. Zhang acknowledged the clear differences between Sanskrit and Chinese but argued that they shared phonological principles.[39] This attention to Buddhist materials and methods was in line with previous justifications of Sanskrit study we have encountered, which asserted that phonology had been neglected by Confucians but maintained in Buddhist circles. It is unclear how seriously Zhang Xianyi took the original context of Buddhist phonological discussion in terms of the relationship between pronunciation and enlightenment. Wang Shizhen's reference to the significance of chanting in particular suggests a perceived link between the process of uttering the text with efficacious pronunciation and a deeper understanding of the *Changes* itself. Taken together, the presentation of multiple readings alongside the intertwining of Buddhist and Confucian discourses highlights the underlying epistemology of a text, which embraced plurality and even uncertainty over rigid singularity.

Zhang left little guidance for his reader in choosing between what he framed as multiple valid readings. In some cases, Zhang's rhyme schemes would include an option that forced a rhyme across an extended passage, whereas the alternatives would force multiple rhymes within one or two short lines. This pattern may suggest that a reader was expected to choose the latter option when quoting an isolated line and opt for the former when reciting a longer passage. Zhang did not explicitly provide a basis for the reader's rhyme selection and seems more concerned with cataloging possibilities than defining a fixed standard. For instance, in one passage, he noted that the pronunciation of the graph <lāi> 來 could be modified in two ways, depending on where one wished to force the rhyme. He further drew attention to four alternative pronunciations from another passage, observing that there were therefore seven possible readings of this single graph.[40] Although these additional four pronunciations would be irrelevant to the specific passage, Zhang evidently was concerned with highlighting the distinctively flexible nature of reading in antiquity. He appears to have believed he was restoring something ancient, rather than creating a convenient shortcut for contemporary readers. He occasionally referred to his readings as being specific to "antiquity" (gu 古), suggesting their perceived difference from contemporary norms.[41] Zhang's brother, in his colophon to Du Yi yunkao, further framed the text as directed against a contemporary trend to "change ancient rhyme readings into modern rhyme readings" (變古韻為今韻), masking the difference between ancient and modern pronunciations.[42] While the inconsistent application of these readings throughout does not demonstrate an understanding of the systematic differences between ancient and modern phonology, it does suggest a conception of reading and pronunciation in antiquity as different from the present.

Zhang Xianyi's study attempted to prove that the entirety of the *Changes* was a rhyming text. In order to do this, Zhang would cite any and all texts to make his point. While the medieval and modern poets he cited may have been imitating ancient rhymes, it is difficult to imagine how they could serve as a source for understanding a rhyme system from over one thousand years earlier. Zhang Xianyi was not the first to link the rhymes of ancient and more recent poetry. Wu Yu 吳棫 (c. 1100–1154), the influential Song dynasty phonologist, similarly used Tang and eleventh-century poets in his seminal study of ancient rhymes, the *Yunbu* (韻補 Rhyme supplement).[43] The extent to which Zhang Xianyi took this approach, particularly in his insistence on the existence of rhymes in prose text, was on a qualitatively different level. It caused even some contemporaries to comment on the "forced" nature of his analysis and provoked the eighteenth-century *Siku quanshu* editors to describe Zhang as "having written this in true ignorance."[44] The linkage of ancient and more recent poetic phonology was, nevertheless, relatively common among sixteenth- and seventeenth-century scholars, who considered literary style, rather than historical period, to provide insight into the rhymes of antiquity.[45]

Zhang Xianyi must have believed the great literary figures of the past to have been capable of perfectly channeling ancient rhymes. Therefore to cite Su Shi 蘇軾 (1037–1101) or Han Yu 韓愈 (768–824) was as relevant as citing a Zhou text. In a discussion of the rhymes in one of the most prosaic sections of the *Changes*, the "Appended Phrases," Zhang added, "When works such as the 'Rhapsody on Sweet Springs' [by Yang Xiong] often likewise conclude with one rhyme at the end of each section, but match with a different rhyme in the middle part, they are all imitating (*xue* 學) the use of rhymes in the 'Appended Phrases.'"[46] Here Zhang saw the *Changes* as the forefather to a particular literary rhyming style. His use of the term *xue* 學 ("to learn" or "imitate") suggests that this later adoption of ancient rhymes was not a natural evolution, but rather that authors of later verse texts were intentionally modeling their style on the *Changes*. The aesthetic value of the *Changes* as a work that could be intoned aloud as verse therefore also justified its usage as a source for poetic composition.

Zhang Xianyi's poetic readings of the Classics were influential for literary practice, and his methods found their way into pedagogical materials and handbooks for the composition of various genres of literature. For example, Zhang Xianyi's contemporary Sun Weicheng 孫維城 (1540–1602) composed a guidebook for writing rhymed poetry entitled *Yunshi bianlan* (韻釋便覽 An explanation of rhymes for convenient perusal). The central argument of this text, which made reference to Zhang Xianyi's work, was that "the Six Classics are all rhyming texts" (*liujing mo fei yun ye* 六經莫非韻也).[47] The author therefore based his categorizations of rhyming for contemporary poetic practice on examples from ancient classical prose texts. In his view, the language of these texts reflected an idealized, not yet corrupted form of language. By recovering this uncorrupted language, originally contained in a prose context, he felt he had determined a better method of rhyming for poetic composition. The poetic reading of the *Changes* appears at its most extreme in the work of the seventeenth-century poet Qu Dajun 屈大均 (1630–1696), who promoted "making poetry out of the *Changes*" (*yi Yi wei shi* 以易為詩), claiming that "those who are not expert in the *Changes* will be incapable of poetry."[48] Qu referred to the

Changes as "the poetry of the ancient sages" on the basis of its perceived rhyming quality, but his proposals to model poetry after the *Changes* were based primarily on the text's cosmological implications, which he hoped his poetry could similarly effect.[49] Qu's efforts, both as author of a commentary on the *Changes* and as a poet, nevertheless reflect this new form of literary interpretation of the Classics, which made verse out of prose.

Contrasting Evidential Learning and Ming Literary Approaches to Classical Rhyming

Sun Weicheng's claim that "the Six Classics are all rhyming texts" can be productively juxtaposed against one of the most well-known arguments regarding the Classics from the Qianlong-period scholar Zhang Xuecheng 章學誠 (1738–1801), who famously declared: "the Six Classics are all history" (*liujing jie shi ye* 六經皆史也).[50] This distinction is telling. The Wanli era scholar saw the Classics as timeless literary works and moreover as a model for poetic composition in the present day. By the late eighteenth century, these texts were seen to belong to a specific historical context, the recognition of which was necessary for comprehending their meaning. Within the field of linguistic study, Gu Yanwu was instrumental in developing the historical approach to phonology, which would become dominant in the eighteenth century. While opera scholars, such as Li Yu, had previously emphasized the existence of historical change in the Chinese language, they did not take great interest in documenting the nature of language in antiquity (see chapter 4). Gu Yanwu, on the other hand, was primarily interested in recovering the specific phonological properties of the ancient Chinese language. Gu did not ignore the rhyming quality of classical works, and he even wrote a text on the phonology of the *Changes*, *Yi yin* (易音 Pronunciations in the *Changes*). Gu would agree with Zhang Xianyi that texts from antiquity could be used to understand ancient rhymes. Gu believed, however, that ancient pronunciations were already gradually being lost in the Qin and Han dynasties, asserting that there was no point in looking to later works to understand the rhyming of antiquity. Further, he was not concerned with the entire text of the *Changes* because, unlike Zhang Xianyi, he held that "it does not rhyme throughout."[51] Gu Yanwu's analysis therefore focused only on sections of the text that reflected a poetic meter or possessed consistent internal rhyme, as opposed to Zhang Xianyi's consideration of inconsistent rhyming within uneven prosaic lines.

Where Gu Yanwu and Zhang Xianyi agreed on the existence of rhyme, their method of documenting that rhyme was vastly different. For example, both Gu Yanwu and Zhang Xianyi noted the rhyme in the passage cited earlier, "a flying dragon is in the sky, it is advantageous to meet with a great man" (<fuī līong dzàe **tiēn**> 飛龍在天, <lì cièn dhà **rēn**> 利見大人). Zhang Xianyi "proved" the existence of this rhyme by extensively citing poetry from throughout the Chinese literary tradition that juxtaposed the graphs "sky" (<tiēn> 天) and "man" (<rēn> 人) as rhymes. Along the way, he posited several alternate pronunciations for both graphs to ensure that a reader could make it rhyme while incanting the text.[52] Zhang's ahistorical method pulled from ancient and modern poetry alike and was based primarily on literary usage. Its unsystematic nature also required that he produce a new proof for every line of the text. Gu Yanwu, on the other hand, expressed the same observation of rhyme in a much more condensed manner, "proving" the rhyme with the following formula: <fuī līong dzàe tiēn> 1 <siēn> 飛龍在天一先, <lì cièn dhà rēn> 17 <jēn> 利見大人十七真.[53] The small font "1 <siēn>" and "17 <jēn>" are two of the rhyme categories to which Gu Yanwu systematically assigned graphs based on their shared phonological properties, which he elsewhere demonstrated through the corroboration of their usage in ancient texts. The graphs within a given category rhymed; these categories were further grouped into sets of "interchangeable rhymes." "1 <siēn>" and "17 <jēn>" were such an example of two categories, which Gu asserted to interchangeably rhyme in ancient practice. Because of the systematic nature of these rhyme categories, Gu had no need in his *Changes* glosses to cite additional evidence supporting the notion that these two particular graphs rhymed. Later Evidential Learning scholars modified Gu's categories and groupings but largely agreed with the premise underlying this systematic classification of ancient phonology.

Gu Yanwu took a considerably more tempered view toward the existence of rhyming in ancient texts than scholars of Zhang Xianyi's era did, observing that "the literary transformations of the ancients were skillful and naturally accorded with pitches. Thus even texts without [consistent] rhyme often had some rhymes, while on the other hand even texts with [consistent] rhyme occasionally did not rhyme. Ultimately, they would not allow rhyme to harm the meaning (不以韻而害意)."[54] For Gu, the texts of antiquity were argumentative, the literary qualities of which were important, but secondary to "the meaning." Forcing the existence of rhymes was, from Gu's perspective, reflective of a modern literary concern.

The key difference between Zhang Xianyi's and Gu Yanwu's approach lay in their understanding of the historicity of ancient language. Gu understood the textual legacy of antiquity to reflect a language specific to that period, a language that systematically differed from that of the present. Hence no matter how much Tang poets may have tried to imitate the ancient style, their chronological distance from the linguistic context of antiquity rendered their poetry unusable as evidence for a discussion of ancient rhyme categories. Zhang, on the other hand, was less interested in ancient texts as repositories of information on a historical language. Instead, he saw them primarily as a canon of verse usage that had been skillfully applied throughout the poetic tradition. While he acknowledged that the pronunciations he documented departed from contemporary spoken norms, Zhang framed these variations as differences in reading practices rather than the fundamental phonological properties of the language. Zhang Xianyi's study, although extreme, was broadly reflective of a contemporary approach to reading classical poetry according to the *xieyun* ("forced rhyme" 叶韻) method. This method involved slightly altering the pronunciation of a given graph to create the appearance of a rhyme when a passage no longer rhymed in the modern language. Like his contemporary Hao Jing, who had argued that graph forms in antiquity were flexible and interchangeable (see chapter 3), Zhang envisioned the ancients as having adopted a fluid approach to the recitation of texts, which prioritized a plurality of rhyming possibilities over a single fixed standard. Scholars such as Chen Di and Gu Yanwu, on the other hand, argued that the divergences in pronunciation between antiquity and the present were systematic and reflective of a different historical stage of the Chinese language. In their view, a single graph generally had just one pronunciation, which it retained regardless of the context. The distinction between these two approaches, although critical to our understanding of the development of historical linguistics in China, was not necessarily clear for a Ming audience. Zhao Yiguang, one of the great philological minds of the Ming and a colleague of Zhang Xianyi's,[55] provides the following survey of recent research into ancient phonology:

> Wu Yu wrote *Yunbu*, a book entirely about sounds that do not rhyme [in the present]. It is clearly evidence-based (*youju* 有據). . . . Recently

there has been Chen Di's *Mao Shi guyin* (毛詩古音 Ancient pronunciations of the *Odes*) and *Qu Song guyin* (屈宋古音 Ancient pronunciations of Qu Yuan and Song Yu), which seem to be somewhat more complete. Before him there was Zhang Xianyi's *Du Yi yunkao*. Although he came before Chen Di, he mainly focused on vast inclusion (*wubo* 務博) and frequently erred. He did not verify as well as Mr. Chen, but still it is worth consulting. I wish to edit the works of Wu Yu, Chen Di, and Zhang Xianyi, making appropriate selections and deletions, and combine them into one book—this would more or less fulfill their intention.[56]

Zhao Yiguang cited Zhang Xianyi's *Du Yi yunkao* as a text to be consulted alongside Chen Di's analyses of ancient rhyming. By the eighteenth century these two works would be seen as representative of two completely different trends in Ming thought: the former an example of misguided notions of the history of language, the latter a direct predecessor to Gu Yanwu's historical phonology. To a Ming audience, however, they may have been achieving similar goals.[57] Even Zhao's criticism of Zhang Xianyi as "focused on vast inclusion" (務博) would have been disputed by some contemporaries. Huangfu Pang, for instance, wrote in his preface to *Du Yi yunkao* that the text "is very much evidence based (*liang you suo ju* 良有所據)," adding that it is not "focused on vast inclusion," as typical of earlier philologists.[58] The notion of "evidence" (*ju*) that both Zhao Yiguang and Huangfu Pang invoked differs from that associated with the eighteenth-century Evidential Learning scholars. Eighteenth-century scholars criticized the tendency of Wu Yu and Zhang Xianyi to cite texts without regard for the era of composition.[59] The sixteenth- and seventeenth-century notion of "evidence," by contrast, tended to see citation of texts across time as a necessary form of corroboration.

Zhao Yiguang ranked the scholarly merit of each text but still considered Wu Yu and Zhang Xianyi's *xieyun* approach to ancient rhyming as belonging to the same category as Chen Di's historically informed method. All three works were distinct from other contemporary philological texts by virtue of their focus on "ancient pronunciation" (*guyin* 古音). Zhao therefore believed it reasonable to compile a new study of ancient rhymes, which cut and pasted from the works of these three scholars. Zhao Yiguang likewise proposed combining *Zhongyuan yinyun*, a rhyme dictionary for composition of northern operatic genres, with Chen Di's study of ancient rhymes for the purposes of "making known antiquity."⁶⁰ For Zhao, one of the most prominent philologists of the late Ming, we need not draw a sharp distinction between the one work devoted to singing application and the other devoted to uncovering the phonological system of antiquity.

Zhao Yiguang understood the language of textual production in antiquity as fundamentally poetic and operatic. What on the surface might appear to be an ancient prose text could be understood as a work of verse, the rhymes of which simply went unnoticed by those with insufficient phonological understanding.⁶¹ Zhao further argued that the distinction of prose and poetry that seemed commonsense to some of his contemporaries was an artificial construction that went contrary to the mode of composition in antiquity. As he explained:

> For the ancients, words (*yan* 言) created literary text (*wen* 文), and literary text had rhymes (*yun* 韻). If it did not rhyme it could not be called literary text. Later generations lost the readings 70–80 percent of the time and altered the graphs 20–30 percent of the time. Thus ever since the Han, that which rhymed was called poetry (*shi* 詩) and that which did not rhyme was called prose (*wen*). . . . The ancients called all [writing] *wen*, and *wen* always had rhymes.⁶²

For Zhao Yiguang, poetry as a category of literature only arose following the breakdown of literary practices postantiquity, during which there emerged forms of writing that did not rhyme. From his perspective, therefore, Zhang Xianyi's reading of the *Changes* was restoring the singular mode of literary production in antiquity by highlighting the text's admittedly malleable rhyming qualities.

In Zhao Yiguang's view, the ancients did not need to go out of their way to write in verse. As he put it, "Whenever the ancients opened their mouths and spoke, it rhymed" (古人出口用韻).⁶³ This striking statement was echoed by contemporaries who believed that the speech of the ancients emerged spontaneously in verse. Qu Dajun, for instance, similarly opined that "whatsoever [the ancient sages] uttered always accorded with *self-so rhyme*" (凡所有言，莫不協乎自然之韻).⁶⁴ Scholars who embraced this conception of language saw later accretions, and in particular the emergence of dialects, as a degraded form of an original pure mode of speech in antiquity. Mao Xianshu (1620–1688), for instance, disputed Gu Yanwu's assertion that discrepancies in ancient rhyming practices were the result of dialect pronunciations.⁶⁵ Mao believed that the sages would have spoken the perfect foundational form of Chinese; these apparent discrepancies were only the result of insufficient phonological understanding among contemporary scholars. A late Ming study of even the more recent poetry of Du Fu (712–770) provided new altered pronunciations for Du Fu's corpus in order to avoid what could be perceived as irregularities of prosody in the original.⁶⁶ Zhang Xianyi himself claimed that the ancients, and even later Tang poets, spoke in literary pattern, which even at its most debased "would not cause people to wash out their ears [for having heard something inelegant]." Zhang hoped to achieve this ideal in his own speech and reported his family members' assessment that he "always spoke in complete literary phrases (出語皆成章), and never uttered vulgar words, even in intimate company."⁶⁷

For Zhao Yiguang and Zhang Xianyi, the ordinary speech of the ancients, which rhymed naturally, would be considered poetry by modern standards. Despite Zhao Yiguang's insistence that poetry as a category was a recent phenomenon, the term for poetry, *shi*, clearly existed in antiquity, as represented most prominently in the classical compilation, the *Classic of Poems*. How, then, was poetry in antiquity differentiated?

Poetry and Music

Ming scholars read the Classics for their literary qualities, embedded in the phonological characteristics of the language of these ancient texts. They also embraced phonology as the key to one of central problems in the study of ancient poetry—recovery of its accompanying music.

The early textual tradition is rife with descriptions of musical and ritual performances of the *Classic of Poems*, suggesting the significant performative aspects of these texts in antiquity.⁶⁸ The majority of references to the *Poems* in the *Analects* refer to the musical qualities of its performance. According to the *Shiji* (史記 Records of the grand historian), Confucius himself sang the *Poems* to his own accompaniment in order to ensure the proper correspondence of poetry and music.⁶⁹ The *Great Preface* (*Daxu* 大序) to the *Poems*, perhaps the single most influential text in the Chinese poetic hermeneutic tradition, illustrates a continuum between speech and song: "The affections are stirred within and take on form in words. If words alone are inadequate, we speak them out in sighs. If sighing is inadequate, we sing them. If singing them is inadequate, unconsciously our hands dance them and our feet tap them." As Stephen Owen observes, this seminal statement posited that the distinction between ordinary speech and (sung) poetry was a matter of emotional intensity, rather than a fundamental difference of expression.[70]

The relationship between the recorded poetic texts of the *Poems* with music and singing was an essential part of its hermeneutic tradition and by no means new to the Ming, but Ming thinkers elaborated this association into a rigorous project of musical reconstruction. The connection between the *Poems* and music became a major trend in its exegesis in the twelfth century. Zheng Qiao 鄭樵 (1104–1162), in particular, initiated an approach to reading the *Poems* that asserted the primacy of "musical setting" (*yuezhang* 樂章) over "meaning of the text" (*wenyi* 文義).[71] Zheng's influential analysis of the *Poems* as a collection of songs was ultimately directed at interpretation of the texts, often rolling back previous moralistic readings. Although he bemoaned the loss of the original music to the *Poems* at the hands of Han scholiasts, Zheng did not attempt to recover the original melodies. Ming thinkers, however, posited a nexus of music, speech, and poetry in more concrete ways than ever before. In their view, the human voice was a precise measure of musical pitch, and the phonological properties of ancient poetry a reliable standard for reconstructing its musical accompaniment.

Ming scholars tended to embrace the notion of a continuum between speech and poetry and extended it from unadorned human speech beyond song to the abstract pitches of musical instruments. Late Ming scholars routinely cited the following famed classical dictum as justification for the unified study of poetry, philology, and music: "Poetry speaks what the mind is intent on, song prolongs this speech. Sound relies on this prolongation, and pitches regulate this sound" (詩言志，歌永言，聲依永，律和聲).[72] This statement suggested to some Ming thinkers that, for the ancients, poetry was inextricable from its musical accompaniment: as one scholar put it, "The *Poems* was based on musical pitches," while another argued that "the 300 pieces [of the *Poems*] are all poetry (*shi* 詩), all tunes (*qu* 曲), all music (*yue* 樂)."[73] Ming scholars also pointed to evidence in the Classics in support of this connection. For instance, in the *Analects*, Confucius comments that "it was after my return from Wei to Lu that music was put right with the Ya and Song [sections of the *Poems*] being assigned their proper places."[74] One Ming reader noted that "if one were to say that music is simply music and the *Poems* simply *Poems*, then the Master should not have understood [the *Poems*] finding their proper place as the putting right of music."[75] Based on this evidence, he went on to argue for the fundamental relationship between graphs (*zi* 字) and pitches (*lü* 律) in the poetry of ancient times.

Ming thinkers deeply theorized the nature of sound in order to justify this linkage. In their view, all sound (*sheng* 聲) was the product of some kind of movement of *qi*, which existed prior to its categorization as tone (*yin* 音), either musical or linguistic. Both music and language were therefore simply differing manifestations of sound-based *qi* (*shengqi* 聲氣). Establishing the fundamental unity of these forms of sound allowed Ming scholars to propose new ways of reconstructing musical pitches and the melodies of antiquity.

Scholars in the sixteenth and seventeenth centuries frequently referred to this originary form of sound as "primordial sound" (*yuansheng* 元聲 or *yuanyin* 元音) (see chapter 1). Widespread interest in "primordial sound" is reflected in numerous contemporary acoustic studies featuring this term in their titles, such as *Wufang yuanyin* (五方元音 Primordial sounds of the five directions), *Taigu yuanyin* (太古元音 Primordial sounds of distant antiquity), *Yuanyin tongyun* (元音統韻 Systematized rhymes of primordial sound), *Dayue lülü yuansheng* (大樂律呂元聲 Primordial sounds of pitch-pipes for grand music), *Dengqie yuansheng* (等切元聲 Primordial sounds of graded rhymes), and *Yuansheng yunxue dacheng* (元聲韻學大成 Complete compilation of rhyme study based on the primordial sound). Primordial sound was conceived of as neither fundamentally linguistic nor musical. Only as it was channeled through either the human vocal cords or a musical instrument could it be more precisely defined. The building block of sound in its undifferentiated quality was generally held to be *qi* ("vital/material force" 氣), a claim that traces back to discussions of music in early China. There existed various proposals for how this *qi* was transformed into musical and linguistic sound. Dong Yue 董說 (1620–1686), for instance, argued that sound was the product of *qi*'s "obstruction." *Qi* in and of itself was without sound (*wusheng* 無聲) and could produce it only when expelled through an enclosed area. Hence, when the legendary Ling Lun created pitch-pipes out of bamboo, he "obstructed the *qi* of heaven and earth with bamboo and produced sound." In the same way, Dong believed humans created sound through the obstruction of the *qi* of heaven and earth as it passed through their "five orifices."[76] Song Yingxing 宋應星 (1587–1666)

similarly posited that *qi* possessed no intrinsic sound. The production of sound was, in his view, a result of the collision of different forms of *qi*. For instance, sounds produced by the human voice resulted from the *qi* contained within a person colliding with that outside on exhalation.[77]

Because of their shared basis in sound-based *qi*, the human voice also came to be seen as a standard for deriving musical pitches and gaining insight into the musical accompaniment of ancient poetry in particular. Ming thinkers advanced new methods of determining musical pitch, with some deriding previous approaches, which were based on ancient measurements and ritual practices.[78] As we saw in chapter 1, certain Ming scholars argued for the *self-so* nature of arithmetically derived sonic categories, both musical and linguistic. Some further contended that the ancient sages had also relied on the human voice in the creation of pitch standards, particularly for establishing the fundamental pitch C (*huangzhong* 黃鐘), from which the other pitches could be arithmetically calculated.[79] Proponents of the human voice as a standard for pitch similarly invoked the notion of *self-so*, focusing on the capability of the unchanging form of the human body to channel what was *self-so*. The notion that the human voice was inherently musical and formed the basis of musical pitch has a long history in the Chinese tradition, stretching back to the earliest clear articulation of this theory in *Wenxin diaolong*.[80] But Ming scholars took these abstract theories of the relationship between music and the voice and translated them into functional plans for the concrete derivation of musical pitch standards.

Why would the human voice provide a more reliable standard? As one scholar, Xing Yunlu 邢雲路 (*jinshi* 1580), observed, "There is no past or present with regard to the human voice, which has remained the same." Scholars such as Xing Yunlu were skeptical of the potential for research into extant vessels to convey the standards described in ancient texts. Similarly to philologists who believed the textual legacy of antiquity was too sparse for research into ancient language, Xing doubted the remaining material legacy was capable of definitively substantiating the measurement standards of antiquity. Instead Xing believed we could make use of the unchanging physical attributes of the human form to deduce musical pitches. In particular, Xing advised that one could intuit the correct intonation of musical pitches by "calming one's mind, contenting one's *qi*, and slowly listening to the rising and falling of the human voice."[81]

Scholars justified the notion of intuitively deducing musical pitch with the claim that humans were the most numinous beings, and therefore the only ones capable of reproducing "primordial sound."[82] Despite the emphasis on the *self-so* nature of sound, humans played an important role in channeling sound. As one sixteenth-century scholar claimed, the "sounds of heaven and earth are unable to emerge of their own" and had to be diverted into rhyming language and musical pitches by the sage-kings of antiquity, who desired to "promulgate the mysteries of heaven and earth, release the harmony of the myriad things, and create a foundation for stirring people's hearts."[83] Another put it more simply: "When humans opens their mouths, the primordial sound is right there" (人開口是元聲).[84]

Some Ming scholars claimed that human beings were the numinous benefactors of heaven and earth's primordial sound, producing utterances that were "more *self-so*" (尤為自然) than those of instruments.[85] Musical instruments represented artifice, as material creations that were capable of imitating (*xiao* 效), resembling (*fang* 彷), or transcribing (*xie* 寫) but not directly channeling the primordial sound.[86] As one scholar argued, "The pitch-pipes are instruments, in other words of the mundane, phenomenal world." The human voice, channeled through its most natural form of expression, poetry, "is the voice of the mind, in other words it is immaterial."[87] In their theoretical endeavors to abandon artifice and reclaim the *self-so* quality of sound, the human voice came to be elevated as the most direct point of access to primordial sound. The widespread belief that the human voice could be used to determine pitches, taking, for instance, the lowest singable pitch as C, had functional significance and even figured in debates for establishing the pitches for ritual music performance at the imperial court.[88]

Can the Music of Antiquity Be Reconstructed via Language?

A central concern within acoustical studies of language and music was the proper setting of text to music. Within the world of contemporary opera composition, guides to pronunciation emphasized the union of musical and linguistic sound. The focus in the case of opera was on the proper phonetic values for singing, rather than the musical accompaniment, which consisted primarily of a repertoire of shared melodies. The melodies of antiquity, however, predated the invention of musical notation in China. Ming scholars posited that these melodies could be reconstructed, based on the premise that there existed a fundamental relationship between musical and linguistic sound, as well as the assumption that the human voice had not changed since antiquity.

Certain scholars in the sixteenth and seventeenth centuries believed speech, literature, and music were unified in antiquity and only separated in a corrupted later world. Wu Jishi argued that the language of the Six Classics could entirely be "harmonized and set to music" on account of their rhyming language.[89] For such scholars, the *Poems* was the best model for understanding this unity. Long before the Ming preoccupation with the unity of language and music in antiquity, scholars had attempted to establish a musical accompaniment to the *Poems*. In his commentary on the early ritual compilation *Yili* (儀禮 Book of etiquette and ceremonial), Zhu Xi, whose interpretations would define the standard for the examination curriculum, provided an example of twelve poems from the *Poems* set to music. Zhu credited the melodies to a contemporary, who in turn claimed that they were a transcription of tunes used at the eighth-century Tang court. An example of a stanza from one poem (Mao 161), both in the original notation and in modern Western musical notation, is provided in figure 5.1.[90]

There is no clear correspondence between a particular graph and a musical pitch in Zhu Xi's scores. For example the graph <wǒ> (我 "I") appears

Figure 5.1 Zhu Xi's musical setting of the *Poems* (Mao 161). The top line of the lyrics is the Chinese text of the poem; the second line is a transcription of its "Ming" pronunciation; the third line represents the standard musical notation Zhu Xi employed. In this notation, a given graph is the first graph of the pitch name (*huang* 黃 = *huangzhong* 黃鍾 [C]). The text of the poetic stanza in translation is: "You, you, call the deer, nibbling the black southernwood of the fields. I have a lucky guest. Let me play my zither, blow my reed-organ, blow my reed-organ, trill their tongues, take up the baskets of offerings. Here is a man that loves me and will teach me the ways of Zhou." Translation from Arthur Waley, trans., *The Book of Songs: The Ancient Chinese Classic of Poetry*, ed. Joseph R. Allen (New York: Grove Press, 1996), 161.

three times: once as the pitch F#, once as E, and once as A. Zhu Xi himself was ambivalent about these melodies. In particular, he believed that the use of only one pitch per graph (直以一聲叶一字) could not capture the full emotional range of the poetry.[91] He instead seems to have preferred a singing style with greater ornamentation, involving multiple notes for each syllable. Zhu Xi's score remained influential and served as a model for one of the most significant subsequent attempts to write musical accompaniment for the *Poems* in the Yuan.[92]

By endorsing a set of tunes that made no effort to integrate the phonology of the poems and even suggesting further ornamentation, Zhu Xi implied that the musical accompaniment to the text was a separate matter from its linguistic qualities. Ming scholars disputed Zhu Xi's melodies as antithetical to the nature of composition in antiquity. For instance, the music theorist Qu Jiusi (1546–1617) transcribed the twelve *Poems* melodies preserved by Zhu Xi, including a complete list of repeated graphs in each poem. Qu's list indicated when these graphs were assigned a different pitch on each repetition in Zhu Xi's score. After each example, Qu exclaimed, "the graph is the same, but the pitch is different. What nonsense!"[93] Qu's contemporary Ge Zhongxuan similarly claimed that Zhu Xi's score "does not consider what pitch [a particular] syllable should be. I am afraid this is not the ancient intention."[94] Ge Zhongxuan carefully associated pitch with pronunciation in his rhyme tables and believed this unity was the key to recovering ancient music. Disputing Zhu Xi's claim that the ancients must have sung multiple notes on a single pitch for emotional expression, Ge argued that the expressive potential of the *Poems* was already complete in its grammatical particles and was not a musical matter.[95] In his view, each syllable should be correlated with a single pitch.

Ming thinkers frequently argued, in contrast to Zhu Xi, that the language and music of the *Poems* were inseparable. One scholar criticized Chen Di's famed historical linguistic study of *Poems* rhymes as "merely aiding in recitation of the text (*fengsong* 諷誦)." By not taking music into consideration, it had missed the true "sounds" (*sheng*) of the poetry.[96] In the preface to a no longer extant work on *Poems* rhymes, Zhu Rangxu 朱讓栩 (1501–1547) similarly claimed that every piece within the *Poems* could be sung (可歌可咏) and warned against isolating the phonological aspects of the text from its musical qualities.[97] During the eighteenth century major Evidential Learning scholars, such as Jiang Yong and Dai Zhen, were also concerned with musical performance of *Poems* but viewed this as a separate matter from phonology. For some sixteenth and seventeenth-century scholars, however, both the linguistic and musical aspects of the text were intertwined under the broader study of acoustics.

The correlation between the syllables and musical accompaniment of the *Poems* was developed even more concretely through the attempts of Ming scholars to compose revised versions of its accompanying music. One of the most widely circulated versions can be found in a text entitled *Yuejing yuanyi* (樂經元義 Original meaning of the Classic of Music) by Liu Lian 劉濂 (*jinshi* 1478), an influential mid-Ming musical scholar, born to a military household in Shandong province. On the premise that the *Poems* was in fact none other than the long-lost *Classic of Music* (樂經 *Yuejing*), Liu provided a set of melodies in which each syllable was assigned a single pitch, which it would retain on each repetition.[98] In this way, the musical accompaniment reflected repetition that existed in the poetry. Figure 5.2 provides a transcription of Liu Lian's musical accompaniment to the same poem cited earlier (Mao 161). In Liu's composition, the correspondence between pitch and graph is evident in the fourth and fifth lines of the poem where the repetition of the two graphs <chuī srāeng> (吹笙) in the text necessitated the musical repetition of the pitch D (for <chuī>) and E (for <srāeng>) in the accompaniment.

Writing a little over a century later than Liu Lian, Wu Jishi provided an even more elaborate example of what the music of the *Poems* could look like if written according to a strict correspondence between phonology and musical pitch. Liu Lian had assigned a pitch to every graph, which it would maintain on each recurrence. For instance each instance of the graph <wǒ>

Figure 5.2 Liu Lian's musical setting of the *Poems* (Mao 161). The repetition of pitch reflecting repetition of graphs in the poem is illustrated. Transcription based on *lülü* notation in Liu Lian, *Yuejing yuanyi*, j. 5, 14a.

我 was set to the pitch C. Phonologically unrelated graphs, however, could be represented by the same pitch. Hence graphs that were phonologically distinct from <wǒ> 我, such as <jī> 之 and <cǔ> 瑟, were likewise represented by the pitch C. Wu Jishi, on the other hand, had created a set of densely cosmological rhyme tables, which delineated twelve rhyme groups correlated precisely to the twelve musical pitches (see chapter 2).[99] The melodies he composed for the *Poems* drew directly from these tables: the pitch he assigned to any given graph in his melodies was prescribed by the pitch assigned to that graph's corresponding rhyme group. Hence because <jī> 之, <wǒ> 我, and <cǔ> 瑟 were in different rhyme groups, they were represented by different pitches (D#, C#, and E, respectively) in Wu Jishi's melody. Conversely, because <srāeng> 笙, <kuāng> 筐, and <ziāng> 將 rhyme (according to Wu Jishi's system of phonological analysis) and were classified as belonging to the C-pitch rhyme group, he therefore assigned all of them the pitch C (see figure 5.3).[100] With this strict correspondence between pitch and phonology, repeated occurrences of the same graph were also necessarily assigned the same pitch.[101] Wu Jishi's musical accompaniment to the *Poems* balanced a cosmological concern for the *self-so* constant of Number underpinning his rhyme tables with the contemporary association of the human voice with "primordial sound," producing a systematic conversion of pronunciation to pitch that might appear less arbitrary than Liu Lian's and Zhu Xi's melodies. It further reflected his conviction that the original relationship between musical pitch and linguistic pronunciation was uncorrupted in antiquity. The resulting tune, however, sounds more like the product of twentieth-century atonal

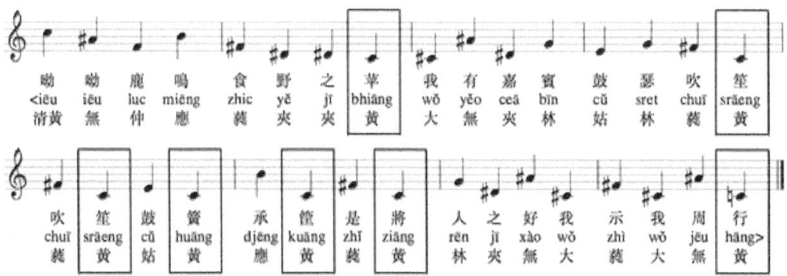

Figure 5.3 Wu Jishi's musical setting of the *Poems* (Mao 161). Recurrences of the pitch C for phonologically related graphs are illustrated. Transcription based on *lülü* notation in Wu Jishi, *Yinsheng jiyuan*, j. 6, 11b.

composition than premodern Chinese ritual music and does not fit any of the eighty-four theoretical modes employed by late imperial Chinese musicians, as it contains three consecutive semitones (B–C–C#).[102] It is perhaps unsurprising that Wu Jishi's composition method appears to have gained few followers.

As strange as the results of Wu Jishi's experiments in phonological music reconstruction were, they reflect a significant contemporary impulse toward unearthing the performative aspects of ancient classical texts. The extensive efforts to reveal the musical setting of ancient music also informed contemporary poetic composition. One seventeenth-century cosmologist argued that the *lü* (律) in *lüshi* (律詩 *lü* poetry) stood not for "regulated," as it is usually understood on account of the strict prosodic requirements of the genre. Instead he claimed that it reflected the alternative meaning of the graph as "musical pitch." This widely composed poetic genre could therefore be performed with music, in his view, based on the inherent relationship between language and musical pitch delineated in the rhyme tables of the eleventh-century cosmologist Shao Yong. To show how this would work in practice, he similarly presented an example of the musical accompaniment for a regulated-verse poem.[103] Although inspired by the cosmological fusion of philology and music theory, his musical composition did not reflect a direct correspondence between pitch and pronunciation. Instead it involved a pattern inspired by the arithmetic derivation of musical pitches, yielding similarly jarring melodies that abandoned the standard pentatonic or heptatonic modes in favor of a melody that included all twelve pitches.

The great late Ming musicologist Zhu Zaiyu proclaimed phonology and music to be unrelated (*bu xiangguan* 不相關), foreshadowing an approach to both fields that would gain currency in the eighteenth century.[104] Evidential Learning scholars for the most part inherited this position and followed the road initiated by Chen Di and Gu Yanwu, who analyzed the language of the *Poems* not in terms of its music, but by comparing rhyme usage both within the text of the *Poems* and throughout other early texts. In the sixteenth and seventeenth centuries there existed another major trend of *Poems* scholarship, which sought to highlight the original unity of music and language, framing the separation of the two fields as artificial. The study of the rhymes of the *Poems* is often upheld as a defining characteristic of the Evidential Learning approach and was also a major source for

Bernhard Karlgren's (1889–1978) innovative historical linguistic studies of Old Chinese. Analysis of rhyming in the *Poems* captivated an earlier Ming scholarly audience as well, but they did not universally see the primary issue as one of historical linguistic change.

Ming thinkers were aware of evidence-based approaches to the rhymes of ancient texts but largely held a different set of priorities. As Zhang Xianyi proposed in his lyrical readings of the *Classics*, there were multiple ways of finessing the pronunciation of a given line to make it rhyme. What mattered most was recognizing the verse underlying the prose, and the music underlying the poetry.

For today's reader, the study of the Classics may bring to mind the close textual analysis of weighty ancient philosophical works. Sixteenth- and seventeenth-century readers certainly attended to the moral lessons contained within such texts. In the Ming, however, these canonical works could also be read as poetic and musical gems. They were meant to be recited aloud and even sung to accompaniment. As models for composition in the present, understanding their linguistic characteristics was essential for the poet who wished to faithfully capture their style. Philological analysis was also necessary for appreciating the artistic merit of the Classics themselves. Innovators like Chen Di made the case for understanding language as constantly evolving, bound to necessary historical change. Many of Chen Di's contemporaries, however, sought universal constants that made the sages and their literary production immediately accessible to a contemporary audience.

PART III

Philology
The Making and Remaking of a Discipline

CHAPTER 6

Afterlives

*Ming Methods and Their Competition in the
Eighteenth and Nineteenth Centuries*

The introduction to this book cited the disparaging remarks applied to Ming texts in the *Siku quanshu*, the signal intellectual project of the late eighteenth century. The ideological and intellectual motivations underlying the *Siku quanshu* editors' criticism of the past have been previously documented.[1] As a court-sponsored venue for establishing and promoting the new values of Evidential Learning, the *Siku quanshu* played a central role in defining the intellectual priorities of its age. Editorial decisions about which texts to include in the *Siku quanshu* and which to bypass or relegate to a summary in its accompanying bibliographical catalog, the *Siku quanshu zongmu* (四庫全書總目 Comprehensive catalog of the *Siku quanshu*), had a concrete effect on the later availability and awareness of Ming texts. Writing in the late nineteenth century, Lao Naixuan 勞乃宣 (1843–1921) observed the difficulty of locating Ming philological texts which had been excluded from the *Siku quanshu* proper. He also affirmed his faith in the accuracy of the editorial evaluation of these excluded texts in the accompanying bibliography, which represented "settled opinion."[2] Promoting precise textual scholarship and critical analysis of ancient texts, Evidential Learning scholars saw little value in the cosmological, metaphysical, and literary modes of philological study that flourished in the Ming.

I have adopted the term *Evidential Learning* throughout this book to refer to the community of late eighteenth- and early nineteenth-century textual scholars. Evidential Learning is the standard English translation of the Chinese term *kaozhengxue* (考證學), which is widely employed in both Chinese and Western discussions of the period. It is worth noting, however, that Qing writers rarely employed the term *kaozhengxue*.[3] The term became prevalent around the turn of the twentieth century and may have reached its current prominence as a result of its usage in Liang Qichao's seminal 1920 *Qingdai xueshu gailun* (清代學術概論 An overview of Qing dynasty scholarship). Thinkers associated with this movement did invoke the terms *kaozheng* and *kaoju* 考據 (lit., "to validate on the basis of evidence") in favorable reference to a particular methodology. Some eighteenth-century philologists further referred to their enterprise as *Ancient Learning* (*guxue* 古學), and nineteenth-century writers would come to apply the term *Han Learning* (*Hanxue* 漢學) to retrospectively assign a label to the textual study of the previous century. The term *kaozhengjia* or *kaojujia* ("the school of *kaozheng/kaoju*") also achieved currency in the nineteenth century, although it was more often used by critics of this method than its proponents.[4] Their methodology typically involved the corroboration of textual evidence with copious historically grounded examples. As we will examine in greater depth in the following chapter, these scholars also explicitly framed their work as belonging to a shared tradition of learning, albeit one not so fixed as the later label of Evidential Learning might suggest.

The emergence of the Evidential Learning methodology as a priority within the field of philology instigated a redefinition of the discipline. Evidential Learning methods were applied to many other fields, including natural science and history.[5] But proper classical philology (*xiaoxue*) came to be focused primarily on ancient texts, with other forms of evidence and fields of knowledge framed as largely irrelevant to the study of language. Evidential Learning philologists were chiefly concerned with the language of antiquity, in particular, as reflected in ancient writings. While Ming thinkers tended to highlight the limitations of this textual legacy, Evidential Learning scholars employed classical texts as the essential source base for corroborating information on the ancient language.

Despite the influence of Evidential Learning rhetoric, Ming methods did not disappear, and major sixteenth- and seventeenth-century texts continued to be reprinted in new editions. This chapter examines the persistence of Ming texts, tracing their influence through the nineteenth century. In following the reception history of books and methods, this chapter considers several questions: Were Ming texts abridged or expanded in later editions? What were the stated goals of circulating Ming books, and who made use of them? Which texts were most sought after, and why did they continue to speak to later readers? On the one hand, Ming methods served as an important alternative for philologists who were dissatisfied with the approach of vocal Evidential Learning practitioners. Ming innovations were also presented in adapted forms, stripped from their original context in order to better fit the scholarly priorities of the time.

The 1770s witnessed a transformation in the production of philological texts.[6] The nature of this shift may be best understood as one of quality, rather than solely quantity. From a quantitative perspective, the 1770s did represent an increase in philological production when compared to the early eighteenth century and previous periods. However, one could make the same argument for the late sixteenth century in comparison to the early sixteenth. Was the late sixteenth century a philological turn of its own? In some sense the answer could be that China experienced multiple philological turns. The meaning and impact of those turns, however, differed. The sixteenth-century turn in intellectual culture witnessed the rise of various communities of learning, which emphasized consultation and corroboration with contemporary specialists in the production of valid knowledge, a topic we will pick up more fully in the next chapter. The valence of philology, however, a field that attracted a disproportionate amount of contemporary scholarly attention, was broadened to include various other fields in response to new concerns about the validity of observed knowledge. The late eighteenth-century turn represented a shift in the boundaries of knowledge, which pared away these other fields from the study of language. While indebted to the emergence of contemporary disciplinary communities in the sixteenth century, eighteenth-century scholars debated the validity of aligning disparate fields in the generation of philological knowledge. By focusing on the eighteenth- and nineteenth-century Qing relationship with the scholarly world of the late Ming, the remainder of this book examines how and why such a transition occurred.

Previous accounts have generally overlooked the considerable influence of Ming philology into the twentieth century, only occasionally highlighting a few exceptional figures for foreshadowing Evidential Learning.[7] This chapter illustrates how Ming methods survived in the Qing as an alternative method of learning for those who disagreed with the premises of Evidential Learning. It further examines how Ming texts came to be adapted in a new intellectual context, in some cases even to meet the needs of Evidential Learning scholars.

Alternative Philologies in the Eighteenth and Nineteenth Centuries

The eighteenth century witnessed a clear narrowing of the boundaries surrounding the field of philology as practiced by the majority of contemporary scholars. Nevertheless the fusion of cosmology, music, and language remained a persuasive form of philological reasoning in some communities. Previous studies of philosophical syncretism between Evidential Learning and Neo-Confucian approaches to knowledge have primarily examined cases in which a single scholar might pursue Evidential Learning-style textual analysis of ancient texts but also subscribe to the moral reading of the Classics according to the standard Learning of the Way commentaries.[8] Less appreciated is the fact that philology itself enjoyed multiple definitions during this period. While proponents of Evidential Learning advocated for a particular definition of the discipline, their opponents maintained or adapted Ming methods of philology. As difficult as it is to imagine on the basis of the *Siku quanshu* discourse, which has had a disproportionate influence on current understandings of the period, some eighteenth-century thinkers looked back to the Ming as the heyday of philology.

Cosmological Approaches

One of the most striking features of Ming philology is its focus on Number, and the linkage of cosmological and musical modes of analysis (see chapter 1). This brand of study remained at the forefront of phonological analysis in the late seventeenth and early eighteenth centuries. During this period, scholars such as Zhao Shaoji 趙紹箕 (fl. 1674), Ma Ziyuan 馬自援 (fl. 1671–1681), Gu Chenxu 顧陳垿 (1678–1747), Xiong Shibo 熊士伯 (fl. 1642–1719), Shi Kui 是奎 (1654–1740), Lin Benyu 林本裕 (fl. 1690–1708), and Pan Lei 潘耒 (1646–1708) composed phonological studies investigating the cosmological origins of sound, which liberally cited from earlier Ming studies. Despite their linguistic expertise, these scholars demonstrated interest and ability in multiple fields, as well as a desire to create systematic links between their study. Gu Chenxu, for instance, first achieved prominence as a mathematician, later composing a study on the arithmetical derivations of musical pitches.[9] He also wrote on phonology. While later Evidential Learning scholars, such as Qian Daxin, would display a similar breadth of scholarly interests, they generally instituted a clear separation of materials and methods in their approach to these varied subjects. Gu Chenxu, on the other hand, applied methods of arithmetic and musical pitch derivation to the classification of linguistic sound in his phonological study, *Bashi zhuzi tushuo* (八矢注字圖說 Diagrams and explanations of the eight-arrow method of annotating graphs). Over the course of the eighteenth century, those who opposed Evidential Learning would continue to adopt such integrative methods, which had developed over the course of the late Ming.

The implications of a cosmology-based approach to linguistic study in the eighteenth century are exemplified by Long Weilin 龍為霖 (1689–1756). Long received his *jinshi* degree in 1706 at the young age of seventeen and subsequently served in posts throughout Yunnan and Guangdong. His acoustic study *Benyun yide* (本韻一得 Apprehending the original rhyme at once), printed in 1751 during a critical period in the formation of Evidential Learning practices, was primarily concerned with phonological analysis but was premised on the fundamental relationship between linguistic and musical sound. Echoing the statements of his Ming predecessors, Long claimed that "the innate primordial sounds of human beings each have a *self-so* unchanging principle. It is not something that can suffer the slightest modification through personal opinion."[10] The key to surpassing "personal opinion" and revealing the *self-so* nature of human speech was to model a phonological system according to the principles and terminology of music theory.

The musical reasoning that informed Long's phonological categories provided a method to refute the renowned seventeenth-century evidential scholar Gu Yanwu's analyses of ancient rhymes. Gu Yanwu famously dismissed the poetry of the postclassical tradition as a valid source for studying the rhymes of ancient poetry, even when such poetry explicitly imitated the ancient style. This stance was a repudiation of the previously dominant mode of analyzing ancient phonology, which since its origins in the twelfth century had taken for granted the applicability of postclassical poetry written in imitation of earlier models. In particular, Gu Yanwu argued that the foremost archaist poet of the eighth century, Han Yu 韓愈 (768–824), did not truly follow practices of ancient rhyming.

Long Weilin believed that his new rhyme classification system, which was based on the relationship of musical pitches, proved that Han Yu had in fact accurately modeled ancient phonology in his rhyme schemes. Long argued that Gu Yanwu's methods were fundamentally flawed because he had insisted on limiting himself to the extant textual corpus of antiquity. He further contended that "of the three thousand ancient poems [from which Confucius supposedly culled three hundred], there are presently only one-tenth preserved—how could we know that there were not rhyming graphs that matched those of Master Han?" Observing that the textual legacy of antiquity had been irreparably damaged by the first Qin emperor's infamous burning of books, Long therefore claimed that it was impossible "to produce evidential research on every single text [that had originally existed] (一一考證)."[11] In this way, Long questioned the very premise of Evidential Learning, as practiced by scholars like Gu Yanwu, that the historical textual record could provide a meaningful basis for philological study. Given that there remained only a small amount of rhyming text from antiquity, how could one systematically describe ancient rhymes on the basis of piecemeal textual evidence? By incorporating methodologies from music, a field with an arithmetical and cosmological basis, Long believed he could surpass these limitations of the textual record.

Long Weilin repeatedly cited seventeenth-century cosmological acoustic studies.[12] Although written well after the peak of acoustic studies in the late Ming, his work followed a similar logic and in its contrast to Evidential Learning illustrates the appeal of combined musico-linguistic studies to late imperial audiences. Musical acoustics was argued to operate according to constant laws as a result of its arithmetical foundation (see chapter 1). If musical and linguistic sound were indeed connected, then these same laws should govern phonology. For late Ming scholars, as well as some in the eighteenth century, this reasoning was more persuasive than a gathering of textual evidence. The notion of a fundamental unity of different varieties of sound provided such scholars with methods of phonological analysis, which in their view shifted the subjective study of linguistic categories in the direction of a precise science.

Although Long Weilin was harshly criticized by the *Siku quanshu* editors who saw his approach as antithetical to Evidential Learning, *Benyun yide* was employed as a reference work and cited in analyses of ancient poetry by his contemporaries.[13] Musico-linguistic analyses remained an alternative path of phonological study to Evidential Learning through the nineteenth century.¹⁴ An exemplary mid-nineteenth-century work, *Guyin leibiao* (古音類表 Categorized tables of ancient pronunciation), was similarly framed as a corrective to Evidential Learning as represented by its leading names, Gu Yanwu, Jiang Yong, and Duan Yucai 段玉裁 (1735–1815), whom the author, Fu Shoutong 傅壽彤 (*jinshi* 1853), criticized throughout the text. Like Long Weilin, Fu Shoutong described the efforts of the Evidential Learning scholars, which were based on collation of classical texts, as "searching for ancient pronunciation in minute remnants."¹⁵ The result of this text-based approach was inevitably "conjecture" (*yi* 臆). A preface to the text likewise claimed that "although researchers of ancient rhymes are increasingly many, they are merely able to create categories according to the Classics and none are able to investigate why they change. . . . [Fu Shoutong] has surely revealed the *self-so* nature of the Heavenly Way."¹⁶ To surpass the limits of ancient texts, Fu proposed another phonological system based on musical pitch. Although his focus on ancient rhymes was in keeping with the philological trends of the time, Fu validated his claims on the basis of the *self-so* connection between music and language, rather than the textual corroboration typical of Evidential Learning scholars.

Cosmology-inspired phonological methods traveled beyond China over the course of the seventeenth and eighteenth centuries, featuring in Korean and Vietnamese discussions of phonology.¹⁷ Scholars involved in developing phonographic writing in other East Asian regions also regularly invoked Shao Yong's methods with claims that such writing systems could corroborate the enormous number of linguistic sounds Shao had calculated.¹⁸ Despite the authoritative position of Evidential Learning conveyed by sources such as the *Siku quanshu* bibliography, alternative cosmological approaches remained a strong undercurrent in philological research across early modern East Asia.

In the face of Western imperialist incursions in the mid-to-late nineteenth century, Chinese scholars increasingly evaluated the premises of Western learning. Although technological and military knowledge demanded the greatest attention, other fields, including linguistics, became loci for epistemological debates about the relative merits of various traditions of learning. One late nineteenth-century scholar, Zhou Yun 周贇 (c. 1835–1911), employed cosmological methods to dispute the validity of the West as a standard for linguistic study. His *Shanmen xinyu* (山門新語 New words from [Zhou] Shanmen) integrated the study of phonology with musical pitches and *Changes* cosmology. Zhou produced similar cosmological diagrams to those of his Ming predecessors but bolstered them with maps of the globe, with the aim of demonstrating why China was geomantically situated to have the best phonology for a universal base of study (see figure 6.1). Zhou claimed to have demonstrated that "only China has received the central *qi* of heaven and earth, and its linguistic sounds therefore reach above to the patterns of heaven and below to the patterns of earth."[19] In the context of late nineteenth-century Western threats to China's sovereignty, Zhou's study had the broader goal of demonstrating that it was in fact the West, typified by its "one-sided partiality" (*pian* 偏), that should follow China, on account of its "centrality" (*zhong* 中). The only cure for the West was to "cause Westerners to recognize their own partiality and transform their partial (linguistic) sounds with the level, rising, falling, and entering tones of China and transform their partial (moral) views with the humaneness, righteousness, ritual, and wisdom of China."[20] Here Zhou established an analogy between the cardinal Confucian virtues he associated with Chinese civilization and the nature of Chinese phonology, both of which benefited from the geomantically superior position of China. Zhou primarily targeted the West but occasionally referenced Evidential Learning thinkers, such as Qian Daxin, as examples of scholars who had mistaken the purpose and methods of philology.[21] In particular, the Evidential Learning thinkers erroneously, in Zhou's view, focused on differences in pronunciation as a distinction between "past and present" (*gujin* 古今) instead of "China and the outside" (*zhongwai* 中外). He further opined that "experts of literary study and Evidential Learning" (詞章考據名家), including Gu Yanwu, were not true "experts in phonology" (非韻學名家). For Zhou, their overreliance on texts had blinded them to the immutable cosmological properties of musical acoustics.[22]

Manchu and Sanskrit

The influence of Buddhist monks and their use of Sanskrit as a tool for phonological analysis was generally denied by the mainstream of the Evidential Learning community. These scholars proposed that the apparent Buddhist traces within the medieval philological tradition had merely obscured the earlier Chinese origins of phonological analysis. They also claimed that the phonetic classification system of Sanskrit was inapplicable

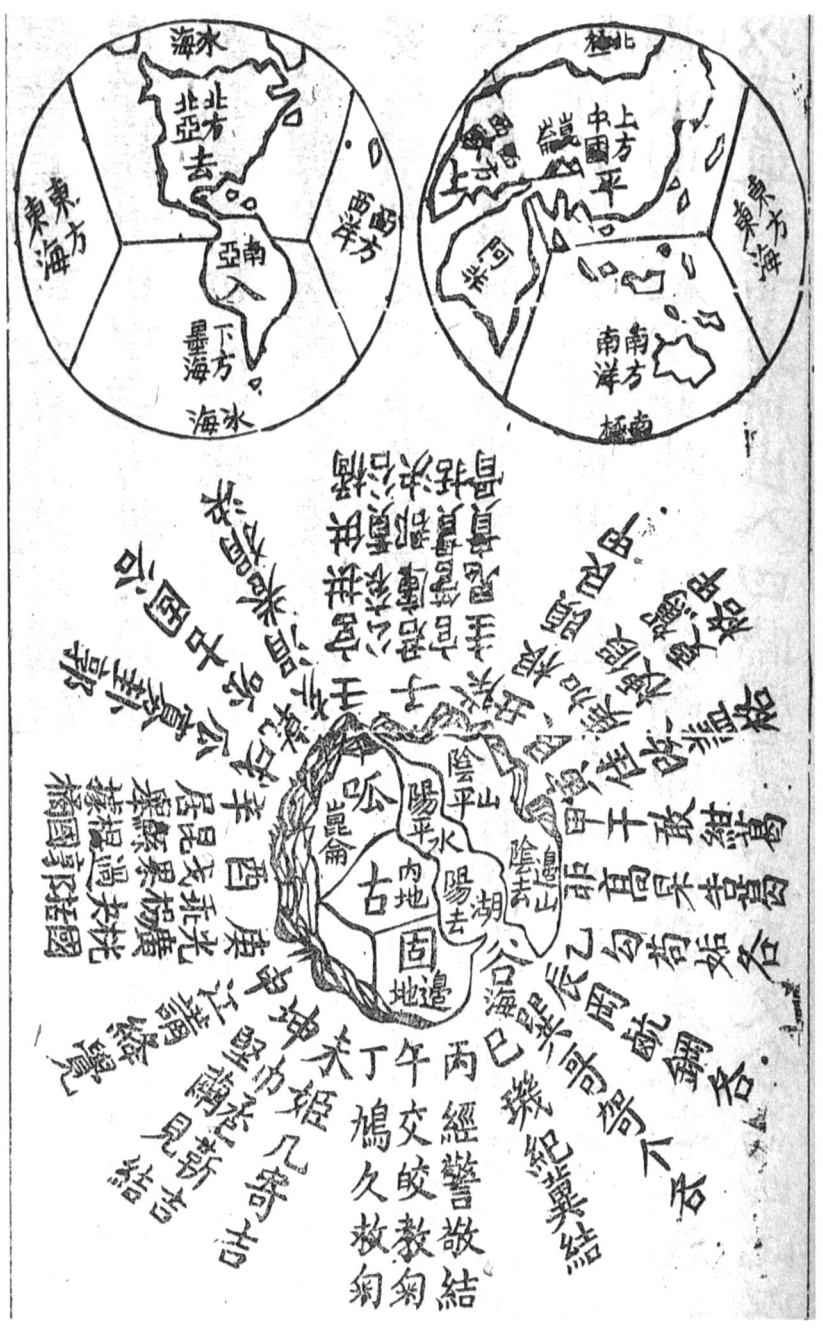

Figure 6.1 Zhou Yun's global linguistic diagram. Zhou Yun, *Shanmen xinyu*, j. 1, *Zhou shi qinlü qieyin*, 36a. (Image courtesy of Harvard-Yenching Library.)

to Chinese.²³ For Evidential Learning classicists, the Ming interaction with Buddhist language practices was symbolic of the corruption of correct Confucian learning that had taken place in the sixteenth century.

Nevertheless, discussion of phonographic writing persisted strongly in the Qing period. This attention to phonographic scripts can be attributed in part to the introduction of the new phonographic "state script" (*guoshu* 國書) of Manchu.²⁴ The discourse surrounding the Manchu state script was deeply influenced by Ming discussions of cosmology and Sanskrit. Late seventeenth- and early eighteenth-century treatises inherited the linkage of cosmology and phonographic writing but added Manchu to existing discussions of Sanskrit and Latin. This link is most explicit in the work of the early eighteenth-century scholar Xiong Shibo, who situated his analysis of Manchu writing with reference to two influential late Ming studies of phonographic script: Zhao Yiguang's work on Sanskrit, and Nicolas Trigault and his collaborators' discussion of Latin (figure 6.2). The imperially commissioned *Tongwen yuntong* (同文韻統 Systematized rhymes of the unified script) of 1750 would later align Manchu, Chinese, Tibetan, and Sanskrit for purposes of transcription. The description of Manchu and phonographic writing throughout this widely circulated text alluded to terminology created within a context of Sanskrit phonological analysis. *Tongwen yuntong* further developed a system for representing each syllable in three parts, resonating with the earlier tradition of tripartite phonetic notation created within the operatic and cosmological phonology of the late Ming (see chapter 4).²⁵

Qing discussions of Manchu remained in dialogue with Ming texts and in some cases explicitly incorporated the late Ming cosmological discourse surrounding phonographic writing. *Dengqie yuansheng*, for instance, was rooted in Shao Yong's cosmological methods and their extension by late Ming scholars. The connection between Manchu script and previous cosmological research is further evidenced by a remarkable text by the Manchu bannerman Du-si-de 都四德 titled *Huangzhong tongyun* (黃鍾通韻 Comprehending rhymes through the pitch C), printed in 1753. As with many works of Ming acoustic study, the title of this text suggests a connection between language and music. Forced to make a choice, *Siku quanshu* compilers assigned the text to the music section of its bibliography. The editors, however, devoted most of their evaluative essay to Du-si-de's phonological claims, which occupy a sizable portion of the original text. Du-si-de argued that Manchu script "contained all graphs and all sounds" and

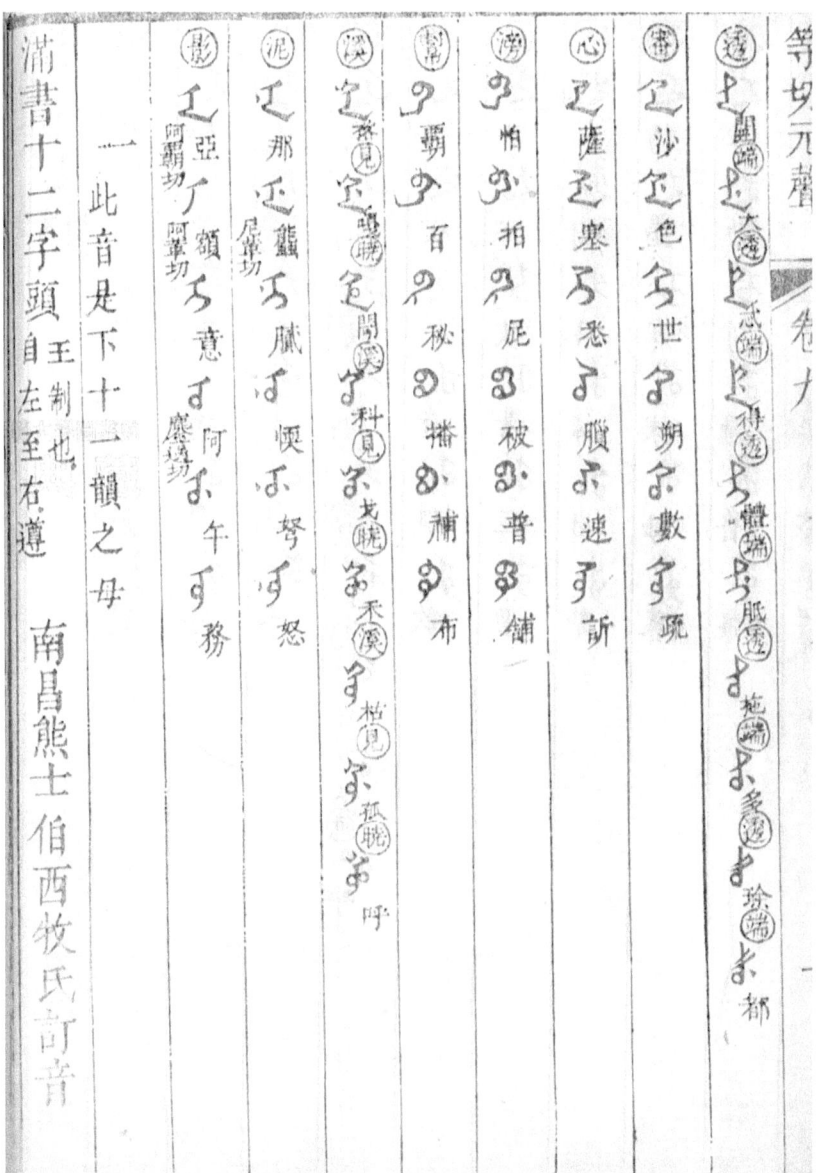

Figure 6.2 Xiong Shibo's phonological discussions of Manchu, Sanskrit, and Latin. Xiong Shibo, *Dengqie yuansheng*, j. 8, *Yue shi shi zimu*, 10a, *Yue Xiru ermu zi*, 2b; j. 9, *Yue qingshu zitou*, 1a. (Images courtesy of the National Taiwan Normal University Library.)

Figure 6.2 (continued)

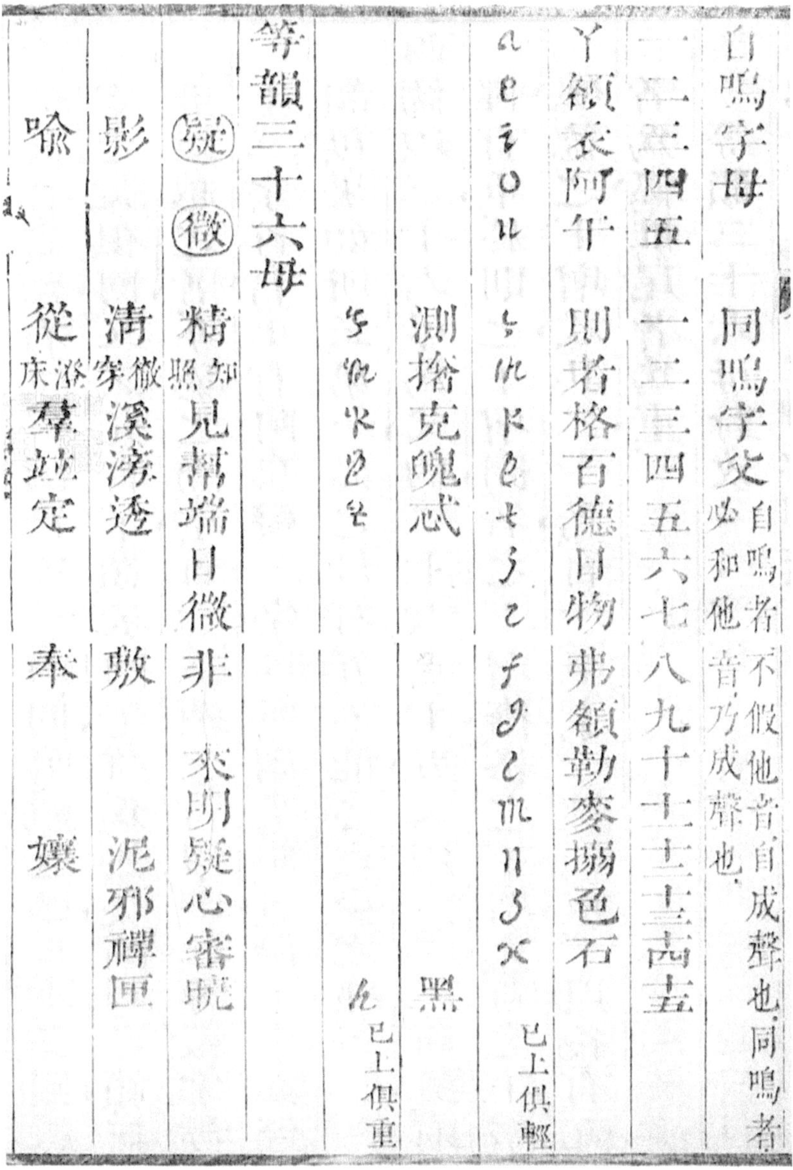

自鳴字母　同鳴字父　自鳴者不假他音自成聲也同鳴者必和他音乃成聲也

一二三四五　一二三四五六七八九十十一十二十三十四十五

丫額衣阿午　則者格百德日物弗額勒麥搦色石

a e i o u　ç ch k p t j v f g l m n s x　已上俱輕

測撦克魄忒　黑

ç' ch' k' p' t'　h'　已上俱重

等韻三十六母

疑　微　精　知照　見　幫　端　日　微　非　來　明　疑　心　審　曉

影　清　徹穿　溪　滂　透　敷　泥　邪　禪　匣

喻　從　澄床　羣　並　定　奉　孃

Figure 6.2 (continued)

was capable of notating any product of sound-based *qi*.[26] Like many Ming acoustic studies, Du-si-de designated a set of twelve finals to correspond with the twelve pitches of the musical scale. Much to the consternation of the *Siku quanshu* editors, he seems to have overlooked the standard organization of the Manchu syllabary according to twelve classes, instead creating his own set of twelve Manchu finals. Du-si-de elaborated this relationship between linguistic and musical pitch in a concentric circle diagram modeled on a seventeenth-century precedent, which aligned each of his Manchu syllable classes with a musical pitch (see figure 6.3).[27] Despite the

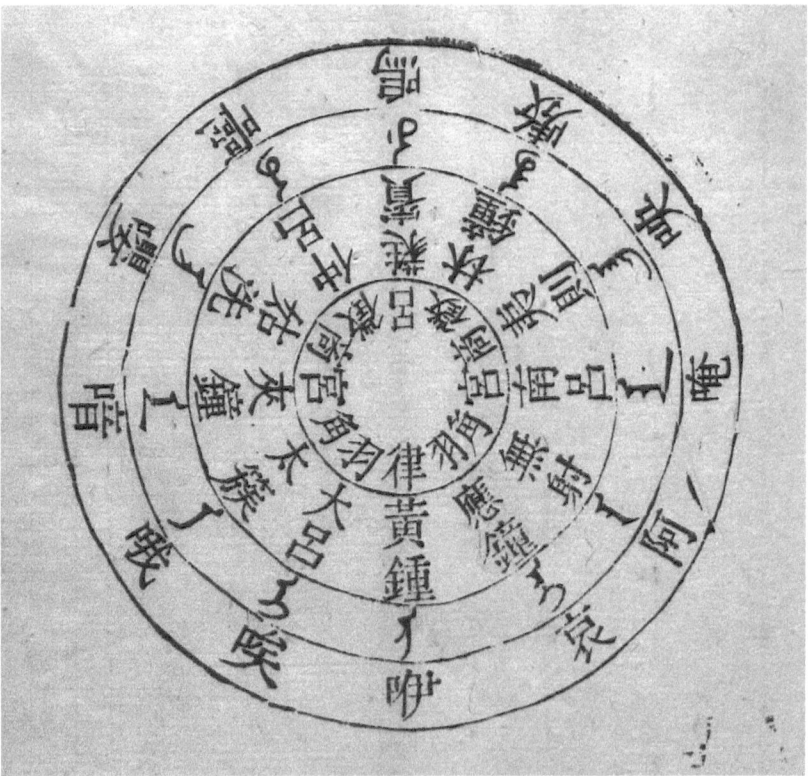

Figure 6.3 Du-si-de's diagram of Manchu-pitch correlations. The outer layer of the circle contains Chinese transcriptions of the Manchu graphs in the second layer. The inner two layers contain names of pitches from the musical scale. Du-si-de, *Huangzhong tongyun*, j. xia, 10a. Seventeenth-century precedents for this style of diagram can be found in Qiao Zhonghe, *Yuanyun pu, juanshou*, 44a; Ge Zhongxuan, *Tailü*, j. 4, j. 5; Fan Tengfeng, *Wufang yuanyin, tushuo*, 4a. (Image courtesy of the Library of Congress.)

negative appraisal of this text in *Siku quanshu*, it appears to have inspired linguistic thinkers to connect music, language, and cosmology through the Manchu script well into the nineteenth century.[28]

Ideological language policies of the Qing state created a practical need for proficiency in Manchu writing among a subset of officials and bannermen, and language scholars capitalized on the potential of this script for phonetic description.[29] The study of Sanskrit persisted during the Qing as well. The prolific late eighteenth-century philologist Zhou Chun 周春 (d. 1815), for instance, authored a text entitled *Xitan ao lun* (悉曇奧論 Treatise on the profundities of Sanskrit writing), which advocated for the relevance of applying Sanskrit methods to the study of Chinese. Like Qing adherents to cosmology, Zhou presented his work as an alternative to Evidential Learning and even tried unsuccessfully to convert major evidential scholars, such as Qian Daxin and Shao Jinhan 邵晉涵 (1743–1796). As Zhou wrote in one such attempt to persuade Qian Daxin, "phonologists of our dynasty tend to promote Gu Yanwu or Mao Qiling. But I believe that phonology must consider the initial spellers (*zimu* 字母) in order to obtain its foundation."[30] The initial spellers Zhou invoked were a set of syllables that had provided the phonological framework of rhyme tables for centuries. The origins of these tables and their spelling methods were decidedly Indic in Zhou's opinion; to claim otherwise, in his view, would be as absurd as denying the foreign origin of Euclid's *Elements*.[31]

Zhou Chun was in frequent communication with the period's Evidential Learning network but occupied an uneasy position in their view. Ruan Yuan 阮元 (1764–1849), a major contemporary practitioner and patron of Evidential Learning, prefaced one of Zhou Chun's philological works and praised aspects of his scholarship. Ruan cautioned, however, that "initial spellers are nothing more than a means to an end" and should not be understood to suggest that "trifling Brāhmaṇ writing (i.e., Sanskrit script)" (區區 婆羅門書) was superior to Chinese.[32] During the mid-eighteenth century a genealogy of Evidential Learning was taking form, featuring foundational figures such as Gu Yanwu, Jiang Yong, and Dai Zhen, who transmitted this learning to Duan Yucai, Qian Daxin, and other later eighteenth-century scholars (see chapter 7). Zhou Chun acknowledged the existence of this lineage but criticized its main constituents as misguided in their approach to philology. Gu Yanwu had claimed that the language of antiquity differed systematically from the present. But Zhou Chun argued that Gu's proposed pronunciations were anything but systematic. By ignoring the principles of "initial spellers," Zhou claimed that Gu Yanwu had created an arbitrary system in which "heaven" (<tiēn> 天) could rhyme with "earth" (<dhì> 地) and "east" (<dūng> 東) could rhyme with "west" (<sēi> 西).[33] Zhou Chun proposed an alternative "orthodox lineage" (*zhengpai* 正派), beginning from Song thinkers such as Shao Yong and Zheng Qiao, and including Ming scholars such as Lü Weiqi, as well as, from more recent times, Li Guangdi and Pan Lei, emphasizing those who recognized the importance of documenting pronunciation by means of phonetic spelling.[34] While the *Siku quanshu* editors would ultimately blame Pan Lei for not following in the footsteps of his teacher Gu Yanwu, Zhou Chun remarked that Pan Lei's only defect was not sufficiently "attacking his teacher's explanations."[35]

This kind of alternative philological lineage that emphasized "spelling" enjoyed currency into the early nineteenth century. Li Ruzhen 李汝珍 (1763–1830), a major phonologist and novelist, was greatly interested in the spelling methods of Indic scripts, which one of the preface writers to his compendious *Li shi yinjian* (李氏音鑑 Master Li's Mirror of sound) connected to the "essence of combining graphs in our state script [i.e. Manchu]."[36] Li Ruzhen, like Zhou Chun, did not fully embrace Ming integrative methods. The prefaces to his *Yinjian* highlighted his skills at astrological divination, not for his ability to apply these techniques to the study of language but as evidence of broad-learnedness.[37] At the same time, Li Ruzhen largely avoided citing Evidential Learning scholars in his encyclopedic tome, preferring to cite Ming philologists, ranging from Learning of the Mind philological thinkers, such as Wang Yingdian, to opera theorists, such as Shen Chongsui.[38] He also collaborated with a contemporary community of philologists who operated outside of the bounds of Evidential Learning circles.[39] While he did not explicitly criticize Evidential Learning, his emphasis on "contemporary pronunciation" (*shiyin* 時音) and citation of Ming scholars (and neglect of Evidential Learning thinkers), as well as his interest in phonographic writing, suggest his conception of an alternative philology.

Li Ruzhen's alternative philology was developed in collaboration with his brother-in-law, Xu Guilin 許桂林 (1779–1822), whom he claimed as his primary influence in phonological studies.[40] Xu departed from the norms of Evidential Learning by embracing the phonographic Manchu syllabary as useful for distinguishing features of ancient phonology.[41] Xu Guilin wrote a preface to Li Ruzhen's *Yinjian*, in which he listed a genealogy of recent philology, similar to that of Zhou Chun's, which highlighted the contribution of the seventeenth-century Hangzhou network and elided the Evidential Learning lineage.[42] Xu Guilin's own phonological work attacked the Evidential Learning methods of his contemporaries.[43] In Xu's view, Evidential Learning scholars, in spite of their self-proclaimed adherence to antiquity, ultimately ended up applying present-day notions to the past, such as their dismissal of "regional pronunciation" (*fangyin* 方音) in the Classics.[44]

Xu Guilin and Li Ruzhen both disputed the criticism of "regional pronunciation" and the overemphasis on antiquity among Evidential Learning scholars. Li Ruzhen boldly defended his focus on "contemporary pronunciation":

> Sound emerges from the mind and is based in what is heavenly-so. It cannot rely on the efforts of humans. . . . If one were to claim that modern pronunciation differs from the ancient and is therefore vulgar (*su* 俗) . . . then we can be thankful that the *fendian* [legendary texts of distant antiquity] were lost, for if they were still extant, then I suppose the Six Classics would also unavoidably be vulgar.[45]

Reflecting on the premise that language had devolved since antiquity, Li Ruzhen observed that language had existed since long before the Classics. Therefore those who claimed language to be in a constant state of decreasing purity were in fact unintentionally lambasting the Classics as much as they were criticizing the present. Li Ruzhen's great encyclopedic travelogue novel, *Flowers in the Mirror* (鏡花緣 *Jinghua yuan*), similarly parodied blind adherence to a perceived language of antiquity.[46] In one chapter, the novel's sojourners arrive at Gentleman's Country (Shushiguo 淑士國), where they encounter an absurd persistence in ancient usage, exemplified by the barkeeper who asks: "Wouldst thou have one flagon of ale, or two?" (酒要一壺乎，兩壺乎).[47] The mid-seventeenth century literary figure Li Yu proposed the notion that the ancients spoke the modern Chinese of their day and if born in the present would surely speak a contemporary version of Chinese (see chapter 4). By contrast, Gu Yanwu, by many accounts the foundational figure of Evidential Learning, had considered recovering ancient pronunciations, radically different from those of his time, for use in contemporary spoken language. While later Evidential Learning scholars tried to walk back this proposal, the association of Evidential Learning with linguistic purification and adherence to antiquity clearly perturbed some contemporary scholars.

Adaptation and Transformation of Ming Texts and Methods

Despite the surprising persistence of Ming methods in some Qing philological circles, the scope of philology within the bulk of extant texts narrowed considerably in the mid-to-late eighteenth century. Even critics of Evidential Learning did not necessarily adopt earlier Ming methods wholesale. Although both Li Ruzhen and Zhou Chun embraced phonographic writing, invoked the concept of *self-so*, and questioned undue attention to ancient language, neither scholar promoted the broader relevance of cosmology to phonology. Zhou Chun, for instance, noted his puzzlement at the inclusion of Shao Yong's cosmological tables in the Ming aria-composition handbook *Xiaoyu pu*.[48] The tightly knit fusion of language-related fields, which had allowed Ming scholars of opera, music, cosmology, and language to find mutual benefit in each other's work, began to unravel in the eighteenth century. Nevertheless sixteenth- and seventeenth-century texts continued to be reprinted in new editions throughout this later period. Such works served different goals and appeared in revised formats within this new intellectual atmosphere.

The Problem: Categorizations and the Siku quanshu Dilemma

The continued circulation of Ming philological texts is evident throughout eighteenth- and nineteenth-century bibliographic catalogs, which routinely listed certain Ming titles. Most unexpected is the regularity with which Wei Jiao's *Liushu jingyun* appears, as well as works of cosmological phonology by Chen Jinmo and Wu Jishi.[49] Ownership, citation, and circulation need not be understood as endorsement. Ming texts acted as a foil for the *Siku quanshu* editors in their codification of Evidential Learning values. Nevertheless, acknowledging Ming scholarship created a dilemma for these scholars. By the mid-eighteenth century, notions of what constituted the discipline of philology had shifted. Compilers of the *Siku quanshu* explicitly acknowledged the struggles they faced in categorizing Ming works. A representative example is the lexicon *Renzi ce* (認字測 Conjectures on recognizing graphs) by Zhou Yu 周宇, a characteristic Ming metaphysical dictionary of Chinese graphs in the vein of Wei Jiao's Learning of the Mind philology, first printed in 1587. The *Siku quanshu* editors wrote of this text that "it is neither philology (*xiaoxue*) nor a record of philosophical sayings (*yulu* 語錄). As there is no category in which it can be placed (*wu lei ke ru* 無類可入) within the *Siku*, it is tentatively appended within the various schools (*zajia* 雜家)."[50] The "various schools" category provided a location for *Siku quanshu* editors to assign texts that did not clearly fit their scheme. It is clear from their evaluation of *Renzi ce* that the editors acknowledged the potential understanding of the text as philological. They were nonetheless definitive in their statement that *Renzi ce* was not philology according to their conception of the term. Seventeenth-century bibliographers, on the other hand, typically placed *Renzi ce* under the philology category.[51] *Renzi ce* was printed in multiple editions and was a highly regarded work of philological scholarship in its time. Two hundred years later it was barely recognized as belonging to the discipline.

Confusion over how to categorize Ming texts can be found throughout the *Siku quanshu* catalog, resulting in the "tentative" (*gu* 姑) placement of boundary-crossing texts into whichever category seemed most appropriate to the editors.[52] This confusion was typically framed not as a neutral recognition of ambiguity, but rather as an accusation of something wrong with the Ming. Qing scholarly criticism of the Ming took many forms, but one clear concern among the *Siku quanshu* editors was a perceived lack of clarity in categories of knowledge. The previous chapters of this book have revealed that Ming scholarship was not truly defined by a lack of clarity but instead adopted a different definition of these categories. As Ming texts continued to circulate over the subsequent centuries, Qing scholars adopted various approaches to accommodate this mode of scholarship within the new disciplinary borders of philology.

Despite the persistent circulation of Ming texts through the eighteenth and nineteenth centuries, a new set of values came to figure in accounts of philological learning, especially within Evidential Learning circles. This shift in the nature of learning is even further evident when we examine later editions of Ming texts, as well as new works inspired by Ming models. Alterations to earlier versions suggest a new conception of the discipline, in which philology pertains to strictly linguistic matters and is not benefited by connections across fields of learning. Texts that had formerly focused on theoretical inquiry into the cosmological basis of sound were stripped of their cosmological framework, with new attention directed toward their description of vernacular phonology, as well as their pedagogical utility. Similarly, while metaphysical inquiry into the construction of graphs was widely repudiated, Ming metaphysical dictionaries were routinely cited as useful sources for ancient graph forms. The sung voice and its relation to spoken language remained an object of study, but one that was increasingly separated from the field of classical studies.

Cosmological Phonology and the Origins of Chinese-English Lexicography

The mid-seventeenth-century rhyme dictionary *Wufang yuanyin* (五方元音 Primordial sounds of the five directions) by Fan Tengfeng 樊騰鳳 (1601–1644) is a representative example of the period's cosmological phonology. Its title indicates the text's focus on "primordial sound" that underlay linguistic and musical sound. The opening sentence of the preface to the first edition cites Shao Yong, whose cosmological influence is visible throughout the paratextual material.[53] Early editions of the text follow this preface with the Yellow River Diagram (*Hetu* 河圖) and a diagram correlating the twelve musical pitches with twelve rhyme groups, adapted from another late Ming philological text.[54]

Despite its condemnation by the *Siku quanshu* editors, as well as the clear influence of cosmology on the theoretical structure of the text, this work enjoyed at least two hundred new editions over the Qing period.[55] The first adaptation of the text took place at the hands of a Chinese bannerman, Nian Xiyao 年希堯 (1671–1738), who revised the text once in 1710 and again in 1727. The most immediately obvious editorial decision Nian made was to remove the paratextual material concerning the cosmological origins of sound, including the original preface. Nian's new preface described in vague terms "additions and deletions" to the original text in order to "broaden the circulation" of this work.[56] As characterized in recent historical linguistic research, some of these emendations were phonological in nature.[57] The deletions appear to have involved the cosmological material as well, perhaps to make the text more palatable to a contemporary audience.

Wufang yuanyin was revised once more by Zhao Peizi 趙培梓 in 1810. Zhao Peizi's edition (titled *Zengbu tibi Wufang yuanyin* 增補剔弊五方元音 Primordial sounds of the five directions, expanded and supplemented with defects removed) notably returned a few token cosmological elements, including the musical pitch diagram. The bulk of the cosmological material, however, remained excised. This later edition emphasized the functional aspects of *Wufang yuanyin* as a text that offered an important alternative to the stroke-based graph lookup method.[58] It altered the entire system of phonological classification in the original, removing cosmologically informed categories and restoring aspects from the mainstream medieval phonological categories. In light of these changes, the inclusion of the diagram at the beginning likely serves as an explanation of the title of the text, rather than an essential part of its epistemological authority.

Of the approximately two hundred documented editions of this text circulating during the Qing, the vast majority were printed on the basis of the later cosmology-reduced adaptations.[59] Such modifications of seventeenth-century texts reflect the changing notion of proper philological study. What had originated as a theoretical inquiry into the nature of sound was reframed as a functional text designed for simple consultation of proper pronunciations. It was in this revised intent that *Wufang yuanyin* came to influence the first Chinese-English dictionaries.

Wufang yuanyin and other cosmological lexicons played an unexpectedly major role in nineteenth-century bilingual lexicographical efforts. We may consider, for instance, the American protestant missionary Samuel Wells Williams's (1812–1884) famed *A Syllabic Dictionary of the Chinese Language*, the full title of which is *A Syllabic Dictionary of the Chinese Language: Arranged According to the Wu-Fang Yuen Yin, with the Pronunciation of the Characters as Heard in Peking, Canton, Amoy, and Shanghai* (Ch. *Han Ying yunfu* 漢英韻府). First printed in 1874, Williams's dictionary described *Wufang yuanyin* as "the groundwork of the present Dictionary," regarding this text as a "vocabulary of the Court Dialect much used in Central and Northern China." Originally framed as a cosmologically based account of all possible sounds, *Wufang yuanyin* came to be seen as reflecting the very particular phonology of the official koiné. Williams employed the system of initials and finals proposed in *Wufang yuanyin* as a structuring device in his own dictionary. Given that Williams's familiarity with the Chinese lexicographical tradition appears limited to the few most famous works of the time, his reliance on *Wufang yuanyin* suggests the widespread influence of this text into the late nineteenth century. Williams did not grasp the original intent of the dictionary and was also reading a version in which the cosmological content had been drastically pared down. Contemporary Chinese readers, whose access to *Wufang yuanyin* would similarly have been primarily limited to later versions, would also likely have been unaware of the extensive cosmological focus of the original text.

Another landmark in bilingual lexicography, Robert Morrison's (1782–1834) six-volume *A Dictionary of the Chinese Language, in Three Parts*, was also based on the convoluted transmission of a work of seventeenth-century cosmological scholarship. Morrison was a member of the London Missionary Society who arrived in Canton in 1807 with the goal of translating the Bible into Chinese. He began studying Chinese under a tutor in London in 1805 and achieved great proficiency in several topolects with the help of additional tutors after his arrival in China. Among his many pedagogical texts on Chinese, Morrison's lexicon assumes a particularly important place, frequently heralded as the first Chinese-English dictionary.[60]

The second of three parts of Morrison's *A Dictionary of the Chinese Language* is titled in Chinese *Wuche yunfu* (五車韻府, Woo-chay-yun-foo in Morrison's Romanization), referring to a work by the great seventeenth-century cosmologist Chen Jinmo. Chen's creation of a numeral system for phonetic notation in *Huangji tuyun* during the late Ming has already been detailed in chapter 1. Shortly after the Qing conquest, Chen Jinmo completed his next cosmological study and dictionary, *Yuanyin tongyun* (元音統韻 Systematized rhymes of the primordial sound). Chen did not have the resources to print *Yuanyin tongyun* during his lifetime and left the twenty-two-*juan* manuscript with his student Hu Shaoying 胡邵瑛. Hu eventually had the text printed in 1708 with the assistance of a colleague, but in a much-reduced format of only ten *juan*. Hu had removed all the cosmological material, leaving only the dictionary proper, titling his version *Wuche yunfu*. In 1714 one Fan Tinghu 范廷瑚 obtained the full manuscript of *Yuanyin tongyun* from Hu Shaoying and printed it in its entirety alongside an additional contemporary lexicographical work, creating a massive twenty-eight-*juan* text. Despite the eventual publication of Chen Jinmo's complete text in 1714, it was the cosmology-free 1708 edition that was republished in 1762 and would go on to influence Robert Morrison's bilingual dictionary.[61]

Morrison wrote that *A Dictionary of the Chinese Language* was "founded" on the *Wuche yunfu*, which he attributed to "Chin Sëen-sǎng 陳先生"

(Mr. Chen, i.e., Chen Jinmo). Describing the phonetic arrangement of the original as "divided with so much minuteness as to puzzle all the Natives whom I ever saw attempt to consult it," Morrison claimed to have rearranged the entries by comparing with other lexicographical works.[62] Whether Morrison consulted *Wuche yunfu* at all remains a matter of debate.[63] Nevertheless the invocation of *Wuche yunfu*, as well as Chen Jinmo's name, attests to the continued association of Chen's work with phonological innovation well into the nineteenth century, and a sense that it could serve a pedagogical goal.

With the cosmological framework removed, important seventeenth-century theoretical texts, such as *Wufang yuanyin* and *Yuanyin tongyun*, enjoyed a new life as introductory materials for foreigners attempting to learn Chinese. Presumably they were also considered useful for Chinese readers. Another British missionary, Alexander Wylie (1815–1887), described *Wufang yuanyin* and *Wuche yunfu* as belonging to the class of phonetically organized dictionary "much more used by students" within China than graphically organized ones.[64] Wu Rulun 吳汝綸 (1840–1903) similarly reported that among northern scholars "every household owns a copy" of *Wufang yuanyin*.[65] Phonetic arrangement was not solely the purview of scholars like Chen Jinmo, but the cosmologists' fascination with sound led to many significant phonological innovations. As a result, cosmological texts came to be reframed in terms of their functional uses.

One of the major contributions of Ming cosmologists was the creation of phonetic notation systems, predicated on the need to transcribe sounds that Chinese graphs could not represent. These systems included the use of numerals and compound graphs to convey phonological information.[66] Both kinds of transcription continued to appear into the nineteenth century, although typically stripped of their cosmological background.[67] Li Ruzhen, for instance, adapted such methods of numerical phonetic notation for educational purposes, transcribing the syllables in his rhyme tables with numbers (see figure 6.4).[68] Li was familiar with seventeenth-century cosmological phonology but did not actively engage in its study.[69] Numeral notation systems initially devised to document all existing sounds in the universe came to be employed as tools for elementary learners, both Chinese and foreign. Remarkably similar systems would arise again in the late nineteenth century as reformers sought alternative modes of writing to facilitate mass literacy (see epilogue). As such, cosmological innovation achieved a new pedagogical function.

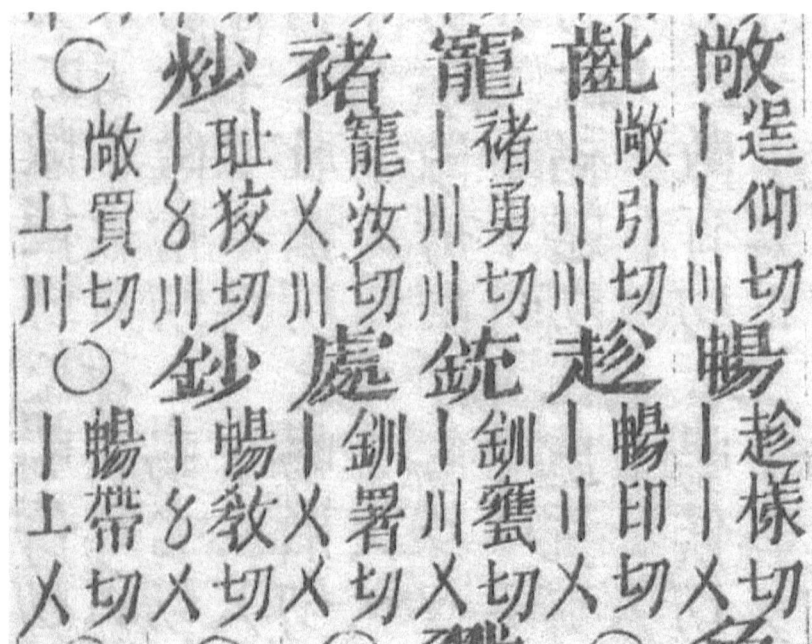

Figure 6.4 Li Ruzhen's transcriptions of syllables in numeral format (including ones the Chinese script could not notate, represented here by empty circles). Li Ruzhen, *Yinjian*, j. 6, 3a. (Image courtesy of the National Taiwan Normal University Library.)

Even Shao Yong's dense cosmological rhyme tables, which had served as the basis for the work of seventeenth-century philologists such as Chen Jinmo and Fan Tengfeng, were reevaluated in the eighteenth century. The Ming interaction with Shao Yong's phonology involved a redirection of its goals, from an exposition of universal processes to an analysis of linguistic sound. In so doing, Ming scholars raised issues with Shao's linguistic categories and worked to align them within a broader phonological tradition that had been irrelevant to Shao's original text (see chapter 1). They nonetheless largely accepted the cosmological underpinning of Shao's work, which posited that linguistic and musical sound were linked by a fundamental numerical relationship. In particular Shao's method of calculating the precise number of theoretically possible sounds captured the attention of Ming scholars who employed similar calculations within their own phonological studies.

Shao Yong's tables were further distanced from their original cosmological intent by eighteenth-century scholars. Li Guangdi, for instance, attempted to historicize Shao Yong's tables, claiming that they recorded what he termed "ancient pronunciation" (*guyin* 古音), which was separate from "present-day official pronunciation" (*jinshi guanyin* 今時官音).[70] Linguists today have continued to examine Shao's rhyme tables, primarily for insights into Song dynasty pronunciation.[71] While Shao Yong himself framed his tables as reflecting all possible sounds of past and present, later scholars increasingly saw them as necessarily constricted by the linguistic sounds Shao would have heard in the world around him. As such they came to be used not as tools for comprehensive linguistic description, but instead for a glimpse into a specific historical stage of Chinese pronunciation.

The Separation of Opera and Classical Phonology

Chen Jinmo's cosmological phonology featured in a major Ming handbook on opera pronunciation, *Duqu xuzhi* (see chapter 4). This handbook in turn went on to influence many later seventeenth-century and early eighteenth-century classicists. Over the course of the Qing dynasty, new regional forms of opera gained prominence and discussions of pronunciation retained an important place among literary figures. By the late eighteenth-century, however, discussions of opera phonology were largely separated and considered irrelevant to classical studies.

Ambivalence concerning the place of opera phonology in the classical study of language is forefronted in the editorial principles of the major Qing dictionary of standard opera pronunciations, *Yunxue lizhu* (韻學驪珠 Brilliant pearls of phonology). Printed in 1792, *Yunxue lizhu* was a rhyme dictionary, which organized the pronunciation of graphs according to categories designed to facilitate the singing of various forms of regional opera. The first item in the editorial principles proclaims that "this book was composed exclusively for singers (*gequzhe* 歌曲者)."[72] This intent was reflected, according to its compiler Shen Chenglin 沈乘麐, in the exceptionally detailed information it presented on place of articulation and associated musical pitch for each graph. Its treatment of the entering tone was also specifically designed to provide convenient lookup for singers to distinguish pronunciation differences between southern opera (which maintained the entering tone) and northern opera (which modified the pronunciation of entering tone graphs).

The editorial principles of *Yunxue lizhu* slightly qualified its opening statement, later averring that "this book is in fact not exclusively for singers, but may even be of some help to librettists (填詞家)."⁷³ Shen Chenglin here observed that just as the pronunciation of entering tone graphs was an issue for singers, librettists must pay attention to such subtleties in order to accurately adhere to either the southern or northern style. Opening a work of opera pronunciation to consultation by librettists was not a great leap. At the end of the editorial principles, however, Shen Chenglin presented a final broader claim: "This book is actually not only useful to singers and librettists. It can even be set on the table in any study—if during the process of writing (*shuxie shi* 書寫時) there are moments of confusion concerning the correct form of graphs or their explanation, it would be permissible to pursue a cursory search [in this text]."⁷⁴ Shen maintained, however, that his dictionary contained only graphs "frequently encountered in the present that are easily recognizable," advising the consultation of more comprehensive lexicons for more challenging contexts.⁷⁵

It appears that the author of *Yunxue lizhu* did envision limited functional applications of the dictionary for composition more broadly. Nevertheless the opening statement that the work was "exclusively for singers," although somewhat qualified by his later admission, is striking in light of the nature of operatic philology in the Ming. Sixteenth- and seventeenth-century opera theorists, such as Shen Chongsui and Wang Jide, sought to devise linguistic systems appropriate for singing, but also reflective of fundamental properties of the Chinese language. This commitment to the field of phonology resulted in contributions aimed at an audience of classicists. Contemporary classicists in turn readily cited and adapted such texts. The opening statement of intent in *Yunxue lizhu* can be understood as a response to this earlier tendency to mix the classical and operatic. In a move indicative of eighteenth-century disciplinary divisions, the author of *Yunxue lizhu* made a point to assure the reader that he saw his text as ultimately unrelated to the realm of classical language study.⁷⁶ Late eighteenth- and nineteenth-century philologists accordingly ignored it. Designed to aid singers and librettists, even the most extended usages its author envisioned did not go beyond literary composition.

As a specialized dictionary aimed at an audience of singers, *Yunxue lizhu* inherited a tradition of functional opera lexicography tracing back to *Zhongyuan yinyun*. Another significant eighteenth-century work of opera phonology, titled *Yuefu chuansheng* (樂府傳聲 Conveying the sounds of sung performance), was unlike any previous text. Its author, Xu Dachun 徐大椿 (c. 1693–1771), was a prominent physician from Wujiang who authored numerous medical studies. As one might expect from someone of his background, Xu was most interested in the physiological aspects of singing and correct pronunciation. On the one hand, Xu Dachun was clearly the inheritor of a Ming discourse on opera phonology. He referred, for instance, to the tripartite division of the syllable into "head, belly, and tail," an innovation first codified in Shen Chongsui's work.[77] In stark contrast to seventeenth-century scholarly attention to opera pronunciation, however, Xu wrote: "Setting musical pitches, lyrics, and rituals are the affair of scholars (*xueshi dafu* 學士大夫). Musical instruments, and the mastery of their associated techniques, are the affair of musical performers (*yuegong* 樂工). But musical modes, pronunciation, and methods of utterance (*koufa* 口法) must be understood by the singers (*changquzhe* 唱曲者)."[78] According to Xu Dachun, "no single person" would be capable of managing all of these tasks. *Yuefu chuangsheng* was primarily concerned with "methods of utterance," which he deemed most relevant to the singers themselves. Xu's relegation of pronunciation from "the affair of scholars" to performance technique represents a telling shift of discourse that would become commonplace in later opera pedagogy texts, such as *Liyuan yuan* (梨園原 Origins of dramatic performance). Xu Dachun did not reflect on contemporary phonological scholarship in *Yuefu chuansheng* and largely referenced foundational works from the medieval tradition for their terminology. His primary concern was to precisely describe the shape of the mouth, and other physiological characteristics, appropriate for each syllable, adopting what Judith Zeitlin has termed a "practice-based approach."[79] Xu did not suggest the potential of this method for application outside of singing or defining a unified common speech, although he did indicate his hope to represent a standard that would render opera intelligible in any region.

Xu Dachun himself framed his work as a text for singers and their instructors, distinguishing it from the concerns of "scholars." Xu's pronouncements on phonetics nonetheless irked later classicists. Jiao Xun 焦循 (1763–1820), a prominent Evidential Learning figure, pointedly referred to Xu as "skilled at medicine and good at singing tunes" but unqualified for philological research. Jiao Xun's comment betrays the fact that he was evidently reading a work of operatic phonology. For Jiao Xun, however, Xu Dachun's conceptualization of phonology in terms of performance practice had limited his understanding of basic linguistic principles.[80] Perhaps as a result of Xu's approach to philology in a manner unbecoming of a philologist, *Yuefu chuansheng* was not even included in the bibliography of the *Siku quanshu*, despite the imperial catalog's inclusion and high praise of his vast medical scholarship. Xu Dachun's reputation as a phonologist was somewhat restored only at the end of the nineteenth century when the reformer Wen Tingshi 文廷式 (1856–1904) observed that it was precisely Xu's proficiency at opera that caused him to yield new insights into phonology.[81] In the age of Evidential Learning, Xu Dachun's physiological-operatic approach to phonology fell on deaf ears. In the period of reform and modernization it claimed new attention.

Although literary scholarship on language was increasingly distanced from classical studies over the course of the eighteenth century, here too there existed exceptions. For instance, one specialized rhyme dictionary for lyric poetry from the mid-eighteenth century claimed inspiration from Gu Yanwu's study of ancient phonology, and in particular Gu's proposition that ancient pronunciations should be restored. The author cited extensively from seventeenth-century philologists and asserted that his work "was intended not only for lyric poetry rhymes" but also aimed to recover the unadulterated fundamental pronunciation of antiquity.[82] Conversely, an early nineteenth-century study of the rhymes of the *Poems* cited Shen Chongsui's tripartite division of the syllable, claiming that "although the lyrics and arias of today are far removed from the songs of antiquity, there is perhaps some similarity passed down orally over time (□□相傳)."[83] In the late Ming many philologists took it for granted that the sung quality of the *Poems* made the study of contemporary opera relevant to an analysis of its phonology. The majority of Qing studies approached *Poems* phonology following the path of historical analysis initiated by Chen Di and Gu Yanwu, but this alternative perspective maintained its persuasiveness for some.

Wei Jiao, Zhao Yiguang, and the Metaphysical Parsing of Graphs

Wei Jiao and his Learning of the Mind readings of the component parts of graphs came under attack in the eighteenth century. As *Shuowen jiezi* assumed a place as the central object of philological research for Evidential Learning scholars, Wei Jiao's alternative was routinely condemned as misguided.[84] Nevertheless, its consistent inclusion in contemporary bibliographies highlights its continued place in the eighteenth-century philological imagination. While the text itself was not reprinted in its entirety during the Qing, isolated entries from the dictionary were cited throughout some of the period's most influential philological works, and an abridged version of the text was produced in the eighteenth century.

Perhaps most unexpected are the citations of *Liushu jingyun*, as well as Wei Jiao's student Wang Yingdian, in the *Kangxi zidian* of 1716. The imperially commissioned dictionary was compiled before the consolidation of Evidential Learning as a widespread scholarly trend. It was nevertheless highly critical of Ming lexicography, and its organizing principles were explicitly framed as a repudiation of this tradition. A comment cited in the dictionary further noted that lexicons such as *Liushu jingyun* "explain ancient graphs on the basis of personal opinion" (以意闡古文) and were therefore unreliable.[85] The compilers nevertheless liberally cited from *Liushu jingyun* and other Ming dictionaries.[86] These citations indicate that the court compilers did not consult *Liushu jingyun* for its explanation of the metaphysical message conveyed by the component parts of graphs. Instead, they appear to have seen value in some of the conventional lexicographic features of the text, including synonym glosses, graph forms, and even pronunciation glosses. These elements are the least original aspect of *Liushu jingyun*; the synonym and pronunciation glosses were largely gleaned from the Ming imperial dictionary *Hongwu zhengyun*, while the graph forms were primarily taken from a set of Song, Yuan, and early Ming reference works. Nonetheless, the court compilers evidently viewed *Liushu jingyun* as a convenient repository of information from these various sources.

In the second half of the eighteenth century, *Shuowen jiezi* became the focus of countless philological studies. This foundational dictionary had been the object of several notable commentaries during the Song and Ming, but the sheer number and depth of commentaries and analyses produced during this period was staggering.[87] Many Evidential Learning thinkers argued that a focus on this lexicon from antiquity allowed them to place the study of graph forms on solid ground, replacing the metaphysical preoccupations of Ming scholars like Wei Jiao. Others argued that these two modes of graphological analysis had shared goals. Gui Fu 桂馥 (1736–1805), for instance, incorporated an array of Ming sources in his magnum opus, *Shuowen jiezi yizheng* (説文解字義證 Corroborating commentary on the meanings of terms in *Shuowen jiezi*). Despite being deeply steeped in the Evidential Learning rhetoric of the age, this text cited from Wei Jiao's lexicographical work, as well as that of Zhao Yiguang, whose reputation had been greatly diminished by Gu Yanwu's fierce repudiation.

Some Evidential Learning scholars continued to follow Gu Yanwu's path, invoking Zhao Yiguang primarily as an example of misguided earlier graph analyses.[88] Gui Fu, on the other hand, cited Zhao Yiguang well over sixty times for corroborative evidence.[89]

This citation of Ming texts of ill repute is evident in other major works of evidential etymological scholarship, such as *Shuowen jiezi judou* (説文解字句讀 Annotated *Shuowen jiezi*) by the eminent Evidential Learning philologist Wang Yun 王筠 (1784–1854), as well as in general studies of the Classics and encyclopedic texts.[90] While the consensus among Evidential Learning scholars seems to have resulted in a negative appraisal of the etymological arguments made by scholars like Wei Jiao and Zhao Yiguang, these texts were typically not viewed as completely devoid of merit. Even in as paradigmatic a field of Evidential Learning as *Shuowen jiezi* studies, the Ming legacy of etymological research served not only as a foil for criticism but also as a source for textual corroboration.

An abridged version of *Liushu jingyun* was included in the compendious eighteenth-century compilation of calligraphic materials *Liuyi zhiyi lu* (六藝之一錄 A record of one of the six arts).[91] A prime example of the fusion of calligraphic practice, epigraphy studies, and philology in early Qing scholarly circles, *Liuyi zhiyi lu* framed the inclusion of Wei Jiao's work in terms of its value for corroboration of ancient graph forms.[92] All the headwords from the original dictionary, and their ancient calligraphic forms, are included. The explanatory entries, however, are drastically shortened. What were originally lengthy philosophical expositions of the intricate relationship of each component of the headword graph are trimmed to brief definitions and pronunciation glosses. This abridgement of Wei Jiao's work may reflect a concern with space in the context of a compilation ultimately geared toward the study of calligraphy. The abridgment is not disclosed, however, and the result was an influential introduction to Wei Jiao's scholarship for later readers, which had effectively removed some of its most distinctive characteristics. It also reflects the perceived value of the text for eighteenth-century readers, less for its insights into the underpinnings of the sagely mind than as an assemblage of ancient graph forms.

The wide range of philological methods adopted over the course of the Qing dynasty suggests that we should not accept one sweeping definition of philology even during the dominance of Evidential Learning in the eighteenth century. Multiple possibilities for the study of language coexisted with the Evidential Learning trend.[93] Integrative methods persisted to a certain degree alongside the rise of a new vision of philology as the evidential study of ancient texts. Evidential Learning practitioners proclaimed the objectivity of their methods and disparaged previous philological schools. Adherents to alternative approaches highlighted inconsistencies and faulty assumptions underlying the Evidential Learning methodology, frequently pulling on the traditions of philological learning that took form in the mid- and late Ming. Eighteenth- and nineteenth-century critics of Evidential Learning rejected the premise that corroboration of ancient sources was sufficient for describing ancient phonology. Scholars continued to build systems of philological knowledge that integrated the study of language with other fields of learning, often based on cosmological assumptions.

Perhaps more significantly for the legacy of Ming philologists, their texts continued to be read and refashioned even by those who disagreed with the methodology they employed. While the fundamental assumptions underlying Ming methods lost credibility within the mainstream of Evidential Learning philology, major court compilations and Evidential Learning tracts still cited Ming philological texts. This citation indicates that the perceived contribution of Ming philology was not only its handy function as a target of criticism. Evidential Learning scholars viewed certain Ming texts as useful compilations of phonological and etymological learning. By divorcing this learning from its original metaphysical, cosmological, and literary contexts, mid-Qing scholars aligned the priorities of Ming philologists with their own.

Ming texts were also published in new editions over the course of the eighteenth and nineteenth centuries, albeit occasionally in vastly altered form. The adaptations of Ming philological texts repurposed these works as pedagogical or corroborative, rendering them barely recognizable in some cases. In so doing, these later editions made Ming learning palatable in a vastly different scholarly environment.

The introduction of the phonographic Manchu script in China further spurred on investigations into the potential of non-Chinese scripts for the description and categorization of linguistic sound. Over the course of the Qing dynasty, phonographic writing came to be valued for its utility as a pedagogical tool for instruction, as opposed to its primarily theoretical role in Ming scholarship. Nevertheless the precedent of in-depth Ming investigations into such scripts was not lost on Qing thinkers.

Kangxi-era scholars cited Ming works on Sanskrit and Latin alongside their inquiries into Manchu writing. Later eighteenth-century scholars also continued to pull directly on this earlier tradition, in dedicated studies of both Sanskrit and Manchu.

Eighteenth- and nineteenth-century scholars appear to have been aware of a substantial body of sixteenth and seventeenth-century philological scholarship. Despite the increasingly evident methodological division between the two periods, later scholars continued to use Ming lexicographic compilations as a base for further research. Prominent voices in the Evidential Learning tradition, especially those associated with the *Siku quanshu* project, routinely remarked on the lack of value in Ming philology. They did not incorporate these texts into the *Siku quanshu* itself and attempted to downplay the role of Ming philologists in the history of the field. Behind this discourse lay considerable interaction with an earlier tradition of linguistic thought. As the following chapter will explore, eighteenth-century scholars built even more directly on the sense of disciplinary community that emerged as a central feature of the late Ming intellectual world.

CHAPTER 7

The Reinvention of Philology

Specialization, Disciplinarity, and Intellectual Lineage

A bibliographical entry in the late eighteenth-century annotated catalog to the *Siku quanshu* praised a certain text as "comprehensive" and "carefully researched," leading the editor to note that on this basis "one may recognize that specialized learning (*zhuanmen zhi xue* 專門之學) is in an entirely different category from dilettantism (*sheliezhe* 涉獵者)."[1] Song dynasty accounts of learning, on the other hand, regularly framed specialization in a negative light, referring to particular texts as "muddled in specialization" or "holding on to the ignorant opinions of specialization."[2] What caused this shift from the denigration of specialized expertise to its veneration as the pinnacle of learning? Did specialization require being narrow-minded and parochial, or was it the key to precise scholarship? The seventeenth-century scholar Fang Yizhi addressed this conflict, acknowledging that "in general if learning is not specialized (*zhuanmen*) it will be imprecise" but expressing concern that it could also lead to "one-sidedness" (*pian* 偏).[3] He therefore envisioned a form of learning he termed "impartial and complete" (*gongquan* 公全), which would combine the strongest elements of specialized and broader learning. The argument in favor of specialization had clearly won by the eighteenth century. But the visible traces of scholarly practice suggest a considerable new emphasis on specialization and expertise emerging already in the sixteenth.

This chapter examines the rise of disciplinary communities in the late Ming as a source of both continuity and disjunction with eighteenth- and nineteenth-century scholarly practices. Communities of scholars, built on mutual citation as well as collaboration, came to be formed in the sixteenth century on the basis of a shared disciplinary interest. One's place within such communities was predicated on expertise. Within the field of philology, the content of this expertise changed over the course of the late imperial period. Ming philologists craved up-to-date research and frequently cited their contemporaries. But the broad valence of "philology" (*xiaoxue*) incorporated methodologies from varied fields of knowledge, from the musical to the cosmological. The shift in knowledge production over the course of the eighteenth century involved a reconfiguration of the discipline. Eighteenth- and nineteenth-century scholars similarly formed contemporary networks of scholarship and valued specialized expertise in philology. But they tended to reframe the boundaries of this philological specialization to focus on language alone, dealing primarily with the language of ancient texts.

The notion of professionalization and specialization as a central feature of the eighteenth-century intellectual landscape has long been recognized.[4] Ming philologists also positioned themselves as specialists, despite the fact that many of them directed methods from fields outside of the directly linguistic to the study of language. They associated and collaborated with other philological experts and formed networks of learning separate from the communities specializing in other subjects. Over the course of the eighteenth century, the notion of specialization and its relationship to the boundaries and methods of the discipline of philology changed. While deeply indebted to the formation of disciplinary communities that emerged in the late Ming, eighteenth-century thinkers increasingly argued for a separation of disciplinary methodologies, as opposed to the integration that had characterized Ming approaches to learning.

This new methodology of textual study, typically referred to as Evidential Learning, would become synonymous with philology for modern historians. As shown in the previous chapter, the definition of "philology" (*xiaoxue*) in fact remained contested through the Qing dynasty, when Ming texts and their methods continued to flourish in various forms. Nevertheless, the Evidential Learning method achieved prominence in court publications and within the writings of the most prolific and influential scholars of the time. This chapter concludes with a preliminary examination of the rise of Evidential Learning and its reshaping of the specialized study of language, reflecting on the implications of the previous chapters for our understanding of Qing scholarly practices and suggesting avenues for further investigation.

Disciplinary Communities and Their Boundaries

The term "discipline" as used in reference to a scholarly subject in modern English is well-attested from the Renaissance and derives from the Latin *disciplina*, which could refer to both "instruction" broadly as well as something akin to a field of learning, with an etymological basis in the transmission of knowledge from master to disciple.[5] The modern Chinese terms for "discipline," *xueke* (學科) and *lingyu* (領域, also meaning nonacademic "fields"), do not appear with this precise meaning in writing before the twentieth century. The *ke* or *xueke* of premodern China primarily indicated subjects tested on the civil service examinations.[6] As an institutionalized curriculum, these subjects formed one kind of disciplinarity in Chinese history. Outside of the examination context, knowledge pertaining to a particular field of knowledge was referred to generally as the "learning" (*xue* 學) or "school" (*jia* 家) of that field. These terms could refer to very specific fields, such as phonology (*yunxue* 韻學), but also to much broader categories, such as classical or literary studies (*jingxue* 經學 and *wenxue* 文學, respectively).

What was a discipline in Chinese history? Within the extensive existing research into varied fields of learning in China, there is little examination of the notion of a discipline, or whether such a term is relevant in the history of knowledge in China.[7] If we are to understand disciplines in their broadest sense as "the nations, provinces, and smaller units on the map of learning at any given time," then the bibliographical categories that had existed since the first century BCE in China would qualify.[8] Distinctions between traditions of learning were by no means new to the Ming, tracing back at least as far as Han dynasty imperial bibliographies, which defined a set of six fields: the six arts (*liuyi* 六藝), philosophical literature (*zhuzi* 諸子), poetry (*shifu* 詩賦), military books (*bingshu* 兵書), mathematical calculations (*shushu* 數術), and technical practices (*fangji* 方技). Each of these was further divided into subfields. For instance, the "six arts" comprised categories for the classical texts in the Confucian tradition, as well as philology.[9] Early seventh-century Tang court scholars codified a new four-part system that in broad strokes would persist into the twentieth century:

Classics (*jing* 經, including philology), Histories (*shi* 史), Masters (*zi* 子, originally containing primarily philosophical texts of the Warring States period), and Literary Collections (*ji* 集). Despite a range of available methods, this four-part system remained popular in the Ming, with one scholar claiming that none of the other methods could equal it in terms of simplicity and comprehensiveness.[10]

The notion that knowledge can be divided into fields of learning has a long history in China and was originally linked to the importance of cataloging materials in the imperial library. Can such divisions on their own be considered disciplines? Accepted definitions of discipline within current studies in the history of knowledge tend to require a set of features in addition to divisions of learning, including "a characteristic method, specialized terminology, a community of practitioners, a canon of authorities, an agenda or problems to be addressed," as well as in some cases professional venues for the publication, sharing, and preservation of knowledge.[11] In tracing the story of disciplinary knowledge in China, there exist multiple significant moments of change, and developments in one field of learning did not necessarily occur simultaneously with those in another. Nevertheless, the broader intellectual concerns of the sixteenth century instigated a widespread shift in the nature of disciplinary knowledge, exemplified by the study of philology but present in other fields as well. This shift witnessed the rise of a community of specialists, who predicated the generation of new knowledge on the basis of recent rather than solely ancient scholarly achievements. This development would prove to be an essential component of the later professionalization of certain disciplines in the eighteenth century.

I have employed the term "disciplinary community" to differentiate an important aspect of scholarly study in the late imperial period.[12] Prior to the sixteenth century, scholars of philology largely positioned their work within a cumulative scholarly tradition. Such thinkers claimed to be contributing to a scholarly project tracing back to antiquity and culminating in their own work. While scholars composing in this model might make sporadic reference to contemporary discussions, they typically presented their accomplishments as either the culmination of a long tradition of scholarship tracing back to ancient times or the direct inheritor of previously lost methods of antiquity. This cumulative approach to scholarship did not disappear in the Ming. What was new in the sixteenth century was a sense that this knowledge could be framed not only in relation to the past, but also within a contemporary field of study.[13]

Recent research has shown how developments in print culture and communication infrastructure enabled new literati networks and provided greater opportunity for interaction among contemporary scholars and literary figures in the sixteenth and seventeenth centuries.[14] In particular, literati engaged with vast peer networks to enhance the prestige of their publications.[15] I have elsewhere documented additional factors contributing to the formation of disciplinary communities in the sixteenth century, including an increasing rejection of the authority of the classical past and a retreat of the court from scholarly patronage.[16] Influential sixteenth- and seventeenth-century philosophers came to question the inherent superiority of antiquity, while Learning of the Way thinkers, local gentry, and officials regularly sought ways to honor living worthies alongside those of the past.[17] The imperial court, which often played an active role in scholarly enterprises in previous (and later) dynasties, had also largely ceased major sponsorship of intellectual projects by the fifteenth century. Ming scholars responded to this lacuna of authority by seeking the approval of a community of contemporary specialists in order to validate their study. The transition from a generalist in conversation with the ancients to a member of a specialized contemporary community is evident in the rhetoric of prefaces, works cited, and other paratextual materials in scholarly texts. It had further implications for scholarly practice, such as collaborative publication.

A common trope in the prefaces of sixteenth-century and later Chinese texts spoke of "awaiting the broadly-learned gentleman" (俟博雅君子) or "a later gentleman" (後之君子) to revise one's work. While this turn of phrase appears in earlier periods, its usage from the sixteenth century on is both quantitatively and qualitatively different. Song scholars might speak of completeness (*bei* 備), which they felt would assist (*zi* 資) later readers.[18] Sixteenth- and seventeenth-century scholars typically presented their efforts in the hopes that contemporary or later scholars would amend (*zheng* 正) or supplement (*bu* 補) them.[19] Rather than declaring completeness, one might herald omission over careless inclusion, anticipating "reevaluation" (*zaikao* 再考).[20] Many scholars suggested their "tentative" (*gu* 姑) inclusion of information with the expectation that a later reader would build on their work.[21] Fang Yizhi, in his philological magnum opus *Tongya*, even affirmed that his corrections to the works of recent scholars were "assuredly what these various masters would have wished for."[22]

The invocation of the later scholar became a staple of the sixteenth- and seventeenth-century preface. More important, the language surrounding this call to later readers increasingly shifted from a proclamation of the work's value to a request for revision. There are instances of scholars from the twelfth through fifteenth centuries hoping for contributions from contemporaries, as well as sixteenth-century scholars asserting their roles as preservers for future generations.[23] But broadly speaking, the figure of the literatus scholar had shifted from a reader of completed past achievements to an active contributor in ongoing research within a particular discipline.

Prefaces to scholarly and literary texts in this period recount extended circulation of manuscripts and revision among peers. The contemporaries acknowledged in these prefaces or cited throughout the body of the text were frequently specialists, that is, scholars with a record of publication within a related field. Citations of recent scholarship were also primarily field-specific; hence the authorities in philology were different from the authorities in medicine, for instance. Literary schools and associations manifested themselves on unprecedented levels during the Ming, and Classics discussions associations flourished at the end of the dynasty.[24] Similarly, schools of contemporary philological thought referenced each other and maintained a level of communication in pursuit of generating new knowledge that is rare in earlier periods. Not just bibliographical traditions of knowledge on the page, disciplines in late imperial China were composed of communities, which actively shared, debated, and contributed to the production of new knowledge.

Differentiation, it has been argued, "is an integral part of how disciplines are constructed."[25] In particular, decisions about where one discipline ends and the next begins are essential for the validation and institutionalization of knowledge.[26] The traces of such debate in China are evident from at least the medieval period, as reflected in shifting bibliographical categorization systems.[27] The late imperial period witnessed the emergence of an extensive discourse surrounding the appropriate boundaries of knowledge. In the Ming, scholars expanded these boundaries within fields such as philology, arguing that only by linking previously unconnected realms of learning could they surpass the limits of human observation and the textual legacy. By the eighteenth century, new intellectual concerns required a further reconceptualization of disciplinary boundaries. These new boundaries were more siloed, limiting the scope of philology only to strictly linguistic issues. They were nonetheless heavily indebted to conceptualizations of disciplinary learning and, in particular, the relevance of contemporary communities of specialized knowledge that emerged in the Ming.

Ming philology was not uniform, but its practitioners largely shared a set of methodological assumptions. Foremost among them was the notion that philological knowledge depended on the expertise of contemporaries and could be validated through correlations with a set of related fields, including, music, cosmology, and literary endeavors. The sixteenth and seventeenth centuries witnessed a transformation in humanistic scholarship with considerable implications for scholarly practice for centuries to come. A sense of contemporary disciplinary community and specialization was central to this transformation.

The better-documented intellectual networks of the eighteenth century shared the late Ming concern with up-to-date information and intellectual community.[28] In contrast to the late Ming, these eighteenth-century communities were often supported by various institutional structures. A strong current within the Qing institutionalization of scholarship involved a redefinition of the categories of knowledge. The remainder of this chapter considers how this new understanding of disciplinary specialization took form.

Intellectual Lineage and the Elevation of Gu Yanwu

One of the clearest manifestations of the shift in philological thinking in the late eighteenth century is the prevalence of a new historical narrative for the origins and development of the discipline. The inclusion of Ming texts in eighteenth-century bibliographies suggests that they could still be seen as part of the philological tradition during the height of the Evidential Learning period. Scholars such as Zhou Chun even attempted to construct an alternative "orthodox lineage" of philology that incorporated major Ming scholars and rejected the leading lights of Evidential Learning (see chapter 6). They did so, however, in opposition to a new intellectual genealogy, which reinvented the history of the field and has in broad strokes informed present-day understandings of scholarly practices in late imperial China. As conventionally recounted in current studies of the history of Chinese philology, the late imperial discipline was formed by a sequence of thinkers, beginning with two or three Ming forerunners but focused primarily on the Qing: Yang Shen (1488–1559), Chen Di (1541–1617), Gu Yanwu (1613–1682), Jiang Yong (1681–1762), Dai Zhen (1724–1777), Qian Daxin (1728–1804), Duan Yucai (1735–1815), Yan Kejun 嚴可均 (1762–1843), and Kong Guangsen 孔廣森 (1751–1786).[29] A survey of twenty-seven philological genealogies of the late eighteenth and early nineteenth centuries shows a high degree of consistency in its adherence to this lineage. All except four include both Gu Yanwu and Jiang Yong, and only two contain neither. In addition, they all present a subset of other prominent Evidential Learning philologists, such as Dai Zhen, Duan Yucai, Kong Guangsen, Qian Daxin, and Yan Kejun.[30] Yang Shen, Chen Di, and Jiao Hong are the almost exclusive representatives of the Ming; major thinkers from antiquity and the medieval tradition are also occasionally included.

This genealogy, which teleologically traces a set of forward-thinking Ming thinkers through to the mature Evidential Learning of the late eighteenth century, has been widely accepted to the present as a straightforward narrative of the history of linguistic and scholarly innovation in China. As should be apparent from the preceding chapters, it is in fact a highly selective history of the field. Evidential Learning scholars' attention to philology (*xiaoxue*) was nothing new. Their approach to the discipline, however, was strikingly different from mainstream approaches in the preceding centuries. In the process of redefining the nature of the field, they rewrote the history of the discipline to include only those whose methods prefigured their own. Like the well-studied twelfth-century Learning of the Way genealogy, the Evidential Learning genealogy of philology established a set of historical figures whose methods they framed as anticipating their approach to the discipline. In the Learning of the Way genealogy, Confucius and Mencius represented the foundational figures in a school of learning that was truly recovered by a set of thinkers only in the eleventh century.[31] The intervening centuries were largely represented as a departure from the original message of these thinkers from antiquity. For Evidential Learning scholars, the progenitor of paleography was the first-century-CE scholar Xu Shen, while for phonology it was the seventh-century Lu Fayan. Within this genealogy, a similar gap of a thousand or more years separated the foundational figures from the next great moment of philological innovation in the late sixteenth and seventeenth centuries at the hands of scholars such as Yang Shen, Chen Di, and Gu Yanwu.

The notion of genealogy was critical to eighteenth-century thinkers.[32] Dai Zhen defined good philological scholarship as based in the "inheritance of teachings" (*shicheng* 師承), in contrast to learning that had "lost its transmission" (*shichuan* 失傳).[33] Qian Daxin and Zhang Xuecheng would elevate this notion of intellectual lineage to a central epistemological position, promoting the concept of "methods of (a particular) school" (*jiafa*

家法) as essential to the creation of new knowledge.³⁴ This attention to lineage culminated in the *Hanxue shicheng ji* (漢學師承記 Record of the inheritance of teachings within Han Learning), first printed in 1818, which traced the revival of this learning from the seventeenth century to the turn of the nineteenth. Genealogies were created not only for specialized fields of learning, such as philology, but more broadly for the Evidential Learning methodology.³⁵ In sketching the emergence and motivations of this genealogy, I focus on the remarkable elevation of Gu Yanwu's position within specialized phonological scholarship, from that of a relatively marginal individual to the central instigator of a new form of knowledge production. This shift reflects changing attitudes toward late Ming scholarship as either a diverse marketplace of scholarly approaches or a benighted age.

Stage 1: The Seventeenth-Century Context

In their own time Chen Di's and Gu Yanwu's prominence as scholars is suggested by references to their work by contemporaries, as well as their intellectual and personal connections to other major literati. Their scholarly presence is perhaps best understood, however, as representing one of many options for philological study in the late Ming. They were not universally acclaimed as models and in fact faced considerable opposition during their lifetimes. This opposition was directed toward the methods they employed, rather than the perceived value of philology as a scholarly enterprise. Chen Di's faith in the textual record of antiquity as a reliable standard for deriving ancient pronunciations was unacceptable to cosmologists who were skeptical of this limited source base (see chapter 1). Gu Yanwu was an active member of intellectual communities in Shanxi, where he formed some of his most important scholarly connections, including to major classicists such as Yan Ruoqu 閻若璩 (1636–1704) and Zhu Yizun 朱彝尊 (1629–1709).³⁶ However, his avoidance of the literary methods promoted by the central scholarly community in Hangzhou kept him isolated from many of the period's most active phonological scholars.

Although Gu Yanwu maintained communication with Hangzhou scholars such as Chai Shaobing and Mao Xianshu, they largely rejected his methods. Their fellow Hangzhou native Mao Qiling further produced voluminous philological writings that disputed the basic premises of Gu Yanwu's work. A supporter of Gu Yanwu reportedly came to blows with

Mao Qiling over this philological dispute, but Mao's methods (aided by imperial patronage) achieved more widespread acknowledgment in his time.[37] Contemporary readers interpreted Mao Qiling's phonological theories as completely incompatible with Gu Yanwu's.[38] Mao saw pronunciation in antiquity as flexible and governed by musical and literary constraints. He included cosmological diagrams of pitch and cited Ming cosmological and literary scholars.[39] Gu Yanwu, on the other hand, saw ancient graph pronunciations as fixed and independent of literary context. It was not an entirely new idea; Chen Di and Jiao Hong had both advanced similar theories in the early seventeenth century. But Gu's development of these theories into systematic groupings of graphs provided the basis for a mode of historical linguistic analysis that would define the Evidential Learning approach to phonology and has lasted to the present.

Gu was paying close attention to the advances in phonology taking place in Hangzhou. He cited the work of Hangzhou scholars throughout his seminal *Yinxue wushu* (音學五書 Five texts on phonology) and engaged in epistolary communications with its leaders. This citation was largely unidirectional, except in the case of scholars such as Mao Qiling, who cited Gu as a foil for criticism. The relatively ecumenical Hangzhou scholars were not isolated from the broader scholarly trends of the period and cited quite broadly from contemporaries outside of their direct network, making the relative neglect of Gu Yanwu more striking. Other encyclopedic compilers of contemporary philological knowledge, such as Chen Jinmo and Fang Yizhi, also neglected Gu Yanwu in their assessments of the philological achievements of their time.[40] The *Rizhi lu* (日知錄 Record of daily-acquired knowledge), a notebook of philological and historical inquiry representative of Gu's later scholarship, no longer cited the Hangzhou scholars and took aim both explicitly and indirectly at several late Ming philologists. This strong departure from the influential scholarly trends of his time would attract eighteenth-century readers to his work but perhaps did not gain him an immediate following among his contemporaries.

Contemporary citation of Gu Yanwu within the extensive phonological scholarship of the late seventeenth century is hard to come by. Even Pan Lei, Gu Yanwu's most illustrious disciple, who would join Gu as a central figure in the Shanxi intellectual world and was responsible for the posthumous publication of *Rizhi lu*, attempted to downplay his teacher's philological accomplishments. Pan rejected Gu's phonological teachings in favor of the cosmological approach practiced by many of his contemporaries. In his monumental phonological study *Leiyin* (類音 Categorizing sounds), Pan averred: "Scholars fond of antiquity perform all manner of investigation [into ancient phonology] but merely get thirty or forty percent of the way there." In case there were any doubt, Pan clarified in a small-font note: "I am here referring to those like Wu Yu, Yang Shen, and my late teacher Gu Yanwu."[41] Gu Yanwu had previously written to Pan of his own misgivings about his earlier work, in some sense giving license to Pan's criticisms.[42] But while Gu believed the errors could be directly solved by broader textual corroboration, Pan rejected Gu's methods altogether, embracing instead the cosmological investigation of sound pioneered by late Ming thinkers.

Commenting in the early eighteenth century, Li Guangdi observed that despite Gu Yanwu's achievements, his work remained little known among contemporaries.[43] The seventeenth century was a lively period of philological experimentation and innovation witnessing the rise of new disciplinary communities specializing in the study of language. Despite his considerable influence in Shanxi and collaboration with local scholars interested in the study of ancient texts, Gu Yanwu was largely isolated from these broader communities of linguistic specialization, and his scholarship was not widely cited in philological texts in his lifetime. Gu's rise to prominence within the genealogy of philology was not a straightforward process but took place over the course of several generations. It is not surprising that his considerable contributions were not universally embraced immediately; great innovation often goes unrecognized in its own time. There is no reason, however, to assume that he would have necessarily been posthumously recognized. The fame of Gu Yanwu as a progenitor of Evidential Learning in some sense says more about his late eighteenth-century supporters than it does about Gu's place in the intellectual world of his age.

Stage 2: Li Guangdi and Jiang Yong

Early eighteenth-century scholars, who were among the first to isolate Gu Yanwu as a crucially significant philological thinker, recognized the diversity of philology in the previous century. Notions of "evidential proof" (*kaozheng*) and "solid learning" (*shixue* 實學) gained new prominence in the early 1700s. This increasing sense of the necessity for concrete scholarship, however, faced competing views of what made scholarship concrete with some thinkers maintaining that cosmological reasoning was a form of "solid learning."[44] The great court scholar Li Guangdi (1642–1718) stood at a crucial transition point in the history of the Evidential Learning lineage.[45] Li Guangdi himself ultimately did not enter the genealogy of Evidential Learning philologists. His methodological approach to the study of phonology was much more in line with previous integrative approaches, based on cosmology, literary usage, and the study of phonographic scripts. He was instrumental, however, in elevating the place of Gu Yanwu, as well as downplaying the efforts of Gu's most outspoken critic, Mao Qiling.

Gu Yanwu interacted with major networks of classicists but was not a leading member within the specialized communities of philological learning. He was not widely credited with the creation of something new and was instead seen as the proponent of one school of phonological analysis. Li Guangdi was one of the first to promote Gu Yanwu above his contemporaries, although he too placed Gu's work within a broader seventeenth-century philological discourse. In this way, Li Guangdi's discussion of Gu Yanwu differs from what would become the standard later genealogical trajectory that identified Gu as the sole significant figure in seventeenth-century philology.

At the age of thirty, Li Guangdi, still "ignorant of phonology," in fact met the elderly Gu Yanwu, who shared with him the core tenets of his linguistic thought.[46] Li was clearly influenced by this meeting but ultimately did not frame his own phonological work as a direct extension of Gu's. For Li Guangdi there existed three major arenas of phonological study (*yunxue* 韻學): ancient phonology, literary phonology, and Manchu phonology (based on phonetic spelling).[47] Only a combination of all three would qualify as a comprehensive study of linguistic sound. Li Guangdi depicted Gu Yanwu as the leading light in the study of ancient rhyming but argued that Gu's neglect of functional literary application required supplement. Li went as far as to propose printing a new version of Gu Yanwu's seminal *Yinxue wushu*, which would contain an appendix of relevant passages from the opera guidebook *Duqu xuzhi* and the Hangzhou scholar Mao Xianshu's writings on literary phonology, in order to generate a more complete study.[48] By the second half of the eighteenth-century, these three sets of writing would be seen as entirely unrelated, with the latter two largely excluded from the history of the discipline.

At the same time that he elevated Gu Yanwu, Li Guangdi also decisively attacked the scholarship of Mao Qiling, criticizing his work as "truly useless."⁴⁹ Mao Qiling's encyclopedic phonological text, *Kangxi jiazi shiguan xinkan Gujin tongyun* (康熙甲子史館新刊古今通韻 Comprehensive rhymes of past and present, newly printed in Kangxi jiazi [1684] by the Historiography Institute), was printed at the approval of the Kangxi emperor by the Historiography Institute, where Mao Qiling was employed. This work was framed as a repudiation of Gu Yanwu and was deeply indebted to Ming musical modes of linguistic analysis, arguing that ancient readings were flexible and dependent on an original correspondence between language and musical accompaniment. Due to its imperial sponsorship, the text was widely promulgated. The original 1684 edition of the text contained a remarkable nineteen prefaces from leading court scholars, such as Xu Qianxue 徐乾學 (1631–1694), overflowing with praise for the work's ingenuity and the Kangxi emperor's perspicacity for sponsoring it. One hundred years later the work was held in almost universal ill-repute. Although it was included in the *Siku quanshu*, it was harshly evaluated by the editors, its flattering prefaces removed, and the work itself retitled as simply *Gujin tongyun* (Comprehensive rhymes of past and present), perhaps to remove its imperial association. Li Guangdi's high official appointment at the Kangxi court may have placed him in a strong position to attack this work, apparently favored at one point by the ruler. Li would put forth a new vision of philology, both in his recorded discussions (語錄 *yulu*) and in a later dictionary commissioned by the Kangxi emperor no less, that would be influential in shaping eighteenth-century philological tastes.⁵⁰

Li Guangdi's influence was recognized by another major philologist of the mid-Qing, Jiang Yong (1681–1762). The case of Jiang Yong, who would himself be elevated to the pantheon of Evidential Learning thinkers, reflects the instability of this lineage even through the first half of the eighteenth century. Like Li Guangdi, Jiang's research operated at the intersection of seventeenth- and eighteenth-century methods. Jiang Yong worked extensively in the tradition of ancient rhyme category study initiated by Gu Yanwu. However, he was familiar with the cosmological approach of Shao Yong through the writings of Pan Lei and Li Guangdi. Although he disputed both of their systems, he did not exclude the relevance of cosmology to linguistic study and even produced a diagram in the model of major late Ming scholars, correlating the initials of the rhyme table tradition with the numerological logic of the He and Luo River diagrams.⁵¹ In his own genealogy of the discipline, Jiang Yong labeled Gu Yanwu as "exceptional" (*techu* 特出) but also included a broad range of sixteenth- and seventeenth-century scholars, including members of the Hangzhou network and Fang Yizhi.[52] Only later, as Evidential Learning values solidified in the late eighteenth century, was Jiang's approach to the discipline portrayed as a straightforward inheritance of Gu Yanwu's methods en route to Dai Zhen. In contrast to Jiang Yong's own discussion of his indebtedness and relationship to a diverse seventeenth-century philological community, later eighteenth-century Evidential Learning thinkers considered Gu Yanwu to be Jiang's only significant influence.

Genealogies of philology in the first half of the eighteenth century tended to be ecumenical in their selection of Ming thinkers. While both Li Guangdi and Jiang Yong incorporated Gu Yanwu into their vision of the complex history of seventeenth-century philology, others rejected Gu's place in such a lineage. Wang Zhi 王植 (*jinshi* 1721), for instance, pointed to seventeenth-century cosmologists as the proper custodians of the philological tradition. He criticized Mao Qiling yet nonetheless attributed some value to his work: namely, his repudiation of Gu Yanwu.[53] Some simply neglected Gu Yanwu's contributions altogether. Gao Wengying 高翁映 (1647–1707), for instance, traced a genealogy that highlighted a vast array of seventeenth-century approaches to philology, from Zhao Yiguang to Fang Yizhi and Nicolas Trigault, but overlooked Gu Yanwu.[54] His contemporary Xiong Shibo was well-versed in Gu Yanwu's writings but, like Gu's student Pan Lei, chose to base his phonological study on the cosmological methods of Shao Yong. His major work, *Dengqie yuansheng*, included an annotated bibliography of significant contemporary phonological studies, analyzing texts from scholars such as Zhao Yiguang and Mao Xianshu but similarly omitting Gu Yanwu. By the eighteenth century, Gu Yanwu's name had noticeably entered the broader philological discourse and came to be vocally promoted by scholars like Li Guangdi and Jiang Yong. Gu nonetheless remained an object of criticism or neglect in some of the period's most widely circulated philological texts.

Stage 3: The Dynastic Placement of Gu Yanwu and the Solidification of the Evidential Learning Genealogy

Li Guangdi and Jiang Yong had highlighted Gu Yanwu's philological achievements, alongside a range of other seventeenth-century figures. By the late eighteenth century, a new genealogical narrative of the field had pared away this range of thinkers, making Gu Yanwu the sole representative of true phonological learning in the previous century. Part of the process of elevating Gu Yanwu's position as a progenitor of Evidential Learning involved downplaying the importance of his contemporaries; it also may have encouraged claiming Gu as a product of the Qing dynasty. Gu Yanwu lived from 1613 to 1682; just under half of his life (thirty-two years) fell during the Ming dynasty, with the other half (thirty-seven years) in the Qing. Most significantly, a preface to his *Yinxue wushu* from 1643 indicates that his phonological magnum opus was at least partially completed during the Ming.[55] Although the work was only printed in the 1660s, portions of the text were evidently circulating much earlier. In the first half of the eighteenth century, Gu's dynastic association remained in question. Dai Zhen, for instance, referred to Gu as a scholar of the Ming. Although he held Gu in high regard for his "pioneering efforts in ancient phonology," he nevertheless contended that in many regards Gu had "not been fully correct."[56] As Gu Yanwu's methods came to be promoted as the origin of the evidential approach to phonology, his dynastic attribution increasingly shifted to the Qing.

By the late eighteenth and early nineteenth centuries, Gu was consistently referred to as a scholar of "the current dynasty" (*benchao* 本朝 / *guochao* 國朝).[57] As Guan Tong 管同 (1780–1831) claimed, "Since the beginning of the dynasty up to the present, phonology has been greatly illuminated. Gu was the creator at first, and Dai Zhen, Duan Yucai, and Kong Guangsen received afterward."[58] Qian Daxin, speaking more broadly of classicist scholarship, criticized previous dynasties, and especially the Ming for neglect of the Han-Tang commentarial tradition. For Qian, the "comprehensive classicists of our dynasty" (*guochao tongru* 國朝通儒), beginning with Gu Yanwu, were the first to revive the methods of Ancient Learning (*guxue* 古學).[59]

The tendency to claim Gu Yanwu as part of a Qing revival of concrete learning is particularly striking when compared with the treatment of Gu's contemporaries. In some respects it may have been a methodological distinction, rather than a temporal one, that earned Gu his dynastic placement. Within the rhetoric of Evidential Learning scholars, the Ming was particularly reviled for its perceived rejection of concrete learning. Regardless of when Gu Yanwu's philological enlightenment actually took place, he was widely regarded as the founding father of the evidential method, which had displaced the misguided scholarly ways of the preceding Ming. Many of Gu Yanwu's contemporaries, on the other hand, were labeled as Ming scholars in eighteenth-century discourse.[60] Fang Yizhi (1611–1671), who was born only two years earlier than Gu Yanwu and whose philological works began to circulate widely in printed form only in the Qing, was typically referred to in late eighteenth-century texts as "Fang Yizhi of the Ming," rather than "Fang Yizhi of the current dynasty."[61] Chen Jinmo (c. 1600–1692), as well, who lived later than Gu Yanwu, and whose second substantial phonological text was completed only in the Qing, was still typically referred to as "Chen Jinmo of the Ming."[62] That Fang Yizhi and Chen Jinmo, among many other contemporaries, remained scholars of the Ming reflects the inconsistent nature of such dynastic designations; it may also suggest a recognition of the clear methodological differences between late Ming cosmological philology and Evidential Learning philology, especially given the clear association of the Ming with intellectual decline in the minds of many late eighteenth-century literati.

The Ming model of philology featured many of the characteristics Qing intellectuals criticized in the scholarly practice of this earlier period: cosmology, Buddhist influence, as well as a perceived decadent literary culture and unclear bibliographical distinctions.[63] Ji Yun 紀昀 (1724–1805), one of the chief *Siku quanshu* editors, famously took issue with the great author of classical tales Pu Songling 蒲松齡 (1640–1715) for writing in a manner that crossed the boundaries of several genres.[64] Where would this hybrid genre fit in the imperial library catalog? We have seen that such issues plagued the catalogers when dealing with Ming philological texts (see chapter 6). Given the tendency of Ming texts to span multiple branches of learning, which heading would it be most appropriate to file them under?

The ecumenical approach of Ming scholars was rejected by those who embraced the new Evidential Learning genealogy. Many Ming thinkers promoted the Indic origins of phonology in China and actively pursued collaboration with Buddhist monks expert in Sanskrit. Evidential Learning thinkers largely attacked this practice.[65] Yao Ying 姚瑩 (1785–1853), for instance, in comparing the accomplishments of Fang Yizhi and Gu Yanwu, claimed that Gu alone was the one "every phonologist of our dynasty venerates." The main difference between the two was that Fang Yizhi's work was "based in the scholarship of Buddhists" and therefore an unacceptable model.[66]

Fang Yizhi's philological study, along with that of many late seventeenth- and early eighteenth-century scholars, was also deeply steeped in cosmology. Even Jiang Yong, later upheld as a pivotal figure of Evidential Learning, was partial to cosmological explanations of language. It was with Dai Zhen and his followers that the cosmological element of linguistic study was largely purged.[67] On its own, the trend to eliminate cosmology from phonology reflects the well-documented anticosmological bent of late eighteenth-century scholars.[68] The birds-eye view of language study, however, shows not only the erasure of cosmology, but also Buddhist and literary impulses. One way to understand this shift would be in terms of the rise of ideological orthodoxy in Qing Confucianism. If philology were to be considered a branch of Confucian classical learning, then all elements that did not conform with their codification of orthodox Confucian learning would need to be purged. Another, more compelling way, I believe, would be to understand this as a shift in the standards of validity. Ming scholars also typically saw their mode of philology as part of Confucian classical study but validated new knowledge on the basis of *self-so* correlations across fields of learning.

The ideal of *self-so* as persuasive proof declined in the eighteenth century. Leading Evidential Learning scholars, such as Qian Daxin and Duan Yucai, rarely referenced the *self-so* nature of their linguistic descriptions, in contrast to sixteenth- and seventeenth-century philologists who tended to repeatedly assert this attribute of their scholarship. This striking discursive shift reflects fundamentally different notions of what it meant to create new knowledge. Both Fang Yizhi and Qian Daxin could make the claim to be specialists who targeted their studies at the refinement of philological learning. For Fang Yizhi, this goal involved the development of an intricate system of *self-so* relationships between language and other fields to validate his linguistic categories. It would be inaccurate to claim that observation played no role within this system. Fang Yizhi read widely in ancient texts and was also interested in the physical production of sound. All these elements, however, were incorporated into the larger *self-so* system of linguistic knowledge he had constructed. Qian Daxin, on the other hand, viewed linguistic phenomena as demonstrable solely on the basis of observation, and in particular the corroboration of ancient texts. A fact could not be true "of itself" but had to be proven with related examples. Instead of referring to their linguistic findings as *self-so*, scholars like Qian Daxin and Duan Yucai adopted a new language of validity, routinely claiming instead that their assertions were "supportable" (*kezheng* 可證) and levying numerous textual examples to serve as this support.[69]

This new genealogy and definition of philology is highly visible in the late eighteenth-century *Siku quanshu* and its accompanying bibliographical category. The only Ming phonological texts included within the *Siku quanshu* proper were the dynastic rhyme dictionary *Hongwu zhengyun* and several texts by the perceived forerunners of Evidential Learning: Yang Shen, Chen Di, and Jiao Hong. Methodological outliers in their own time, the preservation of their writings in the most influential compendium of pre-nineteenth-century texts has reinforced persistent ideas about their significance, as well as the lack of other philological activity in the Ming. The bibliographical catalog accompanying the *Siku quanshu* contained a much broader array of Ming philological texts. While it was by no means comprehensive in its inclusion, many of the most significant texts of the sixteenth and seventeenth centuries were reviewed within this emblematic work of mid-Qing scholarship. The critiques, which served to justify the exclusion of these texts from the *Siku quanshu* itself, painted a dismal picture of the Ming intellectual landscape as a benighted era.

Even in the formative years of the Evidential Learning methodology during the first half of the eighteenth century, major scholars openly credited their inheritance of late Ming philological texts and methods. In the second half of the century, this discourse of indebtedness and constructive interaction largely gave way to repudiation. By the late eighteenth century, Evidential Learning thinkers had come to define philology according to a novel set of methods and associated it with a limited set of ancient and recent thinkers. The historical circumstances of the early twentieth century, when scholar-reformers like Liang Qichao looked to Evidential Learning as an indicator of scientific potential in Chinese history, further reinforced for modern observers the significance of this particular definition and genealogy of philology. Their methods have continued to influence Chinese historical linguistics and shape approaches to the reconstruction of ancient pronunciations. The Ming moment, as we shall see in the epilogue, came to serve a new purpose in the twentieth century, not as methodological inspiration within linguistics, but as the perceived origin of concerns with phonographic scripts and language standardization.

Conclusion: Transition in Notions of Valid Knowledge

Present-day researchers have proposed many theories for why a shift in intellectual priorities occurred during the eighteenth century.[70] A full exploration of the underlying forces behind this transition is beyond the scope of this study. The primary purpose of this book has been to present an alternative understanding of what changed. Rather than seeing the eighteenth century as a pivot away from philosophical speculation in pursuit of moral improvement toward philological study of texts and language, we might alternatively characterize this dramatic period of intellectual transition as a shift in methods of learning and conceptions of disciplinary boundaries. Correct knowledge came to be framed no longer as "so-of-itself," but rather as "supportable" on the basis of textual evidence. This revised picture of the nature of intellectual change in late imperial China suggests new reasons for why such a transition occurred. The following sketch proposes some contributing factors with the intention of providing a basis for future research.

A Conflicted Antiquity: Embracing the New with the Old

The establishment of new disciplinary communities of knowledge in the Ming can be attributed in part to the retreat of the court from scholarly patronage, as well as an increased skepticism toward the inherent validity of antiquity. As a result of the loss of these major sources of authority, scholars pursued an alternative method of demonstrating validity by relying on the expertise of peers. A shift in these factors in the eighteenth century may help explain the new configuration of philology as a more siloed discipline. Antiquity achieved a renewed epistemological status as an antidote to the perceived obsession with novelty in the Ming. Ancient texts assumed a privileged place as "evidence," replacing a previous conception of evidence based on an assumption of *self-so* Coherence that underlay the functioning of the universe. Scholars associated with the imperial court, which had reasserted itself as the center of valid knowledge production, redefined philology as a textual endeavor, paring away the pluralistic influences of Ming linguistic study.

The attention to "antiquity" (*gu* 古) in the eighteenth century was not merely a reaffirmation of an earlier discourse on the value of ancient writings or the moral authority of the ancient sages. As Ori Sela has shown,

Learning of the Way thinkers of the Song and Ming were deeply invested in antiquity and would even pursue philological analyses of the Classics in pursuit of accessing the morality of the sages. But ultimately they saw textual authority as subservient to a mental connection with the Way of antiquity. For many Qing Evidential Learning thinkers, "antiquity," was itself a source of validity, accessible only through careful textual reconstruction of the Classics.[71] For some Evidential Learning thinkers it was also a rhetorical affirmation of communal values in the face of what they characterized as idiosyncratic tendencies in Ming scholarship. Language criticizing the penchant toward the "novel" (*xin* 新) and "divergence" (*yi* 異) abounds in eighteenth-century descriptions of earlier scholarship.[72] Qing scholars routinely charged Ming thinkers in particular with "intentionally establishing divergence" (有意立異) and embracing novelty for its own sake.[73] It is worth considering the implications of "divergence" in this context. In the seventeenth century, "divergence" was also widely invoked in scholarly discourse as a criticism for scholarship that did not match the norms of its field.[74] Evidential Learning thinkers inherited this usage but directed it toward Ming thinkers, who had diverted, in their view, from a way of doing scholarship rooted in the methods of antiquity. It also reflected a perception that late Ming thinkers sought fame through individualistic scholarship rather than scholarly accuracy.

Late Ming scholars did not universally view antiquity as inherently valuable. To be sure, various thinkers intent on "reviving antiquity" (*fugu*) echoed earlier concerns tracing back to the Tang with connecting literary style to morality.[75] Others, like Wei Jiao, attempted to recover ancient practices to get closer to the Way of the ancient sages. Ming thinkers, however, also levied criticisms against foundational figures of the tradition that would have been almost unthinkable in earlier periods.[76] Persistent discussions of antiquity were counterbalanced with a pervasive new discourse of novelty. Evidential Learning scholars, on the other hand, raised the notion of "antiquity" to a key epistemological position, often framed as a response to this Ming attitude.[77] Gu Yanwu, whose methods would greatly inform those of the eighteenth-century Evidential Learning community, famously criticized the leading paleographer of the late Ming, Zhao Yiguang. Gu proposed that the only reason Zhao's work was so popular in its time was because the early seventeenth century "just so happened to be a time when people delighted in the novel and were partial to divergence." Zhao's alterations to texts of antiquity and the methods of "former *ru*" were therefore welcomed by a degenerate culture of novelty.[78] Eighteenth-century claims of a Ming fondness for novelty were not entirely misplaced. Li Zhi, one of the most famous thinkers of the age, famously constructed his self-image as a provocateur by downplaying canonical authority.[79] In so doing, he was an extreme example of a widespread trend.

Evidential Learning thinkers occasionally referred to their scholarship as "foundational learning" (*genben zhi xue* 根本之學).[80] The foundation Qing scholars found lacking in Ming works was a sense of context that formed the new basis of evidence in the eighteenth century and further reinforced the concentration of their efforts on texts from antiquity. Duan Yucai argued that "textual collators who rashly establish an argument on the basis of a single graph or phrase, and who neglect the surrounding text (*bu guan shangxiawen* 不觀上下文) to interpret its meaning, simply relish in despising the ordinary and delighting in the novel."[81] Major Evidential Learning projects, such as *Jingdian wenzi kaoyi* (經典文字考異 Analysis of variation in graphs in the Classics), emphasized a form of textual analysis founded on comparison of examples within a set of ancient texts. The accumulation of contemporaneous sources and examples was how Evidential scholars "proved" their findings.[82]

Even Ming scholars like Zhang Xianyi and Wei Jiao, who devoted great attention to the texts of antiquity, saw no issue with citing texts from much later periods as evidence in support of their reading of early texts. Such thinkers, despite their references to antiquity, adopted the Learning of the Way assumption that there existed a fundamentally ahistorical Coherence linking the past and present.[83] For Wei Jiao, the minds of the ancient sages could be accessed and restored because they were not specific to a historical epoch. Conversely, historical context was essential to the Evidential Learning project. The *Siku quanshu* editors criticized Ming scholars for "wantonly inserting" (*lanru* 闌入) later texts in discussions of antiquity, a quality they routinely characterized as "the inveterate habit of Ming thinkers."[84] This characteristic also frequently led to an appraisal of their work as "scattered" (*boza* 駁雜 or *zarou* 雜糅).[85] In the minds of Evidential Learning thinkers, Ming scholars tended to "cite extensively" (*boyin* 博引) first and ask questions later. By the eighteenth-century, scholars would frequently claim omission over excessive inclusion.[86]

An emphasis on sources from the Han and earlier is reflected not only in the basis of Evidential Learning studies in texts from antiquity, but also in the prevalence of methodological study of *Shuowen jiezi* in the eighteenth century. Contrary to received narratives, this interest in script itself did not represent a stark contrast with Ming scholarly priorities. However, the transition toward heralding *Shuowen* in the eighteenth century is perhaps even more striking in light of the fact that the Han dynasty dictionary was not neglected in the Ming but was in fact the target of active criticism. Ming scholars denounced Xu Shen, author of *Shuowen jiezi*, for misunderstanding the nature of writing in antiquity.[87] Eighteenth-century scholars took a dim view of this disregard for Xu Shen and the early philological tradition.[88] The shifting treatment of *Shuowen jiezi* is reflective of a broader transition in philological reasoning from criticizing to upholding the ancient, and from a notion that scholarly and literary culture had either improved or devolved since antiquity. Dai Zhen criticized the study of graphs after *Shuowen jiezi*, noting that scholarship had become "perverted" (乖) as it increased in distance from antiquity because scholars "rarely observed the foundation of the ancients' creations."[89] Despite their concern with ancient writing, Ming thinkers assumed that the fundamentally ahistorical nature of the ancients' minds allowed for a broader consultation of noncanonical and recent sources.

Context, including historical period of composition and textual corroboration, was an indispensable part of the Evidential Learning methodology. Ming scholars routinely mixed texts from different historical time periods, even when making claims about antiquity. Arguing for a sharp divide between antiquity and the present would have undermined the cosmological and metaphysical foundations of Ming philology, which sought acoustic properties in the sound-based *qi* that had remained constant since the origins of the universe and defined graph forms according to the unchanging processes of the sagely mind. Although the central premise of Evidential Learning philology that the language of antiquity differed systematically from the present had emerged already in the sixteenth century, it was not a proposition that immediately gained wide currency.

The assertion of a historicized "antiquity" as a standard for knowledge production forced a restructuring of the discipline of philology itself. Beginning with the attempts of the eleventh-century cosmologist Shao Yong to link language with a broader set of universal phenomena, philology had increasingly come to be rooted in an integrated nexus of scholarly endeavors. The seminal philological texts of antiquity and the medieval period, however, were more limited in scope, focusing primarily on explicitly linguistic issues.[90] Shifting the model of philology from Shao Yong to Xu

Shen and Lu Fayan had a major effect on the shape of scholarship. Evidential Learning scholars consciously emulated the style of *Shuowen jiezi* in their own writings.[91] In so doing, they brought the field in line with an earlier conception of language study, which was rooted firmly in the explication of graph forms and pronunciations in classical texts.

This increased attention to the historical antiquity was accompanied by a renewed belief in the textual record as a faithful representation of the time of the sages. A primary concern among Ming philologists was the perceived limitation of human perception and the textual legacy, which was only an incomplete reflection of the full textual production of antiquity. Already in the sixteenth century, the study (and production) of forgeries had become increasingly widespread, as scholars questioned and capitalized on the ambiguities of the textual record.[92] Wang Shizhen (1526–1590), who embraced the literary one-upmanship of contemporary forgery, even proclaimed: "Anyone who forges antiquities and [successfully] passes them off must be conversant with antiquity. If someone not conversant with antiquity passes on [a forgery], how could that be the forger's fault?"[93] In the eighteenth century, the study of forgery remained a mainstay of philological study, but the element of literary and scholarly play had been largely replaced with sophisticated linguistic analysis directed toward restoring the putative original version of a corrupted text. This attempt to historicize linguistic sound, script, and meaning significantly undermined the work of Ming scholars. Philology was even rallied to demonstrate that terms such as *yin-yang* and the Five Phases, central to the cosmological studies of Ming scholars, had lacked any cosmological connotation in antiquity.[94] "Evidence" was redefined from information that confirmed the *self-so* Coherence of the universe to the information available in texts.

Scholars active in the Qing court promoted this vision of philology, which eschewed the kind of plurality that defined Ming intellectual endeavors. The role of the Qing court as a locus of scholarly activity is well-documented.[95] The effect of this role on the shape of disciplines is less clearly understood. Ming scholars occasionally criticized the lack of court involvement in scholarly activities. This absence, however, was also in part responsible for the rise of disciplinary communities of knowledge as an alternative source of scholarly validity. The reassertion of court authority in scholarship, as well as attempts to stifle challenges to this authority, did not eradicate alternative modes of learning, and the intellectual world of the Qing was highly diverse in practice. The court was nonetheless able to provide a platform for Evidential Learning, particularly in the context of the *Siku quanshu* project, leading to the overwhelming influence of these thinkers on later understandings of the period.

Communities of philological knowledge, which had begun to form in the Ming, became even more prevalent in the eighteenth century. Perhaps most worthy of note in the construction of what would become the Evidential Learning community is Dai Zhen. As a pivotal figure in the spread of philological learning, Dai shared his vision of a textual evidence-based method with his students and colleagues, molding a community of considerable methodological consistency. The most prominent of Dai's students and collaborators, including Wang Niansun 王念孫 (1744–1832), Kong Guangsen, Qian Daxin, and Duan Yucai, would form the pillars of the Evidential Learning community. Despite their disagreements on issues in Chinese phonology, they shared a set of methodological priorities that separated them from the mainstream trends in sixteenth- and seventeenth-century phonology. Dai's commitment to "antiquity" and "supportable" knowledge, in place of *self-so*, as the standard for new knowledge would become central to later eighteenth-century epistemology.[96]

While considerable work has been done to document significant aspects of eighteenth-century intellectual culture, much remains to be determined: How did the reassertion of the court, alongside other institutions, in intellectual life contribute to new practices of disciplinary learning in the eighteenth century? To what extent do the striking differences in philological methodology between the late sixteenth and late eighteenth century generalize to other fields of learning? Was the eighteenth-century emphasis on intellectual lineage within technical fields primarily a retrospective practice of constructing a historical narrative, or did teachers like Dai Zhen increasingly seek to promote their methods through establishing intellectual successors? It is hoped that incorporating more fully the sixteenth and seventeenth centuries into narratives of eighteenth-century change will illuminate more clearly how and what shifted in this pivotal period.

It is clear that the value of "antiquity" as a standard of validity was increasingly raised as an antidote to the perceived obsession with novelty and integrative system-building among Ming scholars. Nevertheless, eighteenth- and nineteenth-century thinkers were indebted to the sense of disciplinary community, and its emphasis on contemporary scholarship, which had developed in the late Ming. It was in fact a recent scholar, Jiang Yong, who epitomized the right approach to scholarship in the minds of some Evidential Learning scholars. The *Siku quanshu* editor responsible for assessing one of Jiang Yong's phonological works addressed this apparent contradiction, commenting that "it would be impermissible to underestimate [this text] just because it is of recent provenance."[97] The same editor, in a move symbolic of the period's erasure of the Ming contribution, noted conversely that the major seventeenth-century philologists who had preceded Jiang were "unworthy of further discussion." The aim of this book has been to recover the work of these "unworthy" scholars, whose seemingly obscure texts and methods must occupy an important place in our understanding of Chinese intellectual culture.

Epilogue

In a *Foreign Policy* article from May 2016 titled "Chinese Is Not a Backward Language," Thomas Mullaney defended the Chinese writing system against a perceived slight at the hands of science fiction author Ted Chiang's "Bad Character," which appeared earlier that month in the *New Yorker*.[1] Chiang described Chinese graphs as onerous for the learner, a hindrance to literacy, and a setback for digitalization. Mullaney countered that Chinese has been "one of the fastest, most widespread, and successful languages of the digital age." Both positions hinged on assumptions about linguistic efficiency and the implications of the Chinese script for China's modernization.[2] Yet discourse on the efficiency of script forms has a long history in China, which far precedes historical concerns with modernity and the present-day issue of digitalization. The better-known twentieth-century language reform movements resonate with these early discussions in striking ways, suggesting the influence of the Ming moment on China up to the present.

This book has been primarily concerned with the study of language as a window into larger intellectual trends, and in particular the shift from a broader to a more siloed conception of disciplinary knowledge from the sixteenth through eighteenth centuries. Many of the findings within these chapters are also surprising in revealing unexpected attention toward what have often been considered the domain of modern language reformers. This epilogue shifts from the primary intellectual historical argument of the book to highlight some of these later resonances. This discussion is warranted, I believe, given the recent burgeoning of research on modern Chinese language reform, as well as the continued relevance of ideas about the Chinese language in public discourse.[3]

Philology in Chinese history has enjoyed multiple meanings. Late Ming scholars tended to see the philological study of language as predicated on establishing *self-so* correlations across cosmological, musical, and literary branches of learning. The eighteenth-century Evidential Learning approach to philology was based primarily on the corroboration of graphs and pronunciations in ancient texts. The latter looks more familiar to us now as a form of historical linguistics, but there is no reason to assume it would naturally develop into the modern discipline, as practiced in linguistic departments today. Similarly, there was no straightforward path from the linguistic innovations of Ming scholars to the language reform movements of modern China. What on the surface appear to be similar practices often had vastly different goals. For instance, the Ming pursuit of phonographic writing was geared primarily toward a theoretical abstraction of linguistic sound, in contrast to the efforts toward phoneticism for the purposes of mass literacy promoted by twentieth-century reformers. Nevertheless, concrete resonances and linkages suggest the ways in which early modern conceptions of language informed modern language movements, which have strongly shaped the linguistic landscape of China today.

When cast in the light of history, much of what seems daring in the reform movements of the late Qing appears less novel. Late nineteenth-century reformers created systems that replaced Chinese graphs with numbers, a seemingly drastic move that was in fact implemented already by Chen Jinmo in the mid-seventeenth century (see chapter 1).[4] These later reformers carefully documented the number of possible sounds their systems could record, resembling the emphasis on such quantification in the work of Ming cosmologists.[5] The underlying motivations for creating such notation systems differed from the Ming context. Modern reform movements emphasized the importance of mass literacy and national unity, while Ming phonologists were primarily concerned with the theoretical abstraction of sound from script, as well as providing a basis for elite composition and recitation. Nonetheless, the basic techniques reformers employed followed a tradition of phonetic notation that had developed over the course of the Ming and Qing dynasties.

The end of the nineteenth century saw the beginnings of a move toward phoneticization in China, but a less-documented opposing current to this discourse also mirrored Ming discussions. Even among late Qing reformers there were those who remained skeptical of phoneticism. Wen Tingshi, for instance, recounted favorably an anecdote from a meeting of the Romanization Association (Ch. Luomazi hui 羅馬字會 / J. Rōmaji kai ローマ字会), formed in Japan in 1885. This organization was famously concerned with establishing a Romanization system for Japanese (settling eventually on the Hepburn system). According to a Japanese report, which Wen had read, only the Italian ambassador opposed the promulgation of the Roman script, claiming that "the scripts of other nations represent words (辭) but contain no meaning (無意義). The Chinese script creates meaning in the form of its graphs and is capable of encompassing a great many ideas. Hence if the myriad nations used this script, then they would communicate in ideas (通義理)."[6] Wen praised this opinion as "exceptional." The translator and reformer Wang Tao 王韜 (1828–1897) offered that "there is no country on earth with a script as complete as the Chinese. The scripts of other countries only contain sound and cannot contain words."[7] Wang's contemporary reformer Kang Youwei 康有為 (1858–1927) similarly opined that the superficial convenience of phonographic writing was "inferior to the perfect completion of Chinese graphs."[8] This defense of Chinese writing as simpler to understand yet more complete than phonographic alternatives mirrors that of Ming scholars, who were skeptical of the efficiency of such scripts as well as their potential to communicate the full scope of Chinese civilization. Chinese graphs have been put to the test on numerous historical occasions; their defenders indicate that the recent critique of "Bad Character" theories is not just a product of present-day revisionism.

Ming discussions of operatic language and linguistic standards also continue to resonate to the present. Twentieth-century manuals of opera performance technique employed the terminology developed by Sheng Chongsui for discussing pronunciation according to the "head, belly, and tail" of a graph.[9] The usage of a historical technique of instruction for primarily historical operas, as well as the motivation to recover authenticity in performance, makes the adoption of Shen Chongsui's terminology relatively unsurprising. More noteworthy are the striking parallels in conceptions of linguistic unity shared between the opera librettists and twentieth-century reformers, who were similarly concerned with establishing the proper basis for a common language.[10]

The attention to language reform in the late Qing and early Republican era reflected new concerns with mass literacy, national unity, and industrialization. Framed explicitly in response to current events and developed concomitantly with a much broader Eurasian movement of script reform, their innovations should not be understood as developing directly out of earlier discussions of Chinese script and language.[11] In many cases the relationship, if there exists one at all, with premodern discourse is hidden. It does revolutionaries no favors to reveal the origins of their methods in the system they are proposing to overthrow. For the most part, late Qing script reformers did not explicitly frame their work as a development of earlier attempts at phonetic representation in China, making it difficult to ascertain to what degree they were aware of such precedents. Discursive similarities suggest, however, if not direct reading of Ming works, the inheritance of Ming linguistic discussions as mediated through later philological texts.[12]

In the later Republican and early PRC era, reformers increasingly attached importance to generating a historical narrative for script reform in China, which explicitly engaged with Ming precedents. Shortly after the formation of the People's Republic of China, the new Script Reform Press (Wenzi gaige chubanshe 文字改革出版社) was formed in 1956 as the publishing branch of the Committee on Chinese Script Reform (Zhongguo wenzi gaige weiyuanhui 中国文字改革委员会). The press published a set of "historical materials on phonetic scripts" (*pinyin wenzi shiliao congshu* 拼音文字史料叢書) between 1956 and 1958. These materials traced a lineage of script reform practices all the way from the Ming to the development of the pinyin romanization system in the early People's Republic of China (still in use today).

The earliest text included in the compilation was an extant portion of Matteo Ricci's *Xizi qiji* (西字奇蹟 Miracle of Western graphs). Referring to Ricci's work as "the first model of Latin alphabet pinyin in China," its inclusion suggested the beginning of script reform in China as the product of outside stimulus.[13] Zhou Youguang 周有光 (1906–2017), in his Marxist 1961 *Hanzi gaige gailun* (漢字改革概論 An overview of Chinese script reform), similarly traced the origins of pinyin in China to Matteo Ricci and early Jesuit contact.[14] By introducing the Chinese to the Latin alphabet, Matteo Ricci purportedly opened the eyes of Ming scholars to the possibilities of phonographic writing. As described in chapters 1 and 2, when Ricci arrived there were in fact already scholars actively studying Sanskrit writing, as well as experimenting with other forms of phonetic notation, based for instance on numerals and zither compound-graphs. Given the fascination with phonetic representation in Ming China, it seems more likely that the early Jesuit materials included in the "historical materials on phonetic scripts" did not initiate a new interest but instead provided an alternative system that appealed within an existing area of study.

The early PRC promoters of pinyin also devoted substantial attention to the seventeenth-century scholar Liu Xianting, whom they referred to as "the first person in China to research the phoneticization [lit., pinyinization] of writing (*wenzi de pinyinhua* 文字的拼音化)."[15] Liu Xianting studied closely with experts in Sanskrit script and noted his awareness of other phonographic writing systems. He also claimed to have devised a system capable of documenting all possible sounds, including those of the various Chinese topolects. He did not have a substantial influence on Qing philology, and his own phonological studies were in fact lost, if they were ever printed to begin with. He came to be upheld as a model, however, already in the Republican period. Liang Qichao commented that "if [Liu's *New rhyme tables*] had been passed down to posterity, this problem [of how best to Romanize Chinese] might have been solved long before, and much scholarly energy spent on research over the past thirty years might also have been spared."[16] Liang even claimed that the recently created phonetic symbols (*zhuyin zimu* 注音字母) of his own time had adopted aspects of Liu's method based on extant descriptions of the original text, implying that modern script reform had been inspired by seventeenth-century attempts.

Later linguists and reformers explicitly claimed inspiration from Liu Xianting. Luo Changpei 羅常培 (1899–1958), for instance, took part in a systematic effort during the 1930s to document Chinese topolects and saw Liu Xianting as his historical predecessor. Luo argued that Liu Xianting's early interest in documenting topolects was, just like in the present, motivated by a desire to "unify the national language."[17] In a letter to Luo Changpei and his fellow language reformer Li Jinxi 黎錦熙 (1890–1978), Qian Xuantong 錢玄同 (1887–1939) doubled down on this image of Liu Xianting, advocating a commemoration of Liu Xianting's birthyear (1648) as "the founding year of the national language" (國語紀元). Writing in 1933,

Qian noted that in fourteen years they would reach the three-hundredth anniversary of this date, giving them just enough time to make significant progress on the Romanization of Chinese, which they would present at the "300 Year Commemorative Ceremony for the National Language."[18]

Twentieth-century language reformers misinterpreted Liu Xianting's work on nearly all counts and glossed over the original context of Liu's linguistic study. Liu did not explicitly advocate for the use of phonographic writing and criticized the faults of contemporary phonographic scripts. There is no indication that he was interested in unifying a standard spoken language. Instead, he based his phonological study largely on the work of previous Ming cosmologists and expressed his intent to document all possible sounds in the universe. Twentieth-century language reformers had their own motivations for uncovering a history of linguistic reform in China. Liang Qichao's invocation of Liu Xianting served as one of many examples he provided for the emergence of "scientific" thought in China, which could just as well have developed in the direction of natural and physical sciences as the humanities. The Republican language reformers embraced a narrative of China on the path to script reform and linguistic unification, which had only been stifled by the period of Manchu rule. The 1950s PRC scholars extended this narrative a further hundred years into the past. Highlighting the introduction of phonographic writing as a product of Western missionary transmission of the Latin alphabet may have been appealing in light of the early PRC proposal of the Latin alphabet as the basis for pinyin over many alternative options from the preceding decades.[19]

Writing in the Republican period mouthpiece for script reform and linguistic unification, *Guoyu zhoukan* (國語週刊 National language weekly), Zhao Yintang 趙蔭棠 (1893–1970) proclaimed that the phonological studies of the Ming flourished "like a myriad brocade flowers . . . truly impossible to exhaust."[20] As we saw in chapter 7, Evidential Learning scholars rewrote the history of philology in China to feature Gu Yanwu as the pivotal figure in a new trend toward the study of ancient scripts and phonology. Republican era and PRC reformers referenced a different set of key figures from the Ming, not for their attention to antiquity, but for their perceived foresight to envision a phonographic future for China. While this was mostly wishful thinking, there is some truth in twentieth-century narratives that traced the emergence of a fascination with phonographic script and the development of a common language to this period. There are many earlier instances of interaction with phonographic writing in Chinese history, but it was beginning with the Ming that discussions of alternative notation systems achieved a broad currency. The commercialization of literature and spread of regional genres during the Ming also raised new concerns with linguistic unity. As esoteric as their writings appear, the concerns of Ming philologists continue to resurface within China's linguistic practices today.

Acknowledgments

There are too many to thank, whose generosity and support made possible the research, composition, and production of this book. Discussion with many friends and colleagues in both formal and informal settings has improved the book in countless ways. For fear of omission I have not attempted to list everyone; I mention below only a few who were heavily involved in formative stages of the project.

I first must express my deep gratitude to the individuals involved in the original formulation of some of the ideas presented in this book: Peter Bol, Ann Blair, and Michael Szonyi. At a later point, Victor Mair, Willard Peterson, Benjamin Elman, and David Lurie offered important advice. Several of the above, as well as Zev Handel, Mårten Söderblom Saarela, Kathlene Baldanza, Ulug Kuzuoglu, Heng Du, On-cho Ng, Bruce Rusk, Christopher Nugent, Einor Cervone, Ming Tak Ted Hui, and participants in the University Seminar on Neo-Confucian Studies at Columbia University, the Global Archive of Comparison conference at Williams College, and the Early Modern Reading Group at Washington University, among others, read sections of the book manuscript or related articles, providing significant insights.

I would also like to acknowledge the tremendous feedback from the anonymous reviewers. I feel very fortunate to have received such in-depth and constructive comments, which have substantially improved the final version of the manuscript.

It has been a privilege to work with Christine Dunbar, my editor at Columbia University Press, whose guidance has been instrumental at all stages of the book. Many thanks are due as well to Christian Winting, Marisa Lastres, Anita O'Brien, and others at the press who have provided critical support.

Libraries and librarians have played an essential role in the research for this book. I am grateful to the staff of the Harvard-Yenching library, especially Kuniko Yamada-McVey, Xiao-he Ma, James Cheng, and Sharon Yang; Martin Heijdra at the Princeton University East Asian Library; and Joan Wang and Mitsu Nakamura at Washington University. Thanks are due, as well, to the staff of the National Library of China (in particular, Liu Bo), Capital Library (Beijing), Peking University Library, Beijing Normal University Library, National Central Library (Taiwan), Fu Ssu-nien Library at Academia Sinica, National Taiwan Normal University Library, Imperial Household Library of Japan, National Archives of Japan, National Diet Library, Institute for Advanced Studies on Asia (Tōbunken) Library and University of Tokyo Library, Tōyō bunko, Sidō bunko at Keiō University, Seikadō bunko, Sonkeikaku bunko, Jinbunken at Kyoto University, Columbia University Library, and the University of Washington Library.

Funding for research has generously been provided by the Center for Humanities and Information at Pennsylvania State University, Washington University, Fairbank Center for Chinese Studies, Harvard Asia Center, and Reischauer Institute for Japanese Studies. Although primarily dedicated to separate research, my year at the Institute for Advanced Study in Princeton, and conversations with Nicola Di Cosmo and other colleagues (as well as walks in the Institute Woods), played an important role as I completed the last revisions on the manuscript. The final stages of production have also greatly benefited from a subvention from the Geiss Hsu Foundation.

Selected material from the following two journal articles is included in chapters 1 and 7 and is reprinted with the respective journal editors' permission: "From Tradition to Community: The Rise of Contemporary Knowledge in Late Imperial China," *Journal of Asian Studies* 79, no. 1 (2020): 77–101; "New Scripts for All Sounds: Cosmology and Universal Phonetic Notation Systems in Late Imperial China," *Harvard Journal of Asiatic Studies* 78, no. 1 (2018): 1–46.

I am grateful to my family and most especially to Helen, without whose encouragement and patience this book would not have been completed, and whom we must thank for the idea behind the cover design. And to Ran, who entered the world at 3 a.m. the day copyedits on the manuscript were due; I am sure this was just the first of many lessons you will teach me. This book is dedicated to my mother. She has been the greatest influence on my life, my most steadfast supporter and role model. I wish that she had been able to see the completed product, but I know she is as proud of me as I am of her.

Notes

Note on Language

1. For a detailed description of Chao's transcription system, see Yuen Ren Chao 趙元任, *A Project for General Chinese / Tongzi fang'an* 通字方案 (Beijing: Shangwu yinshuguan, 1983). For attempts to transcribe the actual phonetic values of Ming pronunciation, see Li Xinkui 李新魁, *Hanyu dengyunxue* 汉语等韵学 (Beijing: Zhonghua shuju, 1983); Geng Zhensheng 耿振生, *Ming Qing dengyunxue tonglun* 明清等韵学通论 (Beijing: Yuwen chubanshe, 1992); Wang Songmu 王松木, *Mingdai dengyun zhi leixing ji qi kaizhan* 明代等韻之類型及其開展 (Taipei: Hua Mulan chubanshe, 2011).

Introduction

1. Wu Jishi, *Yinsheng jiyuan* 音聲紀元, *Siku quanshu cunmu congshu* 四庫全書存目叢書 (Jinan: Qi Lu shushe chubanshe, 1997) [hereafter *SKQS CMCS*], j. 1, 13b–14a.
2. Similar sequences of phonological study are suggested in Xiao Yuncong 蕭雲從, *Yi cun* 易存, *SKQS CMCS*, [7a]; Fang Yizhi 方以智, *Tongya* 通雅 (Beijing: Zhongguo shudian, 1990), j. 50, 1b; Fang Zhonglü 方中履, *Gujin shiyi* 古今釋疑, *SKQS CMCS*, j. 17, 7a.
3. Rens Bod, *A New History of the Humanities: The Search for Principles and Patterns from Antiquity to the Present* (Oxford: Oxford University Press, 2013), 143.

4. Anthony Grafton, *Joseph Scaliger: A Study in the History of Classical Scholarship* (Oxford: Oxford University Press, 1983); Daniel Stolzenberg, *Egyptian Oedipus: Athanasius Kircher and the Secrets of Antiquity* (Chicago: University of Chicago Press, 2013), 20–21.

5. Mark Edward Lewis, *Writing and Authority in Early China* (Albany: State University of New York Press, 1999); Françoise Bottéro, *Sémantisme et classification dans l'écriture chinoise: Les systèmes de classement des caractères par clés du Shuowen Jiezi au Kangxi Zidian* (Paris: Collège de France, Institut des hautes études chinoises, 1996).

6. The term *xiaoxue* was also employed as a generic term for elementary learning and features in the titles of many primers for young students.

7. Zhao Yiguang 趙宧光, *Shuowen changjian* 說文長箋, *SKQS CMCS, zixu*, 2b–3a.

8. Wu Shilin 吳士琳, *Zhengyun yi* 正韻翼 (at National Library of China), j. 9, 1a. Cf. Dai Tong 戴侗, *Liushu gu* 六書故, *Siku quanshu* 四庫全書 (Taipei: Taiwan shangwu yinshuguan, 1983) [hereafter *SKQS*], j. 16, 5b.

9. For instance, the early seventeenth-century catalog *Dansheng tang cangshumu* 澹生堂藏書目 contains these three main branches of philology in its *xiaoxue* section but also includes additional categories for elementary learning, fusing the two main senses of the term *xiaoxue*. See Qi Chenghan 祁承㸁, *Dansheng tang cangshumu*, [34b]. Cf. Qi's catalog and the range of Ming philological categorizations represented in the bibliographies in Feng Huimin 馮惠民 and Li Wanjian 李萬健, ed., *Mingdai shumu tiba congkan* 明代書目題跋叢刊 (Beijing: Shumu wenxian chubanshe, 1994); and Lin Xi 林夕, ed., *Zhongguo zhuming cangshujia shumu huikan* 中國著名藏書家書目匯刊 (Beijing: Shangwu yinshuguan, 2005).

10. Hu Yinglin, *Huayang boyi* 華陽博議, in *Shaoshi shanfang bicong* 少室山房筆叢 (Beijing: Zhonghua shuju, 1958), 501.

11. It is worth noting that Hu Yinglin also divided philology into more than three subfields, including such related areas as epigraphical studies.

12. Han Qia 韓洽, *Zhuanxue cejie* 篆學測解 (1820 edition at National Library of China), Sima *xu*, 4b–5a. Similar statements concerning the societal significance of lexicography trace back to earlier dictionaries, such as the thirteenth-century *Liushu gu* 六書故. See Dai Tong, *Liushu gu, liushu tongshi*, 1a.

13. Fan Tengfeng 樊騰鳳, *Wufang yuanyin* 五方元音, *Xuxiu Siku quanshu* 續修四庫全書 (Shanghai: Shanghai guji chubanshe, 1995) [hereafter *XX SKQS*], *zixu*, 3b–4a.

14. William H. Baxter, *A Handbook of Old Chinese Phonology* (Berlin: Mouton de Gruyter, 1992), 154–55.

15. Zhao Yiguang, *Shuowen changjian*, j. 50, 33b.

16. Adam Schorr, "The Trap of Words: Political Power, Cultural Authority, and Language Debates in Ming Dynasty China," Ph.D. diss., University of California, Los Angeles, 2004, 36–42.
17. Lü Weiqi 呂維祺, *Tongwen duo* 同文鐸, *XX SKQS, fanli*, 11a.
18. Timothy Brook, *Praying for Power: Buddhism and the Formation of Gentry Society in Late-Ming China* (Cambridge, Mass.: Council on East Asian Studies, Harvard University, 1994). The bulk of philological activity in Ming took place in the Jiangnan region during a time when southern scholars also tended to evince greater divergence from the state than in the North. See Khee Heong Koh, *A Northern Alternative: Xue Xuan (1389–1464) and the Hedong School* (Cambridge, Mass.: Harvard University Asia Center, 2011); and Chang Woei Ong, *Li Mengyang, the North-South Divide, and Literati Learning in Ming China* (Cambridge, Mass.: Harvard University Asia Center, 2016), 27–69.
19. For more on the relationship between philology and literary connoisseurship, see Adam Schorr, "Connoisseurship and the Defense Against Vulgarity: Yang Shen (1488–1559) and His Work," *Monumenta Serica* 41 (1993): 89–128.
20. The original joke hinges on the teacher's confusion of the graphs for "do not improperly" (*wu gou* 毋苟) and "female dog" (*mu gou* 母狗). The classical phrase, which originates in *Liji* 禮記, reads: "When confronted with wealth, do not improperly obtain it; when confronted with calamity, do not improperly avoid it" (臨財毋苟得，臨難毋苟免). The misreading in the joke reads, literally: "When confronted with wealth, the female dog obtains it; when confronted with calamity, the female dog avoids it" (臨財母狗得，臨難母狗免). Youxi zhuren 遊戲主人, *Xinjuan Xiaolin guangji* 新鐫笑林廣記 (1761 edition at Harvard-Yenching Library), j. 2, 10b–11a.
21. See, for example, Feng Menglong, *Feng Menglong's Treasury of Laughs: A Seventeenth-Century Anthology of Traditional Chinese Humour*, trans. Hsu Pi-ching (Leiden: Brill, 2015), 73–75; *Li Zhuowu xiansheng pingdian Sishu xiao* 李卓吾先生評點四書笑 (Taipei: Tianyi chubanshe, 1985), [4a–b]; *Jieyun bian* 解慍編, *XX SKQS*, j. 8, [2–3]; Jiang Guoxiang 蔣國祥, *Tang lüshi yun* 唐律詩韻 (at Taiwan Normal University Library), 15a–b.
22. For example, two provincial exams in 1549 (Fujian and Shaanxi) featured questions on philological matters. See examinations preserved in *Tianyige cang Mingdai kejulu xuankan* 天一閣藏明代科舉錄選刊 (Ningbo: Ningbo chubanshe, 2010). For a typical encyclopedia entry, see Wang Ao 王鏊, *Zhenze zhangyu* 震澤長語, *SKQS*, j. *xia*, 14b–21b.
23. See, for instance, *Qinding Siku quanshu zongmu* 欽定四庫全書總目, j. 30, 28b; j. 37, 14a; j. 43, 27a, 28a, 29b, 33a; j. 44, 12a; j. 65, 17b; j. 69, 16b; j. 123, 23b; j. 134, 11b. Yuming He has documented similar criticism of Ming texts; see Yuming He, *Home and the World: Editing the "Glorious Ming" in Woodblock-Printed*

Books of the Sixteenth and Seventeenth Centuries (Cambridge, Mass.: Harvard University Asia Center, 2013), 1–3.

24. For important exceptions to this general trend, see Bruce Rusk, *Critics and Commentators: The "Book of Poems" as Classic and Literature* (Cambridge, Mass.: Harvard University Asia Center, 2012); Dagmar Schäfer, *The Crafting of the 10,000 Things: Knowledge and Technology in Seventeenth-Century China* (Chicago: University of Chicago Press, 2011); He, *Home and the World*; Bian, *Know Your Remedies;* Nappi, *The Monkey and the Inkpot*; Suyoung Son, *Writing for Print: Publishing and the Making of Textual Authority in Late Imperial China* (Cambridge, Mass.: Harvard University Asia Center, 2018); Ōki Yasushi, *Minmatsu Kōnan no shuppan bunka* (Tokyo: Kenbun shuppan, 2004); Benjamin A. Elman, "Collecting and Classifying: Ming Dynasty Compendia and Encyclopedias (*Leishu*)," *Extrême orient Extrême occident, hors série* (2007): 131–57; and Lin Qingzhang, *Mingdai kaojuxue yanjiu* (Taipei: Taiwan xuesheng shuju, 1983).

25. For a range of interpretations of the transition, see Liang Qichao 梁啟超, *Zhongguo jin sanbianian xueshushi* 中國近三百年學術史 (Shanghai: Minzhi shudian, 1929); Yü Ying-shih, "Some Preliminary Reflections on the Rise of Ch'ing Intellectualism," *Tsing Hua Journal of Chinese Studies* 11 (1975): 105–46; Willard Peterson, *Bitter Gourd: Fang I-chih and the Impetus for Intellectual Change* (New Haven, Conn.: Yale University Press, 1979); Benjamin A. Elman, *From Philosophy to Philology: Intellectual and Social Aspects of Change in Late Imperial China* (Cambridge, Mass.: Council on East Studies, Harvard University, 1984); Kai-Wing Chow, *The Rise of Confucian Ritualism in Late Imperial China: Ethics, Classics, and Lineage Discourse* (Stanford, Calif.: Stanford University Press, 1994); and Kinoshita Tetsuya 木下鉄矢, *Shindai gakujutsu to gengogaku: kōingaku no shisō to keifu* 清代学術と言語学: 古音学の思想と系譜 (Tokyo: Benseishuppan, 2016).

26. See Ori Sela, *China's Philological Turn: Scholars, Textualism, and the Dao in the Eighteenth Century* (New York: Columbia University Press, 2018).

27. Schäfer, *The Crafting of the 10,000 Things*; Roger Hart, *Imagined Civilizations: China, the West, and Their First Encounter* (Baltimore: Johns Hopkins University Press, 2013), 77–130; Ong, *Li Mengyang*.

28. Lin Qingzhang, *Mingdai kaojuxue yanjiu*; Elman, *From Philosophy to Philology*, 215–223; Ch'ien, *Chiao Hung and the Restructuring of Neo-Confucianism in the Late Ming*.

29. Anthony Grafton, *Defenders of the Text: The Traditions of Scholarship in an Age of Science, 1450–1800* (Cambridge, Mass.: Harvard University Press, 1991); Ann Moyer, *Musica Scientia: Musical Scholarship in the Renaissance* (Ithaca, N.Y.: Cornell University Press, 1992); Ann Blair, *The Theater of Nature: Jean Bodin and Renaissance Science* (Princeton, N.J.: Princeton University Press, 1997).

30. This research is summarized in Ann Blair, *Too Much to Know: Managing Scholarly Information Before the Modern Age* (New Haven, Conn.: Yale University Press, 2010), 7.
31. Cf. Elman, *From Philosophy to Philology*; Sela, *China's Philological Turn*.
32. See papers in "Forum: The Two Cultures Revisited; the Sciences and the Humanities in a *Longue Durée* Perspective," *History of Humanities* 3, no. 1 (2018): 5–88; and Ann Blair, "Disciplinary Distinctions Before the '*Two Cultures*,'" *European Legacy* 13, no. 5 (2008): 577–88.
33. Federico Marcon, *The Knowledge of Nature and the Nature of Knowledge in Early Modern Japan* (Chicago: University of Chicago Press, 2015), 251–97.
34. For a critique of this tendency, see Ding Naifei, *Obscene Things: Sexual Politics in Jin Ping Mei* (Durham, N.C.: Duke University Press, 2002), 7–9.

1. The Number of Everything

1. Richard von Glahn, *The Economic History of China: From Antiquity to the Nineteenth Century* (Cambridge: Cambridge University Press, 2016), 295–307.
2. Lucille Chia, *Printing for Profit: The Commercial Publishers of Jianyang, Fujian (11th–17th Centuries)* (Cambridge, Mass.: Harvard University Asia Center, 2003), 184–85.
3. Suyoung Son, *Writing for Print: Publishing and the Making of Textual Authority in Late Imperial China* (Cambridge, Mass.: Harvard University Asia Center, 2018).
4. Ya Zuo, *Shen Gua's Empiricism* (Cambridge, Mass.: Harvard University Asia Center, 2018), 15–17; 133–34.
5. Ge Zhongxuan 葛中選, *Tailü* 泰律 (Yunnan: Yunnan tushuguan, 1914), j. 8, 19b.
6. Yue Shaofeng 樂韶鳳 et al., *Hongwu zhengyun*, *Siku quanshu* 四庫全書 (Taipei: Taiwan shangwu yinshuguan, 1983) [hereafter *SKQS*], *fanli*, 11b–12a.
7. Cf. Han Bangqi 韓邦奇, *Yuanluo zhiyue* 苑洛志樂 (1548 edition, microfilm at Harvard-Yenching Library), j. 2, 33a; Lü Kun 呂坤, *Shenyin yu* 呻吟語, *Siku quanshu cunmu congshu* 四庫全書存目叢書 (Jinan: Qi Lu shushe chubanshe, 1997) [hereafter *SKQS CMCS*], j. 1, 6b; Ge Zhongxuan, *Tailü*, j. 10, 2a; Fang Yizhi, *Siyun dingben* 四韻定本, in *Fang Yizhi quanshu* 方以智全書, vol. 7 (Hefei: Huangshan shushe, 2019), 11.
8. Zhu Xi 朱熹, *Zhu Wengong Yi shuo* 朱文公易說, *SKQS*, j. 19, 31a; Pan Xizeng 潘希曾, *Zhujian ji* 竹澗集, *SKQS*, j. 8, 1b. For similar statements, see Cai Qing 蔡清, *Yijing mengyin* 易經蒙引, *SKQS*, j. 4 *shang*, 33a; Gao Panlong 高攀龍, *Zhouyi yijian shuo* 周易易簡說, *SKQS*, j. 3, 32b; and Shen Yiguan 沈一貫, *Yixue* 易學, *SKQS CMCS*, j. 9, 18a–b.

9. Dagmar Schäfer, *The Crafting of the 10,000 Things: Knowledge and Technology in Seventeenth-Century China* (Chicago: University of Chicago Press, 2011), 240.
10. Michael Puett, "Nature and Artifice: Debates in Late Warring States China Concerning the Creation of Culture," *Harvard Journal of Asiatic Studies* 57, no. 2 (1997): 471–518.
11. Cheng Zongshun 程宗舜, *Hongfan qianjie* 洪範淺解, *Xuxiu Siku quanshu* 續修四庫全書 (Shanghai: Shanghai guji chubanshe, 1995–1999) [hereafter *XX SKQS*], j. 10, 33a.
12. Prior to Zhu Xi there existed other metaphysical codifications of *self-so*, but Coherence became central to this discussion in the Ming. See Zuo, *Shen Gua's Empiricism*, 138–40.
13. Willard Peterson, "Another Look at *Li*," *Bulletin of Sung-Yuan Studies* 18 (1986): 13–32; Zuo, *Shen Gua's Empiricism*, 202–3; Peter Bol, *Neo-Confucianism in History* (Cambridge, Mass.: Harvard University Asia Center, 2010), 163–69.
14. Fang Yingxuan 方應選, *Fang Zhongfu ji* 方眾甫集, *SKQS CMCS*, j. 5, 2a–3a; Fan Tengfeng 樊騰鳳, *Wufang yuanyin* 五方元音, *XX SKQS*, *tushuo*, 4a. A phrase frequently invoked in Ming musicological scholarship ran "Coherence and Number can rely on each other, and cannot be separated from each other" (理數可相倚而不可相違). See, for instance, Xing Yunlu 邢雲路, *Gujin lüli kao* 古今律曆考 (1600 edition, microfilm at Harvard-Yenching Library), j. 63, 3a–9a.
15. Thomas F. Gieryn, *Cultural Boundaries of Science: Credibility on the Line* (Chicago: University of Chicago Press, 1999), 14.
16. Jiao Hong wrote prefaces to both Wu Jishi's *Yinsheng jiyuan* and Ge Zhongxuan's *Tailü*.
17. For a discussion of esotericism as a set of practices ranging from occult philosophy to alchemy, see Wouter J. Hanegraaff, "Esotericism," in *Dictionary of Gnosis and Western Esotericism*, ed. Hanegraaff (Leiden: Brill, 2006), 336–40.
18. Anthony Grafton, *Defenders of the Text: The Traditions of Scholarship in an Age of Science, 1450–1800* (Cambridge, Mass.: Harvard University Press, 1991); Paula Findlen, *Possessing Nature: Museums, Collecting, and Scientific Culture in Early Modern Italy* (Berkeley: University of California Press, 1996); Blair, *The Theater of Nature*; Brian W. Ogilvie, *The Science of Describing: Natural History in Renaissance Europe* (Chicago: University of Chicago Press, 2006). Cf. Daniel Stolzenberg, *Egyptian Oedipus: Athanasius Kircher and the Secrets of Antiquity* (Chicago: University of Chicago Press, 2013), 70.
19. Chen Jinmo, *Yuanyin tongyun* 元音統韻, *SKQS CMCS*, j. 2, 57b.
20. Benjamin A. Elman, *A Cultural History of Modern Science in China* (Cambridge, Mass.: Harvard University Press, 2006), xii; and Aihe Wang, *Cosmology and Political Culture in Early China* (Cambridge: Cambridge University Press, 2006), 5. This early twentieth-century characterization of premodern

Chinese thought is often invoked as an explanation for why there was no scientific revolution in China; for a critique of this claim, see Roger Hart, *Imagined Civilizations: China, the West, and Their First Encounter* (Baltimore: Johns Hopkins University Press, 2013), 111–12.

21. Cf. Hu Qiguang 胡奇光, *Zhongguo xiaoxue shi* 中国小学史 (Shanghai: Shanghai renmin chubanshe, 1987), 181. For a discussion of late Ming phonological innovation in the standardization of "spelling" methods, see Mårten Söderblom Saarela, "Alphabets *Avant la Lettre*: Phonographic Experiments in Late Imperial China," *Twentieth-Century China* 41, no. 3 (2016): 240–43.
22. Ge Zhongxuan, *Tailü*, j. 9, 24a–b; Fang Yizhi, *Tongya* 通雅 (Beijing: Zhongguo shudian, 1990), j. 50, 29b–30a; Qiao Zhonghe 喬中和, *Yuanyun pu* 元韻譜, *SKQS CMCS*, *juanshou*, 31a–35b; Wu Jishi, *Yinsheng jiyuan*, *xu*, 1a.
23. For variations of this phrase, see, for instance, Chen Jinmo, *Yuanyin tongyun*, *xu*, 3a; Long Weilin 龍為霖, *Benyun yide* 本韻一得, *SKQS CMCS*, j. 2, 12a; and Cheng Yuanchu 程元初, *Lülü yinyun guashu tong* 律呂音韻卦數通 (1609 edition at Naikaku bunko), j. 2, 14b.
24. Kenneth J. DeWoskin, *A Song for One or Two: Music and the Concept of Art in Early China* (Ann Arbor: Center for Chinese Studies, University of Michigan Press, 1982), 55–83; Erica Fox Brindley, *Music, Cosmology, and the Politics of Harmony in Early China* (Albany: State University of New York Press, 2012).
25. For the cosmology surrounding discussions of script in early China, see Mark Edward Lewis, *Writing and Authority in Early China* (Albany: State University of New York Press, 1999), 241–86.
26. Hirata Shōji 平田昌司, "'Zhongyuan yayin' yu Song Yuan Ming Jiangnan ruxue–'tuzhong' guannian, wenhua zhengtong yishi dui zhongguo zhengyin lilun de yingxiang" '中原雅音' 與宋元明江南儒学–'土中' 觀念、文化正統意識對中國正音理論的影响, in *Jindai guanhua yuyin yanjiu* 近代官話語音研究, ed. Geng Zhengsheng (Beijing: Yuwen chubanshe, 2007), 52–53.
27. Cf. Zhao Huiqian 趙撝謙, *Huangji shengyin wenzi tong* 皇極聲音文字通, *SKQS CMCS*; Wang Ao 王鏊, *Zhenze zhangyu* 震澤長語, *SKQS*, j. *xia*, 14b–15a.
28. Cao Yin 曹寅, *Lianting shumu* 楝亭書目, *yunxue*, [2b], in *Zhongguo zhuming cangshujia shumu huikan* 中國著名藏書家書目匯刊, ed. Lin Xi 林夕 (Beijing: Shangwu yinshuguan, 2005).
29. Long Weilin, *Benyun yide*, j. 2, 12a; Du Yu 都俞, *Leizuan gu wenzi kao* 類纂古文字考, *SKQS CMCS*, *ba*, 2b; *Qinding Siku quanshu zongmu* 欽定四庫全書總目, *SKQS*, j. 44, 14a; j. 106, 2a; Wu Jishi, *Yinsheng jiyuan*, Jiao *xu*, 2a; Chen Jinmo, *Huangji tuyun*, *SKQS CMCS*, 5b; Ge Zhongxuan, *Tailü*, j. 8, 2a.
30. Lü Weiqi 呂維祺, *Yinyun riyue deng* 音韻日月燈, *zixu*, 1b.
31. Lü Weiqi, *Yinyun riyue deng*, Zheng *xu*, 1b; Fang Yizhi, *Dongxi jun zhushi* 東西均注釋, ed. Pang Pu 龐樸, 296.

32. Han Qia 韓洽, *Zhuanxue cejie* 篆學測解 (1820 edition at National Library of China), j. 16, 26a; Chen Hu 陳瑚, *Quean wen'gao* 確庵文稿, *Siku jinhuishu congkan* 四庫禁燬書叢刊 (Beijing: Beijing chubanshe, 1997), *guwen*, *xu*, *Shuowen xu*, [1b]; Lu Longqi 陸隴其, *Sanyu tang shengyan* 三魚堂賸言, *SKQS*, j. 12, 2b. Wu Jishi argued against this criticism of his work in *Yinsheng jiyuan*, Wu *xu*, 1a.

33. On cosmic resonance, see John S. Major, "Surveying Obscurities," in *The Huainanzi: A Guide to the Theory and Practice of Government in Early Han China*, by Liu An, King of Huainan, ed. John S. Major et al. (New York: Columbia University Press, 2010), 207–13.

34. For the linkage of morality and philology in the Ming, see chapter 3.

35. For more on the usage of the term *topolect* for the Chinese term *fangyan* 方言 as a way of referring to the mutually unintelligible varieties of the Chinese language associated with different regions, see Victor H. Mair, "What Is a Chinese 'Dialect/Topolect'? Reflections on Some Key Sino-English Linguistic Terms," *Sino-Platonic Papers* 29 (1991): 1–31.

36. Ge Zhongxuan, *Tailü*, j. 8, 19b.

37. Wu Jishi, *Yinsheng jiyuan*, *xu*, 2a.

38. Ge Zhongxuan, *Tailü*, j. 8, 2a; Qiao Zhonghe, *Yuanyun pu*, *xu*, 7b–8a, 14b.

39. Fang Yizhi, *Tongya*, j. 1, 1a; cf. Huang Daozhou, *San Yi dongji* 三易洞璣, *SKQS*, j. 13, 11a.

40. Chen Di 陳第, *Mao Shi guyin kao* 毛詩古音考, ed. Kang Ruicong 康瑞琮 (Beijing: Zhonghua shuju, 1988), 7.

41. Wu Jishi, *Yinsheng jiyuan*, *xu*, 1a.

42. Wu Jishi, *Yinsheng jiyuan*, j. 1, 1b.

43. Wu Jishi, *Yinsheng jiyuan*, j. 1, 13a. Confucius referred to his hearing as attuned at age sixty in the *Analects* (2.4). Song dynasty Learning of the Way thinkers glossed this phrase as implying that "when sound enters, his mind comprehends" 聲入心通. See Cheng Shude 程樹德, comp., *Lunyu jishi* 論語集釋, vol. 1 (Beijing: Zhonghua shuju, 1990), 75–76.

44. Zhao Yiguang, *Xitan jingzhuan* 悉曇經傳, in *Xitan jingzhuan: Zhao Yiguang ji qi "Xitan jingzhuan"* 悉曇經傳: 趙宧光及其悉曇經傳, ed. Rao Zongyi (Taipei: Xin wenfeng chubanshe, 1999), *fanli*, 6a. See also Ye Bingjing 葉秉敬, *Yun biao* 韻表, *SKQS CMCS*, *xu*, 6a–8a.

45. Peter K. Bol, "On Shao Yong's Method for Observing Things," *Monumenta Serica* 61, no. 1 (2013): 299; Zuo, *Shen Gua's Empiricism*, 78–79.

46. Fang Yizhi, *Tongya*, j. 50, 30a.

47. *Xunzi* 1.2; Fei Hong 費宏, *Fei Wenxian gong zhai gao* 費文憲公摘稿, *XX SKQS*, j. 10, 45a.

48. Zhao Yiguang, *Xitan jingzhuan*, *zimu zongchi*, 4a; Mao Xianshu 毛先舒, *Xunshu* 潠書 (Shanghai: Shanghai guji chubanshe, 2009), j. 6, 31b; Pan Lei 潘耒,

Leiyin 類音, *SKQS CMCS*, 6a. Li Guangdi picked up this claim in the early eighteenth century; see Li Guangdi 李光地, *Rongcun yulu* 榕村語錄 (Beijing: Zhonghua shuju, 1995), 545.

49. Chen Jinmo, *Yuanyin tongyun*, j. 1, 1b.
50. Ye Bingjing, *Yun biao, xu*, 5a–7b.
51. Li Yu, *Xianqing ouji* 閒情偶記 (1671 edition at Harvard-Yenching Library), j. 7, 34b–35a.
52. There are extremely few references to such a concept in the medieval tradition. The term *yuansheng* seems to have gained wider currency following Cai Yuanding's 蔡元定 (1135–1198) invocation of it in his *Lülü xinshu* 律呂新書, which Zhu Xi often referenced.
53. Dong Yue 董說, *Wenyin fa* 文音發 (at Naikaku bunko), 19a–b, Chen Jinmo, *Yuanyin tongyun*, j. 1, 4a–5a.
54. He Liangjun 何良俊, *Siyouzhai congshuo* 四友齋叢說, *XX SKQS*, j. 37, 1b.
55. For convenience I refer to the term *huangzhong* (黃鐘, lit. "yellow bell"), which is the fundamental pitch of the Chinese musical scale, as the pitch C.
56. Tsuyoshi Kojima, "Tuning and Numerology in the New Learning School," in *Emperor Huizong and Late Northern Song China: The Politics of Culture and the Culture of Politics*, ed. Patricia Ebrey and Maggie Bickford (Cambridge, Mass.: Harvard University Asia Center, 2006), 206–26.
57. The fact that the thirteenth iteration yielded a pitch slightly sharper than C was one of the major issues concerning premodern music theorists. Many solutions were proposed to this problem, including theoretical scales of more than twelve pitches, ranging from 18 to 360 subdivisions of the octave. The solution to this problem accepted today, that is, the logarithmic division of the octave into twelve equal parts, was discovered in China by Zhu Zaiyu in the late sixteenth century.
58. Han Bangqi, *Yuanluo zhiyue*, j. 2, 27b–28a.
59. Ying Huiqian 應撝謙, *Gu yueshu* 古樂書, *SKQS*, j. *shang*, 40b.
60. Zhu Zaiyu, *Yuelü quanshu* 樂律全書, *SKQS*, j. 24, 18b.
61. Zhang Xingyan 張行言, *Shengmen liyue tong* 聖門禮樂統, *SKQS CMCS*, j. 21, 17b; Wu Qiao 吳喬, *Nanguang lu* 難光錄 (Shanghai: Dadong shuju, 1936), 14a; Xu Yangyuan 徐養原, *Wanshi lu jing shuo* 頑石廬經說, *XX SKQS*, j. 7, 21b–24a; Zhang Fengxiang 張鳳翔, *Yuejing jizhu* 樂經集註, *SKQS CMCS*, Wang *xu*, 2a.
62. See Nathan Vedal, "From Tradition to Community: The Rise of Contemporary Knowledge in Late Imperial China," *Journal of Asian Studies* 79, no. 1 (2020): 86.
63. The notion of numbers and quantitative calculation as the basis for objectively empirical claims resonates strongly with assumptions in many fields of present-day learning. See Theodore M. Porter, *Trust in Numbers: The Pursuit*

of *Objectivity in Science and Public Life* (Princeton, N.J.: Princeton University Press, 1994).

64. Huang Zuo 黃佐, *Yuedian* 樂典, SKQS CMCS, j. 17, 15a.
65. Zhao Yiguang, *Xitan jingzhuan, zimu zongchi*, 9a–b. Cf. Chen Jinmo, *Yuanyin tongyun*, j. 1, 13b–14a; j. 2, 6a–8a.
66. In addition to Zhao Yiguang's *Xitan jingzhuan*, see, for instance, Long Weilin, *Benyun yide*, j. 2, 16b.
67. Nathan Vedal, "New Scripts for All Sounds: Cosmology and Universal Phonetic Notation Systems in Late Imperial China," *Harvard Journal of Asiatic Studies* 78, no. 1 (2018): 7–12.
68. See, for instance, Chen Jinmo's citations of Wu Jishi and Fang Yizhi in *Yuanyin tongyun, tongshi*, 56a–57b.
69. Wu Jishi, *Yinsheng jiyuan, xu*, 2a; Fang Yizhi, *Tongya*, j. 50, 1a.
70. Ge Zhongxuan, *Tailü*, j. 10, 13b.
71. Ge Zhongxuan, *Tailü*, j. 10, 13a–b.
72. Vedal, "New Scripts for All Sounds," 16–25.
73. Li Yu, "Character Recognition: A New Method of Learning to Read in Late Imperial China," *Late Imperial China* 33, no. 2 (2012): 4.
74. Ge Zhongxuan, *Tailü*, j. 10, 14a.
75. Qiao Zhonghe, *Yuanyun pu*, Qiao *xu*, 23a–b.
76. Yuan Zirang 袁子讓, *Wuxian tang zixue yuanyuan* 五先堂字學元元, SKQS CMCS, j. 9, 1b, 11b, 14a.
77. Liu Xianting 劉獻廷, *Guangyang zaji* 廣陽雜記 (Beijing: Zhonghua shuju, 1957), 37; Zhao Yiguang, *Xitan jingzhuan, fanli*, 5b; Fang Yizhi, *Siyun dingben*, 9.
78. For Chen's philosophical correspondence with Huang Daozhou, see Chen Jinmo, *Su'an qian* 礪菴槧, SKQS CMCS.
79. K. W. Fung 馮錦榮, "Chen Jinmo (1600?–1692?) zhi shengping ji xixue yanjiu—jian lun qi zhuzuo yu Ma Lixun (Robert Morrison, 1782–1834) *Ying Han zidian* zhi zhongxixue yuan" 陳藎謨 (1600?–1692?) 之生平及西學研究—兼論其著作與馬禮遜 (Robert Morrison, 1782–1834) 《英漢字典》之中西學緣, *Ming Qing shi jikan* 9 (2007): 223, 233, 252–54.
80. Chen Jinmo, *Huangji tuyun*, 47b.
81. Michael Nylan, *The Five "Confucian" Classics* (New Haven, Conn.: Yale University Press, 2001), 223.
82. See, for example, the compilation of diagrams by Lai Zhide 來知德, "Caitu" 採圖, in *Lai Qutang xiansheng Yi zhu* 來瞿唐先生易註 (Ningling: Fu Yongpei Ningyuan tang, 1834), *juanmo*, esp. 45a–48a.
83. For other examples from phonological texts, see Fang Yizhi, *Tongya*, j. 50, 23b; Qiao Zhonghe, *Yuanyun pu, juanshou*, 44a; Ge Zhongxuan, *Tailü*, j. 4, j. 5; and an early seventeenth-century edition of Wu Jishi's *Yinsheng jiyuan* (c. 1616 edition at National Central Library of Taiwan), j. 1, 1a–b.

84. For a more detailed description of the system, see Vedal, "New Scripts for All Sounds," 35–40; and Wang Songmu 王松木, "Yinshu mingli—lun Chen Jinmo *Huangji tuyun* de yuntu sheji yu yinxue sixiang" 因數明理—論陳藎謨《皇極圖韻》的韻圖設計與音學思想, *Wen yu zhe* 23 (2013).
85. Chen Jinmo, *Huangji tuyun*, 3a–b, 55a.
86. Pan Lei, *Leiyin*, j. 1, 1a.
87. Chen Jinmo, *Huangji tuyun*, 5b–6a.
88. See Vedal, "New Scripts for All Sounds," 16–25.
89. Wu Jishi, *Yinsheng jiyuan*, j. 1, 1b; cf. Chen Jinmo, *Huangji tuyun*, 3b.
90. Stolzenberg, *Egyptian Oedipus*, 6.
91. Shen Gua 沈括, *Mengxi bitan* 夢溪筆談, *SKQS*, j. 15, 1b; Wang Anshi 王安石, *Linchuan xiansheng wenji* 臨川先生文集 (Beijing: Zhonghua shuju, 1959), 608.
92. Lewis, *Writing and Authority in Early China*, 197–98.
93. Chen Jinmo, *Huangji tuyun*, 2b.
94. Qu Jiusi, *Yuedao fameng* 樂道發蒙 (at Naikaku bunko), j. 9, 35b.
95. Lorraine Daston and Peter Galison, *Objectivity* (Cambridge, Mass.: MIT Press, 2007), 17.
96. Daston and Galison, *Objectivity*, 47.
97. Zuo, *Shen Gua's Empiricism*, 133–34.
98. Lorraine J. Daston, "Baconian Facts, Academic Civility and the Prehistory of Objectivity," *Annals of Scholarship* 8 (1991): 349–50; Adrian Johns, *The Nature of the Book: Print and Knowledge in the Making* (Chicago: University of Chicago Press, 1998), 428–29.
99. Cf. Daston and Galison, *Objectivity*, 36–37, for the significance of the "self" within the development of objective knowledge in the nineteenth-century West.

2. Letters from the West

1. Ori Sela, *China's Philological Turn: Scholars, Textualism, and the Dao in the Eighteenth Century* (New York: Columbia University Press, 2018), 5–10; Lionel Jensen, *Manufacturing Confucianism: Chinese Traditions & Universal Civilization* (Durham, N.C.: Duke University Press, 1997); Michael Nylan, "Kongzi and Mozi, the Classicists (Ru 儒) and the Mohists (Mo 墨) in Classical-Era Thinking," *Oriens Extremus* 48 (2009): 1–20.
2. Sela, *China's Philological Turn*, 99.
3. Li Guangdi 李光地, *Rongcun yulu* 榕村語錄 (Beijing: Zhonghua shuju, 1995), 409.
4. David Lurie, *Realms of Literacy: Early Japan and the History of Writing* (Cambridge, Mass.: Harvard University Asia Center, 2011), 5.

5. Cf. Zev Handel, *Sinography: The Borrowing and Adaptation of the Chinese Script* (Leiden: Brill, 2019), 189–92.
6. Thomas Mullaney, *The Chinese Typewriter: A History* (Cambridge, Mass.: MIT Press, 2017), 26.
7. For a representative set of approaches, see William G. Boltz, *The Origin and Early Development of the Chinese Writing System* (New Haven, Conn.: American Oriental Society, 1994); Qiu Xigui, *Chinese Writing*, trans. G. L. Mattos and J. Norman (Berkeley: Institute of East Asian Studies, University of California, 2000); Peter Francis Kornicki, *Languages, Scripts, and Chinese Texts in East Asia* (Oxford: Oxford University Press, 2018); and Handel, *Sinography*.
8. Jing Tsu, *Sound and Script in Chinese Diaspora* (Cambridge, Mass.: Harvard University Press, 2010), 21–34.
9. Lurie, *Realms of Literacy*, 357–64; Wiebke Denecke, "Worlds Without Translation: Premodern East Asia and the Power of Character Scripts," in *A Companion to Translation Studies*, ed. Sandra Bermann and Catherine Porter (Hoboken, N.J.: Wiley-Blackwell, 2014), 204–16.
10. Cf. John DeFrancis, *The Chinese Language: Fact and Fantasy* (Honolulu: University of Hawai`i Press, 1984); and Boltz, *The Origin and Early Development of the Chinese Writing System*.
11. Li Nanqiu 黎难秋, *Zhongguo kouyishi* 中国口译史 (Qingdao: Qingdao chubanshe, 2002).
12. W. South Coblin, *A Handbook of 'Phags-Pa Chinese* (Honolulu: University of Hawai`i Press, 2006), 2–3.
13. On knowledge of 'Phags-pa, as well as the role of foreign language study more broadly in the early Ming, see Lotze, "Translation of Empire." On Ming Arabic study, see Weil, "The Vicissitudes of Late Imperial China's Accommodation of Arabo-Persian Knowledge of the Natural World."
14. Norman Wild, "Materials for the Study of the Ssu i Kuan 四夷(譯)館 (Bureau of Translators)," *Bulletin of the School of African and Oriental Studies* 3 (1945): 617–40.
15. Paul F. Copp, *The Body Incantatory: Spells and the Ritual Imagination in Medieval Chinese Buddhism* (New York: Columbia University Press, 2014), 4.
16. Hui Jiao 慧皎, *Gaoseng zhuan* 高僧傳, *Congshu jicheng* (Beijing: Zhonghua shuju, 1991), 116.
17. Richard Salomon, *Indian Epigraphy: A Guide to the Study of Inscriptions in Sanskrit, Prakrit, and the Other Indo-Aryan Languages* (Oxford: Oxford University Press, 1998), 40–41.
18. Robert Hans van Gulik, *Siddham: An Essay on the History of Sanskrit Studies in China and Japan* (Nagpur: International Academy of Indian Culture, 1956); Saroj Kumar Chaudhuri, *Sanskrit in China and Japan* (New Delhi: International Academy of Indian Culture and Aditya Prakashan, 2011).

Chinese-language scholarship has noted in greater depth the degree to which studies of Sanskrit continued in late imperial China. See, for example, Zhou Guangrong 周广荣, *Fanyu "Xitan zhang" zai zhongguo de chuanbo yu yingxiang* 梵语《悉昙章》在中国的传播与影响 (Beijing: Zongjiao wenhua chubanshe, 2004); and Li Bohan 李柏翰, "Ming Qing xitan wenxian ji qi dui dengyunxue de yingxiang" 明清悉曇文獻及其對等韻學的影響, Ph.D. diss., National Tsing Hua University, 2015.

19. These include, most notably, the dictionary *Pianyun guanzhu ji* 篇韻貫珠集 by the monk Zhenkong 真空 and the *menfa* 門法 genre dedicated to explicating medieval rhyme tables.
20. Liu Xianting 劉獻廷, *Guangyang zaji* 廣陽雜記 (Beijing: Zhonghua shuju, 1957), 143.
21. Renchao was from northeastern China, but Zhao Yiguang appears to have met him in the southeast at Tianmu Mountain 天目山, west of Hangzhou. See Zhao Yiguang 趙宧光, *Tanya* 彈雅 (1622 edition at Capital Library in Beijing), *yunxie*, 16b.
22. Zhao Yiguang, *Xitan jingzhuan* 悉曇經傳, *zimu zongchi*, 1a, in *Xitan jingzhuan: Zhao Yiguang ji qi "Xitan jingzhuan"* 悉曇經傳: 趙宧光及其悉曇經傳, ed. Rao Zongyi (Taipei: Xin wenfeng chubanshe, 1999).
23. Nathan Vedal, "Scholarly Culture in Sixteenth and Seventeenth-Century China," Ph.D. diss. (2017), Harvard University, 144–55.
24. The term *fanzi* refers to Brāhmī script specifically in some cases, but Renchao was likely using it as a generic reference to forms of Sanskrit writing, as was typically the case in the Ming.
25. Renchao, *Fajie anli tu* 法界安立圖 (Kyoto: Akitaya Heizaemon, 1654), j. 1.1, 11b–12a.
26. For example, the Sanskrit characters employed in Zhao Yiguang's *Xitan jingzhuan* resemble the Lantsha/Rañjana script used for writing Sanskrit in Tibet and Newari in Nepal.
27. Ryūichi Abe, *The Weaving of Mantra: Kūkai and the Construction of Esoteric Buddhist Discourse* (New York: Columbia University Press, 1999), 396. For an alternative interpretation, see Nicholas Morrow Williams, "Beyond Arbitrariness: Kūkai's Theory of Languages and Scripts," *Journal of the Pacific Association for the Continental Tradition* 4 (2021): 77–94.
28. One earlier exception is Zheng Qiao 鄭樵 (1104–1162), whose influential study of Sanskrit writing was framed in relation to Chinese philology rather than religious enlightenment. See Victor H. Mair, "Cheng Ch'iao's Understanding of Sanskrit," in *China and Beyond: A Collection of Essays*, ed. Victor H. Mair (Amherst: Cambria Press, 2013), 185–205.
29. Tan Zhenmo, "Fomu zhunti fenxiu xidi yiwen baochan xu" 佛母准提梵修悉地儀文寶懺序, in *Shinsan Dai Nihon zoku Zōkyō* 新纂大日本續藏經, ed. Kawamura

Kōshō 河村孝照, vol. 74 (Tokyo: Kokusho Kankōkai, 1975–1989), 556–58, no. 1482 B.

30. Liu Xianting, *Guangyang zaji*, 144; Zhao Yiguang, *Xitan jingzhuan, zimu zongchi*, 11a; Yang Zhenyi 楊貞一, *Shiyin bianlüe* 詩音辯略, *Siku quanshu cunmu congshu* 四庫全書存目叢書 (Jinan: Qi Lu shushe chubanshe, 1997) [hereafter *SKQS CMCS*], *xu*, 1b–2a; Xiong Kaiyuan 熊開元, *Yushan shenggao* 魚山剩稿, *Siku jinhui shu congkan: bubian* 四庫禁燬書叢刊：補編 (Beijing: Beijing chubanshe, 2005), j. 5, 42b.
31. Shen Weirong, "Tantric Buddhism in Ming China," in *Esoteric Buddhism and the Tantras in East Asia*, ed. Charles Orzech, Henrik Sørensen and Richard Payne (Leiden: Brill, 2010), 537–49.
32. *Xitan* originally referred specifically to the Siddham script, but by Ming times it served as a general referent for Sanskrit scripts. Zhao Yiguang's text featured primarily Lantsha/Rañjana rather than Siddham.
33. Zhao Yiguang, *Xitan jingzhuan, fanli*, 17b–20a.
34. Zhao Yiguang, *Xitan jingzhuan, fanli*, 18a.
35. Liu Xianting, *Guangyang zaji*, 143.
36. Liu Xianting, *Guangyang zaji*, 65, 144.
37. Chen Guanzhi 陳冠至, *Mingdai de Suzhou cangshu: cangshujia de cangshu huodong yu cangshu shenghuo* 明代的蘇州藏書：藏書家的藏書活動與藏書生活 (Taipei: Lexue shuju, 2002), 45–46.
38. Timothy Brook, *Praying for Power: Buddhism and the Formation of Gentry Society in Late-Ming China* (Cambridge, Mass.: Council on East Asian Studies, Harvard University, 1994).
39. Zhao Yiguang, *Xitan jingzhuan, zongxu*, 1a.
40. Zhao Yiguang, *Xitan jingzhuan, fanli*, 3a.
41. See, for example, Brook, *Praying for Power*, 83–88; and Edward T. Ch'ien, *Chiao Hung and the Restructuring of Neo-Confucianism in the Late Ming* (New York: Columbia University Press, 1986).
42. Chen Jinmo 陳藎謨, *Yuanyin tongyun* 元音統韻, *SKQS CMCS*, 56b.
43. Cheng Mingshan 程明善, *Xiaoyu pu* 嘯餘譜, *SKQS CMCS, fanli*, 3b.
44. Shang Wei, "Ritual, Ritual Manuals, and the Crisis of the Confucian World: An Interpretation of *Rulin waishi*," *Harvard Journal of Asiatic Studies* 58, no. 2 (1998): 373–424; Sela, *China's Philological Turn*, 6.
45. Zhao Yiguang, *Shuowen changjian*, *SKQS CMCS*, j. 52, 10a.
46. Zhao Yiguang, *Xitan jingzhuan, fanli*, 2b.
47. Yuan Zirang 袁子讓, *Wuxian tang zixue yuanyuan* 五先堂字學元元, *SKQS CMCS*, j. 10, 1b; Wu Jishi 吳繼仕, *Yinsheng jiyuan* 音聲紀元, *SKQS CMCS*, j. 1, 16a–17b.
48. Qian Daxin 錢大昕, *Qianyan tang wenji* 潛研堂文集 (Shanghai: Shanghai guji chubanshe, 2010), j. 15, 14a–15b.

49. See overview in David Prager Branner, "Introduction," in *The Chinese Rime Tables: Linguistic Philosophy and Historical-Comparative Phonology*, ed. Branner (Amsterdam: John Benjamins, 2006), 7–11.
50. Zhao Yiguang, *Xitan jingzhuan, zimu zongchi*, 9a.
51. Zhao Yiguang, *Xitan jingzhuan, zimu zongchi*, 8b.
52. For a description of the no longer extant table, see Zhao Yiguang, *Xitan jingzhuan, fanli*, 11a–b.
53. Zhao Yiguang, *Xitan jingzhuan, fanli*, 3b–4a.
54. Zhao Yiguang, *Shuowen changjian*, j. 33, 31a–31b.
55. Sela, *China's Philological Turn*, 199–204.
56. Zhao Yiguang, *Shuowen changjian*, j. 46, 39a.
57. Zhao Yiguang, *Xitan jingzhuan, fanli*, 3a.
58. Lurie, *Realms of Literacy*, 28.
59. Lurie, *Realms of Literacy*, 204–5.
60. Ge Zhongxuan, *Tailü*, j. 10, p. 16a
61. Fang Yizhi, *Xiyu xinbi* 膝寓信筆 (1888 edition at Harvard-Yenching Library), j. 2, 19a; Fang Yizhi, *Fushan wenji houbian* 浮山文集後編, *Xuxiu Siku quanshu* 續修四庫全書 (Shanghai: Shanghai guji chubanshe, 1995–1999), j. 2, 2a.
62. Wu Jishi, *Yinsheng jiyuan*, j. 1, 11a–b. This instruction appears to be paraphrased from Zhao Yiguang, *Xitan jingzhuan, fanli*, 20a.
63. Wu Jishi, *Yinsheng jiyuan*, j. 2, 1b.
64. For example, Wu Jishi, *Yinsheng jiyuan*, j. 2, 18b.
65. Wen Deyi, *Qiushitang wenji* 求是堂文集, *Siku jinhui shu congkan* 四庫禁燬書叢刊 (Beijing: Beijing chubanshe, 1997), j. 2, 11b.
66. Zhao Yiguang, *Xitan jingzhuan, zimu zongchi*, 4a; Zhao Yiguang, *Shuowen changjian*, j. 67, 20a.
67. Wang Kentang 王肯堂, *Yugangzhai bizhu* 鬱岡齋筆麈, *SKQS CMCS*, j. 4, 39a–40b.
68. Fang Yizhi was somewhat skeptical of Zhao Yiguang's particular proposals. See Fang Yizhi, *Tongya*, juanshou 1, 16b; juanshou 2, 20b.
69. DeFrancis, *The Chinese Language*, 240–41; and Boltz, *The Origin and Early Development of the Chinese Writing System*, 177.
70. Hao Jing 郝敬, *Dushu tong* 讀書通 (1630 edition at Beijing Normal University Library), j. 1, 14a–14b.
71. Zhao Yiguang, *Xitan jingzhuan, fanli*, 4a.
72. Hao's contemporary Chen Shiyuan 陳士元 (1516–1597) similarly commented on the implications of the separation of graphs and meaning in phonographic scripts for the length of written words. See Chen Shiyuan, *Ming yi* 名疑 (Shanghai: Bogu zhai, 1920), j. 4, 31a.

73. Cf. Yuan Zirang, *Wuxian tang zixue yuanyuan*, j. 10, 4b. Yuan appears to have been attempting to understand Sanskrit through the lens of Chinese transcription.
74. Liu Xianting, *Guangyang zaji*, 152–53.
75. On the importance of consulting phonographic writing, see Liu Xianting, *Guangyang zaji*, 211.
76. Liu Xianting, *Guangyang zaji*, 150.
77. Gu Yingxiang cites here a famous statement from the twelfth-century thinker Zheng Qiao. Cf. Zheng Qiao, *Tongzhi* 通志, *Siku quanshu* 四庫全書 (Taipei: Taiwan shangwu yinshuguan, 1983), j. 35, 21a–b.
78. Gu Yingxiang, *Jingzhai xiyin lu* 靜虛齋惜陰錄, *SKQS CMCS*, j. 6, 7a.
79. Gu Yingxiang, *Jingzhai xiyin lu*, j. 6, 6b.
80. Gu Yingxiang, *Jingzhai xiyin lu*, j. 6, 5b.
81. Fang Risheng 方日升, *Gujin yunhui juyao xiaobu* 古今韻會舉要小補, *SKQS CMCS*, houxu, 1b.
82. Chen Shiyuan, *Ming yi*, j. 4, 41a.
83. Wang Kentang, *Yugangzhai bizhu*, j. 4, 39a.
84. Bruce Rusk, "Old Scripts, New Actors: European Encounters with Chinese Writing, 1550–1700," *East Asian Science, Technology and Medicine* 26 (2007): 68–116.
85. Liu Xianting, *Guangyang zaji*, 39. For a similar sentiment, see Zhang Zilie 張自烈, *Zhengzi tong* 正字通, *SKQS CMCS*, chouji xia, 50a.
86. Mårten Söderblom Saarela, "The Manchu Script and Information Management: Some Aspects of Qing China's Great Encounter with Alphabetic Literacy," in *Rethinking East Asian Languages, Vernaculars, and Literacies, 1000–1919*, ed. Benjamin A. Elman (Leiden: Brill, 2014), 169–97.
87. Zhang Taiyan, "Bo zhongguo yong wanguo xinyu shuo" 駁中国用万国新語說, in *Pinyin wenzi shiliao congshu*, vol. 5. (Beijing: Wenzi gaige chubanshe: Xinhua shudian, 1957), 1–2.

3. Script, Antiquity, and Mental Training

1. Hu Qiguang 胡奇光, *Zhongguo xiaoxue shi* 中国小学史 (Shanghai: Shanghai renmin chubanshe, 1987), 229; Mark Elvin, *The Pattern of the Chinese Past* (Stanford, Calif.: Stanford University Press, 1973), 226–27; Yü Ying-shih, "Some Preliminary Observations on the Rise of Ch'ing Confucian Intellectualism," *Tsing Hua Journal of Chinese Studies* 11 (1975): 125–26.
2. Ann Blair, *Too Much to Know: Managing Scholarly Information Before the Modern Age* (New Haven, Conn.: Yale University Press, 2010), 126–27.

3. See, for instance, *Qinding Siku quanshu zongmu*, j. 119, 12b, 48b–49b.
4. There are exceptions to this generalization. Scholars like Tang Shunzhi developed literary theories as an extension of their Learning of the Mind beliefs. See Zuo Dongling 左东岭, *Mingdai xinxue yu shixue* 明代心学与诗学 (Beijing: Xueyuan chubanshe, 2002), 108–48.
5. Sarah Schneewind, *Community Schools and the State in Ming China* (Stanford, Calif.: Stanford University Press, 2006), 104–6, 149.
6. These students include the literary stylists and thinkers Gui Youguang 歸有光 (1507–1571) and Tang Shunzhi 唐順之 (1507–1560), as well as the military strategist Zheng Ruozeng 鄭若曾 (c. 1503–1570).
7. Xu Xiangmei 徐象梅, *Liangzhe mingxian lu* 兩浙名賢錄, *Siku quanshu cunmu congshu* 四庫全書存目叢書 (Jinan: Qi Lu shushe chubanshe, 1997) [hereafter *SKQS CMCS*], j. 4, 35b; Lu Shiyi 陸世儀, *Sibian lu jiyao* 思辨錄輯要, *Siku quanshu* 四庫全書 (Taipei: Taiwan shangwu yinshuguan, 1983) [hereafter *SKQS*], j. 28, 8b–9a; Huang Wan 黃綰, *Huang Wan ji* 黃綰集, ed. Zhang Hongmin 張宏敏 (Shanghai: Shanghai guji chubanshe, 2014), 331–35.
8. Huang Wan, *Huang Wan ji*, 334.
9. Wei Jiao associated with Gui E 桂萼 (d. 1531) in an attempt to ruin Wang Yangming's career. See Jiao Kun 焦堃, "Yōmeigaku to Min no seiji" 陽明学と明の政治, Ph.D. diss., Kyoto University, 2014, 126–27.
10. For another discussion of this text, see Bruce Rusk, "Old Scripts, New Actors: European Encounters with Chinese Writing, 1550–1700," *East Asian Science, Technology and Medicine* 26 (2007): 84–87; and Rusk, "The Rogue Classicist: Feng Fang (1493–1566) and His Forgeries," Ph.D. diss., University of California, Los Angeles, 2004, 167–73.
11. For a description of these principles, see Qiu Xigui, *Chinese Writing*, trans. G. L. Mattos and J. Norman (Berkeley: Institute of East Asian Studies, University of California, 2000), 151–63.
12. Wei Jiao, *Liushu jingyun* 六書精蘊, *SKQS CMCS*, xu, 1b–2a. The phrase in quotation marks is an allusion to a passage in *Mengzi*, 6A7.8.
13. Wei Jiao, *Liushu jingyun*, j. 3, 75b–76a.
14. Wei Jiao, *Zhuangqu yishu* 莊渠遺書, *SKQS*, j. 12, 19b.
15. Wm. Theodore de Bary, *Neo-Confucian Orthodoxy and the Learning of the Mind-and-Heart* (New York: Columbia University Press, 1987), 128–30.
16. Wei Jiao, *Liushu jingyun*, j. 1, 36b, 63b; j. 2, 32b, 40b; j. 3, 3b, 6b, 7a, 7b.
17. Wei Jiao, *Liushu jingyun*, xu, 2a.
18. This example comes from Wang's extant commentary to the *Zhouli*, which serves as one of the major sources for reconstructing his approach to etymology. See Huang Fushan 黃復山, *Wang Anshi 'Zishuo' zhi yanjiu* 王安石《字說》之研究 (Taipei: Hua Mulan wenhua chubanshe, 2008), 175. Cf. Peter K. Bol, "Wang Anshi and the *Zhouli*," in *Statecraft and Classical Learning: The Rituals of Zhou*

in East Asian History, ed. Benjamin A. Elman and Martin Kern (Leiden: Brill, 2010), 239.

19. Wang Anshi, *Linchuan xiansheng wenji* 臨川先生文集 (Beijing: Zhonghua shuju, 1959), 608.
20. Huang Zongxi 黃宗羲, *Ming ru xuean* 明儒學案, *SKQS*, j. 32, 11b.
21. See Wei Jiao, *Daxue zhigui* 大學指歸, *SKQS CMCS*.
22. See examples preserved in Xu Guan 徐官, *Gujin yin shi* 古今印史, *SKQS CMCS*, *moji*, 1a–6b.
23. For contemporary appreciation of seal script and its relationship to seal carving, see Bai Qianshen, *Fu Shan's World: The Transformation of Chinese Calligraphy in the Seventeenth Century* (Cambridge, Mass.: Harvard University Asia Center, 2003), 50–71.
24. Amy McNair, *The Upright Brush: Yan Zhenqing's Calligraphy and Song Literati Politics* (Honolulu: University of Hawai`i Press, 1998).
25. Wei Jiao, *Liushu jingyun*, j. 4, 12a.
26. This interpretation is maintained within the present-day study of historical script forms.
27. Wei Jiao, *Liushu jingyun*, j. 4, 58b; cf. j. 1, 52a.
28. Wei Jiao, *Liushu jingyun*, j. 3, 5a–b.
29. See, for example, Wei Jiao, *Liushu jingyun*, j. 2, 72a–b; j. 3, 3a; j. 4, 57a.
30. "Daxue wen" 大學問, in Wang Yangming 王陽明, *Wang Yangming quanji* 王陽明全集, ed. Wu Guang 吳光, Qian Ming 錢明, Dong Ping 董平, Yao Yanfu 姚延福 (Hangzhou: Zhejiang guji chubanshe, 2010), 1015–16.
31. Wei Jiao, *Liushu jingyun*, j. 2, 32b. The section in single quotation marks is an allusion to a famous passage from *Mengzi*, 6B15.3.
32. Cf. "Lidai bufen zishu shouzi qingkuang jianbiao" 历代部分字书收字情况简表, in *Hanyu da zidian* 漢語大字典 (Wuhan: Hubei cishu chubanshe, 1986–1990), 5460.
33. Wei Jiao, *Zhuangqu yishu*, j. 11, 30a–30b. This version is evidently referring to an earlier manuscript, as the graph "centrality" is now in the third *juan* with "knowledge."
34. Wei Jiao, *Zhuangqu yishu*, j. 4, 41a, 48a; j. 12, 12b, 18b; j. 14, 20b; j. 15, 18b.
35. Wei Jiao, *Liushu jingyun*, *ba*, 1a.
36. For the sake of comparison, the first *juan* on "Heavens" in Wang Yingdian's *Tongwen beikao* contains roughly 530 graphs; the corresponding section in Wei Jiao's *Liushu jingyun* contains roughly 200.
37. Wang Yingdian, *Tongwen beikao*, *SKQS CMCS*, *xuwen*, 13b. For a similar discussion of the relationship between calligraphic art and the Way, see Adam Schorr, "Connoisseurship and the Defense Against Vulgarity: Yang Shen (1488–1559) and His Work," *Monumenta Serica* 41 (1993): 94–102.
38. Lu Deming 陸德明, *Jingdian shiwen* 經典釋文, *SKQS*, *tiaoli*, 2a–6a.

39. Wang Yingdian, *Tongwen beikao*, j. 4, 1b.
40. Wang Yingdian, *Tongwen beikao*, j. 4, 14b. The common interpretation of *xin* was upheld in other major paleographic dictionaries, such as *Liushu tong* 六書統. See Yang Huan 楊桓, *Liushu tong*, SKQS, *xu*, 11b.
41. Xin'an and the Ziyang Academy are generally considered to be strongholds of orthodox Learning of the Way thought in opposition to the Learning of the Mind. *Zhengyun yi* suggests the presence of a Learning of the Mind discourse amid this opposition. See also Qitao Guo, *Ritual Opera and Mercantile Lineage* (Stanford, Calif.: Stanford University Press, 2005), 16.
42. Wu Shilin, *Zhengyun yi*, j. 9, 1a.
43. Wu Shilin, *Zhengyun yi*, j. 9, 2a.
44. His interpretation of the graph *de* 得 "to obtain," for instance, is based on that of Wei Jiao. See Wu Shilin, *Zhengyun yi*, j. 9, 15b–16a. For other examples of citing Wei Jiao, see j. 7, 7b; j. 9, 8b.
45. See, for instance, Dong Yue 董說, *Fengcaoan qianji* 豐草庵前集 (Shanghai: Shanghai shudian, 1994), j. 5, 14a–17a; Gao Panlong 高攀龍, *Gaozi yishu* 高子遺書, SKQS, j. 12, 23a.
46. Brigid E. Vance, "Deciphering Dreams: How Glyphomancy Worked in Late Ming Dream Encyclopedic Divination," *Chinese Historical Review* 24, no. 1 (2017): 5–20.
47. Nathan Vedal, "From Tradition to Community: The Rise of Contemporary Knowledge in Late Imperial China," *Journal of Asian Studies* 79, no. 1 (2020): 88.
48. Xie Zhaozhe 謝肇淛, *Wu zazu* 五雜組, ed. Zhang Yiping 章衣萍 (Shanghai: Zhongyang shudian, 1935), 214.
49. Chu Pingyi, "Philological Arguments as Religious Suasion: Liu Ning and His Study of Chinese Characters," in *Powerful Arguments: Standards of Validity in Late Imperial China*, ed. Martin Hofmann, Joachim Kurtz, and Ari Daniel Levine (Leiden: Brill, 2020), 503–27.
50. Zhao Yiguang, *Shuowen changjian* (1631 edition at Bibliothèque nationale de France), *juanshou shang*, 9a; j. 48, 19b–20a; j. 51, 15a.
51. Mark Edward Lewis, *Writing and Authority in Early China* (Albany: State University of New York Press, 1999), 255, 209.
52. Huang Zongyan 黃宗炎, *Zhouyi xunmen yulun* 周易尋門餘論, SKQS; Qu Dajun 屈大均, *Wengshan yiwai* 翁山易外, SKJHSCK; Qu Dajun, *Wengshan wen wai* 翁山文外, SKJHSCK, j. 2, 4b–5b; Tang Shunzhi, *Tang Jingchuan wenji* 唐荊川文集 (Shanghai: Shangwu yinshuguan, 1922), j. 17, 16b.
53. Daniel Stolzenberg, *Egyptian Oedipus: Athanasius Kircher and the Secrets of Antiquity* (Chicago: University of Chicago Press, 2013), 207–9.
54. David Lurie, *Realms of Literacy: Early Japan and the History of Writing* (Cambridge, Mass.: Harvard University Asia Center, 2011), 29.

55. Rusk, "Old Scripts, New Actors," 112–14; Chu Ping-yi 祝平一, "Liu Ning yu Liu Xun—kaozhengxue yu tianxue guanxi xintan" 劉凝與劉壎 — 考證學與天學關係新探, *Xin shixue* 23, no. 1 (2012): 57–104; Sophie Ling-chia Wei, *Chinese Theology and Translation: The Christianity of the Jesuit Figurists and their Christianized Yijing* (New York: Routledge, 2019).
56. David Porter, *Ideographia: The Chinese Cipher in Early Modern Europe* (Stanford, Calif.: Stanford University Press, 2002), 44–49.
57. Wei Jiao, *Liushu jingyun*, *houxu*, 1b–5b.
58. Wei Jiao, *Liushu jingyun*, *ba*, 1b.
59. Luo Hongxian, *Luo Hongxian ji bubian* 羅洪先集補編, ed. Zhong Caijun 鍾彩鈞 and Zhu Xiangyu 朱湘鈺 (Taipei: Zhongyang yanjiuyuan zhongguo wenzhe yanjiusuo, 2009), 267.
60. Adapted from Richard John Lynn, trans., *The Classic of Changes: A New Translation of the I Ching as Interpreted by Wang Bi* (New York: Columbia University Press, 1994), 67.
61. Xu Guan, *Gujin yin shi*, SKQS CMCS, *xu*, 2b.
62. Gu Yingxiang, *Jingxuzhai xiyin lu*, j. 6, 7b.
63. *Lunyu* 9.3.
64. Gu Yingxiang, *Jingxuzhai xiyin lu*, j. 6, 8a.
65. Wei Jiao, *Zhuangqu yishu*, j. 3, 2b.
66. Wei Jiao, *Zhuangqu yishu*, j. 6, 6a.
67. Xue Hui 薛蕙, *Kaogong ji* 考功集, SKQS, j. 9, 15b.
68. Yang Shen 楊慎, *Zhuanzhu guyin lüe* 轉注古音略 (1532 edition at National Central Library of Taiwan), Gu Yingxiang *xu*, 2b. It is possible that Yang Shen would not have represented his own work in these terms, but Gu Yingxiang's preface reflects the plausible Ming reading of the text as derived from Learning of the Mind methods.
69. See, for instance, Jiao Hong 焦竑, *Guoshi jingjizhi* 國史經籍志, j. 2, 57b; Xu Tu 徐圖, *Xingrensi chongke shumu* 行人司重刻書目, 36b; Chao Li 晁瑮, *Chaoshi baowentang shumu* 晁氏寶文堂書目, *yunshu xia*, 1a; Dong Qichang 董其昌, *Xuanshang zhai shumu* 玄賞齋書目, j. 1, 12a; Xu Bo 徐𤊹, *Xu shi jiacang shumu* 徐氏家藏書目, j. 4, 7a; Zhao Qimei 趙琦美, *Maiwangguan shumu* 脈望館書目, *zi*, 50a; Zhou Hongzu 周弘祖, *Jingu tang shumu* 近古堂書目, *shang*, 8a. These bibliographies can be consulted in Feng Huimin 馮惠民 and Li Wanjian 李萬健, eds., *Mingdai shumu tiba congkan* 明代書目題跋叢刊 (Beijing: Shumu wenxian chubanshe, 1994).
70. See, for instance, Dai Chong 戴重, *Hecun ji* 河村集 (Beijing: Beijing chubanshe, 1997), j. 3, [6a].
71. Han Qia, *Zhuanxue cejie*, *fanli*, 7b.
72. Han Qia, *Zhuanxue cejie*, *fanli*, 9a.

73. See, for example, Wu Renchen 吳任臣, *Zihui bu* 字彙補, *Xuxiu Siku quanshu* 續修四庫全書 (Shanghai: Shanghai guji chubanshe, 1995–1999) [hereafter *XX SKQS*], *xu*, 1a.
74. Li Fu 李紱, *Mutang chugao* 穆堂初稿, *XX SKQS*, j. 18, 18a. Cf. criticisms of *Zihui* and *Zhengzi tong* in Yuan Dong 袁棟, *Shuyin congshuo* 書隱叢說, *SKQS CMCS*, j. 16, 5a; Wang Yingkui 王應奎, *Liunan xubi* 柳南續筆, *XX SKQS*, j. 4, 6b–7a. In an oft-quoted statement, Zhu Yizun 朱彝尊 (1629–1709) referred to the two dictionaries as "lowly primers" (*tuyuan ce* 兔園冊), in contrast to more philologically rigorous lexicons; see Zhu Yizun, *Pushu ting ji* 曝書亭集, *SKQS*, j. 34, 17a.
75. Wu Yuanman here appears to have overlooked Yang Huan's fourteenth-century *Liushu tong*, which set an earlier precedent for grouping human affairs together.
76. Wu Yuanman, *Liushu zongyao* 六書總要, *SKQS CMCS*, *lun* 4a–b.
77. Wu Yuanman, *Liushu zongyao*, *lun*, 2a.
78. Hilde De Weerdt, "Neo-Confucian Philosophy and Genre: The Philosophical Writings of Chen Chun and Zhen Dexiu," in *Dao Companion to Neo-Confucian Philosophy*, ed. John Makeham (New York: Springer, 2010), 228–29.
79. Zhou Yu, *Renzi ce*, *SKQS CMCS*, *xu hou*, 1b.
80. It is worth mentioning that early Song dynasty scholars tried to similarly identify meaning in the ordering of sections (*bu*), albeit not individual graphs, in *Shuowen jiezi*. See Xu Kai 徐鍇, *Shuowen jiezi xizhuan* 說文解字繫傳 (Beijing: Zhonghua shuju, 1987), j. 31–j. 32.
81. See Nathan Vedal, "Later Imperial Lexicons," in *Literary Information in China: A History*, ed. Jack Chen et al. (New York: Columbia University Press, 2021), 84.
82. There are some exceptions, with the archaic form of *zuo* 左, for instance, regularly being glossed on repeat occurrences.
83. Wei Jiao, *Liushu jingyun*, j. 1, 2a–b.
84. For more on "complementary bipolarities" in the Chinese tradition, see Andrew Plaks, *Archetype and Allegory in the Dream of the Red Chamber* (Princeton, N.J.: Princeton University Press, 1976), 43–53.
85. Wei Jiao, *Liushu jingyun*, j. 2, 72a–b.
86. See, for instance, Zhao Yiguang, *Shuowen changjian*, *zixu*, 5a.
87. Bai, *Fu Shan's World*, 50.
88. Bruce Rusk, "Not Written in Stone: Ming Readers of the 'Great Learning' and the Impact of Forgery," *Harvard Journal of Asiatic Studies* 66, no. 1 (2006): 207–11. It is worth noting that Wei Jiao himself seems to have acknowledged the potential for *tongyong* graphs in his commentarial practice. See "Not Written in Stone," 211.

89. Chen Jinmo, *Yuanyin tongyun*, j. 2, 6b.
90. Hao Jing, *Dushu tong*, j. 1, 9b.
91. Hao Jing, *Dushu tong*, j. 3, 5a.
92. Hao Jing, *Dushu tong*, j. 1, 2b.
93. Jiao Hong 焦竑, *Jiao shi bisheng xuji* 焦氏筆乘續集 (Beijing: Zhonghua shuju, 1985), 169.
94. The original context of this passage is Zheng Qiao, *Tongzhi*, j. 35, 6a.
95. Wang Kentang, *Yugangzhai bizhu*, j. 4, 39a.
96. Han Qia, *Zhuanxue cejie*, j. 3, 2b.
97. See, for instance, Li-Hai Tan et al., "Language Affects Patterns of Brain Activation Associated with Perceptual Decision," *Proceedings of the National Academy of Sciences* 105.10 (2008): 4004–09.
98. Peter Burke, "Reflections on the History of Information in Early Modern Europe," *Scientiarum Historia* 17 (1991): 69–70; and Walter Hakala, *Negotiating Languages: Urdu, Hindi, and the Definition of Modern South Asia* (New York: Columbia University Press, 2016), 21.

4. Opera and the Search for a Universal Language

1. Victor H. Mair and Tsu-lin Mei, "The Sanskrit Origins of Recent Style Prosody," *Harvard Journal of Asiatic Studies* 51 (1991): 375–470; Meow Hui Goh, *Sound and Sight: Poetry and Courtier Culture in the Yongming Era (483–493)* (Stanford, Calif: Stanford University Press, 2010), 24–27.
2. Adapted from Meow Hui Goh, "The Rhyme Book Culture of Pre-Tang China," *Journal of Chinese Literature and Culture* 2, no. 2 (2015): 430. For Ming citations, see, for example, Wu Jishi 吳繼仕, *Yinsheng jiyuan* 音聲紀元, *Siku quanshu cunmu congshu* 四庫全書存目叢書 (Jinan: Qi Lu shushe chubanshe, 1997) [hereafter *SKQS CMCS*] j. 1, 21a; Gu Qiyuan 顧起元, *Shuo lüe* 說略, *Siku quanshu* 四庫全書 (Taipei: Taiwan shangwu yinshuguan, 1983) [hereafter *SKQS*], j. 15, 10a; Yue Shaofeng 樂韶鳳 et al., *Hongwu zhengyun* 洪武正韻, *SKQS, fanli*, 2b.
3. Yan Zhitui, *Yanshi jiaxun* 顏氏家訓 (Beijing: Zhili shuju, 1923), j. 7.
4. P. A. Herbert, *Examine the Honest, Appraise the Able: Contemporary Assessments of Civil Service Selection in Early Tang China* (Canberra: Australian National University, 1988), 31.
5. See W. South Coblin, "Marginalia on Two Translations of the 'Qieyun' Preface," *Journal of Chinese Linguistics* 24, no. 1 (1996): 87; Meow Hui Goh, "The Rhyme Book Culture of Pre-Tang China," *Journal of Chinese Literature and Culture* 2, no. 2 (2015): 428.

6. Hirata Shōji 平田昌司, "'Qieyun' yu Tangdai gongling" 切韵' 与唐代功令, in *Dongfang yuyan yu wenhua* 东方语言与文化, ed. in Pan Wuyun 潘悟云 (Shanghai: Shanghai jiaoyu chubanshe, 2005), 326–56.
7. Geng Zhensheng 耿振生, "Bianzhe qianyan" 编者前言, in *Jindai guanhua yuyin yanjiu* 近代官话语音研究, ed. Geng Zhengsheng (Beijing: Yuwen chubanshe, 2007), 1.
8. See Wang Jide, *Qu lü* 曲律, in *Zhongguo gudian xiqu lunzhu jicheng* 中國古典戲曲論著集成 (Beijing: Zhongguo xiju chubanshe, 1959), 4:112; Shen Chongsui 沈寵綏, *Duqu xuzhi* 度曲須知, in *Zhongguo gudian xiqu lunzhu jicheng*, 5:250; Li Yu, *Xianqing ouji*, j. 5, 19a; j. 7, 34a; Gao Wengying 高奣映, ed., *Dengyin Shengwei hehui* 等音聲位合彙 (Shanghai: Shanghai shudian, 1994), *Congshu jicheng xubian* edition, j. xia, 34a; Zhou Deqing 周德清, *Zhongyuan yinyun* 中原音韻, *SKQS*, j. xia, 31a; and He Liangjun 何良俊, *Siyouzhai congshuo* 四友齋叢說, *SKQS CMCS*, j. 15, 14a.
9. Brian Richardson, *Print Culture in Renaissance Italy: The Editor and the Vernacular Text, 1470–1600* (Cambridge: Cambridge University Press, 2011), 66. For accounts of the role of editors in late imperial drama, see Catherine Swatek, *Peony Pavilion Onstage: Four Centuries in the Career of a Chinese Drama* (Ann Arbor: Center for Chinese Studies, University of Michigan, 2002); and Chen Kaishen 陳凱莘, *Cong antou dao qushu: "Mudan ting" Ming Qing wenren zhi quanshi gaibian yu wutai yishu zhi dijin* 從案頭到氍毹:《牡丹亭》明清文人之詮釋改編與舞臺藝術之遞進 (Taipei: Taida chuban zhongxin, 2013).
10. Zang Maoxun, *Fubaotang ji* 負苞堂集 (Shanghai: Gudian wenxue chubanshe, 1958), 56.
11. Zang, *Fubaotang ji*, 62.
12. Tang Xianzu, *Tang Xianzu quanji* 湯顯祖全集, ed. Xu Shuofang 徐朔方 (Beijing: Beijing guji chubanshe, 1999), 1442.
13. Shen Chongsui, *Duqu xuzhi*, 17; Mao Xianshu 毛先舒, *Yun bai* 韻白, *SKQS CMCS*, 20b.
14. He Liangjun, *Qu lun* 曲論, in *Zhongguo gudian xiqu lunzhu jicheng*, 4:10–11. The translation of Ma Zhiyuan's text is from Stephen West and Wilt Idema, trans., *Monks, Bandits, Lovers, and Immortals: Eleven Early Chinese Plays* (Indianapolis: Hackett, 2010), 188.
15. See a similar example in Xu Fuzuo 徐復祚, *Qu lun* 曲論, in *Zhongguo gudian xiqu lunzhu jicheng*, 4:238.
16. For a critique of this tendency, see Ong Chang Woei, *Li Mengyang, the North-South Divide, and Literati Learning in Ming China* (Cambridge, Mass.: Harvard University Asia Center, 2016), 5–6.
17. Katherine Carlitz, "Printing as Performance: Literati Playwright-Publishers of the Late Ming," in *Printing and Book Culture in Late Imperial China*, ed.

Cynthia Brokaw and Kai-Wing Chow (Berkeley: University of California Press, 2005), 286–87.

18. Kevin Conrad Schoenberger, "Resonant Readings: Musicality in Early Modern Chinese Adaptations of Traditional Poetic Forms," Ph.D. diss, Yale University, 2013.

19. Einar Haugen, *Language Conflict and Language Planning: The Case of Modern Norwegian* (Cambridge, Mass.: Harvard University Press, 1966), 9; John Considine, *Academy Dictionaries 1600–1800* (Cambridge: Cambridge University Press, 2014), 12; Mårten Söderblom Saarela, "Manchu, Mandarin, and the Politicization of Spoken Language in Qing China," in *Language Diversity in the Sinophone World: Historical Trajectories, Language Planning, and Multilingual Practices*, ed. Henning Klöter and Mårten Söderblom Saarela (London: Routledge, 2020).

20. Hirata Shōji 平田昌司, *Wenhua zhidu he hanyu shi* 文化制度和汉语史 (Beijing: Beijing daxue chubanshe, 2016), 47–49.

21. Shen Guoyuan 沈國元, *Liangchao congxin lu* 兩朝從信錄 (c. 1628–1644 edition at Harvard-Yenching Library), j. 17, 17b; Qian Qianyi 錢謙益, *Qian Muzhai quanji* 錢牧齋全集 (Shanghai: Shanghai guji chubanshe, 2003), 881; Lu Rong 陸容, *Shuyuan zaji* 菽園雜記, SKQS, j. 10, 9a; Xu Fuzuo, *Huadangge congtan* 花當閣叢談 (Beijing: Zhonghua shuju, 1991), 183. Another late seventeenth-century scholar argued that the focus on *baguwen* in Ming exams resulted in the deterioration of phonological study generally in the Ming. See Jiang Guoxiang 蔣國祥, *Tang lüshi yun* 唐律詩韻 (at Taiwan Normal University Library), 18a.

22. Liu Hainian 劉海年 and Yang Yifan 楊一凡, eds., *Zhongguo zhenxi falü dianji jicheng, yi bian* 中國珍稀法律典籍集成, 乙編, vol. 4 (Beijing: Kexue chubanshe, 1994), 988–89.

23. Richard VanNess Simmons, "A Second Look at the *Tōwa sanyō*: Clues to the Nature of the *Guanhuah* Studied by Japanese in the Early Eighteenth Century," *Journal of the American Oriental Society* 117, no. 3 (1997): 419–26; W. South Coblin, "A Brief History of Mandarin," *Journal of the American Oriental Society* 120, no. 4 (2000): 537–52.

24. Paola Paderni, "The Problem of *Kuan-hua* in Eighteenth Century China: The Yung-chêng Decree for Fukien and Kwangtung," *Annali [dell'Università di Napoli "L'Orientale"]* 48, no. 4 (1988): 258–68.

25. Mårten Söderblom Saarela, "Manchu and the Study of Language in China (1607–1911)," Ph.D. diss., Princeton University, 2015, 384–419.

26. Xu Fuzuo, *Huadangge congtan*, 180. This claim is paraphrased from a mid-Ming text; cf. Lu Rong, *Shuyuan zaji*, j. 4, 8a.

27. Gina Tam, *Dialect and Nationalism in China, 1860–1960* (Cambridge: Cambridge University Press, 2020).

28. Hugh Stimson, *The Jongyuan in Yunn; a Guide to Old Mandarin Pronunciation* (New Haven, Conn.: Far Eastern Publications, Yale University, 1966), 19–20.
29. Xiao Yuncong, *Yun tong* 韻通, *Xuxiu Siku quanshu* 續修四庫全書 (Shanghai: Shanghai guji chubanshe, 1995–1999) [hereafter *XX SKQS*], *ba*, [1a].
30. Wang Jide, *Qu lü*, 110–13.
31. Zhao Yiguang, *Tanya, yunxie*, 20a.
32. *Mengzi*, 3A4.14.
33. Cf. Ge Zhongxuan, *Tailü, waipian*, j. 3, 21b; Shi Shaoxin 施紹莘, *Qiushui an huaying ji* 秋水庵花影集, *SKQS CMCS*, j. 3, 58a; Shen Chongsui, *Duqu xuzhi*, 251.
34. Cf. Elisabeth Kaske, *The Politics of Language in Chinese Education, 1895–1919* (Leiden: Brill, 2008), 41–55.
35. Xu Fuzuo, *Qu lun*, 239.
36. Xu Fuzuo, *Huadangge congtan*, 183–84.
37. Cited in Ning Jifu 宁继福, *Zhongyuan yinyun biaogao* 中原音韵表稿 (Changchun: Jilin wenshi chubanshe, 1985), 240.
38. Ling Mengchu, *Tanqu zazha* 譚曲雜箚, in *Zhongguo gudian xiqu lunzhu jicheng*, 4:259.
39. Xu Fuzuo, *Huadangge congtan*, 182.
40. Wang Shizhen, *Qu zao* 曲藻, in *Zhongguo gudian xiqu lunzhu jicheng*, 4:25.
41. Wang Shizhen does not appear to have had a consistent platform for "correct pronunciation" and elsewhere heralded the pronunciation of Luoyang as the superior language. See Wang Shizhen, *Yanzhou xu gao* 弇州續稿, *SKQS*, j. 40, 10b.
42. Fang Yizhi, *Tongya*, j. 29, 22a.
43. Shen Xiong 沈雄, *Gujin cihua* 古今詞話, *SKQS CMCS bubian, cipin* j. *shang*, 11b.
44. Liu Lian 劉濂, *Yuejing yuanyi* 樂經元義, *SKQS CMCS*, j. 1, 34b; Han Bangqi 韓邦奇, *Yuanluo zhiyue* 苑洛志樂 (1548 edition, at Harvard-Yenching Library), j. 1, 4a.
45. Thomas Bartlett, "Phonology as Statecraft in Gu Yanwu's Thought," in *The Scholar's Mind: Essays in Honor of Frederick W. Mote*, ed. Perry Link (Hong Kong: Chinese University Press, 2009), 198–99.
46. Gu Yanwu 顧炎武, *Yinxue wushu* 音學五書, in *Gu Yanwu quanji* 顧炎武全集, (Shanghai: Shanghai guji chubanshe, 2011), 2:8.
47. Li Guangdi 李光地, *Rongcun xu yulu* 榕村續語錄 (Beijing: Zhonghua shuju, 1995), 902.
48. I have found few references to Fujian pronunciation in Gu Yanwu's extensive writings on phonology.
49. Xu Boling 徐伯齡, *Yinjing jun* 蟬精雋, *SKQS*, j. 7, 8b–9a.
50. Craig Clunas, *Superfluous Things: Material Culture and Social Status in Early Modern China* (Urbana: University of Illinois Press, 1991), 109–15.

51. Pan Lei 潘耒, *Leiyin* 類音, *SKQS CMCS*, j. 1, 10a.
52. Jiang Yong, *Yinxue bianwei* 音學辨微 (Shanghai: Bogu zhai, 1920), 25a. Cf. Kaske, *The Politics of Language in Chinese Education*, 42–43.
53. S. Robert Ramsey, *The Languages of China* (Princeton, N.J.: Princeton University Press, 1989), 9–10.
54. Shen Chongsui, *Duqu xuzhi*, 190.
55. Shen Chongsui, *Duqu xuzhi*, 223.
56. Shen Chongsui, *Duqu xuzhi*, 187, 189.
57. Shen Chongsui, *Duqu xuzhi*, 318.
58. Cheng Mingshan, *Xiaoyu pu* (1662 edition at Harvard-Yenching Library), Ma *xu*, 1b–2a. The "sounds of the heart" is a famous description of "spoken language" (*yan* 言) by Yang Xiong 揚雄 (53 BCE–18 CE), as opposed to writing (*shu* 書), which he defined as the "images of the heart" (心畫). See Yang Xiong, *Exemplary Figures—Fayan*, trans. Michael Nylan (Seattle: University of Washington Press, 2013), 77.
59. See Cheng Mingshan as an editor of Cheng Yuanchu 程元初, *Lülü yinyun guashu tong* 律呂音韻卦數通 (1609 edition at Naikaku bunko).
60. Xiong Shibo, *Dengqie yuansheng*, *SKQS CMCS*, Xiong *xu*, 1b; j. 3, 10b.
61. Shen Chongsui, *Duqu xuzhi*, 249.
62. See Cai Mengzhen 蔡孟珍, "Ming Shen Chongsui zai xiqu yinyunxue shang de gongxian" 明・沈寵綏在戲曲音韻學上的貢獻, *Shengyun luncong* 9 (2000): 255–88; and Li Huei-mian 李惠綿, "Cong yinyunxue jiaodu lun Qingdai duqu lun de chuancheng yu kaizhan" 從音韻學角度論清代度曲論的傳承與開展, *Hanxue yanjiu* 26, no. 2 (2008): 185–218.
63. Shen Chongsui, *Duqu xuzhi*, 209.
64. Translation from Stephen H. West and Wilt Idema, trans., *The Moon and the Zither: The Story of the Western Wing* (Berkeley: University of California Press, 1991), 184.
65. Shen Chongsui, *Duqu xuzhi*, 223–24, 225.
66. Shen Chongsui, *Duqu xuzhi*, 225.
67. Cf. Wu Yuanman, *Liushu zongyao*, *zixu*, 1a; Wang Kentang, *Yugangzhai bizhu*, j. 4, 39b, 40b; Wang Yangming, *Instructions for Practical Living, and Other Neo-Confucian Writings* (New York: Columbia University Press, 1963), 159.
68. Shen Chongsui, *Duqu xuzhi*, 203.
69. Shen Chongsui, *Duqu xuzhi*, 249.
70. Shen Chongsui, *Duqu xuzhi*, 223. Although the term *zixue* can refer specifically to the grammatological study of graphs, it regularly encompassed phonological study, as in this case. The term *zhangju* could refer to the commentaries examination candidates had to gain proficiency in, as well as literary composition more broadly.

71. Patrick Hanan, *The Invention of Li Yu* (Cambridge, Mass: Harvard University Press, 1988); S. E. Kile, "Toward an Extraordinary Everyday: Li Yu's (1611–1680) Vision, Writing, and Practice," Ph.D. diss., Columbia University, 2013.
72. Hanan, *The Invention of Li Yu*, 51; Giorgio Casacchia, "About a 'Book of Rhymes' by Li Yu," *Ming Qing yanjiu* 4 (1995): 45–50.
73. Suyoung Son, *Writing for Print: Publishing and the Making of Textual Authority in Late Imperial China* (Cambridge, Mass.: Harvard University Asia Center, 2018); Yuming He, *Home and the World: Editing the "Glorious Ming" in Woodblock-Printed Books of the Sixteenth and Seventeenth Centuries* (Cambridge, Mass.: Harvard University Asia Center, 2013).
74. Li Yu, *Xianqing ouji*, j. 2, 2b.
75. Li Yu, *Xianqing ouji*, j. 5, 3b.
76. Li Yu 李漁, *Liweng ciyun* 笠翁詞韻, in *Li Yu quanji* 李漁全集, vol. 18 (Hangzhou: Zhejiang guji chubanshe, 1991), 363–64.
77. Li Yu, *Xianqing ouji*, j. 5, 3b–5b.
78. Li Yu, *Liweng ciyun*, 364.
79. Zhou Deqing, *Zhongyuan yinyun*, j. *xia*, 1a, invokes a similar principle.
80. For a typical example of the eighteenth-century articulation of this issue, see Qian Daxin, *Shijia zhai yangxin lu* 十駕齋養新錄, *XX SKQS*, *yulu*, j. *shang*, 9b–11b.
81. Zhou Deqing, *Zhongyuan yinyun*, j. *xia*, 5b.
82. Li Yu, *Liweng shiyun* 笠翁詩韻, in *Li Yu quanji*, 207.
83. Li Yu, *Liweng shiyun*, 208.
84. Li Yu, *Xianqing ouji*, j. 3, 12b.
85. Li Yu, *Xianqing ouji*, j. 3, 13a.
86. Li Yu, *Xianqing ouji*, j. 7, 36b.
87. Li Yu, *Xianqing ouji*, j. 7, 34a. He did, however, dispute the validity of certain distinctions in *Zhongyuan yinyun*.
88. Cf. Kaske, *The Politics of Language in Chinese Education*, 45.
89. Li Yu, *Xianqing ouji*, j. 5, 19a.
90. Long Weilin 龍為霖, *Benyun yide* 本韻一得, *SKQS CMCS*, *xu*, 3b; Xia Dalin 夏大霖, *Qu sao xinyin* 屈騷心印, *SKQS CMCS*, *fafan*, 4a; Xu Jian 徐鑑, *Yin fu* 音泭, *XX SKQS*, 21a; Zhou Chun 周春, *Shisanjing yin lüe* 十三經音略, in *Zhou Songai yishu* 周松靄遺書 (c. 1736–1820 edition at Harvard-Yenching Library), *fu*, 2a; Mei Yingzuo 梅膺祚, *Zihui* 字彙 (1800 edition at Kyoto University, Jinbunken), Qianlong *renxu xu*, 1b.
91. For Li Yu's dates in Hangzhou, see Hanan, *The Invention of Li Yu*, 216n.37.
92. Mao Qiling, *Xihe ji* 西河集, *SKQS*, j. 99, 1a.
93. Wai-yee Li, "Introduction," in *Trauma and Transcendence in Early Qing Literature*, ed. Wilt L. Idema, Wai-yee Li, and Ellen Widmer (Cambridge, Mass.: Harvard University Asia Center, 2006), 15.

94. Qian Lin 錢林, *Wenxian zhengcun lu* 文獻徵存錄, *XX SKQS*, j. 1, 32a.
95. Chai Shaobing 柴紹炳, *Chai shi Guyun tong* 柴氏古韻通, *SKQS CMCS*, *fanli*, 4a–b.
96. Zhong Heng 仲恆, *Ciyun* 詞韻, *SKQS CMCS*, *lunlüe*, 1a–10b.
97. Mao Xianshu, *Xunshu* 潠書 (Shanghai: Shanghai guji chubanshe, 2009), j. 2, 5b–6a.
98. Zhang Minquan 张民权, *Qingdai qianqi guyinxue yanjiu* 清代前期古音学研究, vol. 1 (Beijing: Beijing guangbo xueyuan chubanshe, 2002), 7–13.
99. Chai Shaobing actively criticized Gu's phonological claims in *Chai shi Guyun tong*, *zashuo*, 34b–36b.
100. Mao Xianshu, *Yunbai*, 30a–31a.
101. See Mao Xianshu 毛先舒, *Nanqu rusheng kewen* 南曲入聲客問, in *Zhongguo gudian xiqu lunzhu jicheng*, 7:129–30.
102. Mao Xianshu 毛先舒, *Yunxue tongzhi* 韻學通指, *SKQS CMCS*, 1a–b.
103. Mao Xianshu, *Yunxue tongzhi*, 51a.
104. Mao Xianshu, *Xunshu*, j. 6, 24b–32a.
105. Pan Lei, *Leiyin*, j. 1, 6a; Zhao Shaoji, *Zhuoan yunwu* 拙菴韻悟, *XX SKQS*, 642; Han Qia, *Zhuanxue cejie*, *fanli*, 10b, *shengyun biao*, 3b; Xie Qikun 謝啓昆, *Xiaoxue kao* 小學考, *XX SKQS*, j. 41, 18b.
106. Li Guangdi, *Rongcun xu yulu*, 775.
107. Chen Jinmo, *Yuanyin tongyun*, j. 1, 8b, 34a–35b.
108. Chen Jinmo, *Yuanyin tongyun*, j. 1, 35 a–b.
109. Chen Jinmo, *Yuanyin tongyun*, j. 1, 28b.
110. Chen Jinmo, *Yuanyin tongyun*, j. 1, 54a.
111. Ding Lizhong 丁立中, *Baqian juan lou shumu* 八千卷樓書目, *XX SKQS*, j. 20, 30b; *Qinding Siku quanshu zongmu*, j. 199, 43a; j. 100, 31a; Zhu Xueqin 朱學勤, *Jieyilu shumu* 結一盧書目, j. 4, 25a, in *Zhongguo zhuming cangshujia shumu huikan*.
112. Zhou Hongzu, *Jingu tang shumu*, *shang*, 8a; Qi Chenghan 祁承㸁, *Dansheng tang cangshumu* 澹生堂藏書目, j. 2, 14a; Gao Ru 高儒, *Baichuan shuzhi* 百川書志, j. 2, 6a; Dong Qichang, *Xuanshang zhai shumu*, j. 1, 8b; Zhao Dingyu 趙定宇, *Zhao Dingyu shumu* 趙定宇書目, in *Mingdai shumu tiba congkan*, 1587; Xu Qianxue 徐乾學, *Chuanshi lou shumu* 傳是樓書目, *XX SKQS*, *rizi si ge*, *shu*, 13a.

5. Reading the Classics for Pleasure

1. Ong Chang Woei, *Li Mengyang, the North-South Divide, and Literati Learning in Ming China* (Cambridge, Mass.: Harvard University Asia Center, 2016).
2. Adam Schorr, "Connoisseurship and the Defense Against Vulgarity: Yang Shen (1488–1559) and His Work," *Monumenta Serica* 41 (1993), 113–14.

3. See texts collected in Nagasawa Kikuya 長澤規矩, ed., *Min Shin zokugo jisho shūsei* 明清俗語辭書集成 (Tokyo: Kyūko shoin, 1974-1977); Zhenzhen Lu, "The Vernacular World of Pu Songling," Ph.D. diss., University of Pennsylvania, 2017, 77–145.
4. Bruce Rusk, *Critics and Commentators: The "Book of Poems" as Classic and Literature* (Cambridge, Mass.: Harvard University Asia Center, 2012).
5. Peter K. Bol, *"This Culture of Ours": Intellectual Transitions in T'ang and Sung China* (Stanford, Calif: Stanford University Press, 1992), 17, 100–102.
6. Zhu Xi did theorize proper modes of poetic composition; however, he was primarily concerned with limiting the harmful effects of writing poetry rather than advocating for its utility as a tool for apprehending the Way. See Michael Fuller, "Aesthetics and Meaning in Experience: A Theoretical Perspective on Zhu Xi's Revision of Song Dynasty Views of Poetry," *Harvard Journal of Asiastic Studies* 65, no. 2 (2005): 311–55; Rusk, *Critics and Commentators*, 61–65.
7. Peter K. Bol, "Culture, Society, and Neo-Confucianism, Twelfth to Sixteenth Century," in *The Song-Yuan-Ming Transition in Chinese History*, ed. Paul Smith and Richard von Glahn (Cambridge, Mass.: Harvard University Asia Center, 2003), 267.
8. David L. Rolston, *Traditional Chinese Fiction and Fiction Commentary: Reading and Writing Between the Lines* (Stanford, Calif.: Stanford University Press, 1997), 68–71.
9. Andrea S. Goldman, *Opera and the City: The Politics of Culture in Beijing, 1770–1900* (Stanford, Calif.: Stanford University Press, 2012), 134; Joseph S. C. Lam, "Reading Music and Eroticism in Late Ming Texts," *Nan Nü* 12 (2010): 215–54.
10. Stephen Owen, *Readings in Chinese Literary Thought* (Cambridge, Mass.: Harvard University Asia Center, 1996), 201.
11. Rusk, *Critics and Commentators*, 7.
12. Maram Epstein, *Competing Discourses: Orthodoxy, Authenticity, and Engendered Meanings in Late Imperial Chinese Fiction* (Cambridge, Mass.: Harvard University Asia Center, 2001), 47–49; Rolston, *Traditional Chinese Fiction and Fiction Commentary*, 165.
13. See, for instance, Zhang Yizhong 張以忠, ed., *Chen Mingqing xiansheng pingxuan gujin wentong* 陳明卿先生評選古今文統, *Siku jinhui shu congkan* 四庫禁燬書叢刊 (Beijing: Beijing chubanshe, 1997) [hereafter *SKJHSCK*], j. 2, 75a–89b; Zhang Guoxi 張國璽 and Liu Yixiang 劉一相, *Huigu jinghua* 匯古菁華 (1596 edition at Harvard-Yenching Library), j. 4. Cf. David L. Rolston, "Sources of Traditional Chinese Fiction Criticism" and "Formal Aspects of Fiction Criticism and Commentary in China," in *How to Read the Chinese Novel*, ed.

David L. Rolston (Princeton, N.J.: Princeton University Press, 1990), 15–17, 45–46.
14. Guo Shaoyu 郭紹虞, *Zhongguo wenxue piping shi* 中國文學批評史 (Shanghai: Shanghai guji chubanshe, rev. 1979), 446–52; Rusk, *Critics and Commentators*, 86.
15. See Bruce Rusk, "Not Written in Stone: Ming Readers of the 'Great Learning' and the Impact of Forgery," *Harvard Journal of Asiatic Studies* 66, no. 1 (2006): 215.
16. I use the term "verse" here instead of the more specific "poetry," adopting David Lurie's definition of verse as characterized by "repeated sound patterns" including metrical and phonic elements. See David Lurie, *Realms of Literacy: Early Japan and the History of Writing* (Cambridge, Mass.: Harvard University Asia Center, 2011), 254. Ming accounts do not necessarily refer to the rhymed texts of antiquity as "poetry" (*shi* 詩), making reference instead to their "tonality" (*yin* 音) and "rhyme" (*yun* 韻), as well as their ability to be "sung" (*ge* 歌 or *yong* 詠) or "intoned" (*feng* 諷).
17. Qian Qianyi 錢謙益, *Liechao shiji* 列朝詩集, vol. 8 (Beijing: Zhonghua shuju, 2007), 4578; Zhu Guozhen 朱國禎, *Yongchuang xiaopin* 湧幢小品, *Siku quanshu cunmu congshu* 四庫全書存目叢書 (Jinan: Qi Lu shushe chubanshe, 1997) [hereafter *SKQS CMCS*], j. 21, 19 a–b; Shen Defu 沈德符, *Wanli yehuo bian* 萬曆野獲編, ed. Li Xin 黎欣, vol. 2 (Beijing: Wenhua yishu chubanshe, 1998), 620–21. A variation of the story occurs in Li Le 李樂, *Jianwen zaji* 見聞雜記 (Taipei: Weiwen tushu chubanshe, 1977) j. 10, 47a–b.
18. Zhang Xianyi 張獻翼, *Du Yi yunkao* 讀易韻考, *SKQS CMCS*, Wang *xu*, 1b.
19. For more on these two influential methods of *Yijing* interpretation, see Kidder Smith, Jr., ed., *Sung Dynasty Uses of the I Ching* (Princeton, N.J.: Princeton University Press, 1990).
20. Zhang Xianyi, *Du Yi yunkao*, Wang *xu*, 2a. For missing graphs in this phrase, cf. Wang Shizhen, *Yanzhou xugao*, j. 43, 7b.
21. Zhang Xianyi, *Du Yi yunkao*, Wang *xu*, 2a–b.
22. Zhang Xianyi, *Du Yi yunkao*, *ba*, 1a–b. Translation of the latter passage, which is an allusion to the *Changes* itself, is adapted from Richard John Lynn, trans., *The Classic of Changes: A New Translation of the I Ching as Interpreted by Wang Bi* (New York: Columbia University Press, 1994), 78.
23. The texts of these later studies can be found in Yan Lingfeng 嚴靈峯, ed., *Wuqiubeizhai Yijing jicheng* 無求備齋易經集成, vol. 142 (Taipei: Chengwen chubanshe, 1976).
24. Rusk, *Critics and Commentators*, 85.
25. The meter of *Cantong qi* is not entirely constructed of four-syllable lines, but the text is relatively metrically consistent within any given section.
26. Translation adapted from Lynn, *The Classic of Changes*, 137.

27. Zhang Xianyi, *Du Yi yunkao*, j. 1, 2b–5b.
28. Translation adapted from Lynn, *The Classic of Changes*, 130.
29. The rhyme patterns of the *Yijing* are inconsistent, and there are occurrences of internal rhymes within lines. In such cases, however, there is typically some kind of prosodic or syntactical pattern linking the rhyming graphs. See Richard J. Smith, *Fathoming the Cosmos and Ordering the World: The Yijing (I-Ching, or Classic of Changes) and Its Evolution in China* (Charlottesville: University of Virginia Press, 2008), 23; Edward L. Shaughnessy, "The Composition of the *Zhouyi*," Ph.D. diss., Stanford University, 1983, 142, 181.
30. This pronunciation is attested in the later dictionary, *Zihui*. *Zihui* cites the same passage from the *Yijing* alongside the Buddhist chant, making its gloss likely derived from Zhang Xianyi's interpretation. It could also derive from a lexicon or commentary on *Yijing*, which pre- or postdates *Du Yi yunkao*, although I have been unable to locate such a text. *Zhengzi tong*, which was based on *Zihui*, singled out this gloss as incorrect, and it is not acknowledged in *Kangxi zidian*. This pronunciation was nevertheless evidently later cited in a no longer extant eighteenth-century *Yijing* commentary, inviting Weng Fanggang's 翁方綱 (1733–1818) criticism. See Mei Yingzuo, *Zihui* (1615 edition at Harvard-Yenching Library), *mao*, 9a; Zhang Zilie, *Zhengzi tong*, *SKQS CMCS*, *mao shang*, 23a; Weng Fanggang, *Weng Fanggang zuan Siku tiyao gao* 翁方綱纂四庫提要稿 (Shanghai: Shanghai kexue jishu wenxian chubanshe, 2005), 46.
31. Translation adapted from Lynn, *The Classic of Changes*, 86–87.
32. Zhang Xianyi, *Du Yi yunkao*, j. 6, 10b. Zhang's pronunciation glosses for rhyming graphs are denoted here with square brackets in the Chinese text.
33. Peng Jing 彭靜, "Mingdai Suzhou qujia Gu Dadian xiqu yongyun kao" 明代蘇州曲家顧大典戲曲用韻考, *Korea Journal of Chinese Language and Literature* 47 (2012): 116–17.
34. Zhang Xianyi, *Du Yi yunkao*, j. 6, 10b. Zhang's pronunciation glosses for rhyming graphs are denoted here with square brackets in the Chinese text. The preceding line can be translated as "are there not ideas associated with an age in decline?" Cf. Lynn, *The Classic of Changes*, 86.
35. Zhang Xianyi, *Du Yi yunkao*, j. 5, 1b–2a. Similar instances abound, such as j. 1, 49b; j. 2, 10a; j. 3, 16a, 21b, 22a, 30b; j. 5, 6a.
36. Martin W. Huang, "Author(ity) and Reader in Traditional Chinese *Xiaoshuo* Commentary," *CLEAR* 16 (1994): 47–49; Rivi Handler-Spitz, *Symptoms of an Unruly Age: Li Zhi and Cultures of Early Modernity* (Seattle: University of Washington Press, 2017), 81–84.
37. Zhang Xianyi, *Du Yi yunkao*, Zhang *xu*, 1a.
38. Zhang Xianyi, *Du Yi yunkao*, Wang *xu*, 2a–b.
39. Zhang Xianyi, *Du Yi yunkao*, Zhang *xu*, 1a.

40. Zhang Xianyi, *Du Yi yunkao*, j. 1, 36a–b, 118
41. Zhang Xianyi, *Du Yi yunkao*, j. 1, 23a.
42. Zhang Xianyi, *Du Yi yunkao*, ba, 1b.
43. See Zhang Minquan 張民權, *Songdai guyinxue yu Wu Yu 'Shi buyin' yanjiu* 宋代古音學與吳棫《詩補音》研究 (Beijing: Shangwu yinshu guan, 2005), 99.
44. Yang Shiqiao 楊時喬, *Chuan Yi kao* 傳易考 (1595 edition at Harvard-Yenching Library), j. 1, 76b; *Qinding Siku quanshu zongmu*, j. 44, 10a.
45. See, for example, Pan Wei 潘緯, *Yunxie kao* 韻叶考 (at National Library of China); Hong Sheng 洪昇, *Shi Sao yunzhu* 詩騷韻注 (at National Library of China).
46. Zhang Xianyi, *Du Yi yunkao*, j. 5, 4b.
47. Sun Weicheng 孫維城, *Yunshi bianlan* 韻釋便覽 (1590 edition at Peking University Library), *xu*, 4a.
48. Qu Dajun, *Wengshan wen wai*, j. 2, 30a, 48a.
49. Qu Dajun, *Wengshan wen chao* 翁山文鈔, *SKJHSCK*, j. 1, 14a.
50. For more on this argument, see David S. Nivison, *The Life and Thought of Chang Hsüeh-Ch'eng, 1738–1801* (Stanford, Calif.: Stanford University Press, 1966), 201–4. Li Zhi, the famous late Ming literary figure, had previously asserted that the Six Classics were works of history. He did not develop this claim into a program of learning, as Zhang Xuecheng would later do. See Li Zhi, *Fen shu* 焚書 (Beijing: Zhonghua shuju, 1961), 216.
51. Gu Yanwu, *Yinxue wushu*, 9.
52. Zhang Xianyi, *Du Yi yunkao*, j. 1, 5a–5b.
53. Gu Yanwu, *Yinxue wushu*, 257.
54. Gu Yanwu, *Rizhi lu* 日知錄, in *Gu Yanwu quanji*, 19:801–2.
55. For Zhao's scholarly interaction with Zhang Xianyi, see Zhao Yiguang, *Shuowen changjian*, j. 29, 12a.
56. Zhao Yiguang, *Tanya, yunxie*, 13a–13b.
57. A similar example is Yang Shiwei's 楊時偉 1631 *Zhengyun jian* 正韻牋, which cites from both Wu Yu and Chen Di, a feature that the *Siku quanshu* editors found perplexing. See *Qinding Siku quanshu zongmu*, j. 44, 6a.
58. Zhang Xianyi, *Du Yi yunkao*, Huangfu *xu*, 1b.
59. *Qinding Siku quanshu zongmu*, j. 42, 10a–11b; j. 44, 10a–b.
60. Zhao Yiguang, *Tanya, yunxie*, 20a.
61. Zhao Yiguang, *Tanya, yunxie*, 6a.
62. Zhao Yiguang, *Tanya, tiba*, 10a.
63. Zhao Yiguang, *Tanya, yunxie*, 5b
64. Qu Dajun, *Wengshan wen chao*, j. 1, 14a.
65. Mao Xianshu, *Yun bai*, 51b–52a.
66. For information on Xiao Yuncong's no longer extant *Du lü xi* 杜律細, see Wang Shizhen 王士禎, *Chibei outan* 池北偶談, *Siku quanshu* 四庫全書 (Taipei: Taiwan shangwu yinshuguan, 1983) [hereafter *SKQS*], j. 12, 19b–21a.

67. Zhang Xianyi, "Yantan lun" 言談論, in He Fuzheng 賀復徵, *Wenzhang bianti huixuan* 文章辨體彙選, SKQS, j. 776, 17b–18a.
68. Steven Van Zoeren, *Poetry and Personality: Reading, Exegesis, and Hermeneutics in Traditional China* (Stanford, Calif.: Stanford University Press, 1991), 28–35; Martin Kern, "'Shijing' Songs as Performance Texts: A Case Study of 'Chu ci' (Thorny Caltrop)," *Early China* 25 (2000): 49–111.
69. Sima Qian, *Shiji*, SKQS, j. 47, 28b.
70. Stephen Owen, *Readings in Chinese Literary Thought*, 41–42.
71. Achim Mittag, "Change in *Shijing* Exegesis: Some Notes on the Rediscovery of the Musical Aspect of the 'Odes' in the Song Period," *T'oung Pao* 79, no. 4–5 (1993): 211–12.
72. Adapted from Rusk, *Critics and Commentators*, 26. For Ming uses, see, for instance, Chen Jinmo *Yuanyin tongyun*, *xu*, 1b; Shi Kui 是奎, *Taigu yuanyin* (at Taiwan Normal University Library), j. 4, 23b.
73. Ou Daren 歐大任, *Ou Yubu ji* 歐虞部集, SKJHSCK, j. 7, 10a; Guo Zhengyu 郭正域, *Hebing huangli cao* 合併黃離草, SKJHSCK, j. 18, 23a.
74. Confucius, *The Analects*, trans. D. C. Lau (Hong Kong: Chinese University Press, 2002 reprint), 81.
75. Huang Daozhou, *Rongtan wenye* 榕壇問業, SKQS, j. 11, 25a.
76. Dong Yue, *Wenyin fa*, 19a–b.
77. Dagmar Schäfer, *The Crafting of the 10,000 Things: Knowledge and Technology in Seventeenth-Century China* (Chicago: University of Chicago Press, 2011), 212–16.
78. Huang Yi-Long and Chang Chih-Ch'eng, "The Evolution and Decline of the Ancient Chinese Practice of Watching for the Ethers," *Chinese Science* 13 (1996): 86–87.
79. Han Qia, *Zhuanxue cejie*, j. 15, 32b; Zhu Zaiyu, *Lülü jingyi* 律呂精義, ed. Feng Wenci 馮文慈 (Beijing: Renmin yinyue chubanshe, 1998), 171–89; Liu Lian, *Yuejing yuanyi*, j. 1, 2b; Wang Tingxiang 王廷相, *Wang shi jiacang ji* 王氏家藏集, SKQS CMCS, j. 40, 1a–b; Zhang Yu, *Yayue fawei* 雅樂發微, SKQS CMCS, j. 1, 1a; Tang Shunzhi, *Jingchuan baibian* 荊川稗編, SKQS, j. 42, 4b–5b. As in chapter 1, I hereafter refer to the fundamental pitch *huangzhong* as the pitch C.
80. Judith T. Zeitlin, "Chinese Theories of the Sounding Voice Before the Modern Era: From the Natural to the Instrumental," in *The Voice as Something More: Essays Toward Materiality*, ed. Martha Feldman and Judith T. Zeitlin (Chicago: University of Chicago Press, 2019), 63.
81. Xing Yunlu, *Gujin lüli kao*, j. 35, 7b.
82. Han Qia, *Zhuanxue cejie*, j. 15, 32b; Wu Weizhong 武位中, *Wenmiao yueshu* 文廟樂書 (at Naikaku bunko), j. 2, 26b.
83. Cheng Zongshun, *Hongfan qianjie*, j. 2, 13a.

84. Hao Jing, *Dushu tong*, j. 1, 19a.
85. He Tang 何瑭, *He Wending gong wenji* 何文定公文集 (1580 edition at Harvard-Yenching Library), j. 9, 20b. See also Wu Weizhong, *Wenmiao yueshu*, j. 2, 26b.
86. Tang Shunzhi, *Jingchuan baibian*, j. 42, 2b; Wang Qiao 王樵, *Fanglu ji* 方麓集, *SKQS*, j. 15, 23b; Lu Shiyi 陸世儀, *Sibianlu jiyao* 思辨錄輯要, *SKQS*, j. 22, 7a; Chen Jinmo, *Yuanyin tongyun*, j. 2, 3b.
87. Chen Jinmo, *Yuanyin tongyun*, j. 2, 3b.
88. Xia Yan 夏言, *Xia Guizhou xiansheng wenji* 夏桂洲先生文集, *SKQS CMCS*, j. 12, 70b–71a.
89. Wu Jishi, *Yinsheng jiyuan*, j. 1, 1a, adapting from Guo Zhengyu, *Hebing huangli cao*, j. 18, 22a.
90. In this and the following musical examples, the transcriptions are based on *lülü* notation. The melody by Zhu Xi has been transcribed previously. The subsequent transcriptions are my own. For transcriptions of Zhu Xi's melodies, see Rulan Chao Pian, *Sonq Dynasty Musical Sources and Their Interpretation* (Cambridge, Mass.: Harvard University Press, 1967), 155–73; and Laurence E. R. Picken, "Twelve Ritual Melodies of the T'ang Dynasty," in *Studia Memoriae Belae Bartók Sacra*, ed. Benjámi Rajeczky (Budapest: Aedes Academiae Scientiarum Hungaricae, 1956), 147–73.
91. Zhu Xi, *Yili jingzhuan tongjie* 儀禮經傳通解, *SKQS*, j. 14, 8b.
92. Rulan Chao Pian, *Sonq Dynasty Musical Sources and Their Interpretation*, 11. They were also recorded in the work of Ming musicologists. Cf. Zhang Weiran 張蔚然, "Sanbai pian shengpu" 三百篇聲譜, in Tao Ting 陶珽, ed., *Shuofu xu* 說郛續, *Xuxiu Siku quanshu* 續修四庫全書 (Shanghai: Shanghai guji chubanshe, 1995–1999) [hereafter *XX SKQS*], j. 32, 1a–9a, and Huang Zuo, *Yuedian*, j. 36.
93. Qu Jiusi, *Yuedao fameng*, j. 9, 2a.
94. Ge Zhongxuan, *Tailü*, j. 10, 9b.
95. Ge Zhongxuan, *Tailü*, j. 10, 12a–b.
96. Zhang Weiran, "Sanbaipian shengpu," j. 32, 1a.
97. Zhu Rangxu, *Changchun jingchen gao* 長春競辰稿 (1549 edition, microfilm at Harvard-Yenching Library), j. 1, 23a.
98. Liu Lian, *Yuejing yuanyi*, *xu*, 1a.
99. Wu Jishi, *Yinsheng jiyuan*, j. 5.
100. Wu Jishi further assigned the pitch C to 萍 <bhiēng>, the pronunciation of which he argued would have been altered to <bhiāng> in this verse.
101. The one exception is the change of pitch between the first two syllables. Wu was likely adhering to a compositional practice, which dictates that the first and last note of a melody in a given mode should be the same. He therefore altered the first pitch of this melody, which I believe he would otherwise have written as A#, to match the concluding pitch.

102. Given the quality of the imprint, it is possible that the note I have transcribed as 大 C# could be 太 D. This too results in three consecutive semitones (D–D#–E).
103. Shen Guangbang 沈光邦, *Yi lü tongjie* 易律通解, *SKQS CMCS*, *Shaozi pian*, 91a–92b. For another etymology of *lüshi* relating it to pitch-pipes, see Liu Xizai 劉熙載, *Yi gai* 藝概, *XX SKQS*, j. 2, 21a.
104. Zhu Zaiyu, *Lülü jingyi*, 971.

6. Afterlives

1. R. Kent Guy, *The Emperor's Four Treasuries: Scholars and the State in the Late Ch'ien-lung Era* (Cambridge, Mass.: Council on East Asian Studies, Harvard University, 1987); Chu Hung-Lam, "High Ch'ing Intellectual Bias as Reflected in the Imperial Catalogue," *Gest Library Journal* 1, no. 2 (1987): 51–66.
2. Lao Naixuan, *Dengyun yide waipian* 等韻一得外篇 (c. 1886–1898 edition at Harvard-Yenching Library), 52b.
3. For a rare exception, see Chen Yongguang 陳用光, *Taiyi zhou wenji* 太乙舟文集, *Xuxiu Siku quanshu* 續修四庫全書 (Shanghai: Shanghai guji chubanshe, 1995–1999) [hereafter *XX SKQS*], j. 5, 26b–27a.
4. Wu Minshu 吳敏樹, *Panhu wenji* 柈湖文集, *XX SKQS*, j. 6, 22a; Zhang Weiping 張維屏, *Guochao shiren zhenglüe* 國朝詩人徵略, *XX SKQS*, j. 3, 3a; Tao Shu 陶澍, *Tao Wenyi gong quanji* 陶文毅公全集, *XX SKQS*, j. 42, 2a; Fang Dongshu 方東樹, *Hanxue shangdui* 漢學商兌 (Shanghai: Shanghai shudian, 1994), j. *zhong zhi shang*, 11b. On the terms *Ancient Learning* and *Han Learning*, see Ori Sela, *China's Philological Turn: Scholars, Textualism, and the Dao in the Eighteenth Century* (New York: Columbia University Press, 2018), 1–2, 10–12.
5. Sela, *China's Philological Turn*, 16.
6. Sela, *China's Philological Turn*, 85.
7. Lin Qingzhang's *Mingdai kaojuxue* and Benjamin Elman's *Philosophy to Philology* are notable exceptions. Both studies, however, focus on a discrete set of Ming luminaries who foreshadowed Evidential Learning, in contrast to the Ming thinkers highlighted in the present study, whose methods differed profoundly from Evidential Learning. Ori Sela also observes the limited but significant role of philology for some Song Learning of the Way thinkers; see Sela, *China's Philological Turn*, 94–95.
8. Steven B. Miles, *The Sea of Learning: Mobility and Identity in Nineteenth-Century Guangzhou* (Cambridge, Mass.: Harvard University Asia Center, 2006), 201–36; Sela, *China's Philological Turn*, 78–81.

9. For Gu Chenxu's significance in mathematics, see Catherine Jami, *The Emperor's New Mathematics: Western Learning and Imperial Authority During the Kangxi Reign (1662–1722)* (Oxford: Oxford University Press, 2012), 263.
10. Long Weilin, *Benyun yide*, *Siku quanshu cunmu congshu* 四庫全書存目叢書 (Jinan: Qi Lu shushe chubanshe, 1997) [herefter *SKQS CMCS*], *lunshu*, 2b. For the Ming origins of this discourse, see chapter 1.
11. Long Weilin, *Benyun yide*, j. 7, 20b. Sima Qian claimed that Confucius pared an initial three thousand poems into just three hundred in his compilation of the *Shijing*.
12. Wang Songmu 王松木, "Zhuiru modao de guyin xuejia–lun Long Weilin 'Benyun yide' ji qi yinxue sixiang" 墜入魔道的古音學家—論龍為霖《本韻一得》及其音學思想, *Qinghua zhongwen xuebao* 8 (2012), 98.
13. Cf. Gu Zhen 顧鎮, *Yudong xue Shi* 虞東學詩, *Siku quanshu* 四庫全書 (Taipei: Taiwan shangwu yinshuguan, 1983) [hereafter *SKQS*], j. 5, 6b, 18a.
14. Over the course of this period, Long Weilin's reputation was somewhat restored even within Evidential Learning circles. The prominent Evidential Learning scholar Li Zhaoluo 李兆洛 (1769–1841), for instance, wrote in 1837: "The *Siku* bibliography forcefully criticized the explanations of Pan Lei and Long Weilin. The divisions of syllabic spellers take place within the throat and tongue, however, and the human voice is the primordial sound of heaven and earth. In essence, there are naturally places that correspond [to musical pitch], but one simply should not go too in depth." Li Zhaoluo, *Liushu yunzheng* 六書韻徵 (1838 edition at Columbia University Library), Li *xu*, 1b.
15. Fu Shoutong, *Guyin leibiao*, *XX SKQS*, *zixu*, 5b.
16. Fu Shoutong, *Guyin leibiao*, He *ji*, 1a.
17. Ch'oe Sŏk-chŏng 崔錫鼎, *Kyŏngse hunmin chŏngŭm tosŏl* 經世訓民正音圖說 (Seoul: Yŏnse Taehakkyo Ch'ulp'anbu, 1968); Ch'oe Sŏk-chŏng 崔錫鼎, *Myŏnggok chip* 明谷集 (Seoul: Chŏjakkwŏn cha Minjok Munhwa Ch'ujinhoe: parhaengch'ŏ Kyŏngin Munhwasa, 1995), j. 13, 60b–64a; Chŏng Che-du 鄭齊斗, *Hagok chip* 霞谷集 (Seoul: Chŏjakkwŏn cha Minjok Munhwa Ch'ujinhoe: parhaengch'ŏ Kyŏngin Munhwasa, 1995), j. 2, [25b—28b]; Lê Quý Đôn 黎貴惇, *Vân đài loại ngữ* 芸臺類語 (Taipei: Guoli Taiwan daxue chuban zhongxin, 2011), j. 6, *tiao* 4.
18. Cf. Si Nae Park, "Inscribing and Erasing the Vernacular in Late Chosŏn Linguistic Imaginations," paper presented at annual meeting of the Association for Asian Studies, April 2016.
19. Zhou Yun 周贇, *Shanmen xinyu* 山門新語 (1893 edition at Harvard-Yenching Library), j. 1, *Zhou shi qinlü qieyin*, 45a–b.
20. Zhou Yun, *Shanmen xinyu*, j. 1, *Zhou shi qinlü qieyin*, 57b–58a, 256–55.
21. Zhou Yun, *Shanmen xinyu*, j.1, *Zhou shi qinlü qieyin*, 8a.
22. Zhou Yun, *Shanmen xinyu*, j.1, *Zhou shi qinlü qieyin*, *fanli*, 2b.

23. Qian Daxin, *Qianyan tang ji*, j. 15, 14a–15b.
24. For the significance of Manchu for the development of Chinese philology, see Mårten Söderblom Saarela, *The Early Modern Travels of Manchu: A Script and Its Study in East Asia and Europe* (Philadelphia: University of Pennsylvania Press, 2020).
25. Mårten Söderblom Saarela, "Alphabets *Avant la Lettre*: Phonographic Experiments in Late Imperial China," *Twentieth-Century China* 41, no. 3 (2016): 248–50.
26. Du-si-de, *Huangzhong tongyun*, *SKQS CMCS*, j. *xia*, 8b.
27. The diagram is likely modeled on one presented in Qiao Zhonghe's *Yuanyun pu* or its subsequent adaptation in Fan Tengfeng's *Wufang yuanyin*.
28. Tao Shu, *Tao Wenyi gong quanji*, j. 36, 21a–b; Zhou Zhongfu 周中孚, *Zhengtang dushu ji* 鄭堂讀書記, *XX SKQS*, j. 7, 19b. Cf. the intersection of cosmology and Manchu script in Cunzhi Tang 存之堂, *Yuanyin zhengkao* 圓音正考, *XX SKQS*, *xu*, 1a–8b.
29. David Porter, "Bannermen as Translators: Manchu Language Education in the Hanjun Banners," *Late Imperial China* 40, no. 2 (2019): 1–43.
30. Zhou Chun, *Shisanjing yin lüe* 十三經音略, in *Zhou Songai yishu* 周松靄遺書 (at Harvard-Yenching Library), *fu*, 1a.
31. Zhou Chun, *Shisanjing yin lüe*, *fu*, 8b.
32. Zhou Chun, *Xiaoxue yulun* 小學餘論, in *Zhou Songai yishu*, *xu*, 2a.
33. Zhou Chun, *Shisanjing yin lüe*, *fu*, 3b. This criticism seems to be paraphrasing Jiao Hong's earlier skepticism of the *xieyun* method. Such skepticism in fact directly informed Chen Di's and later Gu Yanwu's historical methods. See Jiao Hong 焦竑, *Jiao shi bisheng* 焦氏筆乘 (Beijing: Zhonghua shuju, 1985), 63.
34. Zhou Chun, *Shisanjing yin lüe*, *fu*, 5a–b. Here Zhou observed that philology was revived during the Ming from a long period of neglect but was also corrupted by many Ming philologists. His approach to the Ming linguistic tradition was thus highly selective.
35. *Qinding Siku quanshu zongmu*, j. 44, 38b; Zhou Chun, *Shisanjing yin lüe*, *fu*, 4b.
36. Li Ruzhen, *Li shi yinjian*, *XX SKQS*, Wu *xu*, 5a.
37. Li Ruzhen, *Li shi yinjian*, Shi *xu*, 1a; Yu *xu*, 2a.
38. A late nineteenth-century edition of *Yinjian* includes a bibliography of the works Li Ruzhen cited, including a substantial number of sixteenth- and seventeenth-century philologists. Only two figures in the works cited were associated with Qing Evidential Learning: Gu Yanwu and Yan Ruoqu. See Li Ruzhen, *Li shi yinjian* (1888 edition at Taiwan Normal University Library), *shumu*.
39. One exception is Ling Tingkan 凌廷堪 (1757–1809), who was sympathetic to Evidential Learning. See Li Ruzhen, *Li shi yinjian*, j. 3, 19b.

40. Li Ruzhen, *Li shi yinjian*, j. 5, 19b.
41. Xu Guilin, *Xu shi shuoyin* 許氏說音, in *Shengyun yaokan* 聲韻要刊 (Beiping: Songyun ge, n.d., at Columbia University Library), j. 2, 3b.
42. Li Ruzhen, *Li shi yinjian*, Xu *houxu*, 1a.
43. Xu Guilin, *Xu shi shuoyin*, j. 3, 1a; j. 4, 1b.
44. Xu Guilin, *Xu shi shuoyin*, j. 3, 3b.
45. Li Ruzhen, *Li shi yinjian*, j. 1, 35b.
46. *Flowers in the Mirror* has elsewhere been interpreted as a "cautionary tale" against the moral flaws of Evidential Learning. See Stephen Roddy, *Literati Identity and Its Fictional Representations in Late Imperial China* (Stanford, Calif.: Stanford University Press, 1998), 201–2.
47. Li Ruzhen, *Jinghua yuan*, *XX SKQS*, j. 5, ch. 23, 29a.
48. Zhou Chun, *Xiaoxue yulun*, j. *xia*, 2b–3b.
49. See, for instance, Wang Wenyuan 王聞遠, *Xiaoci tang shumu* 孝慈堂書目, [13b–14a]; Xu Bingyi 徐秉義, *Peilin tang shumu* 培林堂書目, *jingbu*, 20a; Yao Jiheng 姚際恒, *Haogu tang shumu* 好古堂書目, *jingbu*, 16b–17a; Peng Yuanrui 彭元瑞, *Zhishengdao zhai shumu* 知聖道齋書目, j. 1, 6b; Yao Xie 姚燮, *Dameishan guan cangshumu* 大梅山館藏書目, *jing*, 19a, in *Zhongguo zhuming cangshujia shumu huikan*.
50. *Qinding Siku quanshu zongmu*, j. 128, 23a.
51. Cf. Xu Bo 徐𤊹, *Xu shi jiacang shumu* 徐氏家藏書目, j. 4, 8b; Huang Yuji 黃虞稷, *Qianqing tang shumu* 千頃堂書目, *SKQS*, j. 3, 49a; Xu Qianxue 徐乾學, *Chuanshi lou shumu* 傳是樓書目, *XX SKQS*, *ri zi san ge*, *shu*, 10b.
52. *Qinding Siku quanshu zongmu*, j. 34, 7b; j. 96, 47b; j. 110, 16a; j. 144, 17b; j. 191, 40a.
53. Fan Tengfeng 樊騰鳳, *Wufang yuanyin* 五方元音, *xu*, 1a.
54. Other elements of the phonological structure of the work were adopted from this Ming cosmological text. See Wang Yinfeng 汪銀峰, "Cong 'Yuanyun pu,' 'Wufang yuanyin' yuntu jiegou kan liangzhe zhijian de guanxi" 从《元韵谱》、《五方元音》韵图结构看两者之间的关系, *Hanzi wenhua* 6 (2010): 31–36.
55. *Qinding Siku quanshu zongmu*, j. 44, 48b.
56. Fan Tengfeng, *Wufang yuanyin* (1710 edition at Keio University Library), *xu*, 2b.
57. Zhou Saihua 周赛华, "'Wufang yuanyin' banben kao" 《五方元音》版本考, *Guji yanjiu* 2 (2016): 73–75.
58. Fan Tengfeng, *Zengbu tibi Wufang yuanyin* (Beijing: Longwen ge, 1908, at University of Washington Library), *xu*, 1a.
59. Zhou Saihua, "'Wufang yuanyin' banben kao," 75–80.
60. Huiling Yang, "The Making of the First Chinese-English Dictionary: Robert Morrison's Dictionary of the Chinese Language in Three Parts (1815–1823)," *Historiographia Linguistica* 41, no. 2–3 (2014): 299–322.
61. Wan Xianchu 万献初, "'Wuche yunfu' wenxian yuanliu yu xingzhi kaolun" 《五车韵府》文献源流与性质考论, *Wenxian* 3 (2015): 166–76. Other

noncosmological sections of the text came to circulate independently as well. See Chen Jinmo 陳藎謨, *Gu Tang yun shu* 古唐韻疏 (at Imperial Household Library, Tokyo).

62. Robert Morrison, "Preface," in *A Dictionary of the Chinese Language: In Three Parts*, part 2, vol. 1 (Macao: East India Company Press, 1819–1820), v.
63. Yang, "The Making of the First Chinese-English Dictionary," 312. Compared to *Wufang yuanyin*, Chen Jinmo's *Wuche yunfu* appears to have been lesser known, and the sinologist Stanislas Julien (1797–1873) reported having spent almost fifteen years in search of a copy of text. See Stanislas Julien, "The Late Dr. Morrison's Chinese Dictionary," *Asiatic Journal and Monthly Miscellany* ser. 3, no. 4 (1845): 45–46. Julien may have been unaware that the *Wuche yunfu*, which Morrison consulted, was typically cataloged as *Yuanyin tongyun* in Chinese indexes.
64. Alexander Wylie, *Chinese Researches* (Shanghai: n.p., 1897), 216–17.
65. Wu Rulun, *Wu Rulun wenji* 吳汝綸文集 (Shanghai: Shanghai guji chubanshe, 2017), 346.
66. Nathan Vedal, "New Scripts for All Sounds: Cosmology and Universal Phonetic Notation Systems in Late Imperial China," *Harvard Journal of Asiatic Studies* 78, no. 1 (2018): 1–46.
67. Li Bohan 李柏翰, "Yuntu xingzhi de chongxian–'Yinxue mishu' de bianzhuan linian ji qi yinyun xianxiang" 韻圖形制的重現——《音學秘書》的編撰理念及其音韻現象, *Hanxue yanjiu* 33, no. 1 (2015): 201–2.
68. See Li Ruzhen, *Yinjian*, j. 6; j. 5, 8a, 18b.
69. See, for instance, Li Ruzhen's citation of Fang Yizhi and Shao Yong in *Yinjian*, j. 5, 4a.
70. Li Guangdi 李光地, *Rongcun ji* 榕村集, *SKQS*, j. 29, 13a.
71. See, for example, Zhou Zumo 周祖謨, "Songdai Bian Luo yuyin kao" 宋代汴洛語音考, in *Wenxue ji* 問學集, vol. 1 (Beijing: Zhonghua shuju, 1966), 581–655; Edwin G. Pulleyblank, *Middle Chinese: A Study in Historical Phonology* (Vancouver: University of British Columbia Press, 1984); Hirayama Hisao 平山久雄, "Shō Yō 'Kōkyoku keisei seion shōwa zu' no on'in taikei" 邵雍『皇極経世声音唱和図』の音韻体系, *Tōyō bunka kenkyūjō kiyō* 120 (1993): 49–107; and Richard VanNess Simmons, *Chinese Dialect Classification: A Comparative Approach to Harngjou, Old Jintarn, and Common Northern Wu* (Amsterdam: John Benjamins, 1999), 11–14.
72. Shen Chenglin, *Yunxue lizhu, XX SKQS, XX SKQS, fanli*, 1a.
73. Shen Chenglin, *Yunxue lizhu, fanli*, 3b
74. Shen Chenglin, *Yunxue lizhu, fanli*, 4a. This turn of phrase concerning alternative lexicographical functions came to be adopted in other specialized lexicons, including a major late nineteenth-century dictionary of "correct pronunciation" for southerners. See Sha Yizun 莎彝尊, *Zhengyin qieyun zhizhang* 正音切韻指掌, *XX SKQS, fanli*, 2b.

75. Shen Chenglin, *Yunxue lizhu*, *fanli*, 3a.
76. A similar separation from the world of classical studies is evident in another major contemporary opera dictionary, the *Zhongzhou yinyun jiyao* 中州音韻輯要 (1781).
77. Xu Dachun, *Yuefu chuansheng* 樂府傳聲 (1744 edition at University of Michigan Library), 7b.
78. Xu Dachun, *Yuefu chuansheng*, *xu*, 1a.
79. Judith T. Zeitlin, "Chinese Theories of the Sounding Voice Before the Modern Era: From the Natural to the Instrumental," in *The Voice as Something More: Essays Toward Materiality*, ed. Martha Feldman and Judith T. Zeitlin (Chicago: University of Chicago Press, 2019), 68.
80. Jiao Xun, *Yiyu yuelu* 易餘籥錄 (Shanghai: Shanghai shudian, 1994), j. 5, 3a–4b.
81. Wen Tingshi, *Chunchangzi zhiyu* 純常子枝語 (Yangzhou: Jiangsu Guangling guji keyinshe, 1990), j. 13, 21a.
82. Wu Ning 吳寧, *Rongyuan ciyun* 榕園詞韻, *XX SKQS*, *fanli*, 7a.
83. Mou Yingzhen 牟應震, *Mao Shi guyun zalun* 毛詩古韻雜論, *XX SKQS*, 9a–b.
84. Ji Yun 紀昀, *Ji Wenda gong yiji* 紀文達公遺集 (Shanghai: Shanghai guji chubanshe, 2010), *wenji*, j. 8, 18b–20b; *Siku quanshu zongmu*, j. 43.
85. Zhang Yushu 張玉書 et al., *Kangxi zidian* 康熙字典 (1716 edition at Harvard-Yenching Library), *mao ji shang*, 1b.
86. The *Kangxi zidian* was heavily indebted to the seventeenth-century lexicon *Zhengzi tong*, which frequently cited *Liushu jingyun*. Strikingly, the citations of this Learning of the Mind lexicon in *Kangxi zidian* are different from those in *Zhengzi tong*, suggesting that they were not inherited from *Zhengzi tong* but were more likely the product of the compilers' own research.
87. Sela, *China's Philological Turn*, 85.
88. Zhou Guangye 周廣業, *Jingshi biming huikao* 經史避名匯考, *XX SKQS*, passim.
89. Gui Fu, *Shuowen jiezi yizheng*, *XX SKQS*, j. 2, 12a, and passim.
90. Wang Yun, *Shuowen jiezi judou*, *XX SKQS*, j. 8 *xia* 5b, j. 12 *xia*, 31b; Wu Yujin 吳玉搢, *Shuowen yinjing kao* 說文引經考, *XX SKQS*, passim; Wu Changzong 吳昌宗, *Sishu jingzhu jizheng* 四書經注集證, *XX SKQS*, *Lunyu*, j. 2, 39b, *Lunyu*, j. 5, 43a; Liu Fenglu 劉逢祿, *Shangshu jin guwen jijie* 尚書今古文集解, *XX SKQS*, j. 6, 12b; Wang Hao 汪灝 et al., *Yuding Peiwenzhai Guang qunfang pu* 御定佩文齋廣群芳譜, *SKQS*, j. 9, 1a, j. 73, 1a.
91. Ni Tao 倪濤, *Liuyi zhiyi lu*, *SKQS*, j. 212–16.
92. On the culture of epigraphic scholarship in early Qing, see Bai Qianshen, *Fu Shan's World: The Transformation of Chinese Calligraphy in the Seventeenth Century* (Cambridge, Mass.: Harvard University Asia Center, 2003).

93. Cf. Mårten Söderblom Saarela, "'Shooting Characters': A Phonological Game and Its Uses in Late Imperial China," *Journal of the American Oriental Society* 138, no. 2 (2018): 327–59.

7. The Reinvention of Philology

1. *Qinding Siku quanshu zongmu*, j. 29, 13a–b. For similar articulations, see *Qinding Siku quanshu zongmu*, j. 23, 32b; Zhang Xuecheng 章學誠, *Jiaochou tongyi* 校讎通義, *Sibu beiyao* edition (Shanghai: Zhonghua shuju, 1936), j. 1, 1b.
2. Chen Changfang 陳長方, *Weishi ji* 唯室集, *Siku quanshu* 四庫全書 (Taipei: Taiwan shangwu yinshuguan, 1983) [hereafter *SKQS*], j. 5, 5b; Chen Chun 陳淳, *Beixi da quanji* 北溪大全集, *SKQS*, j. 25, 15a. For an in-depth analysis of specialization in the Song as well as its positive valuation in some circles, see Ya Zuo, "'Ru' Versus 'Li': The Divergence Between the Generalist and the Specialist in the Northern Song," *Journal of Song-Yuan Studies* 44 (2014): 85–137.
3. Fang Yizhi, *Dongxi jun zhushi* 東西均注釋, ed. Pang Pu 龐樸, 203.
4. Benjamin A. Elman, *From Philosophy to Philology: Intellectual and Social Aspects of Change in Late Imperial China* (Cambridge, Mass.: Council on East Studies, Harvard University, 1984).
5. Donald Kelley, "The Problem of Knowledge and the Concept of Discipline," in *History and the Disciplines: The Reclassification of Knowledge in Early Modern Europe*, ed. Kelley (Rochester, N.Y.: University of Rochester Press, 1997), 15.
6. In certain instances, *ke* could refer more generally to a field of learning. See, for instance, Mei Wending 梅文鼎, *Lixue dawen* 曆學答問, *Congshu jicheng chubian* edition (Shanghai: Shangwu yinshuguan, 1936), 17a.
7. For existing research, see G. E. R. Lloyd, *Disciplines in the Making: Cross-cultural Perspectives on Elites, Learning, and Innovation* (Oxford: Oxford University Press, 2009); Joachim Kurtz, "Disciplining the National Essence: Liu Shipei and the Reinvention of Ancient China's Intellectual History," in *Science and Technology in Modern China, 1880s–1940s*, ed. Jing Tsu and Benjamin A. Elman (Leiden: Brill, 2014), 67–91.
8. Donald Kelley, "Introduction," in Kelley, *History and the Disciplines*, 1.
9. Hur-Li Lee, "Praxes of Knowledge Organization in the First Chinese Library Catalog, the *Seven Epitomes*," in *Cultural Frames of Knowledge*, ed. Richard P. Smiraglia and Hur-Li Lee (Würzburg: Ergon Verlag, 2012), 64.
10. Qi Chenghan 祁承爜, *Gengshen zhengshu xiaoji* 庚申整書小記, in *Zhongguo muluxue ziliao xuanji* 中國目錄學資料選輯, ed. Chang Bide 昌彼得 (Taipei: Wenshizhe chubanshe, 1972), 430. Other experiments in categorization

persisted after the Tang. Zheng Qiao, for instance, employed 12 overarching categories, which were further divided into a set of 155 subcategories. Debates about the proper arrangement of a bibliography continued well into the Qing. See David S. Nivison, *The Life and Thought of Chang Hsüeh-Ch'eng, 1738–1801* (Stanford, Calif.: Stanford University Press, 1966), 70.

11. Kelley, "Introduction," 1.
12. A more detailed exposition of the following arguments can be found in Nathan Vedal, "From Tradition to Community: The Rise of Contemporary Knowledge in Late Imperial China," *Journal of Asian Studies* 79, no. 1 (2020): 77–101.
13. For a quantitative demonstration of this shift in discourse, see Vedal, "From Tradition to Community," 79–81.
14. Tobie Meyer-Fong, "Packaging the Men of Our Times: Literary Anthologies, Friendship Networks, and Political Accommodation in the Early Qing," *Harvard Journal of Asiatic Studies* 64, no. 1 (2004): 5–56; William T. Rowe, "Political, Social and Economic Factors Affecting the Transmission of Technical Knowledge in Early Modern China," in *Cultures of Knowledge: Technology in Chinese History*, ed. Dagmar Schäfer (Leiden: Brill, 2012), 25–44.
15. Katherine Carlitz, "Printing as Performance: Literati Playwright-Publishers of the Late Ming," in *Printing and Book Culture in Late Imperial China*, ed. Cynthia Brokaw and Kai-Wing Chow (Berkeley: University of California Press, 2005), 267–303; Suyoung Son, *Writing for Print: Publishing and the Making of Textual Authority in Late Imperial China* (Cambridge, Mass.: Harvard University Asia Center, 2018).
16. Vedal, "From Tradition to Community," 87–93.
17. See texts collected in Nagasawa Kikuya 長澤規矩, ed., *Min Shin zokugo jisho shūsei* 明清俗語辭書集成 (Tokyo: Kyūko shoin, 1974-1977); Zhenzhen Lu, "The Vernacular World of Pu Songling," Ph.D. diss., University of Pennsylvania, 2017, 77–145.
18. For instance, Zhu Xi, *Tongjian gangmu* 通鑑綱目, *SKQS*, j. 9a, 25b; Tang Xuandu 唐玄度, *Jiujing ziyang* 九經字樣, *SKQS*, *xu*, 1b; Jin Lüxiang 金履祥, *Zizhi tongjian qianbian* 資治通鑑前編, *SKQS*, *xu*, 2a; Tang Zhongyou 唐仲友, *Yuezhai wenchao* 悅齋文鈔, *Xuxiu Siku quanshu* 續修四庫全書 (Shanghai: Shanghai guji chubanshe, 1995–1999) [hereafter *XX SKQS*], j. 8, 11b.
19. For instance, Cheng Mingshan, *Xiaoyu pu*, *fanli*, 2b; Feng Dingdiao 馮鼎調, *Liushu zhun* 六書準, *Siku quanshu cunmu congshu* 四庫全書存目叢書 (Jinan: Qi Lu shushe chubanshe, 1997 [hereafter *SKQS CMCS*], 4a.
20. Mao Zhen 茅溱, *Yunpu benyi* 韻譜本義, *SKQS CMCS*, *fanli*, 4b.
21. For instance, Lü Kun 呂坤, *Jiaotai yun* 交泰韻, *SKQS CMCS*, *fanli* 12a; Chen Di, *Mao Shi guyin kao*, 8; Wang Huazhen 王化貞, *Pumen yipin* 普門醫品, *SKQS CMCS*, *fanli*, 10b

22. Fang Yizhi, *Tongya* 通雅 (Beijing: Zhongguo shudian, 1990), *xu*, 8a.
23. For instance, Shi Zhengzhi 史正志, *Shi shi jupu* 史氏菊譜, *SKQS*, 2a; Zhen Dexiu 真德秀, *Xishan wenji* 西山文集, *SKQS*, j. 42, 7a; Gui Youguang 歸有光, *Zhenchuan xiansheng ji* 震川先生集 (1675 edition at Harvard-Yenching Library), j. 2, 5b.
24. On literary associations, see Guo Shaoyu 郭紹虞, "Mingdai de wenren jituan," in *Zhaoyushi gudian wenxue lunji* 照隅室古典文學論集 (Shanghai: Shanghai guji chubanshe, 1983), 518–610. On Classics societies, see Wang Fansen 王汎森, *Quanli de maoxiguan zuoyong: Qingdai de sixiang, xueshu yu xintai* 權力的毛細管作用：清代的思想、學術與心態 (Taipei: Lianjing chuban gongsi, 2013), 89–104.
25. Ellen Messer-Davidow, David R. Shumway, and David J. Sylvan, eds., *Knowledges: Historical and Critical Studies in Disciplinarity* (Charlottesville: University of Virginia Press, 1993), 2.
26. Cf. Thomas F. Gieryn, *Cultural Boundaries of Science: Credibility on the Line* (Chicago: University of Chicago Press, 1999).
27. Evan Nicoll-Johnson, "Fringes and Seams: Boundaries of Erudition in Early Medieval China," Ph.D. diss., University of California, Los Angeles, 2017, 38–158.
28. For earlier concerns with up-to-date information in the Song, see Hilde De Weerdt, *Information, Territory, and Elite Networks: The Crisis and Maintenance of Empire in Song China* (Cambridge, Mass.: Harvard University Asia Center, 2015), 293; and Vedal, "From Tradition to Community," 80–82.
29. For a representative listing of this genealogy, see Liu Zhaoren 刘昭仁, *Daixue xiao ji: Dai Zhen de shengping yu xueshu sixiang* 戴学小记：戴震的生平与学术思想 (Taipei: Xiuwei zixun, 2009), 28.
30. The twenty-seven genealogies consulted are those contained within the prefaces and other paratextual materials of the late eighteenth- and nineteenth-century phonological texts in *XX SKQS*. Texts with no explicit listing of a genealogy have been excluded: An Ji 安吉, *Yun zheng* 韻徵, Qi *xu*, 1a; Wang Niansun 王念孫, *Guyun pu* 古韻譜, *shu*, 1a–3b; Kong Guangsen, *Shi shenglei* 詩聲類, *xu*, 1a–4a; Duan Yucai 段玉裁, *Liushu yinyun biao* 六書音均表, Qian *xu*, 1a–2a, Duan *shu*, 2b–5a, Dai *xu*, 1a–2b, Wu *xu*, 1a–3a; Yao Wentian 姚文田, *Shuowen shengxi* 說文聲系, *xu*, 1a–2a; Yan Kejun, *Shuowen shenglei* 說文聲類, *xumu*, 1a; Qi Xuebiao 戚學標, *Hanxue xiesheng* 漢學諧聲, Huang *xu*, 1a–4a, Qi *xu*, 1a–3a; Mou Yingzhen 牟應震, *Mao Shi guyun* 毛詩古韻, Zhang *xu*, 1a–3b, Mou *xu*, 4a–5a; Zhang Geng 張畊, *Guyun faming* 古韻發明, Wu *xu*, 2a–3a, Zhu *xu*, 4a–5b, Zhang *xu*, 6a–b; Zhang Huiyan 張惠言, *Xiesheng pu* 諧聲譜, *xu*, 1a–4b; Xia Xie 夏燮, *Shu yun* 述均, Xia *xu*, 1a–3a; Shi Yongmai 時庸勱, *Shengpu* 聲譜, Xu *xu*, 1a–2a; Jiang Yougao 江有誥, *Jiang shi yinxue shishu* 江氏音學十書, *fanli*, 1a–b; Xia Xin 夏炘, *Shi guyun biao nianer*

bu jishuo 詩古韻表廿二部集說, *j. shang*, 1a; Chen Li 陳立, *Shuowen xiesheng zisheng shu* 說文諧聲孳生述, *lüeli*, 1a–2b, Xue *shu hou*, 1a; Ding Lüheng 丁履恒, *Xingsheng leipian* 形聲類篇, Ding *shu*, 1a; Fu Shoutong 傅壽彤, *Guyin leibiao* 古音類表, 3a–5a; Long Qirui 龍啓瑞, *Guyun tongshuo* 古韻通說, Ma *xu*, 1a; Pang Dakun 龐大堃, *Guyin jilüe* 古音輯略, j. 1, 3a–5a; Chen Li 陳澧, *Qieyun kao* 切韻考, *xu*, 1a.

31. For a detailed study of the Learning of the Way genealogy, see Thomas A. Wilson, *Genealogy of the Way* (Stanford, Calif.: Stanford University Press, 1995).
32. Huang Chin-hsing, *Philosophy, Philology, and Politics in Eighteenth-Century China: Li Fu and the Lu-Wang School Under the Ch'ing* (Cambridge: Cambridge University Press, 1995), 107–30; Steven B. Miles, *The Sea of Learning: Mobility and Identity in Nineteenth-Century Guangzhou* (Cambridge, Mass.: Harvard University Asia Center, 2006), 95.
33. Dai Zhen 戴震, *Dai Zhen wenji* 戴震文集 (Beijing: Zhonghua shuju, 1974), 62, 90.
34. Nivison, *The Life and Thought of Chang Hsüeh-ch'eng*, 171–74; Qian Daxin 錢大昕, *Qianyan tang ji* 潛研堂集 (Shanghai: Shanghai guji chubanshe, 2010), j. 24, 7b, 12a, 14a.
35. Ya Zuo, *Shen Gua's Empiricism* (Cambridge, Mass.: Harvard University Asia Center, 2018), 236.
36. Bai Qianshen, *Fu Shan's World: The Transformation of Chinese Calligraphy in the Seventeenth Century* (Cambridge, Mass.: Harvard University Asia Center, 2003), 154–56.
37. Quan Zuwang 全祖望, *Jieqiting ji waibian* 鮚埼亭集外編, *XX SKQS*, j. 12, 29a.
38. Mao Qiling 毛奇齡, *Kangxi jiazi shiguan xinkan Gujin tongyun* 康熙甲子史館新刊古今通韻 (1684 edition at Harvard-Yenching Library), Xu *xu*, 9a; Zhou *xu*, 13b.
39. Mao Qiling, *Kangxi jiazi shiguan xinkan Gujin tongyun*, *tu*, 1a; j. 1, 2a.
40. Given the lack of clarity on the precise dating of the circulation of Gu's work, it is possible that Fang Yizhi would not have had access to Gu's main phonological studies.
41. Pan Lei 潘耒, *Leiyin* 類音, j. 1, 11b.
42. Gu Yanwu, *Tinglin shiwen ji* 亭林詩文集, *Sibu congkan* edition (Shanghai: Shangwu yinshuguan, 1922), *wenji* j. 4, 8a–9a.
43. Li Guangdi, *Rongcun xu yulu* 榕村續語錄 (Beijing: Zhonghua shuju, 1995), 902.
44. See, for instance, Shen Qiyuan 沈起元, *Jingting wen'gao* 敬亭文稿, *Siku weishou shu jikan* 四庫未收書輯刊 edition (Beijing: Beijing chubanshe, 1997), j. 4, 15a; Gu Chenxu 顧陳垿, *Bashi zhuzi tushuo* 八矢注字圖說 (manuscript at Taiwan Normal University Library), Wang *xu*, 2a.
45. For Li Guangdi's life and considerable philosophical contributions to Cheng-Zhu learning, see On-cho Ng, *Cheng-Zhu Confucianism in the Early*

Qing: Li Guangdi (1642–1718) and Qing Learning (Albany: State University of New York Press, 2001).
46. Li Guangdi, *Rongcun ji* 榕村集, *SKQS*, j. 33, 5b.
47. Li Guangdi, *Rongcun ji*, j. 20, 17b–19a.
48. Li Guangdi, *Rongcun yulu* 榕村語錄 (Beijing: Zhonghua shuju, 1995), 545. Li was possibly involved in funding the printing of a new edition of the text, as well; see Zhang Minquan 张民权, "Li Guangdi yu 'Yinxue wushu'" 李光地与《音学五书》, *Nanjing shehui kexue: wenshizhe ban* 8 (1996): 69–73.
49. Li Guangdi, *Rongcun xu yulu*, 902.
50. Li Guangdi's extensive discussions of philology can be found in his *Rongcun yulu* and *Rongcun xu yulu*, as well as the imperial dictionary *Yuzhi Yinyun chanwei* 御製音韻闡微 (Imperially commissioned exposition of the subtleties of phonology).
51. Jiang Yong 江永, *Yinxue bianwei* 音學辨微 (Shanghai: Bogu zhai, 1920), 26b–27a, 41a–b.
52. Jiang Yong, *Guyun biaozhun* 古韻標準, *SKQS*, j. 1, 6a, 11a.
53. Wang Zhi, *Yunxue yishuo* 韻學臆說, *SKQS CMCS*, 17b–21a.
54. Gao Wengying, *Dengyin Shengwei hehui* 等音聲位合彙, *Congshu jicheng xubian* edition (Shanghai: Shanghai shudian, 1994), *xu*, 2b–3a.
55. Gu Yanwu, *Yinxue wushu*, 6.
56. Dai Zhen, *Dai Zhen wenji*, 77.
57. Cf. Ding Lizhong 丁立中, *Baqianjuan lou shumu* 八千卷樓書目, *XX SKQS*, j. 2, 24b; Zou Hanxun 鄒漢勛, *Dushu oushi* 讀書偶識, *XX SKQS*, j. 1, 23a; Ruan Yuan, *Rulin zhuan gao* 儒林傳稿, *XX SKQS*, j. 3, 9b; *Qinding Siku quanshu zongmu*, j. 29, 5a; Lu Wenchao 盧文弨, *Baojing tang wenji* 抱經堂文集, *XX SKQS*, j. 11, 9a.
58. Guan Tong, *Yinji xuan wen erji* 因寄軒文二集, *XX SKQS*, j. 4, 8b.
59. Qian Daxin, *Qianyan tang wenji*, j. 24, 11b.
60. Figures born between roughly 1610 and 1625 appear to have been categorized in the *Siku quanshu* as Ming or Qing scholars without a clear correlation to their year of death, although those born before 1615 are more likely to be labeled as Ming. There are exceptions, such as the Hangzhou literary phonologist Shen Qian 沈謙 (1620–1670), who was considered a Ming scholar. Some, such as Xie Wenjian 謝文洊 (1615–1681), were in fact labeled as Ming in one entry and Qing in another. There are also scholars who received a negative appraisal in *Siku quanshu* and whose life falls in the ambiguous period but were nonetheless labeled as "of the current dynasty." Qian Bangqi 錢邦芑 (c. 1600–1673), for instance, produced a study of Chinese graphs roundly criticized by the *Siku* editors. He was still considered "of the current dynasty," further reflecting the somewhat arbitrary nature of such categorizations. Cf.

Qinding Siku quanshu zongmu, j. 37, 30a; j. 43, 39a–b; j. 180, 38b; j. 181, 26a. Only rarely did the *Siku* editors express the reasoning behind their assignment of a dynasty to scholars active during the mid-seventeenth century; cf. *Qinding Siku quanshu zongmu*, j. 14, 10b.

61. Cf. *Qinding Siku quanshu zongmu*, j. 122, 29a; Ding Lizhong, *Baqian juan lou shumu*, j. 12, 21b; Duan Fang 端方, *Taozhai cang shi ji* 陶齋臧石記, *XX SKQS*, j. 13, 8a; Xu Qianxue 徐乾學, *Chuanshi lou shumu* 傳是樓書目, *XX SKQS*, *rizi er ge, xiaoxue*, 8a; Yu Yue 俞樾, *Chaxiang shi san chao* 茶香室三鈔, *XX SKQS*, j. 5, 1b.

62. Cf. *Qinding Siku quanshu zongmu*, j. 44, 23b; Ding Lizhong, *Baqianjuan lou shumu*, j. 11, 2a; Liu Xizai 劉熙載, *Yi gai* 藝概, *XX SKQS*, j. 4, 22b; Qilu zhuren 杞盧主人, *Shiwu tongkao* 時務通考, *XX SKQS*, j. 23, *suanxue* 11, 1a.

63. John B. Henderson, *The Development and Decline of Chinese Cosmology* (New York: Columbia University Press, 1984), 227–58; Huang, *Philosophy, Philology, and Politics in Eighteenth-Century China*, 114; Bruce Rusk, "Not Written in Stone: Ming Readers of the 'Great Learning' and the Impact of Forgery," *Harvard Journal of Asiatic Studies* 66, no. 1 (2006): 190.

64. Leo Tak-hung Chan, *The Discourse on Foxes and Ghosts: Ji Yun and Eighteenth-Century Literati Storytelling* (Honolulu: University of Hawai'i Press, 1998), 163–64.

65. See, for instance, Qian Daxin, *Qianyan tang wenji*, j. 15, 14a–15b.

66. Yao Ying, *Dongming wenji* 東溟文集, *XX SKQS*, *waiji*, j. 1, 37a.

67. Kinoshita Tetsuya 木下鉄矢, *Shindai gakujutsu to gengogaku: kōingaku no shisō to keifu* 清代学術と言語学: 古音学の思想と系譜 (Tokyo: Bensei shuppan, 2016), 55.

68. See Henderson, *The Development and Decline of Chinese Cosmology*.

69. Qian Daxin, *Nianer shi kaoyi* 廿二史考異, *XX SKQS*, *Shiji* j. 1, 6b, and passim; Qian Daxin, *Qianyantang ji*, j. 5, 2a, and passim; Duan Yucai, *Guwen Shangshu zhuanyi* 古文尚書撰異, *XX SKQS*, j. 1, 1b, and passim; Duan Yucai, *Jingyunlou ji* 經韵樓集, *XX SKQS*, j. 1, 5b, and passim; Duan Yucai, *Shuowen jiezi zhu* 說文解字注 (Chengdu: Chengdu guji shudian, 1981), 1 and passim.

70. See sources cited in introduction, n. 25.

71. Ori Sela, *China's Philological Turn: Scholars, Textualism, and the Dao in the Eighteenth Century* (New York: Columbia University Press, 2018), 91–99.

72. Qian Daxin, *Qianyan tang ji*, j. 24, 11a; Li Guangdi, *Rongcun ji*, j. 13, 17a.

73. *Qinding Siku quanshu zongmu*, j. 8, 50b; j. 12, 18a; Jiang Chaobo 蔣超伯, *Nanchun huyu* 南漘楛語, *XX SKQS*, j. 6, 28a.

74. Vedal, "From Tradition to Community," 86.

75. See Daniel Bryant, *The Great Recreation: Ho Ching-ming (1483–1521) and His World* (Leiden: Brill, 2008).

76. As Chu Ming-kin and others have observed, the well-documented Song dynasty skepticism toward classical texts was directed largely toward the commentarial tradition and perceived corruptions to the texts, rather than their inherent authority. See Chu Ming-kin, *The Politics of Higher Education: The Imperial University in Northern Song China* (Hong Kong: Hong Kong University Press, 2020), 54.
77. For a detailed examination of the epistemological implications of "antiquity," see Sela, *China's Philological Turn*, 85–117.
78. Gu Yanwu, *Rizhi lu*, 822.
79. Rivi Handler-Spitz, *Symptoms of an Unruly Age: Li Zhi and Cultures of Early Modernity* (Seattle: University of Washington Press, 2017), 150.
80. *Qinding Siku quanshu zongmu*, j. 36, 6a–b; j. 44, 7a.
81. Duan Yucai, *Jingyun lou ji*, j. 11, 18b.
82. Sela, *China's Philological Turn*, 111.
83. Peter K. Bol, *Neo-Confucianism in History* (Cambridge, Mass.: Harvard University Asia Center, 2010), 168.
84. *Qinding Siku quanshu zongmu*, j. 8, 33a; j. 39, 13b; j. 134, 5b.
85. *Qinding Siku quanshu zongmu*, j. 37, 23b; j. 39, 13b; j. 76, 13a; j. 124, 21b.
86. Zhang Yushu 張玉書 et al., *Kangxi zidian* 康熙字典, *fanli*, 6b–7a; Mao Zhen, *Yunpu benyi*, *fanli*, 4b.
87. Vedal, "From Tradition to Community," 88.
88. *Qinding Siku quanshu zongmu*, j. 43, 32a, 36b; j. 44, 7a.
89. Dai Zhen, *Dai Zhen wenji*, 66.
90. On ideological elements of *Shuowen jiezi*, see Françoise Bottéro, *Sémantisme et classification dans l'écriture chinoise: Les systèmes de classement des caractères par clés du* Shuowen Jiezi *au* Kangxi Zidian (Paris: Collège de France, Institut des hautes études chinoises, 1996).
91. Sela, *China's Philological Turn*, 109.
92. Adam Schorr, "Connoisseurship and the Defense Against Vulgarity: Yang Shen (1488–1559) and His Work," *Monumenta Serica* 41 (1993): 103–8.
93. Translated in Rusk, "Not Written in Stone," 226.
94. Henderson, *The Development and Decline of Chinese Cosmology*, 157.
95. Elman, *From Philosophy to Philology*; Catherine Jami, *The Emperor's New Mathematics: Western Learning and Imperial Authority During the Kangxi Reign (1662–1722)* (Oxford: Oxford University Press, 2012).
96. It is worth noting that Dai did not emphasize the inherent authority of antiquity to the extent that later scholars and students would, a position that attracted some criticism later in the eighteenth century. See Sela, *China's Philological Turn*, 100.
97. *Qinding Siku quanshu zongmu*, j. 42, 52a.

Epilogue

1. Thomas Mullaney, "Chinese Is Not a Backward Language," *Foreign Policy*, May 12, 2016.
2. This discussion also led to heated online debate. See entry and comments to Victor Mair, "Backward Thinking About Orientalism and Chinese Characters," *Language Log*, May 16, 2016, https://languagelog.ldc.upenn.edu/nll/?p=25776.
3. An incomplete sampling of recent studies includes Gina Tam, *Dialect and Nationalism in China, 1860–1960* (Cambridge: Cambridge University Press, 2020); Yurou Zhong, *Chinese Grammatology: Script Revolution and Literary Modernity, 1916–1958* (New York: Columbia University Press, 2019); Ulug Kuzuoglu, "Codes of Modernity: Infrastructures of Language and Chinese Scripts in an Age of Global Information Revolution," Ph.D. diss., Columbia University, 2018; Thomas Mullaney, *The Chinese Typewriter: A History* (Cambridge, Mass.: MIT Press, 2017); Andrea Bachner, *Beyond Sinology: Chinese Writing and the Scripts of Culture* (New York: Columbia University Press, 2014); Elizabeth Kaske, *The Politics of Language in Chinese Education, 1895–1919* (Leiden: Brill, 2008); Jing Tsu, *Sound and Script in Chinese Diaspora* (Cambridge, Mass.: Harvard University Press, 2010); and Edward Gunn, *Rendering the Regional: Local Language in Contemporary Chinese Media* (Honolulu: University of Hawai`i Press, 2006).
4. Cf. Tian Tingjun 田廷俊, *Shumu daizi jue* 數目代字訣 (Beijing: Wenzi gaige chubanshe, 1957); Shen Shaohe 沈韶和, *Xinbian jianzi tebie keben* 新編簡字特別課本 (Beijing: Wenzi gaige chubanshe, 1957); Tsu, *Sound and Script in Chinese Diaspora*, 34–39.
5. Zhu Wenxiong 朱文熊, *Jiangsu xin zimu* 江蘇新字母 (Beijing: Wenzi gaige chubanshe, 1957), 17; Yang Qiong 楊瓊, *Xingsheng tong* 形聲通 (Beijing: Wenzi gaige chubanshe, 1957), j. 4, 6b; Shen Xue 沈學, *Shengshi yuanyin* 盛世元音 (Beijing: Wenzi gaige chubanshe, 1957), 4b.
6. Wen Tingshi 文廷式, *Chunchangzi zhiyu* 純常子枝語 (Yangzhou: Jiangsu Guangling guji keyinshe), j. 27, 3a.
7. Wang Tao, *Wengyou yu tan* 甕牖餘談, *Xuxiu Siku quanshu* 續修四庫全書 (Shanghai: Shanghai guji chubanshe, 1995–1999) [hereafter *XX SKQS*], j. 5, 8a.
8. Kang Youwei, *Guangyi zhou shuangji* 廣藝舟雙楫 (Shanghai: Shangwu yinshuguan, 1937), j. 1, 6b.
9. Wu Mei 吳梅, *Guqu chen tan* 顧曲塵談 (Shanghai: Shanghai shudian, 1989), 131–32; Wang Jilie 王季烈, *Yinlu qu tan* 螾廬曲談 (Shanghai: Shangwu yinshu guan 1928), j. 1, 37a–38a; Lin Jiayi 林佳儀, *Kuntan qingyin: Xu Yanzhi, Zhang Shanxiang de kunqu shengya* 崑壇清音：徐炎之、張善薌的崑曲生涯 (Taipei: Xiuwei zixun, 2019), 115.

10. There are strong parallels, for instance, between sixteenth- and seventeenth-century notions of historical linguistic authenticity (see chapter 4) and those of the twentieth century (documented most recently in Gina Tam, *Dialect and Nationalism in China*).
11. Kuzuoglu, "Codes of Modernity"; Zhong, *Chinese Grammatology*.
12. See, for instance, the case of Lao Naixuan discussed in Nathan Vedal, "New Scripts for All Sounds: Cosmology and Universal Phonetic Notation Systems in Late Imperial China," *Harvard Journal of Asiatic Studies* 78, no. 1 (2018): 45.
13. "Mingmo luomazi zhuyin wenzhang" 明末羅馬字注音文章 (Beijing: Wenzi gaige chubanshe, 1957), inside of title page.
14. Zhou Youguang, *Hanzi gaige gailun* (Beijing: Wenzi gaige chubanshe, 1979), 19.
15. "Liu Xianting" (Beijing: Wenzi gaige chubanshe, 1957), inside of title page.
16. Adapted from Liang Qichao, *Intellectual Trends in the Ch'ing Period*, trans. Immanuel C. Y. Hsü (Cambridge, Mass.: Harvard University Press, 1959), 44.
17. "Liu Xianting," 20–23. Cf. *Guoyu zhoukan* 32–34 (1932).
18. "Liu Xianting," 25–26.
19. Kuzuoglu, "Codes of Modernity," 402. Romanizations proposed by nineteenth-century Protestant missionaries were not included, perhaps to bypass the colonial associations of Latin script.
20. Zhao Yintang, "Zhongyuan yinyun yanjiu xiaoxu" 中元音韻研究小序, *Guoyu zhoukan* 40 (1932): 1b.

Selected Bibliography

Abbreviations

SKQS: *Siku quanshu* 四庫全書. Taipei: Taiwan shangwu yinshuguan, 1983.
SKQS CMCS: *Siku quanshu cunmu congshu* 四庫全書存目叢書. Jinan: Qi Lu shushe chubanshe, 1997.
SKJHSCK: *Siku jinhui shu congkan* 四庫禁燬書叢刊. Beijing: Beijing chubanshe, 1997.
XX SKQS: *Xuxiu Siku quanshu* 續修四庫全書. Shanghai: Shanghai guji chubanshe, 1995–1999.

Philological Primary Sources

An Ji 安吉. *Yun zheng* 韻徵, *XX SKQS* edition.
Chai Shaobing 柴紹炳. *Chai shi Guyun tong* 柴氏古韻通, *SKQS CMCS* edition.
Chen Di 陳第. *Mao Shi guyin kao* 毛詩古音考. Ed. Kang Ruicong 康瑞琮. Beijing: Zhonghua shuju, 1988.
Chen Jinmo 陳藎謨. *Gu Tang yun shu* 古唐韻疏 (at Imperial Household Library, Tokyo).
———. *Huangji tuyun* 皇極圖韻, *SKQS CMCS* edition.
———. *Yuanyin tongyun* 元音統韻, *SKQS CMCS* edition.
Chen Li 陳立. *Qieyun kao* 切韻考, *XX SKQS* edition.

———. *Shuowen xiesheng zisheng shu* 說文諧聲孳生述, *XX SKQS* edition.

Chen Shiyuan 陳士元. *Ming yi* 名疑. Shanghai: Bogu zhai, 1920.

Cheng Mingshan 程明善. *Xiaoyu pu* 嘯餘譜, *XX SKQS* edition.

Cheng Yuanchu 程元初. *Huangzhong yinyun tongkuo* 黃鍾音韻通括 (1609 edition at Naikaku bunko).

———. *Lülü yinyun guashu tong* 律呂音韻卦數通 (1609 edition at Naikaku bunko).

Ch'oe Sŏk-chŏng 崔錫鼎. *Kyŏngse hunmin chŏngŭm tosŏl* 經世訓民正音圖說. Seoul: Yŏnse Taehakkyo Ch'ulp'anbu, 1968.

Cunzhi Tang 存之堂. *Yuanyin zhengkao* 圓音正考, *XX SKQS* edition.

Dai Tong 戴侗. *Liushu gu* 六書故, *SKQS* edition.

Dai Zhen 戴震. *Dai Zhen wenji* 戴震文集. Beijing: Zhonghua shuju, 1974.

Ding Lüheng 丁履恒. *Xingsheng leipian* 形聲類篇, *XX SKQS* edition.

Dong Yue 董說. *Fengcaoan qianji* 豐草庵前集, *Congshu jicheng xubian* edition. Shanghai: Shanghai shudian, 1994.

———. *Wenyin fa* 文音發 (at Naikaku bunko).

Du Yu 都俞. *Leizuan gu wenzi kao* 類纂古文字考, *SKQS CMCS* edition.

Duan Yucai 段玉裁. *Guwen Shangshu zhuanyi* 古文尚書撰異, *XX SKQS* edition.

———. *Jingyunlou ji* 經韵樓集, *XX SKQS* edition.

———. *Liushu yinyun biao* 六書音均表, *XX SKQS* edition.

———. *Shuowen jiezi zhu* 說文解字注. Chengdu: Chengdu guji shudian, 1981.

Du-si-de 都四德. *Huangzhong tongyun* 黃鍾通韻, *SKQS CMCS* edition.

Fan Tengfeng 樊騰鳳. *Wufang yuanyin* 五方元音, *XX SKQS* edition.

———. *Wufang yuanyin* 五方元音. Ed. Nian Xiyao 年希尧 (1710 edition at Keio University Library).

———. *Zengbu tibi Wufang yuanyin* 增補剔弊五方元音. Ed. Zhao Peizi 趙培梓. Beijing: Longwen ge, 1908 (at University of Washington Library).

Fang Dongshu 方東樹. *Hanxue shangdui* 漢學商兌, *Congshu jicheng xubian* edition. Shanghai: Shanghai shudian, 1994.

Fang Risheng 方日升. *Gujin yunhui juyao xiaobu* 古今韻會舉要小補, *SKQS CMCS* edition.

Fang Yizhi 方以智. *Fushan wenji houbian* 浮山文集後編, *XX SKQS* edition.

———. *Siyun dingben* 四韻定本. In *Fang Yizhi quanshu* 方以智全書, vol. 7. Hefei: Huangshan shushe, 2019.

———. *Tongya* 通雅. Beijing: Zhongguo shudian, 1990.

Fang Zhonglü 方中履. *Gujin shiyi* 古今釋疑, *SKQS CMCS* edition.

Feng Dingdiao 馮鼎調. *Liushu zhun* 六書準, *SKQS CMCS* edition.

Feng Huimin 馮惠民 and Li Wanjian 李萬健, eds. *Mingdai shumu tiba congkan* 明代書目題跋叢刊. Beijing: Shumu wenxian chubanshe, 1994.

Fu Shoutong 傅壽彤. *Guyin leibiao* 古音類表, *XX SKQS* edition.

Gao Wengying 高奣映, ed. *Dengyin Shengwei hehui* 等音聲位合彙, *Congshu jicheng xubian* edition. Shanghai: Shanghai shudian, 1994.

Ge Zhongxuan 葛中選. *Tailü* 泰律. Yunnan: Yunnan tushuguan, 1914.

Gu Chenxu 顧陳垿. *Bashi zhuxi shuo* 八矢注字說 (manuscript at Taiwan Normal University Library).

Gu Qiyuan 顧起元. *Shuo lüe* 說略, *SKQS* edition.

Gu Yanwu 顧炎武. *Gu Yanwu quanji* 顧炎武全集. Shanghai: Shanghai guji chubanshe, 2011.

Gu Yingxiang 顧應祥. *Jingzhai xiyin lu* 靜虛齋惜陰錄, *SKQS CMCS* edition.

Gui Fu 桂馥. *Shuowen jiezi yizheng* 說文解字義證, *XX SKQS* edition.

Han Qia 韓洽. *Zhuanxue cejie* 篆學測解 (1820 edition at National Library of China).

Hao Jing 郝敬. *Dushu tong* 讀書通 (1630 edition at Beijing Normal University Library).

Hong Sheng 洪昇. *Shi Sao yunzhu* 詩騷韻注 (at National Library of China).

Hu Yinglin 胡應麟. *Huayang boyi* 華陽博議, in *Shaoshi shanfang bicong* 少室山房筆叢. Beijing: Zhonghua shuju, 1958.

Jiang Guoxiang 蔣國祥. *Tang lüshi yun* 唐律詩韻 (at Taiwan Normal University Library).

Jiang Yong 江永. *Guyun biaozhun* 古韻標準, *SKQS* edition.

———. *Yinxue bianwei* 音學辨微. Shanghai: Bogu zhai, 1920.

Jiang Yougao 江有誥. *Jiang shi yinxue shishu* 江氏音學十書, *XX SKQS* edition.

Jiao Hong 焦竑. *Jiao shi bisheng xuji* 焦氏筆乘續集. Beijing: Zhonghua shuju, 1985.

Kong Guangsen 孔廣森. *Shi shenglei* 詩聲類, *XX SKQS* edition.

Lao Naixuan 勞乃宣. *Dengyun yide waipian* 等韻一得外篇 (c. 1886–1898 edition at Harvard-Yenching Library).

Lê Quý Đôn 黎貴惇. *Vân đài loại ngữ* 芸臺類語. Taipei: Guoli Taiwan daxue chuban zhongxin, 2011.

Li Guangdi 李光地. *Rongcun xu yulu* 榕村續語錄. Beijing: Zhonghua shuju, 1995.

———. *Rongcun yulu* 榕村語錄. Beijing: Zhonghua shuju, 1995.

Li Ruzhen 李汝珍. *Li shi yinjian* 李氏音鑑, *XX SKQS* edition.

———. *Li shi yinjian* 李氏音鑑 (1888 edition at Taiwan Normal University Library).

Li Yu 李漁. *Liweng ciyun* 笠翁詞韻. In *Li Yu quanji* 李漁全集. Hangzhou: Zhejiang guji chubanshe, 1991.

———. *Liweng shiyun* 笠翁詩韻. In *Li Yu quanji* 李漁全集. Hangzhou: Zhejiang guji chubanshe, 1991.

Li Zhaoluo 李兆洛. *Liushu yunzheng* 六書韻徵 (1838 edition at Columbia University Library).

Lin Xi 林夕, ed. *Zhongguo zhuming cangshujia shumu huikan* 中國著名藏書家書目匯刊. Beijing: Shangwu yinshuguan, 2005.

Liu Xianting 劉獻廷. *Guangyang zaji* 廣陽雜記. Beijing: Zhonghua shuju, 1957.

Long Qirui 龍啓瑞. *Guyun tongshuo* 古韻通說, *XX SKQS* edition.
Long Weilin 龍為霖. *Benyun yide* 本韻一得, *SKQS CMCS* edition.
Lü Kun 呂坤. *Jiaotai yun* 交泰韻, *SKQS CMCS* edition.
Lu Rong 陸容. *Shuyuan zaji* 菽園雜記, *SKQS* edition.
Lü Weiqi 呂維祺. *Tongwen duo* 同文鐸, *XX SKQS* edition.
———. *Yinyun riyue deng* 音韻日月燈, *SKQS CMCS* edition.
Mao Qiling 毛奇齡. *Kangxi jiazi shiguan xinkan Gujin tongyun* 康熙甲子史館新刊古今通韻 (1684 edition at Harvard-Yenching Library).
Mao Xianshu 毛先舒. *Yun bai* 韻白, *SKQS CMCS* edition.
———. *Yunxue tongzhi* 韻學通指, *SKQS CMCS* edition.
Mao Zhen 茅溱. *Yunpu benyi* 韻譜本義, *SKQS CMCS* edition.
Mei Yingzuo 梅膺祚. *Zihui* 字彙 (1615 edition at Harvard-Yenching Library).
———. *Zihui* 字彙 (1800 edition at Kyoto University, Jinbunken).
Morrison, Robert. *A Dictionary of the Chinese Language: In Three Parts*. Macao: East India Company Press, 1819–1820.
Mou Yingzhen 牟應震. *Mao Shi guyun* 毛詩古韻, *XX SKQS* edition.
———. *Mao Shi guyun zalun* 毛詩古韻雜論, *XX SKQS* edition.
Nagasawa Kikuya 長澤規矩, ed. *Min Shin zokugo jisho shūsei* 明清俗語辭書集成. Tokyo: Kyūko shoin, 1974–1977.
Ni Tao 倪濤. *Liuyi zhiyi lu* 六藝之一錄, *SKQS* edition.
Pan Lei 潘耒. *Leiyin* 類音, *SKQS CMCS* edition.
Pan Wei 潘緯. *Yunxie kao* 韻叶考 (at National Library of China).
Pang Dakun 龐大堃. *Guyin jilüe* 古音輯略, *XX SKQS* edition.
Qi Xuebiao 戚學標. *Hanxue xiesheng* 漢學諧聲, *XX SKQS* edition.
Qian Daxin 錢大昕. *Shijia zhai yangxin lu* 十駕齋養新錄, *XX SKQS* edition.
Qiao Zhonghe 喬中和. *Yuanyun pu* 元韻譜, *SKQS CMCS* edition.
Qinding Siku quanshu zongmu 欽定四庫全書總目, *SKQS* edition.
Sha Yizun 莎彝尊. *Zhengyin qieyun zhizhang* 正音切韻指掌, *XX SKQS* edition.
Shen Chenglin 沈乘麐. *Yunxue lizhu* 韻學驪珠, *XX SKQS* edition.
Shen Chongsui 沈寵綏. *Duqu xuzhi* 度曲須知. In *Zhongguo gudian xiqu lunzhu jicheng* 中國古典戲曲論著集成, vol. 5. Beijing: Zhongguo xiju chubanshe, 1959–1960.
Shen Xiong 沈雄. *Gujin cihua* 古今詞話, *SKQS CMCS bubian*.
Shen Xue 沈學. *Shengshi yuanyin* 盛世元音. Beijing: Wenzi gaige chubanshe, 1957.
Shi Kui 是奎. *Taigu yuanyin* 太古元音 (at Taiwan Normal University Library).
Shi Yongmai 時庸勱. *Shengpu* 聲譜, *XX SKQS* edition.
Sun Weicheng 孫維城. *Yunshi bianlan* 韻釋便覽 (1590 edition at Peking University Library).
Wang Kentang 王肯堂. *Yugangzhai bizhu* 鬱岡齋筆麈, *SKQS CMCS* edition.
Wang Niansun 王念孫. *Guyun pu* 古韻譜, *XX SKQS* edition.
Wang Yun 王筠. *Shuowen jiezi judou* 說文解字句讀, *XX SKQS* edition.
Wang Zhi 王植. *Yunxue yishuo* 韻學臆說, *SKQS CMCS* edition.

Wei Jiao 魏校. *Liushu jingyun* 六書精蘊, *SKQS CMCS* edition.

Williams, Samuel Wells. *A Syllabic Dictionary of the Chinese Language*. Shanghai: American Mission Press, 1874.

Wu Jishi 吳繼仕. *Yinsheng jiyuan* 音聲紀元, *SKQS CMCS* edition.

———. *Yinsheng jiyuan* 音聲紀元 (c. 1616 edition at National Central Library of Taiwan).

Wu Ning 吳寧. *Rongyuan ciyun* 榕園詞韻, *XX SKQS* edition.

Wu Renchen 吳任臣. *Zihui bu* 字彙補, *XX SKQS* edition.

Wu Shilin 吳士琳. *Zhengyun yi* 正韻翼 (at National Library of China).

Wu Yuanman 吳元滿. *Liushu zongyao* 六書總要, *SKQS CMCS* edition.

Wu Yujin 吳玉搢. *Shuowen yinjing kao* 説文引經考, *XX SKQS* edition.

Xia Xie 夏燮. *Shu yun* 述均, *XX SKQS* edition.

Xia Xin 夏炘. *Shi guyun biao nianer bu jishuo* 詩古韻表廿二部集說, *XX SKQS* edition.

Xiao Yuncong 蕭雲從. *Yun tong* 韻通, *XX SKQS* edition.

Xie Qikun 謝啟昆. *Xiaoxue kao* 小學考, *XX SKQS* edition.

Xiong Shibo 熊士伯. *Dengqie yuansheng* 等切元聲, *SKQS CMCS* edition.

Xu Dachun 徐大椿. *Yuefu chuansheng* 樂府傳聲 (1744 edition at University of Michigan Library).

Xu Guan 徐官. *Gujin yin shi* 古今印史, *SKQS CMCS* edition.

Xu Guilin 許桂林. *Xu shi shuoyin* 許氏說音. In *Shengyun yaokan* 聲韻要刊. Beiping: Songyun ge, n.d. (at Columbia University Library).

Xu Jian 徐鑑. *Yin fu* 音泭, *XX SKQS* edition.

Yan Kejun 嚴可均. *Shuowen shenglei* 説文聲類, *XX SKQS* edition.

Yang Huan 楊桓. *Liushu tong* 六書統, *SKQS* edition.

Yang Shen 楊慎. *Zhuanzhu guyin lüe* 轉注古音略 (1532 edition at National Central Library of Taiwan).

Yang Zhenyi 楊貞一. *Shiyin bianlüe* 詩音辯略, *SKQS CMCS* edition.

Yao Wentian 姚文田. *Shuowen shengxi* 説文聲系, *XX SKQS* edition.

Yao Ying 姚瑩. *Dongming wenji* 東溟文集, *XX SKQS* edition.

Ye Bingjing 葉秉敬. *Yun biao* 韻表, *SKQS CMCS* edition.

Yu Desheng 虞德升. *Zihui shu qiu sheng* 字彙數求聲 (at National Library of China).

Yu Yue 俞樾. *Chaxiang shi san chao* 茶香室三鈔, *XX SKQS* edition.

Yuan Zirang 袁子讓. *Wuxian tang zixue yuanyuan* 五先堂字學元元, *SKQS CMCS* edition.

Yue Shaofeng 樂韶鳳 et al. *Hongwu zhengyun* 洪武正韻, *SKQS* edition.

Zhang Geng 張畊. *Guyun faming* 古韻發明, *XX SKQS* edition.

Zhang Huiyan 張惠言. *Xiesheng pu* 諧聲譜, *XX SKQS* edition.

Zhang Xianyi 張獻翼. *Du Yi yunkao* 讀易韻考, *SKQS CMCS* edition.

Zhang Xuecheng 章學誠. *Jiaochou tongyi* 校讎通義, *Sibu beiyao* edition. Shanghai: Zhonghua shuju, 1936.

Zhang Yushu 張玉書 et al. *Kangxi zidian* 康熙字典 (1716 edition at Harvard-Yenching Library).

Zhang Zilie 張自烈. *Zhengzi tong* 正字通, SKQS CMCS edition.

Zhao Huiqian 趙撝謙. *Huangji shengyin wenzi tong* 皇極聲音文字通, SKQS CMCS edition.

Zhao Shaoji 趙紹箕. *Zhuoan yunwu* 拙菴韻悟, XX SKQS edition.

Zhao Yiguang 趙宧光. *Shuowen changjian* 說文長箋, SKQS CMCS edition.

——. *Shuowen changjian* 說文長箋 (1631 edition at Bibliothèque nationale de France).

——. *Tanya* 彈雅 (1622 edition at Capital Library in Beijing).

——. *Xitan jingzhuan* 悉曇經傳. In *Xitan jingzhuan: Zhao Yiguang ji qi "Xitan jingzhuan"* 悉曇經傳: 趙宧光及其悉曇經傳, ed. Rao Zongyi. Taipei: Xin wenfeng chubanshe, 1999.

Zhong Heng 仲恆. *Ciyun* 詞韻, SKQS CMCS edition.

Zhou Chun 周春. *Zhou Songai yishu* 周松靄遺書 (at Harvard-Yenching Library).

Zhou Deqing 周德清. *Zhongyuan yinyun* 中原音韻, SKQS edition.

Zhou Yu 周宇. *Renzi ce* 認字測, SKQS CMCS edition.

Zhou Yun 周贇. *Shanmen xinyu* 山門新語 (1893 edition at Harvard-Yenching Library).

Secondary Sources

Abe, Ryūichi. *The Weaving of Mantra: Kūkai and the Construction of Esoteric Buddhist Discourse.* New York: Columbia University Press, 1999.

Bachner, Andrea. *Beyond Sinology: Chinese Writing and the Scripts of Culture.* New York: Columbia University Press, 2014.

Bai Qianshen. *Fu Shan's World: The Transformation of Chinese Calligraphy in the Seventeenth Century.* Cambridge, Mass.: Harvard University Asia Center, 2003.

Bartlett, Thomas. "Phonology as Statecraft in Gu Yanwu's Thought." In *The Scholar's Mind: Essays in Honor of Frederick W. Mote,* ed. Perry Link, 181–206. Hong Kong: Chinese University Press, 2009.

Baxter, William H. *A Handbook of Old Chinese Phonology.* Berlin: Mouton de Gruyter, 1992.

Behr, Wolfgang. "Language Change in Premodern China: Notes on Its Perception and Impact on the Idea of a 'Constant Way.'" In *Historical Truth, Historical Criticism, and Ideology: Chinese Historiography and Historical Culture From a New Comparative Perspective,* ed. Helwig Schmidt-Glintzer, Achim Mittag, and Jörn Rüsen, 13–44. Leiden: Brill, 2005.

Bian, He. *Know Your Remedies: Pharmacy and Culture in Early Modern China.* Princeton, N.J.: Princeton University Press, 2020.

Blair, Ann. "Disciplinary Distinctions Before the '*Two Cultures.*'" *European Legacy* 13, no. 5 (2008): 577–88.

——. *The Theater of Nature: Jean Bodin and Renaissance Science.* Princeton, N.J.: Princeton University Press, 1997.

——. *Too Much to Know: Managing Scholarly Information Before the Modern Age.* New Haven, Conn: Yale University Press, 2010.

Bod, Rens. *A New History of the Humanities: The Search for Principles and Patterns from Antiquity to the Present.* Oxford: Oxford University Press, 2013.

Bol, Peter K. "Culture, Society, and Neo-Confucianism, Twelfth to Sixteenth Century." In *The Song-Yuan-Ming Transition in Chinese History*, ed. Paul Smith and Richard von Glahn, 241–83. Cambridge, Mass.: Harvard University Asia Center, 2003.

——. *Neo-Confucianism in History.* Cambridge, Mass.: Harvard University Asia Center, 2010.

——. "On Shao Yong's Method for Observing Things." *Monumenta Serica* 61, no. 1 (2013): 287–99.

——. *"This Culture of Ours": Intellectual Transitions in T'ang and Sung China.* Stanford, Calif: Stanford University Press, 1992.

——. "Wang Anshi and the *Zhouli*." In *Statecraft and Classical Learning: The Rituals of Zhou in East Asian History*, ed. Benjamin A. Elman and Martin Kern, 229–51. Leiden: Brill, 2010.

Boltz, William G. *The Origin and Early Development of the Chinese Writing System.* New Haven, Conn.: American Oriental Society, 1994.

Bottéro, Françoise. *Sémantisme et classification dans l'écriture chinoise: Les systèmes de classement des caractères par clés du* Shuowen Jiezi *au* Kangxi Zidian. Paris: Collège de France, Institut des hautes études chinoises, 1996.

Branner, David Prager, ed. *The Chinese Rime Tables: Linguistic Philosophy and Historical-Comparative Phonology.* Amsterdam: John Benjamins, 2006.

Brindley, Erica Fox. *Music, Cosmology, and the Politics of Harmony in Early China.* Albany: State University of New York Press, 2012.

Brook, Timothy. *Praying for Power: Buddhism and the Formation of Gentry Society in Late-Ming China.* Cambridge, Mass.: Council on East Asian Studies, Harvard University, 1994.

Bryant, Daniel. *The Great Recreation: Ho Ching-ming (1483–1521) and His World.* Leiden: Brill, 2008.

Burke, Peter. "Reflections on the History of Information in Early Modern Europe." *Scientiarum Historia* 17 (1991): 65–73.

Cai Mengzhen 蔡孟珍. "Ming Shen Chongsui zai xiqu yinyunxue shang de gongxian" 明·沈寵綏在戲曲音韻學上的貢獻. *Shengyun luncong* 9 (2000): 255–88.

Carlitz, Katherine. "Printing as Performance: Literati Playwright-Publishers of the Late Ming." In *Printing and Book Culture in Late Imperial China*, ed. Cynthia Brokaw and Kai-Wing Chow, 267–303. Berkeley: University of California Press, 2005.

Casacchia, Giorgio. "About a 'Book of Rhymes' by Li Yu." *Ming Qing yanjiu* 4 (1995): 45–50.

Chan, Leo Tak-hung. *The Discourse on Foxes and Ghosts: Ji Yun and Eighteenth-Century Literati Storytelling*. Honolulu: University of Hawai`i Press, 1998.

Chao, Yuen Ren 趙元任. *A Project for General Chinese / Tongzi fang'an* 通字方案. Beijing: Shangwu yinshuguan, 1983.

Chaudhuri, Saroj Kumar. *Sanskrit in China and Japan*. New Delhi: International Academy of Indian Culture and Aditya Prakashan, 2011.

Chen Guanzhi 陳冠至. *Mingdai de Suzhou cangshu: cangshujia de cangshu huodong yu cangshu shenghuo* 明代的蘇州藏書：藏書家的藏書活動與藏書生活. Taipei: Lexue shuju, 2002.

Chen Kaishen 陳凱莘. *Cong antou dao qushu: "Mudan ting" Ming Qing wenren zhi quanshi gaibian yu wutai yishu zhi dijin* 從案頭到氍毹：《牡丹亭》明清文人之詮釋改編與舞臺藝術之遞進. Taipei: Taida chuban zhongxin, 2013.

Chia, Lucille. *Printing for Profit: The Commercial Publishers of Jianyang, Fujian (11th–17th Centuries)*. Cambridge, Mass.: Harvard University Asia Center, 2003.

Ch'ien, Edward T. *Chiao Hung and the Restructuring of Neo-Confucianism in the Late Ming*. New York: Columbia University Press, 1986.

Chow, Kai-Wing. *The Rise of Confucian Ritualism in Late Imperial China: Ethics, Classics, and Lineage Discourse*. Stanford, Calif.: Stanford University Press, 1994.

Chu Hung-Lam. "High Ch'ing Intellectual Bias as Reflected in the Imperial Catalogue." *Gest Library Journal* 1, no. 2 (1987): 51–66.

Chu Ming-kin. *The Politics of Higher Education: The Imperial University in Northern Song China*. Hong Kong: Hong Kong University Press, 2020.

Chu Pingyi 祝平一. "Liu Ning yu Liu Xun—kaozhengxue yu tianxue guanxi xintan" 劉凝與劉壎 — 考證學與天學關係新探. *Xin shixue* 23, no. 1 (2012): 57–104.

——. "Philological Arguments as Religious Suasion: Liu Ning and His Study of Chinese Characters." In *Powerful Arguments: Standards of Validity in Late Imperial China*, ed. Martin Hofmann, Joachim Kurtz, and Ari Daniel Levine, 503–27. Leiden: Brill, 2020.

Clunas, Craig. *Superfluous Things: Material Culture and Social Status in Early Modern China*. Urbana: University of Illinois Press, 1991.

Coblin, W. South. "A Brief History of Mandarin." *Journal of the American Oriental Society* 120, no. 4 (2000): 537–52.

——. *A Handbook of 'Phags-Pa Chinese*. Honolulu: University of Hawai`i Press, 2006.

———. "Marginalia on Two Translations of the 'Qieyun' Preface." *Journal of Chinese Linguistics* 24, no. 1 (1996): 85–97.
Confucius. *The Analects*. Trans. D. C. Lau. Hong Kong: Chinese University Press, 2002 (reprint).
Considine, John. *Academy Dictionaries 1600–1800*. Cambridge: Cambridge University Press, 2014.
Copp, Paul F. *The Body Incantatory: Spells and the Ritual Imagination in Medieval Chinese Buddhism*. New York: Columbia University Press, 2014.
Daston, Lorraine J. "Baconian Facts, Academic Civility and the Prehistory of Objectivity." *Annals of Scholarship* 8 (1991): 337–64.
Daston, Lorraine J., and Peter Galison. *Objectivity*. Cambridge, Mass.: MIT Press, 2007.
de Bary, Wm. Theodore. *Neo-Confucian Orthodoxy and the Learning of the Mind-and-Heart*. New York: Columbia University Press, 1987.
De Weerdt, Hilde. *Information, Territory, and Elite Networks: The Crisis and Maintenance of Empire in Song China*. Cambridge, Mass.: Harvard University Asia Center, 2015.
———. "Neo-Confucian Philosophy and Genre: The Philosophical Writings of Chen Chun and Zhen Dexiu." In *Dao Companion to Neo-Confucian Philosophy*, ed. John Makeham, 223–48. New York: Springer, 2010.
DeFrancis, John. *The Chinese Language: Fact and Fantasy*. Honolulu: University of Hawai`i Press, 1984.
Denecke, Wiebke. "Worlds Without Translation: Premodern East Asia and the Power of Character Scripts." In *A Companion to Translation Studies*, ed. Sandra Bermann and Catherine Porter, 204–16. Hoboken, N.J.: Wiley-Blackwell, 2014.
DeWoskin, Kenneth J. *A Song for One or Two: Music and the Concept of Art in Early China*. Ann Arbor: Center for Chinese Studies, University of Michigan Press, 1982.
Ding Naifei. *Obscene Things: Sexual Politics in Jin Ping Mei*. Durham, N.C.: Duke University Press, 2002.
Elman, Benjamin A. "Collecting and Classifying: Ming Dynasty Compendia and Encyclopedias (*Leishu*)." *Extrême orient Extrême occident*, hors série (2007): 131–57.
———. *A Cultural History of Civil Examinations in Late Imperial China*. Berkeley: University of California Press, 2000.
———. *A Cultural History of Modern Science in China*. Cambridge, Mass.: Harvard University Press, 2006.
———. *From Philosophy to Philology: Intellectual and Social Aspects of Change in Late Imperial China*. Cambridge, Mass.: Council on East Studies, Harvard University, 1984.
———. "Review of *Historical Truth, Historical Criticism, and Ideology: Chinese Historiography and Historical Culture from a New Comparative Perspective* by Helwig

Schmidt- Glintzer, Achim Mittag, and Jörn Rüsen." *T'oung Pao* 96 (2010): 231–45.
Elvin, Mark. *The Pattern of the Chinese Past*. Stanford, Calif.: Stanford University Press, 1973.
Epstein, Maram. *Competing Discourses: Orthodoxy, Authenticity, and Engendered Meanings in Late Imperial Chinese Fiction*. Cambridge, Mass.: Harvard University Asia Center, 2001.
Feng Menglong. *Feng Menglong's Treasury of Laughs: A Seventeenth-Century Anthology of Traditional Chinese Humour*. Trans. Hsu Pi-ching. Leiden: Brill, 2015.
Findlen, Paula. *Possessing Nature: Museums, Collecting, and Scientific Culture in Early Modern Italy*. Berkeley: University of California Press, 1996.
Fuller, Michael. "Aesthetics and Meaning in Experience: A Theoretical Perspective on Zhu Xi's Revision of Song Dynasty Views of Poetry." *Harvard Journal of Asiastic Studies* 65, no. 2 (2005): 311–55.
Fung, K. W. 馮錦榮. "Chen Jinmo (1600?–1692?) zhi shengping ji xixue yanjiu—jian lun qi zhuzuo yu Ma Lixun (Robert Morrison, 1782–1834) *Ying Han zidian* zhi zhongxixue yuan" 陳藎謨 (1600?–1692?) 之生平及西學研究—兼論其著作與馬禮遜 (Robert Morrison, 1782–1834) 《英漢字典》之中西學緣, *Ming Qing shi jikan* 9 (2007): 209–62.
Geng Zhensheng 耿振生, ed. *Jindai guanhua yuyin yanjiu* 近代官话语音研究. Beijing: Yuwen chubanshe, 2007.
———. *Ming Qing dengyunxue tonglun* 明清等韵学通论. Beijing: Yuwen chubanshe, 1992.
Gieryn, Thomas F. *Cultural Boundaries of Science: Credibility on the Line*. Chicago: University of Chicago Press, 1999.
Goh, Meow Hui. "The Rhyme Book Culture of Pre-Tang China." *Journal of Chinese Literature and Culture* 2, no. 2 (2015): 419–43.
———. *Sound and Sight: Poetry and Courtier Culture in the Yongming Era (483–493)*. Stanford, Calif: Stanford University Press, 2010.
Goldman, Andrea S. *Opera and the City: The Politics of Culture in Beijing, 1770–1900*. Stanford, Calif.: Stanford University Press, 2012.
Grafton, Anthony. *Defenders of the Text: The Traditions of Scholarship in an Age of Science, 1450–1800*. Cambridge, Mass.: Harvard University Press, 1991.
———. *Joseph Scaliger: A Study in the History of Classical Scholarship*. Oxford: Oxford University Press, 1983.
Gunn, Edward. *Rendering the Regional: Local Language in Contemporary Chinese Media*. Honolulu: University of Hawai`i Press, 2006.
Guo, Qitao. *Ritual Opera and Mercantile Lineage*. Stanford, Calif.: Stanford University Press, 2005.
Guo Shaoyu 郭紹虞. *Zhaoyushi gudian wenxue lunji* 照隅室古典文學論集. Shanghai: Shanghai guji chubanshe, 1983.

———. *Zhongguo wenxue piping shi* 中國文學批評史. Shanghai: Shanghai guji chubanshe, rev. 1979.

Guy, R. Kent. *The Emperor's Four Treasuries: Scholars and the State in the Late Ch'ien-lung Era*. Cambridge, Mass.: Council on East Asian Studies, Harvard University, 1987.

Hakala, Walter. *Negotiating Languages: Urdu, Hindi, and the Definition of Modern South Asia*. New York: Columbia University Press, 2016.

Hanan, Patrick. *The Invention of Li Yu*. Cambridge, Mass: Harvard University Press, 1988.

Handel, Zev. *Sinography: The Borrowing and Adaptation of the Chinese Script*. Leiden: Brill, 2019.

Handler-Spitz, Rivi. *Symptoms of an Unruly Age: Li Zhi and Cultures of Early Modernity*. Seattle: University of Washington Press, 2017.

Hanegraaff, Wouter J. "Esotericism." In *Dictionary of Gnosis and Western Esotericism*, ed. Wouter J. Hanegraaff, 336–40. Leiden: Brill, 2006.

Hart, Roger. *Imagined Civilizations: China, the West, and Their First Encounter*. Baltimore: Johns Hopkins University Press, 2013.

Haugen, Einar. *Language Conflict and Language Planning: The Case of Modern Norwegian*. Cambridge, Mass.: Harvard University Press, 1966.

He, Yuming. *Home and the World: Editing the "Glorious Ming" in Woodblock-Printed Books of the Sixteenth and Seventeenth Centuries*. Cambridge, Mass.: Harvard University Asia Center, 2013.

Henderson, John B. *The Development and Decline of Chinese Cosmology*. New York: Columbia University Press, 1984.

Herbert, P. A. *Examine the Honest, Appraise the Able: Contemporary Assessments of Civil Service Selection in Early Tang China*. Canberra: Australian National University, 1988.

Hirata Shōji 平田昌司. "'Qieyun' yu Tangdai gongling" 切韵'与唐代功令. In *Dongfang yuyan yu wenhua* 东方语言与文化, ed. Pan Wuyun 潘悟云, 327–59. Shanghai: Shanghai jiaoyu chubanshe, 2005.

———. *Wenhua zhidu he hanyu shi* 文化制度和汉语史. Beijing: Beijing daxue chubanshe, 2016.

———. "'Zhongyuan yayin' yu Song Yuan Ming Jiangnan ruxue–'tuzhong' guannian, wenhua zhengtong yishi dui zhongguo zhengyin lilun de yingxiang" '中原雅音' 与宋元明江南儒学–'土中' 观念、文化正统意识对中国正音理论的影响. In *Jindai guanhua yuyin yanjiu* 近代官话语音研究, ed. Geng Zhengsheng. Beijing: Yuwen chubanshe, 2007.

Hirayama Hisao 平山久雄. "Shō Yō 'Kōkyoku keisei seion shōwa zu' no on'in taikei" 邵雍『皇極経世声音唱和図』の音韻体系. *Tōyō bunka kenkyūjō kiyō* 120 (1993): 49–107.

Ho, Peng Yoke. *Li, Qi and Shu: An Introduction to Science and Civilization in China*. Leiden: Brill, 1985.

Hu Qiguang 胡奇光. *Zhongguo xiaoxue shi* 中国小学史. Shanghai: Shanghai renmin chubanshe, 1987.

Huang Chin-hsing. *Philosophy, Philology, and Politics in Eighteenth-Century China: Li Fu and the Lu-Wang School Under the Ch'ing*. Cambridge: Cambridge University Press, 1995.

Huang Fushan 黃復山. *Wang Anshi 'Zishuo' zhi yanjiu* 王安石《字說》之研究. Taipei: Hua Mulan wenhua chubanshe, 2008.

Huang, Martin W. "Author(ity) and Reader in Traditional Chinese *Xiaoshuo* Commentary." *CLEAR* 16 (1994): 41–67.

Huang Yi-Long and Chang Chih-Ch'eng. "The Evolution and Decline of the Ancient Chinese Practice of Watching for the Ethers." *Chinese Science* 13 (1996): 82–106.

Jami, Catherine. *The Emperor's New Mathematics: Western Learning and Imperial Authority During the Kangxi Reign (1662–1722)*. Oxford: Oxford University Press, 2012.

Jensen, Lionel. *Manufacturing Confucianism: Chinese Traditions & Universal Civilization*. Durham, N.C.: Duke University Press, 1997.

Jiao Kun 焦堃. "Yōmeigaku to Min no seiji" 陽明学と明の政治. Ph.D. diss., Kyoto University, 2014.

Johns, Adrian. *The Nature of the Book: Print and Knowledge in the Making*. Chicago: University of Chicago Press, 1998.

Kaske, Elisabeth. *The Politics of Language in Chinese Education, 1895–1919*. Leiden: Brill, 2008.

Kelley, Donald, ed. *History and the Disciplines: The Reclassification of Knowledge in Early Modern Europe*. Rochester, N.Y.: University of Rochester Press, 1997.

Kern, Martin. "'Shijing' Songs as Performance Texts: A Case Study of 'Chu ci' (Thorny Caltrop)." *Early China* 25 (2000): 49–111.

Kile, S. E. "Toward an Extraordinary Everyday: Li Yu's (1611–1680) Vision, Writing, and Practice." Ph.D. diss., Columbia University, 2013.

Kinoshita Tetsuya 木下鉄矢. *Shindai gakujutsu to gengogaku: kōingaku no shisō to keifu* 清代学術と言語学: 古音学の思想と系譜. Tokyo: Benseishuppan, 2016.

Koh, Khee Heong. *A Northern Alternative: Xue Xuan (1389–1464) and the Hedong School*. Cambridge, Mass.: Harvard University Asia Center, 2011.

Kornicki, Peter Francis. *Languages, Scripts, and Chinese Texts in East Asia*. Oxford: Oxford University Press, 2018.

Kurtz, Joachim. "Disciplining the National Essence: Liu Shipei and the Reinvention of Ancient China's Intellectual History." In *Science and Technology in Modern China, 1880s–1940s*, ed. Jing Tsu and Benjamin A. Elman, 67–91. Leiden: Brill, 2014.

Kuzuoglu, Ulug. "Codes of Modernity: Infrastructures of Language and Chinese Scripts in an Age of Global Information Revolution." Ph.D. diss., Columbia University, 2018.

Lam, Joseph S. C. "Reading Music and Eroticism in Late Ming Texts." *Nan Nü* 12 (2010): 215–54.

Lee, Hur-Li "Praxes of Knowledge Organization in the First Chinese Library Catalog, the *Seven Epitomes.*" In *Cultural Frames of Knowledge*, ed. Richard P. Smiraglia and Hur-Li Lee, 63–77. Würzburg: Ergon Verlag, 2012.

Lewis, Mark Edward. *Writing and Authority in Early China*. Albany: State University of New York Press, 1999.

Li Bohan 李柏翰. "Ming Qing xitan wenxian ji qi dui dengyunxue de yingxiang" 明清悉曇文獻及其對等韻學的影響. Ph.D. diss., National Tsing Hua University, 2015.

——. "Yuntu xingzhi de chongxian—'Yinxue mishu' de bianzhuan linian ji qi yinyun xianxiang" 韻圖形制的重現—《音學秘書》的編撰理念及其音韻現象. *Hanxue yanjiu* 33, no. 1 (2015): 199–233.

Li Huei-mian 李惠綿. "Cong yinyunxue jiaodu lun Qingdai duqu lun de chuancheng yu kaizhan" 從音韻學角度論清代度曲論的傳承與開展. *Hanxue yanjiu* 26, no. 2 (2008): 185–218.

Li Nanqiu 黎难秋. *Zhongguo kouyishi* 中国口译史. Qingdao: Qingdao chubanshe, 2002.

Li, Wai-yee. "Introduction." in *Trauma and Transcendence in Early Qing Literature*, ed. Wilt L. Idema, Wai-yee Li, and Ellen Widmer, 1–70. Cambridge, Mass.: Harvard University Asia Center, 2006.

Li Xinkui 李新魁, *Hanyu dengyunxue* 汉语等韵学 (Beijing: Zhonghua shuju, 1983).

Liang Qichao 梁啟超. *Intellectual Trends in the Ch'ing Period*. Trans. Immanuel C. Y. Hsü. Cambridge, Mass.: Harvard University Press, 1959.

——. *Zhongguo jin sanbianian xueshushi* 中國近三百年學術史. Shanghai: Minzhi shudian, 1929.

Lin Jiayi 林佳儀. *Kuntan qingyin: Xu Yanzhi, Zhang Shanxiang de kunqu shengya* 崑壇清音: 徐炎之、張善薌的崑曲生涯. Taipei: Xiuwei zixun, 2019.

Lin Qingzhang 林慶彰. *Mingdai kaojuxue yanjiu* 明代考據學研究. Taipei: Taiwan xuesheng shuju, 1983.

Liu Zhaoren 刘昭仁. *Daixue xiao ji: Dai Zhen de shengping yu xueshu sixiang* 戴学小记: 戴震的生平与学术思想. Taipei: Xiuwei zixun, 2009.

Lloyd, G. E. R. *Disciplines in the Making: Cross-cultural Perspectives on Elites, Learning, and Innovation*. Oxford: Oxford University Press, 2009.

Lotze, Johannes S. "Translation of Empire: Mongol Legacy, Language Policy, and the Early Ming World Order, 1368–1453." Ph.D. diss., University of Manchester, 2016.

Lu, Zhenzhen. "The Vernacular World of Pu Songling." Ph.D. diss., University of Pennsylvania, 2017.

Lurie, David. *Realms of Literacy: Early Japan and the History of Writing*. Cambridge, Mass.: Harvard University Asia Center, 2011.

Lynn, Richard John, trans. *The Classic of Changes: A New Translation of the I Ching as Interpreted by Wang Bi*. New York: Columbia University Press, 1994.

Mair, Victor H. "Cheng Ch'iao's Understanding of Sanskrit." In *China and Beyond: A Collection of Essays*, ed. Victor H. Mair, 185–205. Amherst, Mass.: Cambria Press, 2013.

——. "What Is a Chinese 'Dialect/Topolect'? Reflections on Some Key Sino-English Linguistic Terms." *Sino-Platonic Papers* 29 (1991): 1–31.

Mair, Victor H., and Tsu-lin Mei. "The Sanskrit Origins of Recent Style Prosody." *Harvard Journal of Asiatic Studies* 51 (1991): 375–470.

Major, John S, et al., ed. *The Huainanzi: A Guide to the Theory and Practice of Government in Early Han China, by Liu An, King of Huainan*. New York: Columbia University Press, 2010.

Marcon, Federico. *The Knowledge of Nature and the Nature of Knowledge in Early Modern Japan*. Chicago: University of Chicago Press, 2015.

McNair, Amy. *The Upright Brush: Yan Zhenqing's Calligraphy and Song Literati Politics*. Honolulu: University of Hawai`i Press, 1998.

Messer-Davidow, Ellen, David R. Shumway, and David J. Sylvan, eds. *Knowledges: Historical and Critical Studies in Disciplinarity*. Charlottesville: University of Virginia Press, 1993.

Meyer-Fong, Tobie. "Packaging the Men of Our Times: Literary Anthologies, Friendship Networks, and Political Accommodation in the Early Qing." *Harvard Journal of Asiatic Studies* 64, no. 1 (2004): 5–56.

Miles, Steven B. *The Sea of Learning: Mobility and Identity in Nineteenth-Century Guangzhou*. Cambridge, Mass.: Harvard University Asia Center, 2006.

Mittag, Achim. "Change in *Shijing* Exegesis: Some Notes on the Rediscovery of the Musical Aspect of the 'Odes' in the Song Period." *T'oung Pao* 79, no. 4–5 (1993): 197–224.

Moyer, Ann. *Musica Scientia: Musical Scholarship in the Renaissance*. Ithaca, N.Y: Cornell University Press, 1992.

Mullaney, Thomas. "Chinese Is Not a Backward Language." *Foreign Policy*, May 12, 2016.

——. *The Chinese Typewriter: A History*. Cambridge, Mass.: MIT Press, 2017.

Nappi, Carla. *The Monkey and the Inkpot: Natural History and Its Transformations in Early Modern China*. Cambridge, Mass.: Harvard University Press, 2009.

Ng, On-cho. *Cheng-Zhu Confucianism in the Early Qing: Li Guangdi (1642–1718) and Qing Learning*. Albany: State University of New York Press, 2001.

Nicoll-Johnson, Evan. "Fringes and Seams: Boundaries of Erudition in Early Medieval China." Ph.D. diss., University of California, Los Angeles, 2017.

Ning Jifu 宁继福. *Zhongyuan yinyun biaogao* 中原音韵表稿. Changchun: Jilin wenshi chubanshe, 1985.

Nivison, David S. *The Life and Thought of Chang Hsüeh-Ch'eng, 1738–1801.* Stanford, Calif.: Stanford University Press, 1966.

Nylan, Michael. "Kongzi and Mozi, the Classicists (Ru 儒) and the Mohists (Mo 墨) in Classical-Era Thinking." *Oriens Extremus* 48 (2009): 1–20.

———. *The Five "Confucian" Classics.* New Haven, Conn.: Yale University Press, 2001.

Ogilvie, Brian W. *The Science of Describing: Natural History in Renaissance Europe.* Chicago: University of Chicago Press, 2006.

Ōki Yasushi 大木康. *Minmatsu Kōnan no shuppan bunka* 明末江南の出版文化. Tokyo: Kenbun shuppan, 2004.

Ong, Chang Woei. *Li Mengyang, the North-South Divide, and Literati Learning in Ming China.* Cambridge, Mass.: Harvard University Asia Center, 2016.

Owen, Stephen. *Readings in Chinese Literary Thought.* Cambridge, Mass.: Harvard University Asia Center, 1996.

Paderni, Paola. "The Problem of *Kuan-hua* in Eighteenth Century China: The Yung-chêng Decree for Fukien and Kwangtung." *Annali [dell'Università di Napoli "L'Orientale"]* 48, no. 4 (1988): 258–68.

Park, Si Nae. "Inscribing and Erasing the Vernacular in Late Chosŏn Linguistic Imaginations." Paper presented at the annual meeting of the Association for Asian Studies, April 2016.

Peng Jing 彭靜. "Mingdai Suzhou qujia Gu Dadian xiqu yongyun kao" 明代蘇州曲家顧大典戲曲用韻考. *Korea Journal of Chinese Language and Literature* 47 (2012): 97–120.

Peterson, Willard. "Another Look at *Li*." *Bulletin of Sung-Yuan Studies* 18 (1986): 13–32.

———. *Bitter gourd: Fang I-chih and the Impetus for Intellectual Change.* New Haven, Conn.: Yale University Press, 1979.

Pian, Rulan Chao. *Sonq Dynasty Musical Sources and Their Interpretation.* Cambridge, Mass.: Harvard University Press, 1967.

Picken, Laurence E. R. "Twelve Ritual Melodies of the T'ang Dynasty." In *Studia Memoriae Belae Bartók Sacra*, ed. Benjámi Rajeczky, 147–73. Budapest: Aedes Academiae Scientiarum Hungaricae, 1956.

Plaks, Andrew. *Archetype and Allegory in the Dream of the Red Chamber.* Princeton, N.J.: Princeton University Press, 1976.

Porter, David. "Bannermen as Translators: Manchu Language Education in the Hanjun Banners." *Late Imperial China* 40, no. 2 (2019): 1–43.

Porter, David. *Ideographia: The Chinese Cipher in Early Modern Europe.* Stanford, Calif.: Stanford University Press, 2002.

Porter, Theodore M. *Trust in Numbers: The Pursuit of Objectivity in Science and Public Life.* Princeton, N.J.: Princeton University Press, 1994.

Puett, Michael. "Nature and Artifice: Debates in Late Warring States China Concerning the Creation of Culture." *Harvard Journal of Asiatic Studies* 57, no. 2 (1997): 471–518.
Pulleyblank, Edwin G. *Middle Chinese: A Study in Historical Phonology.* Vancouver: University of British Columbia Press, 1984.
Qiu Xigui. *Chinese Writing.* Trans. G. L. Mattos and J. Norman. Berkeley: Institute of East Asian Studies, University of California, 2000.
Ramsey, S. Robert. *The Languages of China.* Princeton, N.J.: Princeton University Press, 1989.
Richardson, Brian. *Print Culture in Renaissance Italy: The Editor and the Vernacular Text, 1470–1600.* Cambridge: Cambridge University Press, 2011.
Roddy, Stephen. *Literati Identity and Its Fictional Representations in Late Imperial China.* Stanford, Calif.: Stanford University Press, 1998.
Rolston, David L., ed. *How to Read the Chinese Novel.* Princeton, N.J.: Princeton University Press, 1990.
———. *Traditional Chinese Fiction and Fiction Commentary: Reading and Writing Between the Lines.* Stanford, Calif.: Stanford University Press, 1997.
Rowe, William T. "Political, Social and Economic Factors Affecting the Transmission of Technical Knowledge in Early Modern China." In *Cultures of Knowledge: Technology in Chinese History,* ed. Dagmar Schäfer, 25–44. Leiden: Brill, 2012.
Rusk, Bruce. *Critics and Commentators: The "Book of Poems" as Classic and Literature.* Cambridge, Mass.: Harvard University Asia Center, 2012.
———. "Not Written in Stone: Ming Readers of the 'Great Learning' and the Impact of Forgery." *Harvard Journal of Asiatic Studies* 66, no. 1 (2006): 189–231.
———. "Old Scripts, New Actors: European Encounters with Chinese Writing, 1550–1700." *East Asian Science, Technology and Medicine* 26 (2007): 68–116.
———. "The Rogue Classicist: Feng Fang (1493–1566) and His Forgeries." Ph.D. diss., University of California, Los Angeles, 2004.
Salomon, Richard. *Indian Epigraphy: A Guide to the Study of Inscriptions in Sanskrit, Prakrit, and the Other Indo-Aryan Languages.* Oxford: Oxford University Press, 1998.
Schäfer, Dagmar. *The Crafting of the 10,000 Things: Knowledge and Technology in Seventeenth-Century China.* Chicago: University of Chicago Press, 2011.
Schneewind, Sarah. *Community Schools and the State in Ming China.* Stanford, Calif.: Stanford University Press, 2006.
———. *Shrines to Living Men in the Ming Political Cosmos.* Cambridge, Mass.: Harvard University Asia Center, 2018.
Schoenberger, Kevin Conrad. "Resonant Readings: Musicality in Early Modern Chinese Adaptations of Traditional Poetic Forms." Ph.D. diss., Yale University, 2013.

Schorr, Adam. "Connoisseurship and the Defense Against Vulgarity: Yang Shen (1488–1559) and His Work." *Monumenta Serica* 41 (1993): 89–128.

———. "The Trap of Words: Political Power, Cultural Authority, and Language Debates in Ming Dynasty China." Ph.D. diss., University of California, Los Angeles, 2004.

Sela, Ori. *China's Philological Turn: Scholars, Textualism, and the Dao in the Eighteenth Century.* New York: Columbia University Press, 2018.

Shang Wei. "Ritual, Ritual Manuals, and the Crisis of the Confucian World: An Interpretation of *Rulin waishi*." *Harvard Journal of Asiatic Studies* 58, no. 2 (1998): 373–424.

Shaughnessy, Edward L. "The Composition of the *Zhouyi*." Ph.D. diss., Stanford University, 1983.

Shen Weirong. "Tantric Buddhism in Ming China." In *Esoteric Buddhism and the Tantras in East Asia*, ed. Charles Orzech, Henrik Sørensen and Richard Payne, 537–49. Leiden: Brill, 2010.

Simmons, Richard VanNess. *Chinese Dialect Classification: A Comparative Approach to Harngjou, Old Jintarn, and Common Northern Wu.* Amsterdam: John Benjamins, 1999.

———. "A Second Look at the *Tōwa sanyō*: Clues to the Nature of the *Guanhuah* Studied by Japanese in the Early Eighteenth Century." *Journal of the American Oriental Society* 117, no. 3 (1997): 419–26.

Smith, Joanna Handlin. *The Art of Doing Good: Charity in Late Ming China.* Berkeley: University of California Press, 2009.

Smith, Kidder, Jr., ed. *Sung Dynasty Uses of the I Ching.* Princeton, N.J.: Princeton University Press, 1990.

Smith, Richard J. *Fathoming the Cosmos and Ordering the World: The Yijing (I-Ching, or Classic of Changes) and Its Evolution in China.* Charlottesville: University of Virginia Press, 2008.

Söderblom Saarela, Mårten. "Alphabets *Avant la Lettre*: Phonographic Experiments in Late Imperial China," *Twentieth-Century China* 41, no. 3 (2016): 234–57.

———. *The Early Modern Travels of Manchu: A Script and Its Study in East Asia and Europe.* Philadelphia: University of Pennsylvania Press, 2020.

———. "Manchu and the Study of Language in China (1607–1911)." Ph.D. diss., Princeton University, 2015.

———. "Manchu, Mandarin, and the Politicization of Spoken Language in Qing China." In *Language Diversity in the Sinophone World: Historical Trajectories, Language Planning, and Multilingual Practices*, ed. Henning Klöter and Mårten Söderblom Saarela, 39–59. London: Routledge, 2020.

———. "The Manchu Script and Information Management: Some Aspects of Qing China's Great Encounter with Alphabetic Literacy." In *Rethinking East Asian*

Languages, Vernaculars, and Literacies, 1000–1919, ed. Benjamin A. Elman, 169–97. Leiden: Brill, 2014.

———. "'Shooting Characters:' A Phonological Game and Its Uses in Late Imperial China." *Journal of the American Oriental Society* 138, no. 2 (2018): 327–59.

Son, Suyoung. *Writing for Print: Publishing and the Making of Textual Authority in Late Imperial China*. Cambridge, Mass.: Harvard University Asia Center, 2018.

Stimson, Hugh. *The Jongyuan in Yunn; a Guide to Old Mandarin Pronunciation*. New Haven, Conn.: Far Eastern Publications, Yale University, 1966.

Stolzenberg, Daniel. *Egyptian Oedipus: Athanasius Kircher and the Secrets of Antiquity*. Chicago: University of Chicago Press, 2013.

Swatek, Catherine. *Peony Pavilion Onstage: Four Centuries in the Career of a Chinese Drama*. Ann Arbor: Center for Chinese Studies, University of Michigan, 2002.

Tam, Gina. *Dialect and Nationalism in China, 1860–1960*. Cambridge: Cambridge University Press, 2020.

Tan, Li-Hai, et al. "Language Affects Patterns of Brain Activation Associated with Perceptual Decision." *Proceedings of the National Academy of Sciences* 105, no. 10 (2008): 4004–9.

Tsu, Jing. *Sound and Script in Chinese Diaspora*. Cambridge, Mass.: Harvard University Press, 2010.

Tsuyoshi Kojima. "Tuning and Numerology in the New Learning School." In *Emperor Huizong and Late Northern Song China: The Politics of Culture and the Culture of Politics*, ed. Patricia Ebrey and Maggie Bickford, 206–26. Cambridge, Mass.: Harvard University Asia Center, 2006.

Turner, James. *Philology: The Forgotten Origins of the Modern Humanities*. Princeton, N.J.: Princeton University Press, 2015.

van Gulik, Robert Hans. *Siddham: An Essay on the History of Sanskrit Studies in China and Japan*. Nagpur: International Academy of Indian Culture, 1956.

Van Zoeren, Steven. *Poetry and Personality: Reading, Exegesis, and Hermeneutics in Traditional China*. Stanford, Calif.: Stanford University Press, 1991.

Vance, Brigid E. "Deciphering Dreams: How Glyphomancy Worked in Late Ming Dream Encyclopedic Divination." *Chinese Historical Review* 24, no. 1 (2017): 5–20.

Vedal, Nathan. "From Tradition to Community: The Rise of Contemporary Knowledge in Late Imperial China." *Journal of Asian Studies* 79, no. 1 (2020): 77–101.

———. "Later Imperial Lexicons." In *Literary Information in China: A History*, ed. Jack Chen et al., 78–89. New York: Columbia University Press, 2021.

———. "New Scripts for All Sounds: Cosmology and Universal Phonetic Notation Systems in Late Imperial China." *Harvard Journal of Asiatic Studies* 78, no. 1 (2018): 1–46.

———. "Scholarly Culture in Sixteenth and Seventeenth-Century China." Ph.D. diss., Harvard University, 2017.

von Glahn, Richard. *The Economic History of China: From Antiquity to the Nineteenth Century.* Cambridge: Cambridge University Press, 2016.

Waley, Arthur, trans. *The Book of Songs: The Ancient Chinese Classic of Poetry.* Ed. Joseph R. Allen. New York: Grove Press, 1996.

Wan Xianchu 万献初. "'Wuche yunfu' wenxian yuanliu yu xingzhi kaolun" 《五车韵府》文献源流与性质考论. *Wenxian* 3 (2015): 166–76.

Wang, Aihe. *Cosmology and Political Culture in Early China.* Cambridge: Cambridge University Press, 2006.

Wang Fansen 王汎森. *Quanli de maoxiguan zuoyong: Qingdai de sixiang, xueshu yu xintai* 權力的毛細管作用：清代的思想、學術與心態. Taipei: Lianjing chuban gongsi, 2013.

Wang Ge 王格. "Lun Wei Zhuangqu 'tiangen zhi xue' de jing yu dong" 论魏庄渠"天根之学"的静与动. *Huadong shifan daxue xuebao* 3 (2012): 116–21.

Wang Songmu 王松木. *Mingdai dengyun zhi leixing ji qi kaizhan* 明代等韻之類型及其開展. Taipei: Hua Mulan chubanshe, 2011.

———. "Yinshu mingli—lun Chen Jinmo *Huangji tuyun* de yuntu sheji yu yinxue sixiang" 因數明理—論陳藎謨《皇極圖韻》的韻圖設計與音學思想. *Wen yu zhe* 23 (2013): 1–52.

———. "Zhuiru modao de guyin xuejia–lun Long Weilin 'Benyun yide' ji qi yinxue sixiang" 墜入魔道的古音學家—論龍為霖《本韻一得》及其音學思想. *Qinghua zhongwen xuebao* 8 (2012): 63–133.

Wang Yangming. *Instructions for Practical Living, and Other Neo-Confucian Writings.* Trans. Wing-Tsit Chan. New York: Columbia University Press, 1963.

Wang Yinfeng 汪银峰, "Cong 'Yuanyun pu,' 'Wufang yuanyin' yuntu jiegou kan liangzhe zhijian de guanxi" 从《元韵谱》、《五方元音》韵图结构看两者之间的关系, *Hanzi wenhua* 6 (2010): 31–36.

Wei, Sophie Ling-chia. *Chinese Theology and Translation: The Christianity of the Jesuit Figurists and Their Christianized Yijing.* New York: Routledge, 2019.

Weil, Dror. "The Vicissitudes of Late Imperial China's Accommodation of Arabo-Persian Knowledge of the Natural World, 16th–18th centuries." Ph.D. diss., Princeton University, 2016.

West, Stephen H., and Wilt Idema, trans. *Monks, Bandits, Lovers, and Immortals: Eleven Early Chinese Plays.* Indianapolis, Ind.: Hackett, 2010.

———, trans. *The Moon and the Zither: The Story of the Western Wing.* Berkeley: University of California Press, 1991.

Wild, Norman. "Materials for the Study of the Ssu i Kuan 四夷(譯)館 (Bureau of Translators)." *Bulletin of the School of African and Oriental Studies* 3 (1945): 617–40.

Williams, Nicholas Morrow. "Beyond Arbitrariness: Kūkai's Theory of Languages and Scripts." *Journal of the Pacific Association for the Continental Tradition* 4 (2021): 77–94.

Wilson, Thomas A. *Genealogy of the Way.* Stanford, Calif.: Stanford University Press, 1995.

Yang, Huiling. "The Making of the First Chinese-English Dictionary: Robert Morrison's Dictionary of the Chinese Language in Three Parts (1815–1823)." *Historiographia Linguistica* 41, no. 2–3 (2014): 299–322.

Yang Xiong. *Exemplary Figures—Fayan.* Trans. Michael Nylan. Seattle: University of Washington Press, 2013.

Yu, Li. "Character Recognition: A New Method of Learning to Read in Late Imperial China." *Late Imperial China* 33, no. 2 (2012): 1–39.

Yü Ying-shih. "Some Preliminary Reflections on the Rise of Ch'ing Intellectualism." *Tsing Hua Journal of Chinese Studies* 11 (1975): 105–46.

Zeitlin, Judith T. "Chinese Theories of the Sounding Voice Before the Modern Era: From the Natural to the Instrumental." In *The Voice as Something More: Essays Toward Materiality,* ed. Martha Feldman and Judith T. Zeitlin, 54–74. Chicago: University of Chicago Press, 2019.

Zhang Minquan 张民权. "Li Guangdi yu 'Yinxue wushu'" 李光地与《音学五书》. *Nanjing shehui kexue: wenshizhe ban* 8 (1996): 69–73.

——. *Qingdai qianqi guyinxue yanjiu* 清代前期古音学研究. Beijing: Beijing guangbo xueyuan chubanshe, 2002.

——. *Songdai guyinxue yu Wu Yu 'Shi buyin' yanjiu* 宋代古音學與吳棫《詩補音》研究. Beijing: Shangwu yinshu guan, 2005.

Zhong, Yurou. *Chinese Grammatology: Script Revolution and Literary Modernity, 1916–1958.* New York: Columbia University Press, 2019.

Zhou Guangrong 周广荣. *Fanyu "Xitan zhang" zai zhongguo de chuanbo yu yingxiang* 梵语《悉昙章》在中国的传播与影响. Beijing: Zongjiao wenhua chubanshe, 2004.

Zhou Saihua 周赛华. "'Wufang yuanyin' banben kao" 《五方元音》版本考. *Guji yanjiu* 2 (2016): 73–80.

Zhou Youguang 周有光. *Hanzi gaige gailun* 漢字改革概論. Beijing: Wenzi gaige chubanshe, 1979.

Zhou Zumo 周祖謨. "Songdai Bian Luo yuyin kao" 宋代汴洛語音考. In *Wenxue ji* 問學集, 581–655. Beijing: Zhonghua shuju, 1966.

Zuo Dongling 左东岭. *Mingdai xinxue yu shixue* 明代心学与诗学. Beijing: Xueyuan chubanshe, 2002.

Zuo, Ya. "'Ru' Versus 'Li': The Divergence Between the Generalist and the Specialist in the Northern Song." *Journal of Song-Yuan Studies* 44 (2014): 85–137.

——. *Shen Gua's Empiricism.* Cambridge, Mass.: Harvard University Asia Center, 2018.

Index

Abe, Ryuichi, 53
abugidas (alphasyllabaries), 50–51, 57, 61, 65
acoustics, 160, 172, 174
alphabetic literacy, 61, 64
alphabets, 50
Analects (Confucius), 153, 154, 242n43
Ancient Learning (*guxue*), 168, 213
animal sounds, 42
astronomy, 11
audiences, literary, 17, 108

Bacon, Francis, 44, 45
"Bad Character" (Chiang, 2016), 224
Bashi zhuzi tushuo [Diagrams and explanations of the eight-arrow method of annotating graphs] (Gu Chenxu), 171
Beixi ziyi [Chen Beixi's interpretation of graphs] (Chen Chun), 82, 95
Benyun yide [Apprehending the original rhyme at once] (Long Weilin), 171, 172
Bible, 65, 188

birds: Chinese script and tracks of, 43, 70; sounds of, 42
Bol, Peter, 137
book catalogs, 3, 236n9
Brāhmī script, 247n24
Buddhism/Buddhist monks, 2, 9, 65, 66, 68, 72, 126; Chan meditation, 51; chanting rhymes and, 141, 265n30; classicist literati collaboration with, 47, 49, 56, 65, 72, 214; introduced to China, 59; Learning of the Mind and, 11; lexicographical works produced by, 51; philosophical compatibility with Confucianism, 145; pilgrimages to India, 50; "rhyme masters/teachers," 51; Sanskrit and, 47, 49, 52–54, 60, 70, 174, 176, 214; Tibetan, 54

Cai Qing, 115–16
Cai Yuanding, 243n52
calendrics, 1, 24, 39, 40
calligraphy, 69, 79, 98, 196
Cang Jie, 123, 125

Cantong qi [Token of the three's unity], 141, 142, 264n25
"Central Plains," of North China, 113, 115, 117
Chai Shaobing, 130, 131, 132, 133, 207
Chao Yuan-Ren, 118–19
Chen Di, 27, 36, 37, 128, 162–63, 194, 266n57; on ancient pronunciation, 150, 208; as perceived forerunner of Evidential Learning, 216; intellectual lineage and, 205, 206; on phonology of ancient Chinese, 5; prominence as scholar, 207
Chen Duxiu, 23
Cheng Hao, 137
Cheng Mingshan, 121
Cheng Yi, 137, 140
Cheng Yuanchu, 24
Chen Jinmo, 21, 23, 25, 29, 35, 62, 120, 184; Buddhist scholarship and, 56; categorized as Ming scholar, 214; chanting rhymes and, 54; Chinese-English lexicography and, 188–89; rhyme tables of, 38–42, 41, 119, 225; on *self-so* nature of Coherence, 43–44; Shen Chongsui and, 121; Shen Chongsui's tripartite spelling method and, 134
Chen Shiyuan, 70, 249n72
Chiang, Ted, 224
"Chinese Is Not a Backward Language" (Mullaney, 2016), 224
Chinese languages: absence of official standard, 108; Cantonese, 33; diversity of mutually unintelligible topolects, 26, 27, 242n35; Mandarin, 33, 115, 142; north–south debate over standards, 108, 113–19, 135; Old Chinese, 163; opera and, 108, 113–19, 135; phonological structure of syllable, 32–33; sounds of, 39; standardization and, 5, 15, 108–13, 115, 116; unified, 6. *See also* topolects
Chinese script/graphs, 23, 43, 46, 55; as index, 102; Japanese readings of, 47, 71; Korean usage of, 71; Learning of the Mind and, 75–83, 84; legendary creator of, 123; meaning conveyed by graphs, 74–75; metaphysical parsing of graphs, 194–96; Ming thinkers' defense of, 69–70; moral principles and, 100; as most *self-so* writing system, 73; opposition to overanalysis of graph forms, 97–102, *98*; oracle bone writing, 79; pronunciation of, 36; reform of, 48, 66, 224, 225; rejection of, 11; Sanskrit compared with, 57, 59, 61, 68–69, 181; "seal script" (*guzhuan*), 52, 79, *80*, *82*; six principles of graph formation, 59; sounds represented outside of, 38; *tongyong* (interchangeable) graphs, 99, 255n88; unification of, 5; visually similar graphs confused, 6, 237n20; Western interest in, 48, 70, 87
Chongding Ma shi dengyin (Ma Ziyuan), 40
Christianity, 86
civil service examinations, 6, 9, 17; commentaries on Classics and, 145; rhymebooks and, 111–12. *See also jinshi* degree
Ciyun [*Ci* rhymes] (Zhong Heng), 131
classical studies (*jingxue*), 136, 139, 186, 194, 201; opera phonology and, 191, 274n76; philology as branch of, 105; rhyme tables and, 51
classicists. *See ru* (classicist, Confucian)
Classic of Changes (*Yijing*), 19, 23, 26–28, 86, 152, 173; "Appended Phrases to the *Classic of Changes*" (*Xici*), 88–89, 143, 147; "Providing the Sequence of

Hexagrams" (*Xugua*), 143;
versification of, 139–48, 265n29
Classic of Poems (*Shijing*), 36, 114, 136,
142, 163; *Great Preface* (*Daxu*) to,
153–54; as long-lost *Classic of Music*
(*Yuejing*), 160; music and, 153–55, 158;
opera and, 194
Classics, 6, 12, 13, 42, 99, 218; aesthetic
qualities of, 139; colloquialisms in,
136; commentarial tradition on, 106;
exegesis of, 105; language of
antiquity and, 183; Learning of the
Mind and, 76, 88; literacy and access
to, 84; natural speech of, 129;
personal cultivation and, 4; philology
subsection of, 134, 202; poetic and
musical elements of, 139, 158;
pronunciations and, 114; as rhyming
texts, 147, 148
Coherence (*li*), 18, 26, 43, 76, 82;
ahistorical notion of, 219; literary
values as distraction from, 137;
mind as, 89; moral self-realization
and, 74; Number (*shu*) and, 20, 29,
240n14; *self-so* quality of, 19–20, 44,
217, 221
colloquialisms, 129, 136
Committee on Chinese Script Reform
(Zhongguo wenzi gaige
weiyuanhui), 227
Confucianism, 2, 49, 137, 215;
corruption of Confucian learning,
176; Learning of the Mind and, 11,
73, 75; Neo-Confucianism, 170;
poetry and, 136; "six arts" and, 201;
synthesis with Buddhist teachings,
55, 145. *See also* literati; *ru* (classicist,
Confucian)
Confucius, 56, 75, 90, 143, 242n43;
ancient poems selected by, 172,
270n11; *Classic of Poems* sung by, 153;

Learning of the Way genealogy and,
206; on music, 154
cosmic resonance (*ganying*), 25
cosmology, 1, 37, 42, 121, 181, 205;
limits of human perception and,
26–28; Number and, 28; origins of
Chinese–English lexicography and,
186–91; philology and, 25, 170–74;
phonetic notation systems and, 46;
phonology and, 21–26; *self-so* quality
of, 26

Dai Tong, 94
Dai Zhen, 10, 159, 181, 205, 206, 212,
213; antiquity as source of validity
and, 220, 222, 281n96; cosmology
purged from linguistic study, 215
Dansheng tang cangshumu (catalog),
236n9
Daston, Lorraine, 44
Dayue lülü yuansheng [Primordial sounds
of pitch-pipes for grand music], 155
Dengqie yuansheng [The primordial
sound of graded rhymes and divided
syllables] (Xiong Shibo), 121, 155,
176, 177–79, 212
Devanāgarī script, 51
"Dialogue on the Entering Tone in
Southern Arias, A" ["Nanqu rusheng
ke wen"] (Mao Xianshu), 132
dictionaries, 3, 18, 75, 76–77, 78, 131–32;
Chinese-English, 186–91; graphs in,
82, 83, 84; opera, 111, 113–19, 131–32,
2742n76; philosophical, 74; in style of
Liushu jingyun, 91
Dictionary of the Chinese Language, A
[*Wuche yunfu*] (Morrison), 188–89
disciplines/disciplinary communities, 2,
9, 10, 12, 169, 184, 185, 198, 199–200;
boundaries of, 201–5; formation in
late Ming, 12

Dong Yue, 155
Duan Yucai, 173, 181, 205, 206, 213; language of validity and, 216
Du Fu, 153
Dun Ren, 109–10, 111
Duqu xuzhi [Prerequisites for aria composition/singing] (Shen Chongsui), 119–20, *124*, 133, 134, 191, 210
Dushu tong [Comprehensive analysis of reading] (Hao Jing), 99
Du-si-de, 176, 180
Du Yi yunkao [A study of the rhymes in reading the *Changes*] (Zhang Xianyi), 139–48, 151, 265n30

efficiency, of writing systems, 73, 75, 224; culturally/historically contingent notions of, 48, 50, 67; indexing methods in late Ming and, 102; phonographic versus graph-based, 47, 70, 74, 100
Elman, Benjamin, 269n7
empiricism, 31, 43
encyclopedias, 75
entering tone (*ru*), 33, 106, 114; language standardization and, 115; north-south pronunciation differences, 191; opera arias and, 132; in Wu Jishi's rhyme tables, *63*, *64*
Erya [Approaching elegance] (lexicon), 92
esotericism, 43
etymology, 5, 88, 91, 136, 196; folk etymologies, 85; "principles of graph formation" and, 77
Evidential Learning (*kaozhengxue*), 21–22, 43, 86, 91, 134, 229, 271n38; antiquity as source of validity, 218, 222; cosmology in linguistic study and, 171, 172–73; dominance in eighteenth century, 196–97; Ming precedents, 169–70, 269n7; "foundational learning" and, 219; Hangzhou philologists and, 132; historical change in Chinese language and, 128; intellectual lineage (genealogy) and, 206, 207, 210–16; linguistic purification associated with, 183–84; literary approaches to classical rhyming and, 148–53; metaphysical parsing of graphs and, 194–96; methods applied to many fields, 168; musical performance of *Poems* and, 159–60, 162; Neo-Confucian syncretism with, 170; operatic phonology and, 193, 194; Sanskrit study and, 181; *Siku quanshu* and, 167, 199; specialized language study reshaped by, 200; modern scientific "objectivity" and, 45
evidential research (*kaojiu*), 23

falling tone (*qu*), 33, 97–98, 106; in Wu Jishi's rhyme tables, *63*, *64*
Fang Yizhi, 27, 29–30, 62, 65, 212, 215; Buddhist scholarship and, 214–15; categorized as Ming scholar, 214; on corrections to recent scholars, 203; on link between spoken languages, 35–36; phonographic scripts studied by, 61–62, 66; on specialized learning, 199; on universality of language, 30
fanqie method, 33, 40, 106, 116; division of syllable into two parts, 120, 121, 127
Fan Tengfeng, 186, 190, 271n27
Fan Tinghu, 188
Faxian, 50
Figurists, 87

[308] INDEX

Five Phases, 28, 221
Flowers in the Mirror [*Jinghua yuan*] (Li Ruzhen), 183, 272n46
Fu Shoutong, 173

Galison, Peter, 44
Gao Wengying, 212
genealogy, 206–7, 212, 277n30; elevation of Gu Yanwu and, 209, 211–12; of Evidential Learning, 181–82, 205–7, 210–16
geomancy, 27, 62, 69, 174
Ge Zhongxuan, 26–27, 35, 36, 37, 42, 159
Goh, Meow Hui, 107
grammatology, 3
graphs. *See* Chinese script/graphs
Great Learning, (*Daxue*), 79, 99
Great Yu [Da Yu] (mythical first emperor), 38
Guangyun [Expanded rhymes], 92, 128
Guan Tong, 213
Gu Chenxu, 170, 171
Gui Fu, 195, 196
Gui Youguang, 251n6
Guoyu zhoukan [National language weekly], 229
Gu Yanwu, 7, 117, 133–34, 148–50, 162, 173, 271n38; on ancient and postclassical poetry, 171, 172; criticized for overreliance on texts, 174; as perceived founder of Evidential Learning, 132, 181, 183, 213–14; on restoration of ancient pronunciation, 194; on rhyming and dialect pronunciation, 152–53; stages in elevation of, 205–16, 229; Zhao Yiguang criticized by, 218–19; Zhou Chun's criticism of, 181–82

Gu Yingxiang, 68–70, 89–90, 91, 250n77, 254n68
Guyin leibiao [Categorized tables of ancient pronunciation] (Fu Shoutong), 173

Han Bangqi, 31
Han dynasty, 43, 59, 60, 90, 148, 219, 220; classicists of, 106; imperial biographies in, 201
Hangzhou philologists, 132, 183, 207, 208, 212
Han Learning (*Hanxue*), 168
Hanlin Academy, 131
Han Qia, 92, 94, 133
Hanxue shicheng ji [Record of the inheritance of teachings within Han Learning], 207
Han Yu, 147, 171, 172
Hanzi gaige gailun [An overview of Chinese script reform] (Zhou Youguang), 227
Hao Jing, 67, 99–100, 249n72
He Liangjun, 109–10, 111
heptatonic scale, 32, 162
hermeneutic traditions, 153, 154
hexagrams, 19, 143
Hong Sheng, 132
Hongwu emperor, 111
Hongwu zhengyun [Correct rhymes of the Hongwu reign], 18, 84, 90, 111, 195, 216
Hongzhi emperor, 112
Hooke, Robert, 45
Huang Daozhou, 38
Huangfu brothers (Chong, Xiao, Pang, and Lian), 140
Huangfu Pang, 151
Huangji jingshi shu [Book of the august ultimate traversing the ages] (Shao Yong), 34–35

Huangji tuyun [Supreme principles for diagramming rhymes] (Chen Jinmo), 38, *41*, 120, 188
Huang Yanbo, 131
Huangzhong tongyun [Comprehending rhymes through the pitch C] (Du-si-de), 176, 180–81, *180*
Huangzhong yinyun tongkuo [A comprehensive examination of the initials and rhymes based on the pitch C] (Cheng Yuanchu), 24
Hui Muslims, writing system of, 69
Hu Shaoying, 188
Hu Yinglin, 3, 236n11

indexing methods, 102
India, 50
Indic scripts, 52, 56, 69, 182. *See also* Sanskrit language
individualism, 13, 218
"initial spellers" (*zimu*), 181, 182
innovation, 8, 13, 21, 26; cosmology and, 45, 189; lack of, 73; posthumously recognized, 209
insects, sounds made by, 42
institutions, role of, 9, 201
Interpreters Institute (Huitong guan), 49

Japan, 60, 226
Jesuit missionaries: Latin alphabet and, 46, 49, 72, 227–28; origins of pinyin and, 227
Jiang Yong, 118, 159, 173, 181, 222–23, 279n50; Gu Yanwu's reputation and, 209, 211–12; intellectual lineage and, 205, 206
Jiao Hong, 206, 208, 216, 240n16, 271n33; on ancient pronunciation, 208; cosmology in linguistic study and, 21; as perceived forerunner of Evidential Learning, 216; intellectual lineage and, 206; on moral principles in graphs, 100
Jiao shi Yilin [Master Jiao's forest of *Changes* interpretation], 141
Jiao Xun, 193
jing (classical) category, 137, 138
Jingdian wenzi kaoyi [Analysis of variation in graphs in the Classics], 219
jinshi degree, 76, 99, 107, 171. *See also* civil service examinations
Ji Yun, 214
Julien, Stanislas, 273n63
jokes, 6, 237n20

Kangxi emperor/period, 131, 198, 211
Kangxi jiazi shiguan xinkan Gujin tongyun [Comprehensive rhymes of past and present, newly printed in Kangxi jiazi] (Mao Qiling), 211
Kangxi zidian (Qing court dictionary), 94, 195, 265n30, 274n86
Kang Youwei, 226
Karlgren, Bernhard, 163
Kircher, Athanasius, 70
knowledge, 13, 73, 74, 89, 169, 224; "acquired through hearing and seeing" (*wenjian zhi zhi*) 17–18, 118; "acquired through virtuous nature" (*dexing zhi zhi*), 18; action united with, 80–81; boundaries of, 9; communities of, 9, 10, 217, 221; cosmology and, 28; division into fields of learning, 202; graph representing, 81, 83, 252n33; history of, 10; intellectual lineage and, 206–7; interconnectedness of, 1–2; linguistic, 11, 13; "man-made," 19, 20, 61; sensory and system-building methods, 17–18; specialization and, 10, 204; standards of validity, 118;

textual, 5; transition in notions of valid knowledge, 217–23; transmission from master to disciple, 201; modern science, 44. *See also* *self-so* (*ziran*) knowledge

knowledge production, 2, 8, 45, 200, 204, 220

Kong Guangsen, 205, 206, 213, 222

Korea, 46, 173

Kūkai, 53, 67

Kumārajīva, 50

Lalitavistara sūtra, 53

language, 42, 184; of antiquity, 4–5; cognition in relation to, 101–2; cosmology and, 24, 133; history of, 74; imperial court involvement in, 5; of infants, 29; koines, 42–43, 112, 187; music of antiquity reconstructed through, 157–62; music related to, 24, 34, 44, 138, 162, 173; "national language," 118, 119, 228–29; nature of, 1, 9, 12; Number and, 30, 34–37; opera and, 105; *self-so* features of, 11, 171; as sound-based *qi*, 30, 155; sounds of, 23; standardization of, 5. *See also* Chinese languages; phonographic writing; pronunciation; syllables

Lantsha/Rañjana script, 247n26, 248n32

Lao Naixuan, 167

Latin language/alphabet, 48, 61, 68, 198, 226; colonial associations of Latin script, 283n19; Jesuits and, 46, 49, 72; Ricci and, 227–28; in Wu Jishi's rhyme tables, 64, *64*; in Xiong Shibo's *Dengqie yuansheng*, 176, 177–79

Learning of the Mind (*xinxue*), 11, 73–75, 83, 131, 185, 252n36; efficiency of information retrieval and, 102; philological trends within, 88–91; proposals for abandonment of literary practice, 138; unity of knowledge and action (*zhixing heyi*), 80; Wei Jiao and philology in, 75–83

Learning of the Way (*daoxue*), 17–20, 24, 74, 90, 203, 242n43; Coherence (*li*) concept and, 219; early Qing court and, 131; Evidential Learning and, 170; genealogy of, 206; on literary values and morality, 137; *Luoshu* diagram and, 39; "methods of the mind" (*xinfa*) and, 78; pursuit of sages' morality, 218; sequential ordering and, 94–95; *zhong* (centrality, equilibrium) concept, 115

legibility versus alegibility, 60–61, 87

Leibniz, Gottfried Wilhelm, 70

Leiyin [Categorizing sounds] (Pan Lei), 209

level tone (*ping*), 33, 106; in Wu Jishi's rhyme tables, 63, *64*

Lewis, Mark Edward, 86

lexicography, 82, 131; Chinese-English lexicography, 186–91

Liang Qichao, 23, 168, 216, 228, 229

Li Guangdi, 117, 133, 182, 190–91, 209–11, 279n50

Li Jinxi, 228

Li Mengyang, 136

Lin Benyu, 170

Ling Lun, 155

Ling Menchu, 116

Ling Tingkan, 271n39

linguists/linguistic study, 1, 3, 29, 150, 216, 225; cosmology and, 42, 173; evidential research and, 23; Qing, 8

Linnaeus, Carl, 44

Lin Qingzhang, 269n7

Li Ruzhen, 182, 183, 184, 271n38; numeral notation system of, 189, *190*

Li shi yinjian [Master Li's Mirror of sound] (Li Ruzhen), 182–83, 271n38
literacy, mass, 73, 189, 225
literary studies (*wenxue*), 201
literati, 1, 5, 17, 19, 118, 125; Buddhism and, 65; collaboration with Buddhist monks, 47; print culture and, 203; utility of phonographic scripts and, 66. *See also* Confucianism; *ru*
Liu Lian, 159, 160
Liu Ning, 86
Liushu benyi [Original meaning of the six principles of graph formation] (Zhao Huiqian), 93
Liushu gu [Origins of the six principles of graph formation] (Dai Tong), 93, 94, 236n12
Liushu jingyun [Essential meanings of the six principles of graph formation] (Wei Jiao), 76–77, 82, 83, 85, 184; dictionaries in style of, 91; Lu Ao's postface to, 88; metaphysical parsing of graphs and, 195–96, 274n86; thematic categories in, 92, 93, 95–97, 96
Liushu tong [System of the six principles of graph formation] (Yang Huan), 93, 255n75
Liushu zongyao [Comprehensive summary of the six principles of graph formation] (Wu Yuanman), 93
Liu Xianting, 51, 54, 68, 71, 228–29
Liu Xie, 138
Liuyi zhiyi lu [A record of one of the six arts], 196
Liu Zongzhou, 131
Li Yu, 29, 126–30, 132, 148
Liyuan yuan [Origins of dramatic performance], 193
Li Zhaoluo, 270n14
Li Zhi, 219, 260n50

Long Weilin, 171, 172, 173, 270n14
Lu Ao, 88
Lu Deming, 141
Lu Fanchao, 131
Lu Fayan, 106, 118, 206, 221
Lülü xinshu (Cai Yuanding), 243n52
Lülü yinyun guashu tong [Comprehending the twelve musical pitches, syllable initials and rhymes, and the numbers of the *Yijing* trigrams] (Cheng Yuanchu), 24
lunar calendar, solar terms of, 62
Luo Changpei, 228
Luo Hongxian, 88–89
Luo River diagram, 38–39, 39, 211
Lurie, David, 47, 60, 87
Lü Weiqi, 35, 182
Lu Xiangshan, 89

Manchu language, 68, 71, 176, 182–83, 197; as Qing state language, 71, 181, 182; in Xiong Shibo's *Dengqie yuansheng*, 176, 177–79
Mao Qiling, 130, 181, 207–8, 210–11, 212
Mao Shi guyin kao [An investigation of ancient pronunciation in the Classic of Poems] (Chen Di), 27, 151
Mao Xianshu, 130, 131, 132–33, 152–53, 207, 210, 212
Marcon, Federico, 12
mathematics, 11, 38
Ma Ziyuan, 170
Mencius, 115, 206
Mencius, 114–15
menfa ("methods of study") genre, 37, 247n19
"methods of the mind" (*xinfa*), 77–78, 81
Mingdai kaojuxue (Lin Qingzhang), 269n7
Ming dynasty, 5, 34; afterlives of texts/methodologies from, 12; cosmology

and, 43; disciplinary communities in, 199–200; fall of, 12; as heyday of philology, 170; intellectual culture of, 1–2, 75; intersection of classical and literary learning in, 136; linguistic standardization and, 111; literary/scholarly efflorescence of, 17; loyalists of fallen Ming, 131; resituated in China's intellectual history, 7–11; scholarly identity in, 46

Ming pronunciation, ix, 235n1

Mongolia, 46

Mongolian language, 49

morality/moral cultivation: antiquity as source of validity, 218; calligraphic forms and, 79, 84, 89, 101, 102; Classics and, 4; Coherence and, 20–21, 26, 74; dictionaries and, 83, 90, 91–92, 94, 97; language of antiquity and, 4–5, 99–100; Learning of the Mind and, 74, 80, 81, 85, 94; literary composition as form of, 137, 138; "methods of the mind" (*xinfa*) and, 78; philology and, 2, 5, 12–13, 26, 76, 88, 90, 98; phonology and, 176

Morrison, Robert, 188–89

Mullaney, Thomas, 47, 224

music, 5, 42, 120, 121, 184, 193, 205; *Classic of Poems* and, 136; Classics and, 139; cosmology in linguistic study and, 171; entering tone (*ru*) and, 114; language related to, 24, 34, 44, 138, 162, 173; pitches, 1, 24; poetry and, 153–57; *self-so* properties of harmony, 30; *self-so* quality of, 26; as sound-based *qi*, 30; verse as, 12. *See also* opera; pitch

Nanqu zhengyun [Correct rhymes for southern arias] (Mao Xianshu), 132

nationalism, 135

natural history, Japanese (*honzōgaku*), 12

natural science, 168, 229

Nepal, 247n26

neurolinguistics, 102

neuroscience, 29

Nian Xiyao, 186

nondiscursive senses of writing, 11, 21, 73, 83, 86–88, 101

Number (*shu*), 19, 20, 28–30, 42, 170; as finite constraint on language, 34–37; objectivity of, 30–34; *self-so* nature of, 31, 37, 161; sound and, 29, 121

numerology, 23, 62, 140

octave, twelve equal divisions of, 31, 243n57

Old Chinese, 163

Old Uyghur script, 48

"one school of thought" (*yi jia zhi xue*), 31

opera, 13, 105–6, 157, 182, 184; aria dictionaries as classical lexicons, 113–19; classical assimilation of opera theory, 130–34; at intersection of music and language, 138; Kunqu (Kun opera), 119, 120, 123, 126, 131; librettists, 2, 12, 125–26, 133, 192; linguistic standardization and, 108–13; popularity of, 135; separation from classical philology, 191–94; twentieth-century language reformers and, 226–27; as universal standard of language, 126–30. *See also* music; pitch

Owen, Stephen, 154

Palace of Eternal Life [*Changsheng dian*] (Hong Sheng), 131

paleography, 3, 111, 206, 218, 253n40

Pan Lei, 42, 118, 133, 170, 182, 270n14; cosmology of Shao Yong and, 212; Gu Yanwu's reputation and, 208–9
patronage, 17, 203
pentatonic scale, 32, 162
Peony Pavilion [*Mudan ting*] (Tang Xianzu), 109, 132
People's Republic of China (PRC), 227, 228, 229
perception, limits of, 26–28, 44, 45, 50
'Phags-pa script, 49
philology, 1, 8, 11, 12, 13, 73, 154; antiquity as source of validity, 220–21; Buddhist, 55; civil service examinations and, 125, 260n70; classical, 55; as "classical" field, 46, 47, 215; Classics and, 84, 105, 134; "concrete learning" and, 75; cosmological approaches to, 170–74; as evidential study of ancient texts, 168, 197; importance in late imperial China, 2–7; literary issues incorporated into, 137, 138; Manchu syllabary and, 176, *177–79*, 182–83; modern language reform and, 13; as moral pursuit, 11–12; music theory and, 162; opera theorists and, 130–34, 191–94; "philological turn," 7, 169; Qing use of Ming texts/methods, 184–96; as "research into rhymes," 110; Sanskrit study and, 49, 145; specialized expertise in, 200. See also *xiaoxue*
Philosophy to Philology (Elman), 269n7
phonemes, 32–33, 65, 110, 133
phonetic legibility, 11, 60–66
phonetic notation, 37, 42; of Chen Jinmo, 38, *41*, 188; Chinese-English lexicography and, 188, 189; cosmology and, 46, 189; phonographic writing and, 65; pinyin and, 228; tripartite, 176
phonographic writing, 8, 11, 26, 45, 60, 176, 184; abstraction of linguistic sound and, 225; of China's neighboring states, 46, 48–49; Chinese script compared favorably with, 21, 47, 48, 50, 226; disadvantages in culture of logography, 66–71; Ge Zhongxuan's system, 36; Jesuit missionaries and, 49; notation of sound, 70; as pedagogical tool, 197; phonetic legibility of, 60–66, *63–64*; rhyme table phonology and, 59; as transcription tool, 65. See also Latin language/alphabet; Manchu language; Sanskrit language
phonology, 5, 6, 18, 27, 65; Buddhist monks and, 54; codification of tones, 106; cosmology and, 21–26; Indic origins of, 214; in Korea and Vietnam, 173; lack of knowledge about, 6; literary context of, 106; music and, 171–72; opera and, 111, 127, 130–34; "originary," 19; origins of Chinese-English lexicography, 186–91; pitch and, 161; pronunciation of graphs and, 36; Sanskrit, 50, 55, 56; script and, 42; topolects and, 116. See also *fanqie* method
Pianyun guanzhu ji (Zhenkong), 247n19
pinyin Romanization system, 13, 65, 227, 228
pitch (*lü*), 24, 121, 140; Chinese tones and, 62; classification of linguistic sound and, 171; human voice as precise measure of, 154; Manchu graphs correlated with, 176, 180, *180*; pitch C of musical scale (*huangzhong*), 30–31, 33, 156, 161, 243n55, 267n79,

268n100; rhyme groups and, 186. See also music; opera

poetry/poets, 2, 6, 13, 106, 113, 128, 201; as aspect of Confucian learning, 136; Classics and, 139; moral values and, 138; music and, 153–57; poetry societies (*shishe*), 131; prose in relation to, 152

Portuguese language, 63

Prémare, Joseph Henri Marie de, 86

progress, 11, 23

pronunciation, 4, 50, 105, 174; in *Classic of Changes*, 144, 145, 146, 265n34; "common" (*tongyu* or *tongyin*), 109; "correct" (*zhengyin*), 109, 117, 118, 129, 273n74; "elegant" (*yayan* or *yayin*), 109; "official" (*guanhua* or *guanyin*), 108, 112; in opera, 112, 113, 114, 134, 191; "originary," 18; phonetic spelling and, 182; pitch and, 162; regional, 19, 27, 60, 106, 118, 129, 183; of Sanskrit syllables, 52; Shen Chongsui and theorization of, 119–26, *124*; singing, 12, 29, 32, 123; Tang bureaucratic appointments and, 107. See also *fanqie* method

pronunciation, ancient (*guyin*), 28, 45, 117, 120, 151, 225; Chen Di and, 27, 36; loss of, 148; Evidential Learning and, 173; flexibility of, 208; Gu Yanwu and, 117; Jiao Hong and, 21; opera theory and, 110; phonological corruptions and, 125; restoration of, 194; Shao Yong's rhyme tables and, 191; Zhao Yiguang and, 56, 114

Protestant missionaries, 187, 283n19

qi ("vital/material force"), 27, 174; ideal balance of, 115; sound-based, 30, 155–56, 180, 220

Qian Bangqi, 279n60

Qian Daxin, 10, 174, 181, 205, 206, 213, 222; language of validity and, 216; as specialist, 215.

Qianlong emperor, 7

Qian Xuantong, 228–29

Qiao Zhonghe, 37, 271n27

Qieyun [Divided rhymes] (Lu Fayan), 92, 106, 107

Qin dynasty, 5, 148

Qingdai xueshu gailun [An overview of Qing dynasty scholarship] (Liang Qichao), 168

Qing dynasty, 5, 65, 75, 112, 143, 172, 213; Evidential Learning (*kaozhengxue*), 45; institutionalization of scholarship in, 205; language standards and, 111; Manchu as state language, 71, 181, 182; Ming texts/methods adapted and transformed in, 184–96; persistence of Ming methods under, 168; philology under, 8, 10–11, 13, 221; phonographic writing studied in, 176; poetry societies (*shishe*) in, 131

Qionglin yayun [Elegant rhymes of celestial forest], 110

Qu Dajun, 147–48, 152

Qu Jiusi, 44, 159

Qu Song guyin [Ancient pronunciations of Qu Yuan and Song Yu] (Chen Di), 151

Qubilai Khan, 49

Renchao, 51, 52–53, 57, 70, 247n21, 247n24

Renzi ce [Conjectures on the recognition of graphs] (Zhou Yu), 95, 185

Republican era, 227, 228

rhymes/rhyme tables, 24, 25, 32, 33, 36, 84, 127; Buddhist monks as "rhyme masters/teachers," 51, 54; "chanting rhymes" (*chang yun*), 54, 141; Chen Jinmo's rhyme tables, 38–42, *41*; civil service examinations and, 111–12; in *Classic of Changes*, 141, 142–43, 145–46; dictionaries of, 92, 186; graded rhymes (*dengyun*), 51; Liu Xianting's rhyme table system, 68; rhyme dictionaries, 61; rhyme groups, 27; Sanskrit rhyme tables, *58*; Tang rhyme tables, 57; Wu Jishi's rhyme tables, 62–64, *63–64*; *xieyun* ("forced"/"harmonized") rhyming method, 36, 150, 151, 271n33

Ricci, Matteo, 49, 227–28

rising tone (*shang*), 33, 98, 106; in Wu Jishi's rhyme tables, *63*, *64*

Rizhi lu [Record of daily-acquired knowledge] (Gu Yanwu), 208

Romanization Association (Japan), 226

Romanization systems, 13, 65, 226, 228, 229, 283n19

Rongcun yulu (Li Guangdi), 279n50

ru (classicist, Confucian), 2, 9, 46–47, 49, 55, 56, 60; centrality of philology to, 47; crisis of *ru* identity, 55; *fo* (Buddhism) in opposition to, 47; Ming *ru* identity, 59; opera and, 12, 106, 110–11; pronunciation debates and, 105, 120; Sanskrit study and, 53–54, 60. *See also* Confucianism; literati

Ruan Yuan, 181

Rusk, Bruce, 137, 139, 141

Sanskrit language, 11, 34, 47, 48, 71, 72, 198, 228; alphasyllabary of, 61, 65; chanting in, 145; Chinese transcriptions of, 57, 250n73; debate about writing systems and, 46; Dhāraṇī chants, 61; Evidential Learning scholars and, 174, 176; Indic origins of Chinese phonology and, 214–15; "legibility" of, 61; "numinous" origin of writing system, 52–53, 70; Qing-period study of, 181; religious study of, 50–53; rhyme tables, *58*; scripts used in writing, 53, 247n24, 247n26; secular study of, 53–60, *58*; sounds of, 65; unfavorable comparison with Chinese, 67, 68–69; in Xiong Shibo's *Dengqie yuansheng*, 176, *177–79*. *See also* Buddhism/Buddhist monks

Sapir-Whorf hypothesis, 101–2

Schäfer, Dagmar, 19

science, modern, 21, 44

Script Form Press (Wenzi gaige chubanshe), 227

Sela, Ori, 217–19

self-so (*ziran*) knowledge, 11, 19, 25, 49–50, 184, 215–16, 222; Coherence and, 19–20, 240n12; human voice as standard for pitch and, 156; "man-made" in contrast to, 19, 20, 43; music–language connection and, 173; origins of sound and, 120; *self-so qi*, 27; universal categories and, 45; modern scientific "objectivity" and, 44, 45; writing systems and, 73

Shanmen xinyu [New words from Zhou Shanmen] (Zhou Yun), 173–74, *175*

Shao Jinhan, 181

Shao Yong, 24, 34–35, 37, 114, 120, 220; cosmological tables of, 121, 184, 190, 212; numerology of, 62; phonology and, 141; rhyme tables of, 162

Shen Biao, 120

[316] INDEX

Shen Chenglin, 191
Shen Chongsui, 119–26, 127, 132, 133, 134, 182; terminology applied to pronunciation, 226; on tripartite division of syllable, 193, 194
Shen Jiao, 133
Shen Qian, 131, 279n60
Shen Yue, 106
Shi Guizhang, 131
Shiji [Records of the grand historian] (Sima Qian), 153
Shi Kui, 170
Shi Sao yunzhu [Commentary on the rhymes of the *Shijing* and *Lisao*] (Hong Sheng), 131–32
Shuowen changjian (Zhao Yiguang), *98*
Shuowen jiezi [Explanation of simple and compound graphs] (Xu Shen), 59, 60, 77, 82, 194–96, 255n80; Learning of the Mind and, 85–86, 90; methodological study of, 219–20; as progenitor of script-based lexicography, 92; "read as" (*duruo*) method, 106
Shuowen jiezi judou [Annotated *Shuowen jiezi*] (Wang Yun), 196
Shuowen jiezi yizheng [Corroborating commentary on the meanings of terms in *Shuowen jiezi*] (Gui Fu), 195
Siddham script, 53, 248n32
Siku quanshu [Complete library of the Four Treasuries], 7, 147, 167, 170, 172, 173, 182, 222–23, 266n57; antiquity as source of validity, 219; categorizations and dilemma of, 184–86; Evidential Learning and, 222; *Huangzhong tongyun* negatively appraised in, 176, 180–81; *Gujin tongyun* negatively appraised in, 211; Ming and Qing scholars categorized in, 279–80n60; on specialization versus dilettantism, 199; status of Ming contributions and, 216, 223; *Wufang yuanyin* condemned by, 186. *See also* Evidential Learning
Siku quanshu zongmu [Comprehensive catalog of the *Siku quanshu*], 167, 185, 216
Sima Qian, 270n11
Sima Yan, 3–4
singing (*ge*), 113
Song dynasty, 17, 20, 38, 55, 85; cosmology studies in, 43; lexicographic texts under, 92; Northern Song, 107; pronunciation in, 191; return to "ancient-style prose" and, 138; scholarly completeness and preservation as goal, 203; specialization viewed negatively in, 199
Song Lian, 137
Song Yingxing, 155–56
sound (*sheng, yin*), 24, 129, 183; articulation of, 33; finite number of, 35; of nonhuman animals, 42; notation of, 70; origins of, 19, 120; primordial sound (*yuansheng, yuanyin*), 30, 32, 44, 155, 157, 161, 186, 243n52; *self-so* quality of, 27, 91, 157; sound-based *qi*, 30, 155–56, 180, 220
specialization/specialized learning, 199–200
Stolzenberg, Daniel, 43
Story of the Western Chamber [*Xixiang ji*] (Wang Shifu), 123
Sun Weicheng, 147, 148
Sun Zhi, 131
Su Shi, 147
Syllabic Dictionary of the Chinese Language, A (Williams), 187

syllables, 42, 54, 59, 65; division into two parts, 33, 106, 120, 121, 123, 127; division into three parts, 121–23, 127, 133, 193, 194; four-syllable line poetry, 142, 264n25; graphs and, 67, 68, 120, 122; musical pitches and, 24, 34; opera theory and, 108, 109; phonological structure of, 32–33; possible number of, 35; rhymebooks and, 110; Sanskrit, 52

Taigu yuanyin [Primordial tones of distant antiquity] (Shi Kui), 24, 155
Tailü [Grand pitches] (Ge Zhongxuan), 24
Tang dynasty, 42, 51, 53, 107; literary models reconceptualized in, 137; music at Tang court, 158; poets of, 150; regular script (*kaishu*) and, 79; return to "ancient-style prose" and, 138; rhyme table tradition of, 57
Tangong, 139
Tang Shunzhi, 251n6
Tang Xianzu, 109, 111, 132
Tangyun (rhyme book), 42
Tan Zhenmo, 54
"Ten Masters of Xiling," 131
textual study, 7, 22, 200
Tibet, 46, 66, 247n26
Tibetan language, 72
tones, 24, 32, 62–63, 63–64, 113, 174. See also entering tone; falling tone; level tone; rising tone
Tongwen beikao [A complete study of unified script] (Wang Yingdian), 83–84, 85, 88, 92, 252n36
Tongya (Fang Yizhi), 203
topolects, 26, 27, 43, 112, 116, 228; entering tone (*ru*) and, 33; opera and, 113, 118, 130
translation, 49, 50, 60, 117

Translators Institute (Siyi guan), 46, 49
Trigault, Nicolas, 49, 212
"Two Cultures" (scientific and humanistic), 9–10

Vietnam, 173

Wang Anshi, 78–79, 85, 86, 251n18
Wang Deyuan, 84
Wang Gen, 79
Wang Jide, 114, 192
Wang Kentang, 66
Wang Niansun, 222
Wang Shizhen, 117, 140–41, 145, 221, 259n41
Wang Tao, 226
Wang Wei, 137
Wang Yangming, 73, 74, 75, 83, 85, 88; on knowledge and unity of all things, 81; polarity with Wei Jiao, 76, 90, 251n9; variant graph forms and, 99
Wang Yingdian, 83–84, 182, 195
Wang Yun, 196
Wang Zhi, 212
Wang Zongmu, 83
Warring States period, 202
Way, the, 82, 84, 88, 89, 96
Wei Jiao, 88, 89, 91, 94, 184, 185, 194–96; critical responses to graph analyses of, 97–101; Learning of the Mind and, 75–83, 92, 94; methods and legacy of, 84–87; on sagely intent behind graphs, 82, 87, 97, 99, 100, 125; students of, 83–84; Way of the ancient sages and, 218. See also *Liushu jingyun*
Wei Liangfu, 120
Wei Ximing, 76, 83, 88
wen (literary) category, 137, 138
Wen Deyi, 65

Weng Fanggang, 265n30
wenjiao ("literary" or "cultured" teachings), 137
Wen Tingshi, 226
Wenxin diaolong [The literary mind and the carving of dragons] (Liu Xie), 138
Wen Zhengming, 140
Williams, Samuel Wells, 187–88
writing systems. *See* Chinese script/ graphs; phonographic writing
Wu Baipeng, 131
Wufang yuanyin [Primordial sounds of the five directions] (Fan Tengfeng), 155, 186–88, 189, 271n27
Wu Jishi, 1, 26–28, 35, 42, 184; on music of the *Poems*, 160–62, *161*, 268nn100–101; phonographic scripts used by, 65; rhyme groups of, 62–64, *63–64*; on rhyming language of the Classics, 158
Wu Renchen, 131
Wu Rulun, 189
Wu Shilin, 84–85
Wu Yu, 146, 150, 151, 209, 266n57
Wu Yuanman, 94, 255n75
Wu Zetian, Empress, 112
Wylie, Alexander, 189

Xia dynasty, 38
xiangshu ("Image and Number"), 23
xiaoxue ("lesser learning"), 3, 10, 21, 236n6, 236n9. *See also* philology
Xiao Yuncong, 114
Xiaoyu pu [Formularies for the remnants of howling], 121, *122*, 184
Xie Wenjian, 279n60
xieyun ("forced"/"harmonized") rhyming method, 36, 150, 151, 271n33
Xing Yunlu, 156

Xiongnu language, 100
Xiong Shibo, 121, 170, 176
Xitan ao lun [Treatise on the profundities of Sanskrit writing] (Zhou Chun), 181
Xitan jingzhuan [Authoritative study of Sanskrit script] (Zhao Yiguang), 54, 58, 247n26, 248n32
Xizi qiji [Miracle of Western graphs] (Ricci), 227
Xu Dachun, 192–93, 194
Xu Fen, 131
Xu Fuzuo, 115, 116
Xu Guilin, 182–83
xunguxue ("study of glosses"), 3
Xu Qianxue, 211
Xu Shen, 206, 220–21

Yang Huan, 255n75
Yang Shen, 91, 136, 205, 206, 209, 216, 254n68
Yang Shiwei, 266n57
Yang Xiong, 77, 106, 147, 260n58
Yan Kejun, 205, 206
Yan Ruoqu, 207, 271n38
Yan Zhitui, 106
Yao Ying, 214
Yellow River Diagram (*Hetu*), 186
Yili [Book of etiquette and ceremonial], 158
Ying Huiqian, 31
Yinsheng jiyuan [Recording the origins of sound] (Wu Jishi), 24, 28, 62, *63–64*
Yinxue wushu [Five texts on phonology] (Gu Yanwu), 208, 210, 213
yin-yang binary, 28, 120, 127, 140, 221
Yi yin [Pronunciations in the *Changes*] (Gu Yanwu), 148
Yongzheng emperor, 112
Yuan Changzuo, 70

Yuan dynasty, 48–49, 92, 107, 109, 113
Yuanqu xuan [Selection of Yuan plays] (Zang Maoxun, editor), 109
Yuansheng yunxue dacheng [Complete compilation of rhyme study based on the primordial sound], 155
Yuanyin tongyun [Systematized rhymes of primordial sound] (Chen Jinmo), 155, 188, 189
Yuanyun pu (Qiao Zhonghe), 271n27
Yuan Zirang, 35, 37
Yuefu chuansheng [Conveying the sounds of sung performance] (Xu Dachun), 192, 193–94
Yuejing yuanyi [Original meaning of the Classic of Music] (Liu Lian), 160, *160*
Yunbu [Rhyme supplement] (Wu Yu), 146, 150
Yunshi bianlan [An explanation of rhymes for convenient perusal] (Sun Weicheng), 147
yunxue ("study of rhymes"), 3
Yunxue lizhu [Brilliant pearls of phonology] (Shen Chenglin), 191–92
Yuzhi Yinyun chanwei [Imperially commissioned exposition of the subtleties of phonology], 279n50

Zang Maoxun, 109
Zeitlin, Judith, 193
Zengbu tibi Wufang yuanyin [Primordial sounds of the five directions, expanded and supplemented with defects removed] (Zhao Peizi), 187
Zhang Bangqi, 90
Zhang Jin, 141
Zhang Jingguang, 131
zhangju (phrase and line), 126, 260n70
Zhang Taiyan, 71
Zhang Xianyi, 139–47, 148, 149–53, 163, 265n32, 265n34
Zhang Xuecheng, 148, 206, 260n50
Zhao Peizi, 187
Zhao Shaoji, 133, 170
Zhao Yiguang, 5, 33–34, 91, 116, 195–96, 247n21; on ancient speech as poetry, 153; Buddhist methods and, 65, 126; on Chinese graphs' challenges for readers, 67; commentary on *Shuowen jiezi*, 86; Gu Yanwu's criticism of, 218–19; intellectual lineage and, 212; on opera and pronunciations, 114–15; on relation of prose and poetry, 152; on research into ancient phonology, 150–51; script reform and, 66; secular Sanskrit study and, 53–60, 64; on sound and graphs, 62; variants of ancient graph forms and, 97–98, 100
Zhao Yintang, 229
Zheng Qiao, 154, 182, 247n28, 250n77, 276n10
Zheng Ruozeng, 251n6
Zhengyun jian (Yang Shiwei), 266n57
Zhengyun yi [An aid to correct rhymes] (Wu Shilin), 84, 253n41
Zhengzi tong [Comprehensive correction of graphs], 94, 265n30, 274n86
Zhenkong, 247n19
Zhong Heng, 131
Zhongyuan yinyun [Tones and rhymes of the central plains] (Zhou Deqing), 109, 113–14, 115, 117–18, 121; as authoritative standard, 130; Chen Di's study of ancient rhymes and, 151–52; in Qing bibliographies, 134
Zhongzhou quanyun [Complete rhymes of the central states], 121
Zhongzhou yinyun jiyao (opera dictionary), 2742n76
Zhou Chun, 181–82, 183, 184, 205
Zhou Deqing, 113, 114, 115, 116, 128

Zhou dynasty, 79
Zhouli, 251n18
Zhou Youguang, 227
Zhou Yu, 95, 185
Zhou Yun, 173–74
Zhu Rangxu, 159
Zhu Xi, 74, 75, 99, 140, 240n12, 243n52, 263n6; musical setting of *Classic of Poems*, 158–59, 268n90
Zhu Yizun, 207, 255n74
Zhu Yuanzhang, 5
Zhu Zaiyu, 31, 162, 243n57
Zihui bu [A supplement to the *Assemblage of Graphs*] (Wu Renchen), 131
Zihui [Assemblage of graphs], 82, 92, 94, 102, 265n30
Zishuo [Explanations of graphs] (Wang Anshi), 78
zixue ("study of graphs"), 3
Ziyang Academy, 84–85, 253n41
Zou Shouyi, 83
Zuo, Ya, 18

GPSR Authorized Representative: Easy Access System Europe, Mustamäe tee 50, 10621 Tallinn, Estonia, gpsr.requests@easproject.com